PENGUIN BOOKS

UNDERSTANDING ORGANIZATIONS

Charles Handy is, these days, a writer and broadcaster. He has been an oil executive, an economist, a professor at the London Business School and a consultant to a wide variety of organizations in both the public and private sectors. He has also been the Warden of St George's House in Windsor Castle, a private study centre concerned with ethical and social issues, and was for two years the Chairman of the Royal Society of Arts. He is known to many for his 'Thought for the Day' broadcasts on BBC Radio 4's *Today* programme.

Understanding Organizations was his first book, originally published in 1976 and now in its fourth edition. Since then he has published a further ten books, including *Inside Organizations*, *Understanding Schools as Organizations* (with Robert Aitken), *Understanding Voluntary Organizations*, *Gods of Management*, *The Age of Unreason*, *The Empty Raincoat* and *The Hungry Spirit*. A collection of his 'Thoughts for the Day' is published under the title *Waiting for the Mountain to Move*. His work has focused on the changing shape of work and organizations and what this might mean for our futures. Several of his books are published in Penguin.

Charles Handy

Understanding Organizations

Fourth Edition

Penguin Books

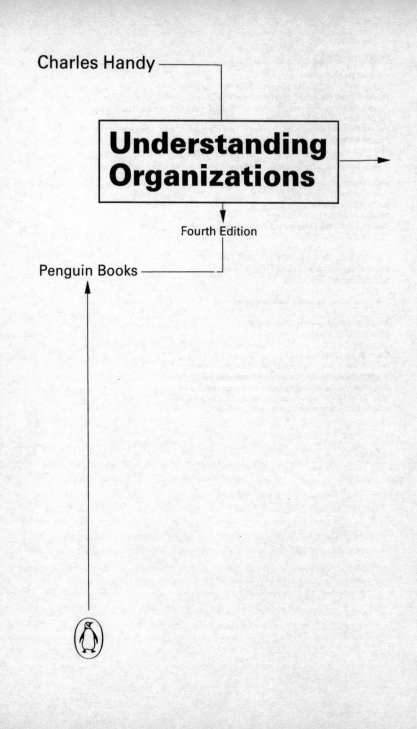

PENGUIN BOOKS

Published by the Penguin Group
Penguin Books Ltd, 80 Strand, London WC2R 0RL, England
Penguin Putnam Inc., 375 Hudson Street, New York, New York 10014, USA
Penguin Books Australia Ltd, 250 Camberwell Road, Camberwell, Victoria 3124, Australia
Penguin Books Canada Ltd, 10 Alcorn Avenue, Toronto, Ontario, Canada M4V 3B2
Penguin Books India (P) Ltd, 11 Community Centre, Panchsheel Park, New Delhi – 110 017, India
Penguin Books (NZ) Ltd, Cnr Rosedale and Airborne Roads, Albany, Auckland, New Zealand
Penguin Books (South Africa) (Pty) Ltd, 24 Sturdee Avenue, Rosebank 2196, South Africa

Penguin Books Ltd, Registered Offices: 80 Strand, London WC2R 0RL, England

www.penguin.com

First published 1976
Fourth edition 1993
Reprinted with a new Foreword and a new Introduction 1999
21

Printed in England by Clays Ltd, St Ives plc
Filmset in 9/11pt Linotron Times

→ Contents

6 Contents

→ Foreword

Nothing in this book has not been said before, it's just not been read before. This observation about an earlier edition of *Understanding Organizations* captures well the reason for its enduring success. Charles Handy writes in a way that makes important subjects accessible and real. In his writing we find our colleagues at work and ourselves. We recognize aspects of organizational life we have taken for granted and stopped thinking about. We can identify with his messages and empathise with his humanity. We may also be challenged by his metaphorical illustrations and always relieved to know that in his writing there is no retreat into muddled jargon.

The themes in *Understanding Organizations* were well chosen for their generic and durable character. Fashions in analytical vocabulary have come and gone since this book was first published in 1976, but people are still concerned about how to motivate their subordinates, peers and bosses; how to influence and lead; how to build and run effective teams; and how to develop people and organizations.

Throughout the book the reader is encouraged to relate the concepts and frameworks to her experience or his organizational setting. This constant reflective character makes the book more of a personal journey than an impersonal trek through endless academic knowledge. The 'so what' challenge is well represented in Part Two, where we are encouraged to think about putting knowledge into practice. This double hurdle of scholarship and relevance is the other implicit message in a study of management and organizations now regarded by many as one of the most successful of its generation.

Andrew M. Pettigrew
Warwick Business School
1998

→ New Introduction to the Fourth Edition

When I first sat down to write the first edition of this book, nearly twenty-five years ago now, there were few books published on management or organizations, and almost none in Britain. Those that did exist were mostly written for academics and not for the practising executive. Most of those engaged in the real business of managing and organizing things thought that it was mostly a matter of common sense and that you either had the knack of leadership and administration or you didn't. Sadly, common sense was not all that common and by the time you discovered that you did not have the knack of leadership it was often too late.

I commented at that time that there were three occupations in Britain for which no training or qualifications were needed – those of parent, politican and manager. I went on to say that, unfortunately, they are three of the most important roles in our society. Few of us would want to be treated by a doctor who had learnt only in the hard school of life, as managers used to, in case we were one of the doctor's learning mistakes. Society suffered much when the school of hard knocks was the only school for its managers.

I wrote the book because I felt that common sense and intuitive leadership needed to be backed up by a better understanding of how human communities worked. I felt then, and I feel now, that organizations are not inanimate objects staffed by inconvenient things called individuals who would be much easier to deal with if they really were just human resources, a name we gave them in the hope that they would be as docile as our fork-lift trucks or as programmable as our computers. Words like 'strategy', 'structure' and 'systems' can easily deceive one into thinking that if you get those things right, the rest will follow.

Organizations, of course, are not objects. They are micro-societies. Those who lead them have to understand the needs and motivations of the people in them. Rulers can only rule effectively with the consent of those whom they govern, which means that they have to think about power and the sources of power, about the constituencies and factions they can rely on and about the techniques of communication and persuasion, in other words – politics. They have to work with the grain of the place, which means understanding the values and nature of its culture: 'the way things work around here'. This book is about all these things.

Things are different today. Parents and politicians still enter their roles largely unprepared, but managers are increasingly expected to have acquired some fundamental skills and knowledge before they are entrusted with any significant responsibility. There were two MBA programmes in Britain when I started to write the book; there are now over one hundred. The bookstores are crammed with volumes of varying size and quality directed at the practising executive, full of the latest nostrums or gimmicks. Not all of them are good. Sometimes we seem to have substituted witch-doctoring for old-fashioned common sense. Because management is now defined as a skill, we can be tempted to think that it can be taught in the same way as computing or cooking. It can't. It can only be learnt, and learnt, even now, in the school of experience. But experience guided and enlightened by understanding is likely to be a gentler experience for everyone and to lead to a shorter learning cycle. That is why this book is still essential reading for anyone interested in organizations and how to make them work better. Revisiting the book while preparing this new introduction I have realized how most of its essential messages and insights are still key, although the context has changed over time, as Part Three makes clear.

I have been gratified to notice, however, that the language that people use in organizations has begun to change. The old engineering language of constructing, commanding and controlling is giving way to a more political language of leading, co-ordinating and persuading. We talk more of groups and teams than of hierarchies, of consulting people more than of ordering them and of visions as much as of bottom lines. In which case this book, which has long argued that this is the way it should be, becomes a more immediate guidebook to the future.

My hope is that it is as pleasurable to read as it is useful, for there is no reason why study should not be pleasing, even fun at times. I have larded it with anecdotes and examples from my own and others' experience, partly because theory that is not grounded in reality is empty fancy, but also because I hope to tempt you to add your own anecdotes to mine. This way the book becomes as much yours as mine and I hope that you will be pleased by the result.

Diss, Norfolk
1998

Part One

The Concepts

1 ➤ About This Book

1 Introduction

1.1

I came to the study of people in organizations expecting certainty and absolute knowledge in the behavioural sciences. I anticipated that I would find laws governing the behaviour of people and of organizations as sure and as immutable as the laws of the physical sciences. I was disappointed. I found concepts and ideas abounding. I found, too often, ponderous confirmation of the obvious and weighty investigation of trivia. But the underlying unalterable laws were not there, organizations remained only patchily efficient, and the most exciting of the ideas did not always work.

This disappointment initially brought dismay and disillusionment. But then I came to realize that, perhaps with some exceptions in physiological psychology, the study of people in organizations is not to do with predictive certainty – for two very good reasons:

1 The multiplicity of variables impinging on any one organizational situation is so great (Figure 1 suggests over sixty) that data on all of them sufficient to predict the precise outcome of that multiple inter-relationship would never in practice be forthcoming.
2 What seems to be the inherent ability of the human being to override many of the influences on his behaviour.

Organizational phenomena, I realized, should be explained by the kind of contextual interpretation used by an historian. Such interpretation would allow us to predict 'trends' with some degree of confidence. To add precise quantities to those trends, as in the physical sciences, would, however, be inappropriate and unrealistic.

As individual human beings we should take delight in this lack of certainty since it carries with it a guarantee of ultimate independence. As managers, or potential organizers of people, we can take comfort in the facts that:

1 Most of the variables remain constant most of the time.
2 Most individuals do not override the influencing factors most of the time.
3 Most interpretations will be valid for the future as well as the past.
4 Prediction tends to improve as the object of study turns from individuals to collections of individuals.

Box 1.1

Until well into the seventeenth century, surgery was performed not by doctors but by barbers who, untaught and unlettered, applied whatever tortures they had picked up during their apprenticeship. Doctors, observing a literal interpretation of their oath not to inflict bodily harm, were too 'ethical' to cut and were not even supposed to watch. But the operation, if performed according to the rules, was presided over by a learned doctor who sat on a dais well above the struggle and read what the barber was supposed to be doing aloud from a Latin classic (which the barber, of course, did not understand). Needless to say, it was always the barber's fault if the patient died, and always the doctor's achievement if he survived. And the doctor got the bigger fee in either event.

There is some resemblance between the state of surgery four centuries ago and the state of organization theory until recently. There is no dearth of books in the field; indeed, organization theory is the main subject taught under the heading of 'management' in many of our business schools. There is a great deal of importance and value in these books – just as there was a great deal of genuine value in the classical texts on surgery. But the practising manager has only too often felt the way the barber must have felt. It is not that he, as a 'practical man', resisted theory. Most managers, especially in the larger companies, have learned the hard way that performance depends upon proper organization. But the practising manager did not as a rule understand the organization theorist, and vice versa.

From Drucker, *The Practice of Management*, 1954

1.2

Figure 1 is a schematic way of illustrating why the study of organizational effectiveness is likely to be complicated. Over sixty different variables are listed there. Most managers could suggest a few more or would group them differently. Looking at this complexity one can begin to understand why the organizational theorist will tend to focus on one group of variables, e.g. the motivation to work, in an attempt to get hold of *something*, and why the pragmatic manager will respond to the academic's theories by saying, 'Yes, that's all very well but it doesn't help my particular situation.'

The diagram should also reveal the dangers of the lure of the familiar. Because we know what to do about competition, for instance, or about unions, we selectively focus on that variable or group of variables in any problem situation. Unfortunately selective focusing, if done by habit, also unfocuses a lot of other variables. I have often myself been swept up in enthusiasm for a new form of training (group dynamics is one example), only to find in the cold light of practice that it deals with only

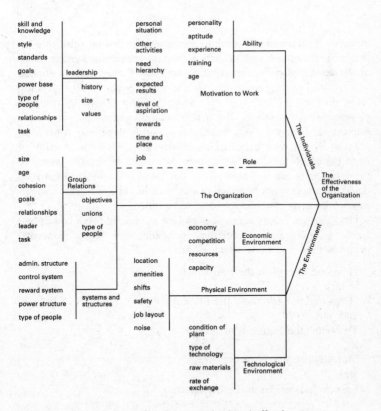

Figure 1   Some factors affecting organizational effectiveness

one aspect of a much more complex situation. The consultant firm that links its prestige to dealing with one set of variables (e.g. systems and structures), because that is where its operational experience lies, runs the risk of doing a superlative job on an irrelevant issue. It is of little use regulating the clocks when the house is burning down.

'Reductionism', as it is called, the disentangling of each variable in turn, may suit some academics and analysts but will not do for the manager who has to put the lot together and make it work. Beware the manager who hawks one patent cure. He has not studied Figure 1.

2 The utility of organizational theory

2.1

Analysis is an important prerequisite of action. It is no substitute for action, and analysis without action or implementation remains mere analysis and is often seen as irritating sophistry. Or just as the centipede was reduced to lying on its back in a ditch by pondering the question 'How do I use my legs?', so excessive management analysis can lead to management paralysis. But action without analysis becomes mere impulse. In fact, very little behaviour is purely impulsive. Most individuals, by the time they reach maturity, have built up an array of concepts which they use to interpret the data they observe. Many of these concepts are not part of our conscious awareness. Often they could more accurately be called beliefs, hunches or assumptions; sometimes even myths, stereotypes and superstitions.

Organization theory seeks to substitute a coherent set of conceptual frameworks for these collections of assumptions. These concepts, properly used and understood, should:

Help one to *explain* the Past which
in turn
Helps one to *understand* the Present
and thus
To *predict* the Future which leads
to
More *influence* over future events
and
Less *disturbance* from the Unexpected.

2.2

Do not underrate the value of the conceptual understanding of the present. One of the stereotyped assumptions of our culture is that man is master, or should be, of his environment. When anything goes wrong, or goes in an unexpected direction, we are apt to blame the individual – ourselves or someone else. This tendency towards individualism has, in my experience, caused a great deal of unnecessary trauma and personal anxiety in organizations. In fact, as Figure 1 demonstrates, the individual and his abilities are only one part of many forces bearing on a situation. A proper understanding of the relevant concepts of organization theory has brought much comfort to individuals in tension as well as allowing them to carry out the analytical task of the manager, which is:

To identify the key variables in any situation;
To predict the probable outcomes of any changes in the variables;
To select the ones he can and should influence.

Even if this yields only knowledge of the negative, that it will be useless to do such and such in such and such a situation, the manager will benefit. For in organizations, as in life, we progress as much by knowing what *not* to do as by recognizing what we must do.

Box 1.2

'The centurion answered and said . . . "I say to this man, go and he goeth, and to another come and he cometh, and to my servant, do this and he doeth it." ' (Matthew 8:9)

The centurion in the Bible was explaining his organizational model. It was one which worked for him in his time and place. He assumed that it applied to everyone, everywhere.

We all of us carry around some organizational model in our minds, unstated, unformulated but very powerful none the less. We got it from our first organization, perhaps, or from the early books and films we read. For many, those first organizations were schools or armies, or just the home. They shaped our ideas of authority, of what you can expect of other people, of how close you can get to them and how you behave.

Such models, lurking in the unconscious, can be dangerous in the wrong place. We need to understand the models in our mind.

2.3

This book contains:

Some of the conceptual frameworks that I have found most useful in the interpretation of organizational phenomena;
A discussion of their application to particular types of organizational problems.

This book is eclectic. It is not a comprehensive review of all the ideas that have been put forward, though ideas for further study are suggested in Part Three. But it is a coherent set of concepts. The concepts are interpretative devices, not precise definitions in the tradition of the physical sciences. Many of them will, and should, accord with the intuitive assumptions and beliefs of successful managers.

I am reminded of a student on a management development programme. He had made half-a-million pounds by his own efforts by the time he was 35. 'Why are you coming here as a student?' I asked him. 'With your success record you should join the faculty.' 'Not so,' he replied, 'I have come to find out why I was so successful.' He understood that if he could not explain his success he could not repeat it.

So it is with the interpretative devices of organization theory. Organizations have existed for thousands of years. Many have succeeded. Many have failed. The aim of organization theory is to explain the difference. To conceptualize and understand what works well so that it can be repeated. To generalize from the particular and to perceive the common thread in the tangled skein of individual incidents. If this book, therefore, can help the individual reader to re-interpret his own experience so that he can better understand it and generalize from it, then it will have achieved its aim. To distort Pope's dictum about wit

> Theory is Nature to advantage dressed,
> What oft was thought, but ne'er so well expressed.

2.4

The theme of this book could be said to be that diagnosis lies at the heart of effective management. There are lucky managers, of course; those whose favourite remedy just happens to be appropriate for the organizational malaise; those who find an organization in the bloom of health and vitality when no pill can harm or help; those few who, by force of will and personality, drag a sick constitution through to health. Most of us, however, would do better to rely on an accurate reading of the interplay of variables in Figure 1. To do this we need understanding, or theories, of the way the variables affect each other. We need to know those which we can alter and how by altering them we shall change the total situation.

This book should help towards that understanding. It will suggest some linking mechanisms, some charts for reading the signs of difficulty or success in organizations and for relating them to possible causes. But although understanding helps the diagnosis, gives better predictive ability and more power to influence the future, it nevertheless remains true that to understand all is not to resolve all. Diagnosis brings dilemmas. It is seldom possible to optimize on all the variables. What is good for the organization is not always good for all its members. Not all the variables are equally susceptible to change. 'Effectiveness' too is an umbrella-word It leaves 'effectiveness for what or for whom?' unanswered, although the nature of goals and objectives feeds back into the set of influencing factors (see Figure 1 again).

There is no theory that unlocks these dilemmas. Diagnosis clarifies but seldom solves. This remains a question of judgement – the ultimate justification of the managerial role. Do not look, therefore, in this

---

Box 1.3 Diagnosis or functional myopia?

As director of a general management programme I was once in search of a so-called multi-disciplinary problem which would help the participants to understand the interlinking nature of the functional areas of management. It seemed to me that the recent much-publicized failure of a nationally known firm would provide a good example. I suggested this to my colleagues on the teaching staff of the programme.

'Excellent idea,' said the economist, 'a classic example of the failure to forecast a peaking of the demand curve.'

'Of course,' said the accountant, 'this organization has never understood the concept of cash-flow – an excellent case-study.'

'I should be delighted to be involved,' said the organization theorist, 'it only goes to show how inflexible a centralized organization can become.'

'It's a bit too obvious, that's the only trouble,' said the marketing man, 'with their distribution system and pricing policy disaster was inevitable.'

If all were right, I wondered, could any one of them be more right than the others?

book or in organization theory for detailed advice on how to manage. Look rather for interpretative schemes to clarify your organizational dilemmas.

3   The nature and history of organization theory

The study of people in organizations is no new phenomenon. Confucius was an expert, so were the Greeks and all civilizations who discovered how to organize large numbers of people fruitfully. Aristotle had insights into organization theory which should not be ignored.

In more modern times people have started to think about people in organizations more systematically. It was, at first, fashionable to regard organizations as machines, machines with human parts. Machines could be designed, directed, controlled, speeded up or slowed down. That made them very convenient. They could be 'managed' by an outside agent. Indeed, much of the language of management was at one time borrowed from engineering and, later, from electrical and electronic engineering with its talk of interlocking systems and feedback loops. It is a seductive language because it suggests that organizations are, or can be, devices under our control which we can use to implement our wishes.

Although there are many managers today who still like to use this language and would like to think that it works, the thinking about organizations has moved on a long way from those early days. Looking back now it is possible to distinguish seven schools of thought, none of which has proved to be wholly wrong, but none of which is wholly right. Like organizations themselves, the theory of organizing started out simple but got steadily more complicated. Perhaps it should not now be called a theory at all.

The seven schools of thought are:

1 Scientific Management. Building on the pioneering studies of F. W. Taylor (see Box 1.4), a man who was, by all accounts, quite a character, this school set out to prescribe how organizations *should* work. It produced some simple-sounding injunctions – plan ahead, count things and movements, allocate tasks and responsibilities, limit your span of control, review results. Commonsensical though it was, it was a big step forward for the time (1880s), but people had been left out of the equation – they were not to be so easily regimented, nor was the world outside so neat and stable as these rules assumed.

Box 1.4   F. W. Taylor and Scientific Management

F. W. Taylor, the father of Scientific Management, was fascinated by the inefficiencies of much of the manual work that he observed. Most famously he studied the work of pig-iron handlers, men who carried heavy pieces of iron around the steel-works at the end of the last century. He went on to look at the people who shovelled coal in those steel-works and marvelled, for instance, to discover that they used the same size of shovel to lift rice coal at 3½ pounds to the shovel as they did for Massaba Range coal at 38 pounds per shovel. He discovered by experiment with the workers that there was an optimum load of 22 pounds per shovel which would permit them to lift the maximum tonnage each day. He therefore arranged for there to be a range of shovels of different sizes adapted to the types of coal. The final result was that Bethlehem Steel, where the experiments took place, were able to reduce their workforce from 600 to 140 and to pay the remaining 140 men 60 per cent higher wages provided that they met their precisely calculated targets each week.

In bricklaying, he describes how an expert bricklayer, called Frank Gilbreth, was able, after 18 months of careful experiment, to show his bricklayers how to lay a brick with five motions instead of eighteen by such simple devices as building a platform to hold the bricks at a height convenient to the bricklayer instead of placing them on the ground. (Gilbreth later developed his ideas into a full-scale classification of all possible movements, which he called 'therbligs', his name spelt backwards).

It is obvious, really, and it was the beginning of time and motion study and of industrial engineering. It is still true. Simple things can always be done more simply.

Taylor, however, made the mistake of pressing his point too far. 'The law is almost universal,' he said, '. . . that the man who is fit to work at any particular trade is unable to understand the science of that trade without the kindly help and co-operation of men of a totally different education.' That statement was an invitation to regard organizations as systems to be devised by some to be worked by others.

See further: F. W. Taylor, *Scientific Management*, 1947.

2 Human Relations. Chester Barnard, a businessman who could write books as well as think clearly about what he was doing, was the first to insist that organizations were not machines but co-operative communities. People had to be persuaded. Authority really came from the people you led not from those above. That was in the 1930s. Then came studies in productivity, notably at the Hawthorne plant of Western Electric, which showed how

important the informal group was, and the hearts and minds of its people.

3 Bureaucratic. Max Weber wrote about bureaucracy in Germany in 1910 but it was not until the 1940s that his work was translated and debated in America and the English-speaking world. His description, and apparent support for, bureaucracy as a necessary part of organizing was not well-received. No one, it seems, approves of bureaucracy except, interestingly, lots of people in organizations who like to know where they stand, what they have to do, who is in charge and what the rules are. We should be careful not to throw out all the concepts of bureaucracy along with its name.

4 Power, Conflict and Decisions. Philip Selznick, studying the Tennessee Valley Authority in the 1950s, realized that organizations were not as logical as they seemed, even the supposedly democratic ones. Different parts of them have different goals and fight to secure them. Power, its quantity and its distribution, began to be studied, as did conflict and the way in which decisions are actually made instead of the way they *should* be made. Simon and March pointed out that human beings were inevitably limited in intelligence, information and even in time. People did not usually go for the best possible solution but for one that would just about do. Organizations, they suggested, could best be understood by looking at how decisions are taken and by the way the organization talks to itself, its vocabulary.

5 Technology. Joan Woodward, in Britain, then threw another spanner in the works, in the 1960s, by pointing out that the technology of the work you are doing makes a huge difference to the type of organization you can use. As Burns and Stalker, also from Britain, suggested, routine or mechanistic operations need a lot of bureaucracy whereas one-off products or 'organic' work arrangements need temporary groups and delegated responsibility. Lawrence and Lorsch extended this by adding in the environment. A stable environment needed a bureaucratic organization while a fast-changing one required a more flexible one to deal with it. Obvious, as so often, with hindsight, but a shaft of insight at the time.

6 Systems. It was all getting complicated. It was tempting then to subscribe to open systems theory. This theory views organizations as open systems which take in resources of all sorts, work on them and push them out, transformed. In systems thinking everything affects everything else, everything is part of something bigger and

nothing can stand on its own or be understood on its own. Rather like economics, systems thinking explains everything but predicts little, although writers like Peter Senge, building on Jay Forrester's model-building in Industrial Dynamics, are helping to make it more practically useful.

7 Institutional. Meanwhile, the sociologists and the anthropologists of organizations were beginning to insist that each organization was a unique bit of history, with its own goals, sitting in its own environment, with its own ways of doing things and its own patterns of influence. All the other schools of thought, therefore, apply in some measure. Organizations are not naturally co-operative places, they do need bureaucratic rules, but logic will not necessarily prevail because different people see things differently and have different priorities and, anyway, the technology and the market-place make some things impossible and some things essential even if you wished that they weren't. 'Culture' became the fashionable word for this school of thought, with its implication that every organization had its own way of doing things but with the implied corollary that their way was not necessarily the best way or the only way.

All the schools of thought have contributed something useful. It is wise to be eclectic, to pick from each anything that helps, to compile the sort of personal anthology which is what this book aims to be. My own biases show through if I group the many topics covered by the book under the headings of People, Power and Practicalities as in Figure 2. Organizations are to me, first and foremost, fascinating collections of people. The challenge is to make them productive and useful communities. That requires the use of power in its many guises, as well as an understanding of the context of the organization, of its history and of its purpose – the politics of the practical you might say, or the organization as it really is. I call these the practicalities, because what is the use of all our understanding if we cannot turn it into something practical and useful?

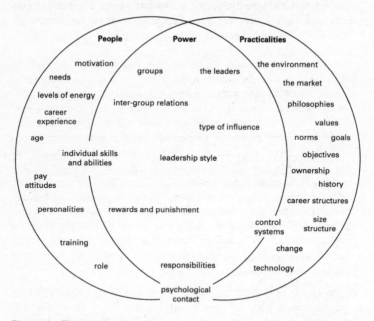

Figure 2   The relationship between people, power and practicalities

Gareth Morgan, in a fascinating book, *Images of Organization*, takes another tack, suggesting that it is metaphor and analogy which gives us our understanding of organizations. He explores a range of different metaphors, looking at:

Organizations as machines;
Organizations as organisms;
Organizations as brains;
Organizations as cultures;
Organizations as political systems;
Organizations as psychic prisons;
Organizations as flux and transformation;
Organizations as instruments of domination.

The way you think, he emphasizes, governs the way you act. Make sure, therefore, that you get your thinking straight first, and realize, always, that there is more than one way of thinking about a problem. Each metaphor, he suggests, is valuable because it offers insight. We should not be blinkered in our thinking but pursue 'the injunction of metaphor'. There is no one right answer when you are dealing with organizations. That may not seem a comforting thought to some, but I have always found it a liberating and an exciting one.

Box 1.5

Fred Taylor did not only measure pig-iron carriers and coal shovellers, he would, on his cross-country walks, constantly experiment with his legs to discover how to cover the greatest distance with a minimum use of energy, or the easiest way to vault a fence, or the ideal length of a walking stick.

Recounting this, Gareth Morgan explains that Taylor grew up in a well-to-do but puritan household which emphasized work, discipline, tidiness and the ability to keep one's emotions in check. Taylor's life was dominated thereafter by the need for control, a man who wanted to master every aspect of his life, even constructing a canvas that hung by two poles over his bed to keep his brain cool while he slept and so prevent nightmares.

He carried this personal obsession into his recipes for organization, recipes which happened to meet the mood of the time and were, for many years, very influential. We are all, in some way perhaps, the prisoners of our past and our models of organizations just reflections of our childhood. There is no truth, only personality. It is a sobering thought for any would-be theorist.

See Morgan, *Images of Organization*, 1986

---

4   How to use this book

4.1

Part One contains a set of models, or frameworks, for the better understanding of people and organizations. I have selected six, the six which I have found most useful. Some of them, like 'motivation' and 'leadership', are topics common to all books on organizations. Others, like 'power and influence' and 'politics' are strangely rare. The frameworks overlap. It is not possible to talk about leadership without talking about motivation, or about politics without mentioning groups. Different models, sets of concepts, can be used to describe the same phenomena. This is as it should be. There are different angles from which we view the world. The view will be slightly different from each, the truth will be a combination of all.

Part Two looks at some key and current organizational issues in the light of the concepts introduced in Part One. Part of the intention is to demonstrate how the theories can be applied to the practices. Too often the two are kept in watertight compartments. One bookcase for the theoretical models, another for the tips and hints on current practice. The discussions in this part are not intended to be a review of best current practice but rather an interpretation, often a provocative one, of the implications of some of the theories that we say we all subscribe to.

Part Three is for those who wonder about the sources of my ideas, concepts and theories, or for those who wish to pursue any topic in greater depth. For each chapter in Parts One and Two there are notes which:

(a) Give a brief and sketchy overview of the relevant field of theory;
(b) Suggest a few sources which I have found particularly helpful or stimulating;
(c) Give references to the major studies mentioned in the text.

I have kept the main text uncluttered by footnotes or references in the, perhaps erroneous, belief that the average reader will be more interested in the ideas than in detecting their ultimate origin; that the resulting models and conclusions are more useful than the process of muddling through that led me to them. For the more persistent reader Part Three should provide a short-cut to the original sources and to further reading. But I have not attempted to give any kind of survey of the literature or a complete bibliography. Others have done this much better than I could and some of them will be listed in this section.

I have attempted to keep the matter, the layout and the style of Parts One and Two as concise as possible. The leisurely style of the Russian novel must be inappropriate for the busy student of organization theory. And I would rather that the extra time should be spent in mulling over the ideas, in re-reading them, in seeking to apply them to personal experience, than in marvelling at the depth of my learning or the number of my examples.

4.2   How to learn from this book

This book has been written in the belief that a better understanding of organizations and the way they work will help to lead to more effective organizations. But it would be naïve to believe that this understanding will result merely from the reading of the text. Were that to be so then the plethora of books, journals and newspapers would by now have produced a much wiser and more understanding world than the one we observe today.

The process of understanding, or learning, is more complicated than that. There is some general agreement that it consists of four main stages.

Questioning. The individual begins to ask himself – is there a problem? What kind of a problem? What do I need to know in order to be able to deal with it. Without some form of questioning the individual will be reduced to taking it on trust that the dogma of the teacher is both apposite and useful. In all likelihood learning without questioning will be short-lived and under-utilized. It will be more akin to ritual or rote than true re-appraisal. Children will learn the verses of a poem one evening for repetition the next morning only to forget them by evening, for their learning had not been preceded by questioning. It was not connected with their experience. In our learning we work from experience outwards, not inwards from models.

Conceptualization. The nature of the problem having once been explored, the individual must conceptualize it. He must learn how to set this one experience of the problem in a more general context or framework. If he does this he will be able not only to explain the first problem but all others like it. Conceptualization elevates the particular to the universal. Without concepts the isolated experience becomes mere anecdote, an experience talked of but not learnt from. Only if the next experience is *precisely* the same as the preceding one can the lessons of the first be applied to the second.

Experimentation. The thesis of Chapter 1 has been that better understanding leads to better prediction which could lead to more effective action. It is this action consequent on conceptualization that is here called experimentation. Here the individual as scientist is testing his hypothesis. Having intuitively formulated the general law of gravity as little children, we are constantly experimenting from it as a base. These acts of experimentation test out the conceptualization and, if successful, implant the concepts more firmly in one's mind. If we do not experiment with the concepts they will remain remote theory, of as much use as hieroglyphs to the average man.

Consolidation. This is the final stage. The concepts are internalized and begin to mesh in one's mind. The experimental phase is past, and the new hypotheses become the basis for future action. They have become part of one, so that habitual behaviour is altered and affected. The lesson has been learnt.

For a self-developing individual such consolidation is but the start of a new exploration, a fresh cycle of understanding. But without the consolidation phase the conceptualization and the experimentation together become mere interesting suppositions, not useful in practice. Throughout this book the reader should continually push himself through this cycle of learning. Some of the boxes contain exercises which may help.

Box 1.6   Two nuggets of wisdom

Seek simplicity – and, having found it, suspect it.
James Conant

Common sense is that layer of prejudice laid down before the age of 18.
Einstein

The boxes in Parts One and Two are not crucial to the text except when the text specifically refers to them. They are intended to flesh out the rather bare bones of the main text by providing examples, fuller definitions of key concepts, and interesting research studies. They have been boxed in order to keep the supporting material out of the way of the main argument. Read them for interest rather than from vital necessity.

The book is most sensibly read from beginning to end, since the language of Part Two is explained in Part One. But the index should lead you to a discussion of any particular topic or problem.

Finally: only some of my intellectual debts are acknowledged in Part Three. No one can study and teach in this area, can work in and with organizations and their managers, without unconsciously picking up other people's amendments to one's own views. The original sources of many ideas get lost in time. The evidence for some new insight may be recalled but its provenance forgotten. In these and other ways, many unnamed, unknown or forgotten people have contributed to this work. In particular my colleagues at the London Business School, my critical but stimulating students, the many managers and executives that I have known, have all had more of a share in shaping the ideas in this book than they were aware of or I can keep tally of.

2 ── On the Motivation to Work

1 Introduction

The hermit sitting in his mountain cell and confronted one day with the Sunday newspaper might be pardoned for wondering why all those people were doing all those things. Why this eager striving to be President of the United States? Why this restless urge to merge, or, with fortunes made, to return again to the fray of business and create yet another empire? Why do all these people buy and sell their houses so ardently, enriching the middlemen but disrupting families? Why do they change their jobs, divorce their mates, chase the sun or sue their neighbour? Why do they work so hard? Why do they work when they do? Why, come to that, do they work at all?

There must be many pressures and facts which can be called upon to explain any particular set of circumstances. But is there any one set of forces, any general mechanism *within* each of us which pushes us one way or the other? Can we, by looking at the *internal decision process*, answer those questions about work for any given individual or set of individuals? Is man at work dominated by sexuality and aggression, or is he engaged on an endless pursuit of happiness? Does it make a difference if the 'he' is a 'she'? Are women different from men in the way they decide their priorities? The body of knowledge about this internal decision process carries the generic title of motivation theory.

'Motivate' is one of those ambiguous words. The dictionary calls it a transitive verb. It normally has a subject and an object. X motivates Y, Y is motivated by X. But is X a thing or a person? Can *you* motivate someone? Or is it only money, or hunger, or status, or need for affection? Are you motivated by a lack of something, in the sense that thirst equals lack of liquid, or only by the thing, e.g. water? Or is it a mixture? We use the word ambiguously. Does this mean we are unsure of what we really mean by it?

If we could understand, and could then predict, the ways in which individuals were motivated we could influence them by changing the components of that motivation process. Is that manipulation – or management? Certainly such understanding could lead to great power since it would allow the control of behaviour without the visible and unpopular trappings of control. Early work on motivation was indeed concerned to find ways by which the individual could be 'motivated' to apply more effort and talent to the service of his or her employer. It is only fair to add that many of these theorists were also concerned to find an answer to the problem that was consistent with the essential dignity and independence of the individual.

We should perhaps be relieved that no guaranteed formula of motivation was found. But there is now a much better understanding of the process by which the individual reaches decisions on the apportionment of his or her ambitions, time, energy and talent. The decision is often unconscious or instinctive, physical as when we go in search of food, or more psychological, as when we seek security under threat; or it may be a conscious and deliberate decision to leave or join a firm, to satisfice or to optimize. The process, we shall discover, is complex and particular. Particular to individuals and to situations. Thus no general formula can be guaranteed to work, but understanding of the process will help to explain some of the problems and difficulties of people at work.

Understanding of the process should make for better decisions affecting people in organizations, better decisions in the sense that they are taken with more knowledge of the implications and likely outcomes.

It is this kind of understanding that this chapter seeks to provide. It will start with a review of the earlier approaches to motivation, each of them with a grain of truth, but none of them sufficient in themselves. *Early motivation theories* will then suggest *another approach* and a look at *the psychological contract – its application*, and finally *a summary and implications*.

Box 2.1

All men seek one goal; success or happiness. The only way to achieve true success is to express yourself completely in service to society. First, have a definite, clear, practical ideal – a goal, an objective. Second, have the necessary means to achieve your ends – wisdom, money, materials, and methods. Third, adjust your means to that end.

Aristotle, 384–322 B.C.

2   Early motivation theories

2.1

These approaches can be categorized under three headings.

Satisfaction theories. The assumption here is that a satisfied worker is a productive worker.

Incentive theories. The assumption of these theories is based on the principle of reinforcement, what might crudely be called the 'carrot' approach. Individuals will work harder given specific reward or encouragement for good performance.

Intrinsic theories. Man is not an animal, say these theorists. He will work best if given a worthwhile job and allowed to get on with it. The reward will come from the satisfaction in the work itself.

2.2   Satisfaction theories

There is very little evidence that a satisfied worker actually works harder. However there is strong support for the suggestion that a satisfied worker tends to stay in the same organization. There is also evidence that satisfaction correlates positively with mental health. This suggests that paying attention to conditions of work and worker morale will reduce staff turnover and absenteeism but will not necessarily increase individual productivity. Herzberg's findings (summarized in *3.2*) suggest a reason for this.

Under this heading can be grouped those theories that hold that people work best when they like their leader, or are satisfied with their work group.

It has been suggested that where satisfaction does correlate with productivity, it may be the productivity that caused the satisfaction rather than the other way round. (See Chapter 6, section *3.1*.)

2.3   Incentive theories

Incentive theories suggest that the individual will increase his efforts in order to obtain a desired reward.

Although based on the general principle of reinforcement, most of the studies in this area have concentrated on 'pay' or 'money' as a motivator. To some extent this concentration is justifiable in that money acts as a 'stand in' for many other rewards such as status and

Box 2.2

What are the two most important factors in your job? (%)

	Young urban professionals	All other workers
money	22	40
independence	40	35
gratifying work	50	32
liking co-workers	14	25
pleasant environment	11	25
contribution to public good	33	15
important career step	10	15
don't know/no answer	3	3

The Chivas Regal Report, 'Working Americans: Emerging Values for 1990s'

In Britain, The Industrial Society surveyed 1063 adult workers in 1989 and found that respondents rated having an interesting and enjoyable job, security and a feeling of doing something worthwhile, more important than basic pay as motivators.

The Industrial Society, 'Blueprint for Success', 1989

independence. This situation may, however, be more true of America, where most of the studies were done, than of Europe.

Incentive theories undoubtedly *can* work if:

(a) The individual perceives the increased reward to be worth the extra effort;
(b) The performance can be measured and clearly attributed to the individual;
(c) The individual wants that particular kind of reward;
(d) The increased performance will not become the new minimum standard.

These theories often work well for the owner-manager or, at the worker level, in unit or small-batch manufacturing. If, however, any of the first three conditions does not apply, the individual will tend to see the reward as an improvement to the general climate of work and will react as under *Satisfaction theories*. Condition (d) of course, if violated, will only create a serious credibility gap.

2.4   Intrinsic theories

These theories derive their *raison d'être* from some general assumptions about human needs along lines originally advocated by Maslow. Maslow categorized human needs as follows:

Self-actualization needs;
Esteem needs;
Belonging and love needs;
Safety needs;
Physiological needs.

He postulates that needs are only motivators when they are unsatisfied. He further suggests that these needs work, roughly, in the kind of hierarchy implied by the listing above. The lower-order needs (physiological and safety) are dominant until satisfied, whereupon the higher-order needs come into operation. There is considerable intuitive support for this conceptualization. If you are starving, your needs for esteem or status will be unimportant; only food matters. When adequately warm, further heat will not motivate you, i.e. the need does not operate as a motivator. Unfortunately the research evidence does not support the idea that needs become less powerful as they are satisfied, except at the very primitive level. Aldefer, who has simplified Maslow's needs down to three categories – the need for existence, the need to relate to others and the need for personal growth – is at pains to point out that each of us may have different levels of each kind.

The assumption of the intrinsic theorists (e.g. McGregor and Likert) is that the higher-order needs are more prevalent in modern men and women than we give them credit for. In particular that we can gain a lot of satisfaction from the job itself, provided that it is *our* job, i.e. we have some degree of freedom in determining what the job is and how we will do it. This approach would say that involvement or participation will in general tend to increase motivation, provided that it is genuine participation. Rewards tend to lie in the task itself or in the individual's relations with the group. The ideal is to create conditions where effective performance is a goal in itself rather than a means to a further goal. The manager is a colleague, consultant and resource, rather than a boss.

These theories are appealing but there is evidence to suggest that they do not work too well when:

The technology prevents the individual from having control over his or her job design, i.e. at shop-floor level in process, mass or large batch production;

Box 2.3

Gail Sheehy has written revealingly about the differences between male and female life patterns. 'If women had wives to keep house for them to stay home with vomiting children, get the car fixed, fight with the painters, run to the supermarket, reconcile the bank statement, listen to everyone's problems, cater the dinner parties, and nourish the spirit each night, just imagine the possibilities for expansion, the number of books that would be written, companies started, professorships filled, political offices that would be held, by women.'

Or, as Joan Collins once said, 'every working woman needs a wife'. Gail Sheehy goes on, however, to point out that while both male and female can demonstrate behaviour that is *initiating* and behaviour that is *responsive*, our culture emphasizes initiating behaviour at the expense of responsiveness in young men and the reverse for young women. When talking about the first half of their lives, Sheehy notes, men talk about the actions they have initiated, women about the people they have responded to.

Reported by Gail Sheehy in *Passages*, 1976

The individual does not have strong needs for self-actualization, or alternatively likes authoritarian masters.

One would expect therefore to find these intrinsic theories working best where individuals of intelligence and independence were working on challenging problems, e.g. in R and D laboratories or in some consulting firms. The evidence supports this supposition.

2.5 Underlying assumptions

These theories all stem from some underlying assumptions about people. To a large extent unproven, they tend to represent the dominant mood or climate of opinion at that time. Schein has classified them as follows, and it is interesting to note that the categories follow each other in a sort of historical procession, starting from the time of the industrial revolution.

The rational-economic assumption. We are primarily motivated by economic needs. We are essentially passive animals to be manipulated, motivated and controlled by the organization. Our feelings are essentially irrational; organizations must be so organized that these feelings and unpredictable traits are controlled (McGregor's Theory X Assumptions). *But*, fortunately, not all of us are like this. There are those who are self-motivated, self-controlling and in charge of their emotions. This group must assume responsibility for the management of the others.

The social assumption. We are essentially social animals and gain our basic sense of identity from relationships with others. As a result of the necessary rationalization of work much of the meaning has gone out of work itself and must be sought in the social relationships of the job. Management is only effective to the extent that it can mobilize and rely on these social relationships. Issues of leadership style and group behaviour are therefore of great importance.

The self-actualizing assumption. We are primarily self-motivated and self-controlled. We seek to be mature on the job and are capable of being so. External controls and pressures are likely to be seen as reducing our autonomy and therefore will affect our motivation. Given a chance, people will voluntarily integrate their own goals with those of the organization.

The complex assumption. Schein comes down in favour of what he calls 'complex man'. People are variable. We have many motives which have at any one time a hierarchy, but the particular hierarchy may change from time to time and situation to situation. We do not necessarily have to find fulfilment of all our needs in any one situation. We can respond to a variety of managerial strategies. Whether we will or not, will depend upon our view of their appropriateness to the situation and to our needs.

The psychological assumption. This is a category suggested by Levinson, following Jacques and Zaleznik. A person is a complex, unfolding, maturing organism who passes through physiological and psychological stages of development. We evolve an ego ideal towards which we strive. The most powerful motivating force in us, over and above such basic drives as hunger, sexuality, aggression, is the need to bring ourselves closer to our ideal. The greater the gap between our perception of ourselves in reality and our ego ideal the more angry we are with ourselves and the more guilt we feel. Work is part of our identity, our ego ideal, and opportunities must be provided for us to work towards our ego ideal in work if we are to be 'motivated'.

2.6

The kind of theory that we subscribe to will colour all our views about management and people in organizations. Satisfaction and incentive

Box 2.4

Theory X and Theory Y

Douglas McGregor in the 1950s enunciated two sets of propositions and assumptions about man in the organization.

Theory X

1 The average man is by nature indolent – he works as little as possible.
2 He lacks ambition, dislikes responsibility, prefers to be led.
3 He is inherently self-centred, indifferent to organizational needs.
4 He is by nature resistant to change.
5 He is gullible, not very bright, the ready dupe of the charlatan and the demagogue.

The implications for management are:

1 Management is responsible for organizing the elements of productive enterprise – money, materials, equipment, people – in the interest of economic ends.
2 With respect to people, this is a process of directing their efforts, motivating them, controlling their actions, modifying their behaviour to fit the needs of the organization.
3 People must be persuaded, rewarded, punished, controlled, their activities must be directed.

Theory Y

1 People are not by nature passive or resistant to organizational needs. They have become so as a result of experience in organizations.
2 The motivation, the potential for development, the capacity to assume responsibility, the readiness to direct behaviour towards organizational goals, are all present in people. It is a responsibility of management to make it possible for people to reorganize and develop the human characteristics for themselves.
3 Management is responsible for organizing the elements of productive enterprise in the interest of economic ends, but their essential task is to arrange the conditions and methods of operation so that people can achieve their own goals best by directing their own efforts towards organizational objectives.

From McGregor, *The Human Side of Enterprise*, 1960

theories, assumptions that people are rational-economic, will lead to a bargaining approach, to preoccupation with the extrinsic conditions of work, money and fringe benefits. Believers in intrinsic theories, in self-actualizing or psychological theories, will be more concerned with creating opportunities for individuals to develop and realize their talents, with providing the right climate for work and the right type of work.

At this point it might be helpful to the reader to pause and reflect upon his or her assumptions about people and the appropriate theory of motivation. For we are now going to complicate the whole issue, to pour more variables into the mix than are assumed even by Schein's complex assumption or Levinson's psychological one. Working from a basic model of a person's decision-making process we shall proceed piecemeal towards a better and fuller understanding of how people answer the three questions posed at the beginning of this chapter. The resulting picture will be complicated and intricate. This is only in line with the intricacies of reality, but for most operational purposes psychological reality is too complex. We are reduced to thinking in stereotypes or over-simplifications in order to get anything done and to avoid the paralysis of analysis. This process of reduction is, however, a better base for action if we understand the underlying complexity and if we confront our other prejudices, assumptions and stereotypes along the way.

3   An alternative approach

3.1

Faced with the variety of all the approaches to motivation it is possible to begin to build up an admittedly theoretical model but a model which seeks to explain some of the apparent contradictions or lack of support in the research studies, and pull together the various strands of the different theories.

The bare bones of the basic model are set out in Figure 3. In this form the model is most understandable if it is regarded as the way the individual deals with *individual* decisions, to do or not to do something, to go or not to go, to apportion or not to apportion time, energy and talents. This approach is based on the idea that we are self-activating organisms, and can, to some degree, control our own destiny and our own responses to pressures, that we can select our goals and choose the paths towards them. Some versions of this approach have in fact been given the name of path-goal theories (Georgopoulos).

Figure 3   The individual decision

The model in this form merely states that each individual has a set of *needs* and of *desired results*. That we decide how much 'E' (which stands for effort, energy, excitement, expenditure, etc.) to invest by doing a calculation. The process of calculation is not often as cold-blooded or deliberate as this description would suggest, but more of that anon. Let us first add some flesh to the model.

3.2   Individual needs

Almost all theories of motivation make some assumptions about individual needs, or drives. They have been categorized, listed, and titled in a variety of ways. Some of the most useful lists are:

1 Maslow's hierarchy of needs; simplified by Aldefer.
2 Roethlisberger and Dickson amplify Maslow. They add on to physiological and safety needs the following:
   Friendship and Belonging Needs;
   Needs for Justice & Fair Treatment;
   Dependence – Independence;
   Needs for Achievement.
3 Herzberg's two-factor theory. Herzberg maintains, on the basis of his research studies, that in any work situation you can distinguish between the factors that dissatisfy and those that satisfy. The interesting thing is that they are not the opposites of each other. Dealing with the dissatisfying factors does not turn them into satisfying or motivating factors. In general, the dissatisfying factors are things to do with conditions of work – company policy and administration, supervision, salary, interpersonal relations and physical working conditions. He called these the *hygiene* or *maintenance* factors. They are the necessary conditions of successful motivation. The satisfiers are achievement, recognition, work itself, responsibility and advancement. These he called the *motivators*. Good hygiene deals with

the question 'Why work here?', only the motivators deal with 'Why work harder?'

4 McClelland. McClelland and his co-workers have looked at the way people think, in many cultures and many sections of society. They have grouped the responses into three categories each representing an identifiable human motive or need. These are:

   Need for affiliation;
   Need for power;
   Need for achievement.

Most people have some of each in their thoughts, but seldom in the same strength.

The need for power. Most managers have a high need for power (as defined by McClelland's tests). High need for power by itself will often lead to unconstructive authoritarianism. Combined with, in particular, need for achievement it can lead to productive and satisfying results. Some degree of need for power seems to be a *necessary* condition for managerial success. Having it, however, does not guarantee success!

The need for affiliation. The individual with a high need for affiliation *alone* will tend to be more concerned with developing and maintaining relationships than with decision-making. These sort of people are often seen as ineffective helpers, probably because they are not task-oriented enough. However, some need for affiliation is probably present in most. It is present but is seldom dominant in successful individuals.

The need for achievement. The individual with high scores on this need will like personal responsibility, moderate and calculated risks, feedback on how he is doing. Unless moderated by other needs the high need-achiever may tend to become too individualistic to be very successful in any organization where other people's contentions need to be harnessed.

5 Robert Ardrey, working from his observations of animal populations arrived at three basic needs (*identity*, *security* and *stimulation*) in his book *The Territorial Imperative*.

These categories of needs should not be thought of as exclusive. Anyone can add to these lists. Nor need we feel confined to lists of three or five. My own list embraces all the needs mentioned above since they all seem to operate at one time or another. One psychologist, Murray, listed thirty needs which perhaps is too wide a spread to be useful in analysis. The valuable aspect of most of these particular lists is that ways have been developed of measuring them. The really important points to remember about needs are:

That each individual has their own set, sets that may differ widely;
That the relative importance of each need in the set can change over
time. For instance, in times of redundancy, the security needs suddenly
come to the fore so that there is little point in relying on self-
actualization as a motivator.

It is interesting to speculate on the origins of particular need hierarchies, or individual differences. This would lead us deeper into personality and behaviour theory than would be appropriate in this
section. But at least we can list the influencing factors that must be
thought of in any consideration of an individual's set of needs.

Heredity/early environment. Recognized by all theorists as crucially
important, it is notoriously hard to disentangle the effect of one from
the other. Physical talents are more easily attributed to heredity, aspiration levels and ego ideals to environment.

Education. By changing an individual's set of models through his or her
educational surroundings the priority rating of needs can be changed.
McClelland has also applied an educational approach to the raising of
levels of need for achievement.

The individual's self-concept. The individual's assessment of his or her
personal capacities, of their place in society, of their degree of aspiration, will affect the strength of each need. The self-concept itself is
largely the result of early environment, education, and the people we
have chosen to model ourselves on – parents, teachers, friends.

Experience. The individual's experience in life, our age, the degree to
which we have in the past satiated some needs, will all affect our
current need set. Needs not satisfied by experience at the appropriate
stage in life can often remain dominant unnaturally long. The forty-
year-old adolescent may never have had the opportunity in adolescence
to satisfy the needs for play and rebellion appropriate to that age.

3.3 The motivation calculus

This calculus is the heart of the whole problem. It is the mechanism
by which we decide how much 'E' we expend on any particular activity
or set of activities.

Most motivational theories have been concerned with the expenditure of *effort*. This word has perhaps too narrow a connotation. There
do appear to be a whole set of words, characterized by the fact that
they start with 'E', which help to widen the application of motivation

Box 2.5

Holland has described how people with different orientations tend to choose different work environments to suit their skills and needs.

1 *Realistic* The realistic person seeks objective, concrete goals and tasks and likes to manipulate things – tools, machines, animals and people. They are best suited by agriculture, engineering, outdoor conservation work and similar practical jobs.

2 *Intellectual* Ideas, words and symbols are important to these people, who are best suited to tasks requiring abstract and creative abilities, suggesting science, teaching or writing.

3 *Social* These people are best known for their interpersonal skills and interest in other people. Social work and counselling are possible careers and so is the organization of others.

4 *Conventional* The conventional person copes with life by following the rules and selecting goals approved of by society and customer. Accounting, office work and administration often suit them well.

5 *Enterprising* High energy, enthusiasm, dominance and impulsiveness are the hallmarks of these people, leading to occupations such as sales, politics, entrepreneurial business or foreign service.

6 *Artistic* The artistic person uses feelings, intuitions and imagination to create forms and products, leading most obviously to the performing arts, or writing, painting and music.

From Holland, *Making Vocational Choices*, 1973

theory. They include for instance, the word 'energy'. There is some ground for believing that we have finite quantities or levels of energy – whether or not this is true we can certainly decide how to apportion our own individual stock of energy and we do so decide. Motivation theory has to explain that decision. So too it must be with excitement, enthusiasm, emotion, expenditure of time, expenditure of money, expenditure of passion.

The calculus is different for each individual. We have all seen instances where, when everything seems the same to everybody, one man appears to decide to invest all his energies and efforts while the rest of us hang back. For each individual the calculus has three separate elements:

(a) The strength or *salience* of the need;
(b) The *expectancy* that 'E' will lead to a particular result;
(c) The *instrumentality* of that result in reducing the need in (a).

To give an example: a person who has a high need for power if given a task to do and promised promotion at the end of it will expend energy on the task to the degree that he or she believes:

That good performance will lead to promotion (expectancy);
That promotion will satisfy his power needs (instrumentality).

If either of these conditions does not apply we will not expend energy over and above that needed to keep us employed (assuming that our need for security is operating). This example brings out two other important elements of the calculus:

It is *subjective*. The individual makes it personally and no one else's guess is necessarily right.
The relationship between strength of need, expectancy and instrumentality is *multiplicative*, i.e. if one is zero the whole sum is zero.

There are two further aspects of this calculus that are worthy of note:

1 The act of calculation can range from unconscious all the way to totally conscious or deliberate. The unconscious we label 'instinct', the conscious 'calculating'. When the calculus is unconscious or instinctual the individual will react to the most immediate need. The desire for another drink, although irrational, will prevail if the calculus is kept at the instinctual level. The time-span covered by the calculus can vary from the immediate to decades of years. That is, the calculus can take into account results over the next half-hour or over the following day, or following year. The longer the period the more the needs that have to be considered, e.g. desire for health versus need for a drink.

It is possible that psychological maturity in an individual shows up in a more conscious calculus and in a lengthening time-span for the pay-off of expenditure. Small children appear to make almost instinctive calculations aimed at almost immediate results. As they grow up the calculus seems to become more conscious, and often as a result more complicated, and their time-span for pay-off rather longer. Occasionally, for the highly analytical or the emotionally insecure, the possible variations of 'E', of obtainable results, and of differing time-spans, result in a paralysis of the calculus, which shows up as inertia, with-drawal or breakdown. In such cases it may help the individual to cut down the available alternatives, or to reduce the time-span, thus per-mitting the calculus to function again (holidays, for instance, often have this effect).

Let no one think, however, that life is an endless series of such calculations. No thinking person would ever get out of bed in the morning if that were so. Most decisions in life are based on precedent. Similar situations call forth similar reactions without the need for a deliberate activation of the calculus. We are concerned here with the precedent-setting decisions, the new decisions, the decisions to change or to do something for the first time, to leave or join a group, to double one's efforts or cease trying.

3.4   Results

It should be clear that the calculus becomes difficult if not impossible if the anticipated results are unclear. In such a situation the individual must either make up his or her own mind about the probable outcome or, more usually, will make no calculation at all. It is in the light of this that we should look at the principles underlying such managerial *desiderata* as 'management by objectives' and participative manage-ment. If individuals are given some say in deciding on the desired results they will at least be able to complete a personal calculation. The model also explains, however, the finding that if individuals are *rewarded* according to their performance against those same results they will normally set the standard lower than if rewards are *not* tied to performance against standards, i.e. management by objectives *can* lower performance. 'Obviously so,' the calculus would say, 'why ex-pend energy to achieve higher results when the instrumentality (i.e. the likelihood of getting rewarded) is greater with lower results?' *Ergo*: set the results lower. Interestingly, high-need achievers, who get their satisfaction from job performance, set only moderately high standards. Interestingly, too, the most common finding on objective-setting is that the one most important factor in raising performance is the setting of any objectives at all. Without knowledge of *intended* results it is impossible to complete the calculus. Further, without knowledge of actual results there is no check that the calculations were correct or justified. Leavitt and Mueller (1951) amongst others have demon-strated that performance improves in relation to the quantity of feed-back or knowledge of results. They also observed that absence of any knowledge of results was accompanied by high hostility and low

---

Box 2.6   Evidence for the calculus

Kolb, Winter and Berlew found that when business school students were committed to a new goal (instead of having it imposed) and also got more feedback from each other, the percentage of successful students rose from 5 per cent to 61 per cent.

Kay, French and Myer found that when specific goals for self-improvement were included in appraisal interviews 62.5 per cent were achieved compared with 27.3 per cent when they were not included.

Row and Russell demonstrated in an experimental game situation that constant *failure* to achieve targets resulted in individuals ultimately setting lower targets for themselves than when they were reasonably successful in meeting their targets, i.e. we lower our goals if we find we cannot reach them.

Hoppe found that *success* in a problem-solving exercise led to a rise in the level of aspiration for 69 per cent, while *failure* led 50 per cent to lower their aspirations.

Lewin pointed out in 1936 that goals are not accepted by the individual unless they are thought to be attainable. He also underlined the fact that one's colleagues, or peer groups, have a big influence on the level of our goals. A high-achieving group will raise the aspirations of all its members.

Gebhard demonstrated that continued success increased the desirability of the goal. In other words, if you think that your effort or energy will be rewarded (high expectancy and high instrumentality) it is only natural to feel that it is all worthwhile (increased salience).

---

confidence. On the other hand, a high level of feedback, no matter whether it was good or bad, brought with it high confidence and friendly attitudes. To set objectives and then forget about them is only going to produce frustration. To use an analogy, the golfer who does not count his shots is only there for the walk. Without knowledge of the score the motivation calculus will soon dry up.

3.5

The basic model is now more complicated, and looks like Figure 4.

Figure 4

People do not, it must be repeated, go through this calculus every time they take a decision. It is useful to remember it only because it is the ultimate and underlying decision-making mechanism. *Each calculus, however, operates within the limits of a contract, a psychological contract* that each individual has with each group that plays any part in his or her life.

4 The psychological contract

Just as in most work situations there is a legal contract between the organization and the individual which states who gives who what in consideration for what, so there is an implied, usually unstated psychological contract between the individual and the organization, be it work organization, social organization or family. This psychological contract is essentially a set of expectations. We have a set of results that we expect from the organization, results that will satisfy certain of our needs and in return for which we will expend some of our energies and talents. Similarly the organization has its set of expectations and its list of payments or outcomes that it will give to us.

Three important things follow from this:

1 Most individuals belong to more than one kind of organization. They will have more than one psychological contract. It is not necessary for us to seek to satisfy all our needs under any one contract and few do. You cannot assume, for instance, as a manager that all your workers have put their self-actualizing or achievement needs into their contract with you.

2 A contract which is not perceived identically by both parties becomes the source of trouble, conflict or litigation. The organization's view of the psychological contract, for instance, is often more

all-embracing than the individual's. This may lead to a feeling of exploitation by the individual, or, by the organization, to a feeling of lack of co-operation or involvement on the part of the individual.

3 The motivation calculus of the individual only becomes predictable if and when the psychological contract is viewed in similar terms by both parties. When this happens people talk as if they understand the 'motivation' of the individual.

4.1   The appropriate psychological contract

It is possible to categorize organizations according to the type of psychological contract which predominates. These categories are:

Coercive;
Calculative;
Co-operative.

4.2   Coercive contracts

Organizations where this kind of contract predominates are prisons, concentration camps, coercive unions, custodial mental hospitals. The individual is held as a member against his will, by forces beyond his control. The psychological contract is not therefore voluntarily entered into. The method of control is rule and punishment, power is in the hands of a small group, the individual's task is to conform and to comply in return for which he will avoid punishment. These organizations strengthen their control by depriving the individual of much of his personal identity (through uniforms, numbers, lack of contact with the outside world) and by emphasizing conformity. It is unfortunately true that some institutions, e.g. some schools and hospitals and even factories, can today fall under this heading. If this is the dominant psychological contract the expectation of any 'E' forces must be limited to those which can be called forth by fear of punishment.

4.3   Calculative contracts

In these organizations the contract is a voluntary one. There is usually a fairly explicit exchange of goods or money for services rendered. The control is retained by the management of the organization but is expressed mainly in their ability to give desired things to the individual. 'Desired things' include not only money, but promotion, social opportunities, even work itself. Studies have shown that the vast majority of people would go on working even if they had no economic need to do so, so that the availability of a place to work over and above the material rewards is a desired reward under this type of contract. Most industrial organizations have this as the dominant psychological contract for most of their employees. It is a perfectly realistic form of contract, but increases in 'E' under this contract have to be paid for by the organization in some way or other. If the organization seeks to get more 'E' for the same pay (by, for example, threatening to remove the availability of work from an individual) the contract will seem to the individual to have become a coercive one and he or she will tend to adjust their side of the contract accordingly.

4.4 Co-operative contracts

Under this type of contract the individual tends to identify with the goals of the organization and to become creative in the pursuit of those goals. In return, in addition to just rewards, we are given more voice in the selection of the goals and more discretion in the choice of means to achieving them. The management relinquishes a large amount of day-to-day control but retains ultimate control partly through the right of selection of people, partly through the allocation of financial resources which gives it a power of veto on certain of the goals.

There is a distinct trend on the part of many managements to move the psychological contracts of their organizations in this direction. They are on occasions surprised and offended when these kinds of gestures are rebuffed. What is often not realized is that:

1 Organizational goals which are meaningful to the management and worthy of commitment may not seem so meaningful lower down in the hierarchy.
2 Sharing responsibility for goals and decisions brings cares as well as delights. Not all individuals will want those cares as part of their psychological contract for that part of their life.

In short, you cannot impose a psychological contract on anyone without it coming to be seen as coercive. Freedom of entry into the contract is one of the prerequisites of the co-operative contract.

4.5 The application of the psychological contract

The psychological contracts that apply in different organizations are seldom as clear-cut as the categorization above would imply. Furthermore, there is likely to be more than one type of contract operating in one organization, perhaps even a different contract for each manager.

Box 2.7 What subordinates want in a job compared with their superiors' estimates (%)[a]

	As men	As foremen		As general foremen	
	Rated the variables for themselves	Estimated men would rate the variables	Rated the variables for themselves	Estimated foremen would rate the variables	Rated the variables for themselves
Economic variables					
steady work and steady wages	61	79	62	86	52
high wages	28	61	17	58	11
pensions and other old-age security benefits	13	17	12	29	15
not having to work too hard	13	30	4	25	2
Human-satisfaction variables					
getting along well with the people I work with	36	17	39	22	43
getting along well with my supervisor	28	14	28	15	24
good chance to turn out good-quality work	16	11	18	13	27
good chance to do interesting work	22	12	38	14	43
Other variables					
good chance for promotion	25	23	42	24	47
good physical working conditions	21	19	18	4	11
total number of cases[b]	2499	196	196	45	45

[a] From Kahn. 'Human relations on the shop floor' in Hugh-Jones (ed.), *Human Relations and Modern Management*, 1958
[b] Percentages total over 100 because they include three rankings for each person

This variety can well be confusing to the individual at the other end of the contract when he or she finds that different parts of the organization have differing expectations.

It is often appropriate for the contract to change as the task changes. The contract in R and D for example might well differ from the contract on the shop floor. Often, however, the contract changes because the individual manager has different *assumptions about the nature of man in general*, and the way we go about our motivation calculus. These are the stereotypes and over-simplifications referred to earlier (this chapter, section 2.5) which colour so much of our approaches to people and their management.

5   Summary and implications

5.1   A summary of the principal arguments thus far may be helpful

Early theories of motivation were either:

Satisfaction theories;
Incentive theories;
Intrinsic theories.

Although each worked in some situation, none was universally valid. They were based on underlying assumptions about the nature of people:

Rational-economic;
Social;
Self-actualizing;
Complex;
Psychological.

Figure 5 is a model of the way motivation affects our decisions.

Figure 5

This decision model operates within a psychological contract which can be:

Coercive;
Calculative;
Co-operative,

but is likely to be a mix of all three, with one dominant. The nature of the contract operating within any one group will often depend on the manager's assumptions about people in general.

5.2   The implications

We have suggested:

That each individual has a motivation calculus mechanism which is used for precedent-setting decisions;
That this mechanism operates within the limits of a psychological contract implied between an individual and the group or organization;
That 'motivation' will happen when the psychological contract as viewed by the organization and by the individual is the same, irrespective of the actual nature of the contract;
That therefore there is no 'right' theory of motivation, but only the individual and the particular circumstances.

What are the implications of this? Have we not torn down some admittedly simplistic views of people and motivation but ones that were at least operational, and left behind a model too complicated and variable to be usable?

There is that danger. But the over-simplified views with their stereotyped assumptions did not seem to be leading to better or more effective organizations. Complexity has its problems but at least some general implications are clear:

1 Managers need to think more deeply and more clearly about their view of the psychological contract operating in their organization. What one asks of people, how one controls people, how one organizes people, how one rewards people, all depend on the psychological contract. If out of line with that contract they will work less well and may produce unintended effects.
Moral: The psychological contract will be a significant factor in the choice of leadership style and the organization of work.
2 If managers wish to change the method of control or the method of influence in their organization they must be aware that they are

changing the psychological contract. For instance, decentralization involves a change in the responsibility levels for many people. You cannot just *assume* that this is desired by everyone for its own sake.

Moral: The psychological contract often lies at the heart of any change problem.

3 If the desired outcome of a decision reached by means of the motivation calculus is not working out, i.e. if we find that our expectancy calculation is wrong and 'E' does not lead to the expected results, we experience what is called 'dissonance'. 'Dissonance' is the discrepancy between what is and what we would like to be. It is for most people a form of psychological discomfort or stress. If not resolved, all the symptoms of stress will emerge. (These will be discussed in Chapter 3.) To resolve the dissonance we can:

Increase 'E';
Re-calculate the expectancy, i.e. lower the target result;
Re-calculate the instrumentality, i.e. decide we do not need the result after all.

Dissonance will be more fully discussed in Chapter 5. Here we must note that this sort of dilemma can be seen in objective or budget setting all the time. The motivation calculus model explains how it is that each of us can behave in one of the above ways. If we are to choose the 'increase E' alternative we will only do so if we feel committed to the results level. In other words 'budgets' will tend to work as a device to raise performance only if implemented under a certain type of psychological contract. Under other contracts they will be seen as a control device and the individual will resolve any dissonance by one of the other methods.

Moral: The motivation calculus explains much of the trouble about budgets.

6 Money

It would be inappropriate to write a chapter on motivation without some discussion of the role of money or pay as a motivating agent. Unfortunately, as one recent review concluded, 'Although it is generally agreed that money is the major mechanism for rewarding and modifying behaviour in industry . . . very little is known about how it works.'

The reason should be obvious. The value of money as a motivator will depend upon the individual calculus, the salience of the needs affected by money, the expectancy that any 'E' will lead to more money, and the instrumentality of money in meeting the need.

A full review of the role of money is impossible here, but some important points need to be made.

Money is all-embracing. None of the well-known categorizations of needs include money. Money is often, however, assumed to be instrumental in satisfying each and every one of the needs, from hunger to self-actualization. But the extent to which this is true will vary from individual to individual and probably from culture to culture. Most self-reported lists of needs do not put money top of the list, though this too may represent a cultural bias ('money is bad but the things that money buys are all right').

Money is the basis for comparison. Money can be measured precisely. Most other motivating agents cannot be. Therefore money is uniquely useful as a measure of comparison. Comparison with the past, comparison with other organizations, comparison with other people. Since money accompanies increases in status, responsibility, success, independence, or security, money is the element that is measured and talked about, not the underlying factor. It has been frequently observed that we are more concerned about comparisons in our disfavour than we are pleased about comparisons in our favour. In other words, we use money as a comparative measuring stick. When *any* of the comparisons are unfavourable, inequitable, we are dissatisfied. When they are favourable we put it down to 'luck'. In a sense it is not money that is a hygiene factor, as Herzberg argues, but 'equity'. The absolute levels of pay are not often an issue but the equitable level, in relation to others, to one's own pay curve, to future expectations and self-concept. Jacques' idea of using 'time-span of discretion' as a basis for equity will be discussed in Part Two. Many union arguments are about equity, not money as such. Lawler's finding that, in the absence of information we overestimate our colleagues' pay and *then* are dissatisfied, reinforces the argument that it is equity not money that matters.

Money as reinforcement. We know from research with animals that reinforcements of some desired object if given at *regular* periods have little effect as motivators. Pay, therefore, given in annual increments, is likely to be seen as a condition of work rather than related to particular effort. Only a few categories of sales people experience money tied directly to particular pieces of effort. They are known to be highly motivated by money.

Incentives, tied to piece-rates, often work well, for a time, but there is some evidence that it is the variety and control over output that is as motivating as the extra money. Moreover, piece-rates bring feelings of insecurity if tied to the individual, but are too spread out in their effect if tied to a group.

In spite of all the difficulties it will be argued in Part Two that pay is a much simpler, and ultimately less costly, way of *rewarding* people in some parts of the organization than security, status or job satisfaction. But the implications for equity, or perceived inequity, have to be considered.

7 In conclusion

Having got this far in an overview of motivation theory the reader may perhaps be experiencing, as I did, a sense of disappointment with much of the work in this field. I had hoped that motivation theories would reveal to me the true purpose in my life and my *raison d'être*. I expected that I would be able to answer and deal with the perplexities of the hermit described in the opening paragraph. Instead man is treated as a semi-conscious mechanism responding to a variety of impulses in a partly predictable way. This wasn't me, I cried, although I could recognize many of my colleagues in the model along with those hordes of imagined but anonymous workers out there in organizations.

From this position of disappointment I came to recognize that motivation theory is useful as a way of understanding how most individuals, *given who they are*, go about taking the short- and medium-term decisions in their life. In organizations these are the important decisions for anyone seeking to activate the 'E' forces or to direct them towards any specific objective. But the proviso is important, for motivation is a process that works within me as I am. But 'me', the essential identity that is 'me', *that* must be explained in other terms. The result, however, is crucial to the working of motivation processes in that my 'self' is the case within which the process operates. 'I' *am* one party to each psychological contract, 'I' *do* have a set of needs of varying salience, but how did this come about? Through the chance accident of heredity or environment? Did I have any say in it, or was I a powerless victim?

7.1 The self-concept

This problem of the 'self', of the self-concept, of the ego-ideal and how it is formed underlies all the work on motivation. Levinson indeed has suggested, as mentioned previously, that the pull of the ego-ideal, of one's vision of what one could be, is the basic motivating drive. Karen Horney has argued that the central core of neurosis lies in the tendency of the neurotic to judge himself or herself in terms of an unattainable ideal, that feelings of worthlessness and self-hatred come from setting one's ego-ideals too high – a thing that high need-achievers are careful not to do. Without being quite so prescriptive as Levinson it is easy to understand how one's notion of what one ought to be can affect the salience of different needs. When I changed my career from that of an organization executive to educationalist and academic I found myself that my revised self-concept had forced me to downgrade some materialist needs and to resurrect others, such as the respect of my colleagues.

Box 2.8   Tolstoy on reinforcing the self-concept

Whatever a man's position may be, he is bound to take a view of human life in general that will make his own activity seem important and good. People usually imagine that a thief, a murderer, a spy, a prostitute, knowing their occupation to be evil, must be ashamed of it. But the very opposite is true. Men who have been placed by fate and their own sins or mistakes in a certain position, however irregular that position may be, adopt a view of life as a whole which makes their position appear to them good and respectable. In order to back up their view of life they instinctively mix only with those who accept their ideas of life and their place in it. This surprises us when it is a case of thieves bragging of their skill, prostitutes flaunting their depravity or murderers boasting of their cruelty. But it surprises only because their numbers are limited and – this is the point – we live in a different atmosphere. But can we not observe the same phenomenon when the rich boast of their wealth, i.e. of robbery; when commanders of armies pride themselves on their victories, i.e. on murder; and when those in high places vaunt their power – their brute force? We do not see that their ideas of life and of good and evil are corrupt and inspired by a necessity to justify their position, only because the circle of people with such corrupt ideas is a larger one and we belong to it ourselves.

From Tolstoy, *Resurrection*

We understand only a little about the formation of the self-concept. Some of its aspects are:

1 The self-concept comes largely from our selection of models in life. Adolescence and early adulthood are often times when we are rejecting old models and seeking new ones. Parents get discarded, and

sometimes reinstated. Individual teachers can have an importance out of all proportion to either their salary or their status in society. The boy brought up in the same village all his life, a member of the village school group, will have a constantly consistent set of models and will have little difficulty in arriving at a self-concept. The boy lifted by his intelligence into another class of models has a difficult choice to make. Richard Hoggart in *The Uses of Literacy* has described how the grammar-school boy from a working-class home uses two different accents, one at school, one at home, to separate out the two influences on his life. It is hard for parents to bear their rejection as models, to have little influence on the self-concept of their own flesh and blood, yet the increasing mobility and flexibility of our society is bound to present more young people with more possible models.

2 The self-concept is not formed without trauma. Adolescence is a difficult time. As the shepherd in *A Winter's Tale* comments: 'I would there were no age between ten and three-and-twenty, or that youth could sleep out the rest: for there is nothing (in the between) but getting wenches with child, wronging the ancientry, stealing, fighting. . .'

3 The formation (by the mass media perhaps?) of what has come to be called a youth culture with its own norms, values and symbols has presented young people with another, and very powerful, model for their self-concept. The generality of young people becomes what is called a 'reference group'. We may have different reference groups for different things: in one study by Miles adolescent girls chose their peer group reference group (other girls) as most important in matters of taste in clothes, books, etc., but parents were preferred as a reference group in more important matters. For example, faced with the problem of which of two boys to date when she liked them both equally, only one-third accepted the recommendations of friends rather than parents.

4 The influence of the peer group may be over-emphasized, but certainly the difficulty of choosing models or reference groups can result in much alienation, withdrawal, and rebellion which is hard to deal with. Ken Loach's 1971 film, *Family Life*, based on the work of Laing, is an excellent record of one family's experiences of this problem.

5 As we grow older we tend to fix on a self-concept. We then tend to find ways of protecting that selection by surrounding ourselves with people whose self-concept is roughly the same and who confirm ours as being sensible. So we go to live amongst similar kinds of people,

Box 2.9 Origins and Pawns

An Origin is a person who feels that he or she is director of his or her life. Origins feel that what they are doing is the result of their own free choice; they are doing it because they want to do it, and the consequences of their activity will be valuable to them. They think carefully about what they want in this world and choose the most important goals, ruling out those that are too easy or too risky . . . aware of their abilities and limitations. In short, an Origin is master of his own fate.

A Pawn is a person who feels that someone or something is in control of his or her fate. Pawns feel that what they are doing has been imposed on them by others. They are doing it because they are forced to, and the consequences of the activity will not be a source of pride. Since external factors are felt to be in control, Pawns do not consider carefully the possible goals in life nor concern themselves with what they can do to further their cause. Rather they hope for lady luck to smile on them.

Which are you? An Origin or a Pawn?

From de Charme, *Personal Causation*, 1968

select newspapers which reflect our values, join clubs and go on holidays where our self-concepts will not be challenged. Criticisms of our chosen self-concept can be ignored, either by rejecting the source of it ('he's only an old fool') or by physically avoiding the chance of incurring it, e.g. by not mixing out of one's chosen group. But a different and/or traumatic experience can often cause us to revise our ideal self-concept, our ego-ideal. For many people the war was such an experience – they found a new set of models and after the war changed the direction of their lives completely. A sabbatical, a big educational programme, a stay in hospital or in prison, can have a big effect on an individual's concept. This is not always comfortable. It may involve a whole change of life since the psychological contract no longer works the same way – the things that you liked about the job, the security, the regular hours, are now perhaps examples of what you don't want to be. A girl who marries out of her own *milieu* is often confronted by a new set of models, with resulting changes in her self-concept which may take years to re-settle itself. The publicity given to the women's movement can be seriously unsettling to many women if it presents new models for their self-concept.

The parts, or roles, that we take on in life are in part determined by our self-concept but they in their turn can influence it. And just as 'one man in his time plays many parts' sequentially, so too can we live separate lives simultaneously. So the dictatorial manager can be the docile husband, or the commandant of a Nazi concentration camp have a contented home life. This interaction of roles and its effects will be discussed more fully in the next chapter; here let us only take notice of the fact that we can 'flow into' a role, which really means that we alter our self-concept so as to have a better fit between the requirements of the role and the way we see ourselves to be.

7.2 Psychological success

It has been suggested, particularly by Argyris, that an individual seeks continually to increase his self-esteem, or to enhance his self-concept. He does this by searching for psychological success. Psychological success is experienced by us if:

> We set a challenging goal for ourselves;
> We determine our own methods of achieving that goal;
> The goal is relevant to our self-concept.

The experience of psychological success makes us feel more competent, gives us a more competent identity. In general the more competent someone feels the more likely he is to take risks in areas important to himself, and the less he feels the need to go around protecting his self-concept in the ways described earlier. 'We are all worms,' said Churchill once, 'but I do believe that I am a glow-worm.'

Psychological failure on the other hand leads to a lowering of goals, an urge to protect one's self-concept and avoid exposing it to possible damage. Failure tends to breed future low achievement just as success tends to breed further success. The man accustomed to failure, when he does succeed, tends to 'quit while he is ahead'; he has a fear of success.

It is an important aspect of psychological success that the individual should feel that it is due to his or her efforts or energy that the goal was achieved. If the achievement was fortuitous, or the means were decided for him, then the feeling of success is reduced. Vice-versa, the experience of psychological failure is reduced if the blame can be laid at the door of fortune, the system, or another colleague. In the jargon, this is called Attribution Theory.

The theory then is that psychological success becomes one of the needs, if not the main need, for the individual. If you believe this the consequences for the motivation calculus are big:

If a goal is not relevant to an individual's self-concept, i.e. does not meet his need for psychological success, the whole sum of the calculus will be reduced and less 'E' will be expended;

If the means of achieving the goal are not chosen by the individual the goal will not satisfy his need for psychological success and again the whole sum of the calculus will be reduced.

Box 2.10   Unemployment's threat to psychological success

Peter Warr of the University of Sheffield has listed the nine likely psychological effects of unemployment, as established by research.

1 Financial anxiety – two-thirds of working-class people have their income reduced by a half or more.
2 Loss of variety – there are fewer places to go to, fewer things to do. Most unemployed people sleep more and do more housework and television-watching.
3 Loss of traction – there is less structure in life to draw one along, and fewer goals and tasks that have to be done.
4 Reduced scope for decisions – there is more freedom but less to be free about, fewer options.
5 Less skill development – there is usually less outlet for one's skills.
6 More psychological threats – more rejections from job interviews, credit applications, and social meetings.
7 More insecurity – particularly about the future.
8 Less interpersonal contact – social contacts are cut because of lack of money and there is no work to go to.
9 Loss of status – and the self-concept that goes with a work-role.

These factors, Peter Warr points out, do not apply to all people equally. Those who were *less* committed to the job, who were older or younger, those who were middle-class, female and healthy: these all seemed to suffer less than the others. To be working-class, middle-aged and totally committed to your job was bad news when unemployment hit.

P. Warr, 'Work, Jobs and Unemployment'.
Bulletin of the British Psychological Society, 1983

In other words we need to know not only the need profile of an individual in any psychological contract but we must also have a picture of his or her self-concept and the directions in which he or she wishes it to move. However, although we may well agree that psychological success is a need to be found in all individuals, we might well want to dispute its pre-eminent position in Everyman's need hierarchy. For some of us, psychological success may no longer be, or never have been, very important, whilst for others it may be *the* crucial need.

In conclusion, therefore, let us recognize that the motivation calculus gives some understanding about the process by which individuals decide to apportion 'E'. But the things that influence that calculus, that affect the salience of the needs, are many and various. The self-concept of the individual, the role that we are in, our psychological contract, our perceptions of the situation are all involved. We need to go much further than the process of motivation to understand the behaviour of people in organizations.

3 ►|On Roles and Interactions

1 Introduction

Think of all the roles that you, or any individual, carry in life. Perhaps, executive, father, wife, gardener, golfer, scapegoat, go-between. Which of them is most essentially you? Or, remove them all and what of you is left? Ask the ten people who know you best to write a description of you. Will they differ very much? Who are you? Are you the same person in all your roles, or would your daughter not recognize you in your office? Are you anything over and above a collection of role performances? Should you be?

Many novels have been built around this problem of identity. Much has been suffered by individuals in sorting out the confusion of their ideas. Would you be different now if you had been cast in different roles in life – female instead of male or vice versa, teacher not manager, chemist not clerk? To what extent does one's role shape the kind of person one is? Does the situation make the person or the person make the situation?

Motivation theory gives us some clues as to why people behave as they do. But not enough. Role theory, the study of the individual and his roles, will provide a few more clues. Or, rather, it will provide another language, another framework, to help us understand why the world is not as easy a place to manage as it should be, why individuals suffer stress and strain, why organizations breed misunderstandings and conflict. It will provide one way of linking theories about individuals to theories about organizations.

It has been argued that the main result of all the improvements in communications, in social mobility, in education, in affluence and opportunity, has been to make a lot more roles available to each and any of us. No longer, born into a community, will we take over our father's occupation, live in his house and marry down the street. Who knows now where our children will live, marry and work, or what they will be? Pre-determined roles may have been boring, or restrictive, but they led to certainty and to security, to a consistent self-concept. Role variety, role opportunity, role diversity are no doubt desirable, but they bring in their train complexity and uncertainty, insecurity and strain. Within organizations, the size and complexity of their operations, the rate of change and speed of impact, have made more complex the roles of the individual. The dominance of the work organization has increased in our society, bringing with it the problems of combining the work role and the family role, the career role and the social role. The individual is the crunch point in all these pressures. How does he or she react? Can it be predicted? Can he or she be helped? How do organizations help or hinder? These are the concerns of this chapter.

It will in turn discuss *the concepts of role theory*, *role stress*, *the implications of stress*, and will then turn to the implications of role theory in considering:

individual *perceptions* of other people;
individual *interactions* with other people.

1.1

Any individual, in any situation, occupies a role in relation to other people. Her performance in that role will depend on two sets of influences:

The forces in herself – her personality, attributes, skills;
The forces in the situation.

To a degree, these two sets of influences are interactive. A personality is influenced by the situations to which it is exposed. The situation in its turn depends to a degree on the personalities involved. Much argument in psychology centres around the effect that the situation or the environment can have on behaviour or personality. Much of the argument in leadership theory (discussed in Chapter 4) centres on the influence that an individual can exert on the situation. In this chapter, the focus will be largely on the effects of the situational forces – how can the concepts of role theory help us to understand and predict the behaviour and performance of individuals?

2 The concepts of role theory

2.1 Role set

The particular individual with whom one is concerned in the analysis of any situation is usually given the name of *focal person*. He has the *focal role* and can be regarded as sitting in the middle of a group of people, with all of whom he interacts in some way in that situation. This group of people is called his *role set*. For instance, in the family situation, an individual's role set might be as shown in Figure 6.

The role set should include all those with whom the individual has more than trivial interactions. There are usually more people involved in any role set than one initially expects, which is one reason why it is often a salutary experience to draw one's own role set in a given situation.

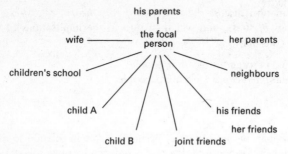

Figure 6

2.2   Role definition

The definition of any individual's role in any situation will be a combination of the *role expectations* that the members of the role set have of the focal role. These expectations are often occupationally defined, sometimes even legally so.

The role definitions of lawyers and doctors are fairly clearly defined both in legal and in cultural terms. The role definitions of, say, a film star or a bank manager are also fairly clearly defined in cultural terms, too clearly perhaps.

Individuals often find it hard to escape from the role that cultural traditions have defined for them. Not only with doctors or lawyers is the required role behaviour so constrained that if you are in that role for long it eventually becomes part of *you*, part of your personality. Hence there is *some* likelihood that all accountants *will* be alike or that all blondes are similar – they are forced that way by the expectations of their role (see Box 3.6).

It is often important that you make it clear what your particular role is at a given time. The means of doing this are called, rather obviously, *role signs*. The simplest of role signs is a uniform. The number of stripes on your arm or pips on your shoulder is a very precise role definition which allows you to do certain very prescribed things in certain situations. Imagine yourself questioning a stranger on a dark street at midnight without wearing the role signs of a policeman if you need any further understanding!

In social circumstances dress has often been used as a role sign, to indicate the nature and degree of formality of any gathering, and occasionally the social status of individuals present. The current trend towards blurring these role signs in dress is probably democratic but it also makes some people very insecure. Without role signs who is to know who has what role?

We must all at times have been confused or even angry to find that we have not recognized some important personage, have been patronizing to the Chairman or rude to the Minister, because he was not wearing the appropriate kind of dress or uniform.

Place is another role sign. Managers often behave very differently outside the office and in, even to the same person. They use a change of location to indicate a change in role from, say, boss to friend. Indeed, if you wish to change your roles you must find some outward sign that you are so doing or you won't be permitted to change – the subordinate will continue to hear you as his boss no matter how hard you try to be his friend. In very significant cases of role change, e.g. from student to graduate, from NCO to officer, from bachelor to married man, the change of role has to have a very obvious *sign*, hence *rituals*. It is interesting to observe, for instance, some decline in the emphasis given to marriage rituals. This could be taken as an indication that there is no longer such a big change in role from single to married person, and therefore no need for a public change in *sign*.

In organizations, office signs and furniture are often used as role signs. These and other perquisites of status are often frowned upon, but they may serve a purpose as a kind of uniform in a democratic society. For roles without signs often lead to confused or differing expectations of the role of the focal person.

2.3 Role ambiguity

Role ambiguity results when there is some uncertainty in the minds, either of the focal person or of the members of his role set, as to precisely what his role is at any given time. One of the crucial expectations that shape the role definition is that of the individual, the focal person, themselves. If his or her conception of the role is unclear, or if their conception of the role differs from that of the others in the role set, there will be a degree of role ambiguity. Is this bad? Not necessarily, for the ability to shape one's own role is one of the freedoms that many people desire, but the ambiguity may lead to role stress which will be discussed later on. The virtue of job descriptions is that they lessen this role ambiguity. Unfortunately job descriptions are seldom complete role definitions except at the lower end of the scale. At middle and higher management levels they are often a list of formal jobs and duties that say little about the more subtle and informal expectations of the role. The result is therefore to give the individual an uncomfortable feeling that there are things left unsaid, i.e. to *heighten* the sense of role ambiguity.

Box 3.1   Role ambiguity and the manager

In a study by Norman Maier and two colleagues, a number of vice-presidents in several organizations were each asked to select an immediate subordinate with whose work they were thoroughly familiar, and to define his role (including major responsibilities, priorities among these, and qualifications required by the job). The subordinates were then requested to define their own roles independently but with respect to the same variables. The agreement between the members of the pairs was of the order of 35 per cent.

Adapted from Maier, Read and Hoover, 'Breakdowns in boss–subordinate communication', Foundation for Research on Human Behaviour, 1959

The four most frequently cited instances of role ambiguity in a work situation are:

Uncertainty about how one's work is evaluated;
Uncertainty about scope for advancement;
Uncertainty about scope of responsibility;
Uncertainty about others' expectations of one's performance.

Looking at role ambiguity from the other side, from the point of view of the members of the role set, lack of clarity in the role of the focal person can cause insecurity, lack of confidence, irritation and even anger among members of his role set. One list of the roles of a manager identified the following:

Executive, planner, policy-maker, expert, controller of rewards and punishments, arbitrator, exemplar, representative of the group, scapegoat, counsellor, friend, teacher.

If it is not clear, through role signs of one sort or another, which role is currently the operational one the other party may not react in the appropriate way – we may in fact hear quite another message if the focal person speaks to us, for example, as a teacher and we hear her as an executive. The section on interactions spells out this problem in more detail.

2.4 Role incompatibility

Role incompatibility results when the expectations of the members of the role set are well-known but are incompatible as features of the same role. For instance, an individual's superior may make it clear that he wants a tight-structured rule-oriented form of leadership, while his subordinates want a loose, relaxed, friendly style. The expectations of an individual's line superior and those of the staff superior are another frequent source of role incompatibility.

Perhaps, however, the most difficult form of role incompatibility is that which results from a clash between other people's expectations of one in one's role and one's own self-concept. The most clear-cut examples exist in the ethical issues, where company practice and standards may differ from an individual's personal standards. More subtle, but more intrusive, are the pressures that result when we feel that the role requirements or expectations are 'just not us', when we are forced to act in a way which, in a psychological rather than an ethical sense, gives the lie to our personal identity. Some research has indicated that successful managers have a strong definition of their identity, are, in a sense, self-centred, yet it is also clear that to succeed in the middle layers of large organizations it is usually necessary to be organization-centred. This suggests that many successful managers must, at some time in their careers, go through a period of this particular form of role incompatibility. The consequences and methods of dealing with it will be discussed under *role stress*.

2.5 Role conflict

Role conflict results from the necessity for a person to carry out one or more roles in the same situation. The expectations of each role may be quite clear and the expectations be compatible for each role, but the roles themselves may be in conflict. The career woman, for instance, often finds that she is expected to fulfil at one and the same time the expectations attached to being a woman and the expectations attached to a male stereotype of successful executives. The two roles

Box 3.2   Role conflict in the Mikado

KO-KO: Pooh-Bah, it seems that the festivities in connection with my approaching marriage must last a week. I should like to do it handsomely, and I want to consult you as to the amount I ought to spend upon them.

POOH-BAH: Certainly. In which of my capacities? As First Lord of the Treasury, Lord Chamberlain, Attorney-General, Chancellor of the Exchequer, Privy Purse, or Private Secretary?

KO-KO: Suppose we say as Private Secretary.

POOH-BAH: Speaking as your Private Secretary, I should say that as the city will have to pay for it, don't stint yourself, do it well.

KO-KO: Exactly – as the city will have to pay for it. That is your advice.

POOH-BAH: As Private Secretary. Of course, you will understand that, as Chancellor of the Exchequer, I am bound to see that due economy is observed.

KO-KO: Oh! But you said just now, 'Don't stint yourself, do it well.'

POOH-BAH: As Private Secretary.

KO-KO: And now you say that due economy must be observed.

POOH-BAH: As Chancellor of the Exchequer.

KO-KO: I see. Come over here, where the Chancellor can't hear us. [They cross the stage.] Now, as my Solicitor, how do you advise me to deal with this difficulty?

POOH-BAH: Oh, as your Solicitor, I should have no hesitation in saying, 'Chance it.'

KO-KO: Thank you. [Shaking his hand.] I will.

POOH-BAH: If it were not that, as Lord Chief Justice, I am bound to see that the law isn't violated.

KO-KO: I see. Come over here where the Chief Justice can't hear us. [They cross the stage.] Now, then, as First Lord of the Treasury?

POOH-BAH: Of course, as First Lord of the Treasury, I could propose a special vote that would cover all expenses, if it were not that, as Leader of the Opposition, it would be my duty to resist it, tooth and nail. Or, as Paymaster-General, I could so cook the accounts that, as Lord High Auditor, I should never discover the fraud. But then, as Archbishop of Titipu, it would be my duty to denounce my dishonesty and give myself into my own custody as First Commissioner of Police.

KO-KO: That's extremely awkward.

W. S. Gilbert, *The Mikado*

are in conflict. All managers have a variety of roles from amongst those listed in *2.3*. Many of these roles are in conflict. Many successful male executives find that the role of husband/father and the role of manager are in conflict. Although in different role sets the roles can encroach on each other in such a way as to cause conflict, both cannot be done well at the same time.

It is useful to separate role conflict (conflicting roles) from role incompatibility (conflicting expectations) but the end result is the same – *role stress*.

2.6 Role overload

Another form of role conflict is what can best be described as *role overload*. Most people can handle some measure of role conflict. That is a collection of roles that do not precisely fit. There comes a time, however, when the number of roles that one person has to handle becomes just too much. He or she then experiences role overload. This is not the same as work overload. Work overload can often mean that there is just too much to do in one role. It has its own problems – often of weariness resulting in stress – but is of a different order from role overload which is concerned with variety as well as quantity.

The transition from executive to manager is often accompanied by a change in the problem of work overload into one of role overload. Overtime is a feasible strategy for dealing with work overload, but it may be, and often is, an inappropriate strategy for role overload. This can be confusing to the individual who has successfully employed this strategy as an executive only to find it fail as a manager.

2.7 Role underload

A neglected but very real problem in the lower parts of the organization is *role underload*. This form of role conflict arises when an individual feels that the role definition is out of line with his self-concept – out of line, that is, in terms of his capacity to handle a bigger role or a greater set of roles. It occurs, for instance, when the recruiting arm of an organization takes on a new graduate and, by means of their talk about opportunities, can even enlarge the individual's self-concept. This concept then suffers a rude shock when the recruit is given a job which, in the opinion of the individual, is well below his capacities. Whether it is or not becomes irrelevant – it is the individual's perception that causes role underload. Individuals placed in auditing roles in organizations – quality control, part of the finance department, some computer sections – often suffer from role underload. Indeed they are placed in positions where, if all goes well, they should not be needed!

Delegation often, when first practised, creates a feeling of underload. The delegating manager feels naked and un-needed. Role underload is the form of role conflict which perhaps most seriously threatens an individual's self-concept. As will be seen it is the most insidious, but most ignored, perverter of organizational efficiency.

3   Role stress

It is now pertinent to look at the implications of these varieties of role problems and to examine some of the ways of dealing with them.

3.1   Role stress

All of them, role ambiguity, incompatibility, conflict, overload and underload, lead to role stress. Stress can be good, stress can be bad. Most people need some form of stress to bring out their best performance, but if the stress is of the wrong form, or too much, it becomes damaging. One of the major tasks of management in organizations is to control the level of stress.

For convenience we shall define beneficial stress as *role pressure* and harmful stress as *role strain*. Unfortunately there is no clear way of distinguishing between them except by their effects.

3.2   Symptoms of role strain

When role strain exists for the focal person, he will normally exhibit some of the following symptoms:

Tension. Often expressed by irritation, excessive preoccupation with trivia, great attention to precision, or periods of sickness. Tension focuses attention on the immediate, polarizes situations into 'black' and 'white' extremes, leads to stereotyped responses and increases sensitivity to rumours and group pressures.

Low morale. Often expressed as low confidence in the organization, expressions of dissatisfaction with the job, or a sense of futility.

Communication difficulties. Often the individual is hard to talk with or even breaks off communication entirely. He becomes silent and withdrawn. Absenteeism is an extreme form of this symptom.

You cannot, of course, assume that the reverse is true, that because these symptoms appear there must be role strain. There are other forms of organization diseases that will cause these symptoms. But if role strain seems to underlie those behaviour patterns the next step is to identify the types of role problem. This can sometimes be done by looking at the mechanisms employed by the individual to ease the strain.

3.3   Strategies for dealing with role strain

There are some general strategies which could be better described as coping rather than solution strategies:

1 *Repression*. The individual refuses to admit that there is any problem, although all the symptoms are there. Laughter or jocular behaviour is often a symptom of repression; so is excessive drinking or smoking.
2 *Withdrawal*. The individual retreats behind a psychological barrier, or leaves the organization.
3 *Rationalization*. The individual decides that the conflict is inevitable and that she must live with it.

There are also separate strategies for each type of role problem. If the problem is one of *role ambiguity*, the individual will attempt to clarify his or her role definition:

By enforcing their expectations on other members of the role set;
By asking for clarification, either specifically or by precedent, from key members of the role set – particularly line and staff superiors.

Role incompatibility problems can be resolved for the individual:
By deciding privately to give preference to the more important or salient of the members of a role set and down-grading the expectations of the others. We will decide, for instance, between our line and our staff superior, usually in terms of their political importance for us;
By asking for a resolution of the incompatibility from the affected parties. (We may not always be in a position to do this.)

Role conflict is eased for someone:
By reducing the salience or importance of one of the roles so that poor performance in that role is no longer a bother to himself, e.g. reduce the salience of the father role and therefore allow himself to opt out of it;
By an agreed compartmentalization of her life so that the roles do not overlap and by setting up rules and procedures to maintain those compartments and their relative priorities, e.g. weekends kept for the family.

Role overload can be reduced:
By down-grading the importance of some of the roles and turning in low performance in those areas, but accepting that as consistent with the reduced importance of those goals;
By an agreed re-assignment of role responsibilities and priorities.

Role underload can be made easier for the individual:
By exerting his irritant powers (described as *negative power* in Chapter 5) to increase his visibility and felt presence in the organization;
By taking on someone else's role in addition to her own.

Looking at these solution strategies it will be seen that in each case the first strategy is always a unilateral strategy. Sometimes this involves the unilateral re-definition of priorities (one way of resolving dissonance), in other cases it means the unilateral re-definition of responsibilities and scope of the job. Unilateral strategies invite retaliation from others involved, and are often only steps to an escalation of the problem. Unfortunately under conditions of strain (which often means tension or withdrawal) unilateral strategies come more naturally to mind than co-operative ones.

The second set of strategies are (with the exception of role underload) all co-operative ones. There is good evidence that close and positive inter-personal relationships with members of one's role set can mitigate substantially the effects of role problems. A given degree of role conflict is experienced as carrying less strain when there are positive relations with the others involved. Unfortunately role problems work to cause deterioration in inter-personal relations. Decreased trust, liking and respect for fellow-workers often follows role incompatibility or role conflict. This tendency leads on to unilateral solutions which tend to be self-defeating.

In the case of role underload there appears to be no co-operative strategy that the individual can initiate, apart from asking for an enlargement of the role – a strategy seen as presumptuous or arrogant. The first unilateral strategy – the use of negative or irritant power – is so tempting that it is hard to resist trying it. Most individuals find that they are in a position to initiate new systems, rules or procedures which will effectively give them more prominence in the organization and so re-define their role. These strategies are all legal, indeed since they often appear to be synonymous with a desire for increased efficiency, they are even approved of. But if originating from role underload they effectively act to hamper the natural workings of the organization.

The second strategy, take-over, can seldom be done co-operatively and therefore results either in inter-personal conflict or duplication of effort – or both.

Since role underload is so potentially harmful to our self-concept, it is hard to resist attempts to enlarge our own jobs. Indeed, put that way, it might seem actually beneficial. But in fact most people in underload positions can *only* enlarge their jobs by encroaching on the roles and responsibilities of others since they will tend to be in the middle or lower reaches of the organization.

Box 3.3   Roles and stress

In a study of 100 young coronary patients Russek and Zohman found that 25 per cent had been working at two jobs and an additional 45 per cent had been on jobs requiring sixty hours or more per week. In 91 per cent of the cases prolonged emotional strain preceded the attack.

Margolis *et al.* examined a representative sample of 1,496 employed persons. They found that work overload was significantly related to: escapist drinking, absenteeism, low motivation, lowered self-esteem, and an absence of suggestions to employers.

Kahn *et al.* found that men who suffered from role ambiguity experienced lower job-satisfaction, higher job-related tension, greater futility and lower self-confidence.

Shirom *et al.* collected data on 762 male kibbutz members in Israel. They found a significant relationship between role conflict and abnormal electro-cardiograph readings, but for the managers only. As they moved down the ladder of occupations the relationship between role conflict and abnormal readings decreased. Physical work (e.g. in agriculture) produced the lowest correlations.

Mettlin and Woelfel discovered that the more complex an individual's communication network, the more symptoms of stress were exhibited.

Pincherle studied 2,000 UK managers attending a medical centre and found evidence of physical stress symptoms being linked to age and level of responsibility, particularly responsibility for people.

Reported in Cooper, *Psychology and Management*, 1981

4 The implications of stress

4.1

Stress can be either stimulating (pressure) or harmful (strain). The dividing line will depend partly on the situation and the role problems it creates, partly on the individual and the degree to which he can tolerate and even gain benefit from stress.

4.2 Situations leading to stress

There are five organizational situations that are likely to create role problems, and therefore stress, for the individual:

1 *Responsibility for the work of others*. The role ambiguity, incompatibility and conflict that are inherent in the typical 'management' situation have already been touched upon. In a sense, a manager's task is always to reconcile overlapping or conflicting objectives – of groups and organization, of groups and individuals, of self and superiors. One study has shown that role stress increases as rank in the organization increases.

2 *Innovative functions*. The major role problem encountered by people responsible for innovative activities is that of conflicting priorities. In general the power centres in the organization are in favour of the *status quo* – this will impart a high degree of role ambiguity to the manager of an innovative function – is he or is he not supposed to innovate? He will also find considerable conflict between the routine administrative aspect of his job and the creative side – two types of work with different psychological demands, hard to combine in the one individual.

3 *Integrative or boundary functions*. The role of the co-ordinator, linkman or outside contact appears to be particularly stressful. This is perhaps due to the lack of control that she has over their demands or their resources. She often becomes the focal point for inter-group conflict either within the organization or between the organization and its environment.

4 *Relationship problems*. People who have difficulties with their boss, their subordinates or their colleagues exhibit, not surprisingly, symptoms of stress. One study found that individuals under pressure complained of lack of feedback and consideration from their managers. For some people, particularly those with a technical orientation, the need to work with and through other people is a worrying

complication to their life, soon becoming a burden if there are difficulties. Morris actually talks of the 'cross of relationships' borne
by the manager, with colleagues on either side, bosses above and
subordinates beneath. For some this cross is stimulating; for many
it is a stressful complication to life.

5 *Career uncertainty*. If future career prospects become doubtful, the
uncertainty can quickly become stressful and spread to affect the
whole of one's work. The possibilities of redundancy, of peaking-out
or of being promoted into too hot a seat are particular problems for
middle-aged middle managers. The rapid changes in technology, in
markets and in corporate structures make this source of personal
stress an area of growing concern and importance.

Box 3.4   Four types of stress

Karl Albrecht identifies four categories of stress.

Time stress. The feeling that there is not enough time available to do the
things one has to do. Deadlines press, work piles up. Techniques of
time-management can help by setting priorities and planning one's days.
Time stress can result from role overload. Some people thrive on it.
Some cultivate a '*mañana*' attitude.

Situational stress. Role stress in its various forms, sometimes accentuated
by the personalities or actors involved in a particular situation. The
strategies listed in this chapter should help.

Anticipatory stress. Commonly called 'worry', sometimes called 'free-
floating fear'. This is the feeling that some unknown disaster is about to
happen, that no news is bad news or that the worst possibility is the most
likely one. Boxing one's worry is one device, like the slave in *Gone with
the Wind*: 'Thursday's mah worryin' day. Ever' Thursday, ah sets down
for a while and ah worries about things.'

Encounter stress. The anxiety about dealing with one or more people
whom one finds difficult, unpleasant or possibly unpredictable, or the
kind of mild panic that comes when the conventional rules of social
behaviour no longer seem to apply. The instinctive reaction is to retreat
behind one's official role, or to adopt as much formality as possible, to
write instead of meeting, for instance.

From Albrecht, *Stress and the Manager*, 1977

4.3   Stress – personality variables

It is obviously important for the organization to choose people for
inherently stressful roles who will be able to tolerate the stress. Several

personality variables are known to be involved in the management of stress. These are:

1 *Sociability*. The person who builds strong inter-personal bonds finds stress more tolerable than the independent individual who develops relationships which, while often congenial, are seldom deep-rooted enough to withstand conditions of tension. The independent or autonomous person often withdraws from inter-personal relationships when things get tough and resorts to unilateral methods of resolving role problems.

2 *Emotional sensitivity*. People who are emotionally sensitive tend to feel more tension in any given conflict or ambiguous situation than those with lower sensitivity. Complete insensitivity will tend to produce bad interpersonal relationships, so the 'happy mean' is required here.

3 *Flexibility/rigidity*. There is evidence that members of a role set will apply pressure where it is seen to be effective. Thus people seen to be flexible will tend to have more pressure applied to them than those whose steadfastness has already demonstrated the futility of pressure.

In general, the strong-minded relatively insensitive individual *feels* less tension. The individual with deep inter-personal relationships can *withstand* more tension. The tough executive will better survive the pressures of organizational life, but sometimes at the cost of damaging the interpersonal relationships which should make the organization more effective and more tolerable. They may also kill themselves in the process.

4.4 Stress – implications for organizations

It is probably impossible to design an organization that will have no role problems and therefore no stress. It is too easy and too dangerous, however, to go to the other extreme and leave it to the individuals involved to live with all the role confusions and conflicts that abound in organizations, be they businesses, hospitals, schools or, worst of all perhaps, charitable organizations. Stress should not be the battle honour of the committed executive. Type A people, the thrusters, provide the dynamism of the organization but, left alone, they can do enormous hurt to themselves and to others.

Left to themselves, individuals will too often:

Adopt the unilateral solution – causing role problems elsewhere; or carry the strain outside the organization, into the home or the bar

Box 3.5   Type A and Type B

Friedman and Rosenham first distinguished between Type A and Type B people. Individuals with certain behavioural traits were found to be more susceptible to coronary heart disease (Type A) than the low-risk Type B individuals.

Type A people are characterized by 'extreme competitiveness, striving for achievement, aggressiveness, haste, impatience, restlessness, hyper-alertness, explosiveness of speech, tenseness of facial musculature and feelings of being under pressure of time and under the challenge of responsibility'. Type B were more laid back.

A national sample in the United States of 3,400 men (without heart disease) was judged by a panel of psychiatrists and rated A or B. Two and a half years later Type A men aged between 39 and 49 had 6.5 times the incidence of coronary heart disease of the Type B men. Between 50 and 59 the incidence was 1.9 times higher. When a similar study was done on Benedictine and Trappist monks the same sort of difference emerged!

In 1976 Howard *et al.* looked at 236 managers and found that extreme Type A behaviour was associated with a range of known risk factors (high blood pressure, cholesterol, triglycerides, uric acid, smoking and lack of fitness).

(and the home, at least, was not intended to be the litter bin for the organization's problems); or try to contain the stress within themselves with breakdown or breakup.

Individuals need, therefore:

To understand the value of co-operative solutions to role problems (superiors can help by initiating meetings of those involved or by clearer task and job descriptions);

To create 'stability zones' for themselves for proper rest, recreation and outside stimulus (organizations can help by making these culturally acceptable at all levels);

To get a better perspective on their problems, by having a clearer definition of their priorities and purposes in their work and lives (organizations can help with better objective-setting and career planning and advice).

5   Perceiving people

5.1

Role theory is the key to the tricky area of how we perceive other people. If we know someone very well, a friend, a relation or a close colleague, then we tend to know them as a person, with all their individual differences. E. M. Forster has differentiated between flat characters and round characters in novels. 'The test of a round character is whether it is capable of surprising in a convincing way. If it never surprises, it is flat. If it does not convince it is a flat pretending to be round. It has the incalculability of life in it.' He went on to label most of the characters in Dickens as flat in comparison with those of Tolstoy and Jane Austen. Those people that we know well become round characters, but a great amount of time in organizations is spent with people who, to us, are flat since we shall never get to know them well enough to know their hidden depths.

In interacting with someone that we do not know in the round we have to make some assumptions as to what kind of person they are, what their motives are, what their likely reaction or behaviour is going to be in any situation. In order to do this we:

Collect data;
Fit the information into categories;
Make some predictions.

Categories. Let us first consider the categories. Categories are a way of organizing material and as such are very useful. But they have their dangers, for with those categories go a certain set of assumptions or predictions. 'Professors are absent-minded', 'Blondes are willing', 'Chinese are superstitious', 'Brown-skinned men are violent', 'Older men are less ready to change'. These are stereotypes. Stereotypes we know to be inaccurate. We cannot preface any of the above statements with 'All' for we know there to be exceptions to each of them. However, stereotyping does happen to be an easy way to think. If we can fit someone into a stereotyped category then he becomes predictable and easier to deal with. Box 3.11 shows how pupils, given a slightly different stereotype of a teacher, reacted quite differently to the same behaviour, influenced by the prediction they had made from the stereotype. Knowing the role of an individual, that he is a doctor, or a professor, or a steelworker, let's make all sorts of quick assumptions about him.

Box 3.6 The effects of occupational roles

Terman and Miles examined personality differences between the sexes in the American culture and concluded:

The males directly or indirectly manifest the greater self-assertion and aggressiveness; they express more hardihood and fearlessness, and more roughness of manner, language and sentiments. The females express themselves as more compassionate and sympathetic, more timid, more fastidious and aesthetically sensitive, more emotional in general . . . severer moralists, yet admit in themselves weaknesses in emotional control and (less noticeably) in physique.

Waller did a study of 'What Teaching Does to Teachers'. He summarized his impressions:

There is first that certain inflexibility or unbendingness of personality which is thought to mark the person who has taught. That stiff and formal manner into which the young teacher compresses himself every morning when he puts on his collar becomes, they say, a plaster cast which at length he cannot loosen . . . One who has taught long enough may wax unenthusiastic on any subject under the sun . . . The didactic manner, the authoritative manner, the flat, assured tones of voice that go with them, are bred in the teacher by his dealings in the classroom. If these traits . . . are found among the generality of teachers, it is because these traits have survival value in the schools of today. If he does not have them when he joins the faculty, he must develop them or die the academic death.

Merton commented about the impact of performing the bureaucratic role on the occupant of that role:

The bureaucrat's official life is planned for him in terms of a graded career, through the organizational devices of promotion by seniority, pensions, incremental salaries etc., all of which are designed to provide incentives for disciplined action and conformity to the official regulations. The official is tacitly expected to, and largely does, adapt his thought, feelings and actions to the prospect of this career. But these very devices . . . also lead to an over-concern with strict adherence to regulations which induce timidity, conservatism and technicism.

Data. In order to place someone in a category we need information about them. This information may be public reputation, published fact or private hearsay. All of this data would be prior information which would allow you to build up a picture of the individual and make some assumptions about him or her before they arrive. But we also use clues – dress, speech, actions, gestures. It used to be said that by the time an Englishman had entered a room and greeted his hostess every other Englishman would have decided where he came from, where he was educated, how much he earned and how he earned it. Role signs are, of course, a very useful source of data. If escaping criminals were to use the role signs of priests by donning clerical collars and dark suits, they would be trying to suggest a particular stereotype, and all the

---

Box 3.7   Roles and symbols

Farr's Law of Mean Familiarity . . . can be expressed as a curve, but is much clearer set down as follows: The Guv'nor addresses:

Co-director Michael Yates as *Mike*;
Assistant director Michael Yates as *Michael*;
Section manager Michael Yates as *Mr Yates*;
Second assistant Michael Yates as *Yates*;
Apprentice Michael Yates as *Michael*;
Night-watchman Michael Yates as *Mike*.

From S. Potter, *One-upmanship*

---

assumptions about behaviour that go with that stereotype. Most people are, however, remarkably unscientific in their collection of perceptual data. For instance:

1 We collect very little. The outcome of most interviews appears to be decided in the first three minutes. We form a stereotype from the first available perceptual information and regard that as adequate. For some people, the simple information that X is a Jew, or black, or a student at LSE, is enough to enable them to make a whole range of predictions about their behaviour, many of which will be false. The students in Box 3.11 needed only a change of one adjective to change their stereotype.

2 We are very prone to the sin of *selective perception*. We only perceive what we want to perceive. We look for data to support our initial assumptions, and neglect or do not notice contradictory evidence. Since we cannot register all the data that our senses can bring us, we focus on what we want to see and ignore, do not see, things or behaviour that do not fit our categories. Confronted with the same shop-window, the housewife may easily 'see' a quite different collection of objects from that 'seen' by her husband. In a management game used at the London Business School the instructions for the groups included, for one group, the words 'You report to the head of group X'. In nearly every exercise this group did not realize their supposedly subordinate position. They had not ignored or disobeyed the instruction, they literally did not perceive it. They 'selected it out' of their perceptual screen.

3 The order in which the data is collected is important. Box 3.8 offers some evidence to support the view that the earlier information, if

received, colours that which comes after it. In part this is probably due to rapid stereotyping based on very little information.

4 Our own roles colour our perceptions. The same set of facts viewed from different angles will look different. This is another kind of selective perception.

Dearborn and Simon conducted an experiment on this theme with a group of executives who represented different functional areas of business. These areas included sales, accounting, production and others. The executives were given a description of a management situation and asked to identify the principal problem of the company described in the case. The case was designed to encourage them to take a company-wide view. The majority of the executives identified the principal problem as one related to their own functional role. Thus 83 per cent of the sales executives mentioned sales as the most important problem facing the company while only 29 per cent of the non-sales executives did so. Another experiment, of a different type but on the same theme, was by Bagley. Mexican and US schoolteachers were given stereoscopes (binoculars which project a different image to each eye). They were all presented with the same two pictures simultaneously – one of bullfighters and one of baseball players. Most of the Mexicans saw the bullfighters, most of the US teachers saw only the baseball players. National roles had coloured their perception.

5.2 Implications of role perception

The implications of the way we perceive other people and their roles are various and important. Some of the more interesting ones are mentioned below.

The snares of stereotyping. In *She Stoops to Conquer* Charles Marlow is under the impression that he is staying at an inn and that Mr Hardcastle is the innkeeper. Marlow therefore treats Hardcastle according to his stereotype of the role of a landlord. In reality, however, Hardcastle is Marlow's prospective father-in-law and he behaves in the manner appropriate towards a future son-in-law. The ensuing bewilderment and frustration on the part of the two characters who receive data that so vehemently conflicts with their stereotypes of the other's role is great entertainment for the audience, who are party to the role confusion.

Box 3.8

The picture below is a well-known 'ambiguous' picture. It can be seen as a young girl or as an old woman. Hofstede describes how he showed half of a class a slightly altered version of the picture, for only five seconds, in which only the young girl could be seen. He then showed the remaining members of the class another version of the picture, again for only five seconds, in which only the old woman could be seen. After this preparation he showed the full ambiguous picture to everyone.

The results were, he says, amazing. Most of those 'conditioned' by seeing the young girl first saw only the young girl in the ambiguous picture, and those 'conditioned' by seeing the old woman saw only the old woman. He then asked each group to try to help the others to see what they saw until everyone saw both images. Each group found great difficulty in getting its views across to the other, with considerable complaints about each other's 'stupidity'.

From Hofstede, 'Motivation, Leadership and Organization. Do American Theories Apply Abroad?', *Organizational Dynamics*, Summer 1980

If individuals do not give clear data on their role they run the risk of either confusing, or antagonizing, those with whom they come in contact, or, more often, of being stuck with a stereotype which they did not want.

I recall my first experience of unwanted stereotyping. Participating for the first time in a group learning experience in the USA, I said nothing at all for the first three hours, feeling that the others, who were all American, had more to contribute than I. I was therefore astonished in a feedback session to discover that in spite of saying nothing they still had a clear impression of me as a social snob, intellectually arrogant, conservative, narrow-minded, unfriendly and effeminate! In not providing them with any contrary data they had stuck me with their, largely unfavourable, stereotype of the Englishman. Thereafter, in new encounters, I went to some lengths to provide early data to offset the initial stereotyping!

Unilateral decisions to behave differently from one's role stereotype are not always popular. The manager who does not behave as a manager, the parson who leaves off his collar in the pub, will initially cause role confusion which will be resented. The experiment recounted in Box 3.10 shows what happens in families when the children unilaterally re-define their role. The consultant, in industry, often suffers from role confusion. Seeing himself as a helper he is often perceived as a spy, disrupter of established order, or advance redundancy man. If unused to the experience he may be surprised at the antagonisms aroused by this alternative stereotype of his role.

In general, it is wise to remember that people have to place other people in roles and stereotypes in order to make predictions about them. They will act on whatever information is available, be over-influenced by what they receive first and will be hard to sway from their first impressions. If anyone is not content with the stereotype likely to be provided by existing information she would do well to provide alternative data, or clearer role signs, as quickly as possible.

The halo effect. There is a strong tendency for people to conform to other people's perceptions of them. The bishop tends to behave as bishops are expected to behave, the father begins to conform to the stereotype of a father. The children who are perceived to be bright do in fact become bright (see Box 3.9). Those who are thought to be malcontents tend to become malcontents. If you wish your children to be clever, treat them as if they were clever. If you desire your subordinates to become responsible, behave to them as if they already were responsible. The timid new officer finds himself demonstrating unsuspected bravery in action, because that is part of the role requirement.

There appear to be two reasons for this readily observable phenomenon:

1 People tend to enforce their expectations on the role occupier. The teacher applies higher standards and more encouragement to the pupils he or she regards as talented, thus making them reach ever higher. The officer is forced by his NCO to give orders and take command in certain situations. The Cabinet Minister finds his car waiting for him, the speaking engagements arranged, the appointments set up. It is usually easier in the short-run to conform to the expectations of the role than to change the role. Not living up to role expectations is regarded either as failure or deviancy. Deviant behaviour unaccompanied by demonstrable success is regarded as failure. Only a very self-confident person will be deviant, i.e. over-throw the role expectations. It is often easier for the child to bring

his performance up to the teacher's expectations than to change the expectations.

Box 3.9   Role expectations and the self-fulfilling prophecy

There have been a number of studies of the self-fulfilling prophecy in educational contexts, but the most famous study is that of Robert Rosenthal and Lenore Jacobson, social psychologists at Harvard University. Rosenthal is concerned with the positive self-fulfilling prophecy which states that if children are predicted to improve they will do so, although the *negative* form, whereby pupils deteriorate in work or behaviour as a result of the teacher's expectation, is obviously of at least equal educational significance. The results of Rosenthal's experiment are very complicated in detail, but the main findings can be briefly summarized.

The pupils of an American elementary school were given the 'Harvard test of inflected acquisition'. The teachers were told that this test would single out those pupils who could be expected to make dramatic academic progress. Actually the test was simply an intelligence test. Rosenthal selected *at random* 20 per cent of the pupils, who, the teachers were informed, were the spurters. After the teachers were given the names of the alleged spurters no further action was taken until the pupils were all re-tested for intelligence one year later. If the teachers believed that the alleged spurters would indeed bloom academically, then they might so influence events that the prediction would come true. The results supported such an interpretation. After one year the children nominated as spurters did make marked gains in intelligence. Spurters in the first grade gained on average fifteen IQ points more than did other pupils and in the second grade the spurters gained on average nine IQ points over the others. In these two grades one-fifth of the pupils not nominated as spurters gained over twenty IQ points whereas almost half the spurters did so. The spurters also made marked gains in reading as assessed by the teacher. Rosenthal was able to show that more teacher time was not devoted to the spurters and attributes the result to the quality of the teacher-student interactions.

Reported by Hargreaves in *Interpersonal Relations and Education*, 1972

---

2 Most individuals do not like ambiguity. A new role has lots of ambiguity. Joining a firm, moving into a new level of management, going away on secondment to another institution, are all situations fraught with ambiguity. Explicit role expectations by the 'significant others' (people who matter to the occupant of the role) are one way of resolving the ambiguity. Thankfully, the newcomer does all that he

or she is asked or expected to do. The best way to make a newcomer feel insecure, in a university, in a graduate entry scheme, after mergers or on transfer, is to provide no structure, no rules, no role prescriptions. On the other hand, a detailed programme, instructions on when to eat, how to get things done, the provision of a very competent secretary, will induce feelings of security and compliance. Educational institutions discovered long ago that busy students are contented students, at least as long as they are busy.

The implications of the halo effect are considerable. Self-fulfilling prophecies of a positive or negative kind can readily be created by treating people as if they already are what you want them to become. Assumptions that men are animals lead to treating them like animals and to their behaving like animals, thus justifying your assumptions. Positive self-fulfilling prophecies do not work so infallibly as the negative kind. The basic ability has to be then called out. In Rosenthal's experiment on IQ levels (Box 3.9) not all the supposed spurters prospered. One child had regressed six IQ points by the end of the year. But when people talk of the job making the man, they are pointing to an individual living up to his role expectations. It is probable that not enough people find their role expectations hard to attain – the negative prophecy is more prevalent than the positive, for positive prophecies require faith and trust. Yet if, as has been asserted, the average individual during his lifetime uses only 20 per cent of his talents, it is stimulating to reflect what a burst of 'E' forces could be released in most of us by the use of revised role expectations.

6   Interacting with people

6.1

Our interactions with people are affected to a large extent by the way we perceive them, the things they say and what they do. Our perceptions are in turn affected by our roles *vis-à-vis* them and our view of their roles. Personality, inter-personal skills, the structure of the situation, the qualities of the leader are other factors that affect our interactions. Here we are concerned with the intervening effect of roles and the perception of roles on the behaviour of individuals. We shall consider the interactions of an individual with another individual and the interactions of an individual in a group.

6.2 Interacting with individuals

We have seen that the first thing that anyone does in a new interaction is to place the other individual in some sort of role. The kind of role may vary. It may be occupational (the personnel manager), or social (a worker), or behavioural (a drunkard), or mixed (a snobbish banker). In this way we can make predictions about how they will react and the attitudes they will carry.

When the roles are unclear, the individuals will probe, like two strangers at a cocktail party, to find categories and structures into which they can fit the other. Unless they can find some congruent way of defining the situation, communication will be impaired. If the personnel manager sees herself as advising, but is regarded as telling, she will be resented and will not understand the resentment. This need for an agreement on the relative roles within any particular situation can be illustrated by thinking of each individual as being in one of the metaphorical roles of *parent*, *adult*, *child*. If the individual X intends to relate to the individual Y as Adult to Adult, but is heard by Y as a Parent speaking to a Child, the interaction will result in misunderstanding and possibly resentment. When my wife says to me 'Where did you put the scissors?' my reaction to her simple question will vary depending on which of the relationships depicted in Figure 7 seems to me to be operating. If I hear her speaking to me as a mother to a naughty child I might reply, resentfully, 'I haven't the slightest idea, you used them last.' If I hear her as an inefficient child looking for help, I could reply, 'Don't you know that they are always in the top left-hand drawer.' If, however, it's Adult to Adult I might reply in the same vein, 'I think I left them on the sitting-room table.'

Figure 7

We can also use the need for role classification to influence the situation in the way we want it. Amidst a group of strangers at a party a friend deliberately created ambiguity and even hostility by answering 'nothing' to the repeated question 'What do you do?' When they said 'Oh, you're self-employed, are you?' he replied, 'No, I do nothing.' This blocking response gave them no way of placing him and thus frustrated further communications. Others will experiment with new roles, allowing people to mistake them for a television personality, or claiming to be a distinguished author. The role definition will colour the whole interaction. Or you can force a role definition on someone. 'You are well-known, Sir, for your knowledge of . . .' is an approach that casts the other in the role of expert. He may find the role definition so pleasing that he will carry out the role requirements.

Box 3.10 Confused role expectations in the family

Garfinkel once asked some of his students to behave in their own homes as if they were lodgers and to report back the results:

. . . family members were stupefied. They vigorously sought to make the strange actions intelligible and to restore the situation to normal appearances. Reports were filled with accounts of astonishment, bewilderment, shock, anxiety, embarrassment and anger, and with charges by various family members that the student was mean, inconsiderate, nasty or impolite. Family members demanded explanations: What's the matter? What has got into you? Did you get fired? Are you sick? What are you being so superior about? Why are you mad? Are you out of your mind or just stupid? One student acutely embarrassed his mother in front of her friend by asking if she minded if he had a snack from the refrigerator 'Mind if you have a little snack? You've been eating little snacks around here for years without asking me. What has got into you?' One mother, infuriated when her daughter spoke to her only when she was spoken to, began to shriek in angry denunciation of the daughter for her disrespect and insubordination and refused to be calmed by the student's sister. A father berated his daughter for being insufficiently concerned for the welfare of others and for acting like a spoiled child.

Adapted from Garfinkel, *Studies in Ethnomethodology*, 1967

Many of the rituals of greetings – introductions, indications of appropriate dress or degree of informality – are ways of clarifying role situations, of saying who is who and who is expected to do what and when. But in addition to our attempts to define the role relationships we also look for cues as to how they are behaving in those roles. Are they warm and friendly, or suspicious, or threatening? I once worked in a large open-plan office. One morning the manager came in and walked quickly through to his partitioned office in the corner. As he went past he said 'Good morning, Tony' to my neighbour but said nothing to me. As soon as he had entered his office, Tony turned to me. 'I wonder what was the meaning of that,' he said, 'is he softening me up for a body-blow later this morning, or does he have it in for you and is warning you by ignoring you?' The alternative explanation, that the man was in a hurry and had not noticed me, was too superficial to satisfy Tony's needs for cues as to his boss's feelings.

Box 3.11   Reputations matter

Harold Kelley conducted an experiment to test the effect of prior impressions on perception and behaviour. At the beginning of a psychology class some students at the Massachusetts Institute of Technology were informed that their usual instructor was out of town and that a substitute would take his place. The students were then given, in the form of a note, some information about the replacement instructor:

Mr . . . is a graduate student in the Department of Economics and Social Science here at MIT. He has had three semesters of teaching experience in psychology at another college. This is his first semester teaching EC.70. He is 26 years old, a veteran and married. People who know him consider him to be a rather cold person, industrious, critical, practical and determined.

For half the students in the class this prior information contained the words 'very warm' instead of 'rather cold'. At the end of class the students were asked to rate the instructor on a number of traits and it was found that those students who received the 'warm' information rated the instructor as more considerate, more informal, more sociable, more popular, better natured, more humorous and more human than did the students who received the 'cold' information.

Furthermore, since the class took the form of a discussion group, Kelley was able to record the number of times any student initiated verbal interaction with the instructor, 56 per cent of the students with the 'warm' information participated as against only 32 per cent of those with the 'cold information'.

Adapted from Kelley, 'The warm-cold variable in first impressions of people', *Journal of Personality*, 1950

Non-verbal communication is in fact as important, if not more so, than the actual words used. Non-verbal cues are often the best ways we have of ascertaining the goals, intentions and expectations of the other party in the interaction. Anyone who has the opportunity should study or record an interaction with the sound turned off (videotape can be used effectively for this purpose). You will be surprised at the amount that you will uncover about the overtones in the interaction. Detailed studies have been done of eye contact, of physical proximity and of features in interactions in order to demonstrate the ways we have of communicating without words. Mime is a crucial element in the training of actors for this sort of reason. An awareness of the non-verbal cues we give to people is certainly a useful piece of knowledge for anyone who has a lot of interactions with relative strangers.

Like dogs in a garden, our aim in sniffing each other out in interaction situations is to find answers to the following questions:

What is the other's role?
How does he or she perceive their role?
What are the other's goals?
What does he or she expect to gain from the interaction?
What are his or her immediate intentions?
How is he or she going to behave towards me?

The answers to these questions can result in quite false outcomes. Laing has identified three levels of complication: the direct perspective (my thoughts), the metaperspective (what I think you think of me), and the metametaperspective (what I think you think I think). To make it clearer let us look at one of Laing's examples:

Direct Perspective

John does not love Mary	Mary does not love John

Metaperspective

John thinks Mary loves him	Mary thinks John loves her

Metametaperspective

John thinks that Mary thinks that he loves her	Mary thinks that John thinks that he loves her

Neither wants to hurt the other; rather than resolve the misunderstanding, they might well get married.

Manager–subordinate relationships can easily get into this kind of tangle. If a manager thinks (falsely) that a favourite subordinate dislikes him he can easily behave in such a way that the subordinate begins to think the manager dislikes him. In this way they both are convinced of the other's dislike although the apparent dislike is only a reaction to their interpretation of the other's feelings. If Laing's systematization of the problem appears complicated it is nothing to the complications that underlie many of the role relationships in real life.

The problem of perspective and the dangers of misperception become heightened when there is a mix of cultures. The cultures can be the obvious national ones, as in Box 3.12, or the less obvious ones of staff and line, professional and manager. A piece of behaviour that means one thing to you may be interpreted quite differently by the other person inducing a false metaperspective. What is a *salient* characteristic of the role in my view may not be salient to you. English people who have been brought up to associate articulate ability with intelligence are prone to think inarticulate people stupid. This has led them into difficulties when they encounter the inarticulate scientist, or the silent but efficient engineer, and mistakenly write them off as unintelligent. In perceiving and being perceived it is necessary to find out what the other person regards as salient clues to any role.

Box 3.12   Cross-cultural metaperspectives

We were negotiating with our French partners. The moment of agreement on intentions had arrived. The Frenchmen immediately pushed a document across the table asking us to sign our agreement to our stated intentions in quadruplicate. Reacting like typical Englishmen we regarded this request for a signature at this stage as somehow reflecting on our integrity. After all we had *said* that we agreed to their suggested course of action and at this stage no legal documentation was necessary. Clearly the other side did not trust us. Huffily we replied that signatures were not necessary. So, thought the French, reared in a bureaucratic tradition, they will not sign. What does this mean? Clearly they do not trust us and want to retain room for manoeuvre. It is common practice to record the process of negotiations by signature at each stage.

The meeting was rescued from this cross-cultural misperception only by the intervention of an American who was able to discern that cues were being misinterpreted.

6.3   Interacting with groups

The working of groups is discussed in a later chapter. Here it needs to be recognized that group situations confront the individual with considerable role problems and identity problems, which in turn cause problems for organizations.

The problem for organizations. Individuals must be organized in groups in order to make most effective use of their mix of skills and abilities, but *too much* emphasis on the group may blunt the individual contribution; whilst too much emphasis on the autonomous individual may hinder the development of group identities.

The problem for individuals. Groups, or families, are desirable psychological homes. Without them individuals can become too egocentric to be effective in organizational situations and can deprive themselves of the richness of interpersonal relationships. To submerge oneself in a group too far may involve the sacrifice of some of one's individuality.

Only those who have worked or lived in a small group can fully understand the force of group pressures on an individual. The group pressures need not be explicit, they can be implicit, in that merely being 'out of line' with the group can be itself a pressure towards conforming. Groups tend to develop an identity of their own. The general nature of group pressure is to require the individual to share in this identity, to be one of the group, even if this means subordinating some part of his identity (see Box 3.13).

In simplistic terms this means conforming to the group norms, its customs and standards. Individuals have the choice of:

Complying as a matter of convenience but without real conviction (compliance);
Fully accepting the group norms (internalization);
Rejecting the norms, or the group, or both (counter-conformity).

There is good evidence that group pressure towards conformity or acceptance of norms is strong on the individual, particularly:

When the issue is ambiguous, not clear-cut;
When the individual is in prolonged physical proximity to the other members of the group;
When the individual lacks support for *his* views or behaviour.

Individuals differ in the degree to which they are affected by group pressure to conform. In particular:

More intelligent people conform less readily;
Conformists tend to be more anxious and to lack spontaneity;
Conformists lack self-confidence;
Autonomous people conform less readily;
Conformists tend to be conventional in their social values.

In order to preserve some of his identity the individual will seek a role in the group. There are numerous ways of classifying the possible roles. We shall list only some of them here, as illustrations.

Some, following Wallen, take a behaviourist view in stating that everyone could choose between the roles of:

Friend and helper;
Strong fighter;
Logical thinker.

Box 3.13   Group pressures for conformity

Crutchfield devised an experimental way of testing these pressures. Five subjects at a time are seated in individual booths, screened from one another. Each booth has a panel with a row of numbered switches which the person uses to signal his judgements on items presented on a screen. Also displayed on his panel are signal lights which indicate what judgements the other four members are giving to the item. No one is permitted to talk during the session.

In fact the subjects are being deceived by the experimenter. There are no electrical connections between the five panels. The signals to each individual are in fact given by the experimenter from a master panel so that he can present any combination of four choices to each individual before that individual makes his choice. The individual can then follow the majority (conform) or remain independent. In a one-hour session as many as fifty items can be presented to the five subjects, items of fact or logic, opinion or attitude. Some of the general findings are:

1 When two figures, one a third larger than the other, are presented a large proportion of people will go along with a majority which appears to say that the smaller figure is in fact larger. In a sample of fifty military officers 46 per cent conformed.
2 Among the military officers not a single one, questioned privately, agreed with the statement 'I doubt whether I would make a good leader'. Under group pressure in the test situation 37 per cent expressed agreement.
3 There are large individual differences in degree of conformity.
4 Over an hour-long session some individuals grow more conforming, some grow more independent, though the overall average remains fairly constant.
5 When re-tested privately afterwards, some but not all of the conformity was reversed. The amount retained varied widely for individuals.

From Crutchfield, 'Conformity and Character', *American Psychology*, 1955

In fact, in any group situation, we probably opt for a mixture of all three. But we are likely to have a characteristic pattern of behaviour, whether recognized by us or not, which can be diagrammatically represented by placing ourselves within a triangle formed by putting these three styles at the assumed points, as in Figure 8. It is worth reflecting how much variability there is in fact in your behaviour, whether your colleagues would agree on your assessment, and whether that style is that which the group needs for its particular task. Most groups need a combination of all three; lacking one, they may force an individual into an unaccustomed role, as when the staff adviser finds that, as temporary leader, he has to abandon his favourite stance of 'logical thinker' and become a 'strong fighter'.

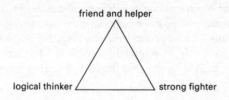

Figure 8

Every group needs some admixture of the three elements if it is to (a) do its task, (b) maintain itself as a group. Who provides which element will be in part determined by the organizational roles and in part by the personalities of the individual. A new form of role problem can arise:

If individuals are competing for one of the categorizations;
If an individual's behavioural role is out of line with their organizational role (e.g. staff assistant is a strong fighter).
More whimsical lists include the following roles:

The comedian. He or she is valuable in relaxing tension, in providing a willing butt for other members of the group and in particular the chairman. When, however, the task becomes dominant the comedian is often discarded as being no longer necessary. People who are insecure often can find this role a quick way of establishing an identity within a group. It brings popularity – is threatening to no one. Unfortunately, the comedian's role is a hard one to escape from. Many people are overlooked in groups because they initially seized on this role.

The organizer. Usually taken by an extrovert character at the outset when the group is relieved that any leader should emerge. He or she establishes their identity within the group by becoming their spokesperson or leader on anything that does not call for the presence or action of the formal leader. Physical arrangements, social activities and a lot of chore-like jobs come his or her way and are willingly taken on.

The commentator. Not a popular role since it involves some threat to the other members. The occupant, often clever but disillusioned, takes it upon him- or herself to maintain an occasional commentary on the proceedings, e.g. 'By my reckoning we have now spent one hour discussing the opening paragraph of the report . . .' This activity is often useful but is seldom seen to be so by the other group members.

The deviant. One way to establish one's identity is to exploit any differences that there may be between you and the group. For instance, a reputation for always asking for definitions can be exploited, sometimes humorously, to give someone an early role in a group. Others make a role out of always opposing anything. To become a common enemy is a sure way of attracting attention. Members of minority groups often use this fact to gain the role of legitimate deviant.

Belbin builds a whole theory of group effectiveness around the set of required roles (or patterns of behaviour) in any task-performing group. These will be studied in more detail in the chapter on the workings of groups. In *Games People Play* Eric Berne has built a semi-serious analysis of group games around role caricatures such as the Rapist, Frigid Woman, etc. The general message is clear – roles are important in groups because they give out signals about the behaviour that is expected and required. A mature group allows people to switch roles from time to time. There is nothing worse than being locked for ever in a role into which you stumbled by accident. It can be a problem for children in school – to escape from the role in which they cast themselves during their first terms – and it is no less a problem as life goes on. Roles are powerful framing devices and need to be taken seriously.

7   Summary and implications

7.1

This chapter has introduced the concepts of role theory as a way of understanding the dilemmas and problems of individuals as members of organizations, groups and pairs. The concepts were:

Role set – the people with whom the *focal person* interacts;
Role definition as a result of *role expectations*;
Role ambiguity – unclear role expectations.

Role conflict – conflicting or overlapping roles;
Role overload – too many roles;
Role underload – too few roles.

In the organization, role problems manifested themselves in:

Individual tension;
Low morale;
Poor communications.

Strategies for resolving these problems were either:

Coping mechanisms – repression, withdrawals, rationalization;
Unilateral strategies;
Co-operative strategies.

Role stress is inherent in organizations:

It can be healthy (role pressure) or unhealthy (role strain);
It occurs mainly in management, innovative or integrative areas;
Some personalities have a higher tolerance for stress than others.

Roles are important to interactions since they provide *categories* into which we can fit data about people and make some assumptions. In seeking for role clarification we often rely on inadequate information, reject conflicting evidence, and are biased by early impressions. This can lead to:

The problem of role confusion;
The halo effect.

When interacting with individuals, separately or in groups, we continually seek for *role clarification* since lack of congruence between the role perceptions of the interacting parties will lead to misinterpretations.

In group interactions, roles are a way of protecting the individual and his identity from the undoubted pressures towards conformity exerted by a group. They also signal the kind of contribution expected from each individual.

7.2 The implications of role theory

Role theory is much better at explaining situations than predicting them. But, as Chapter 1 emphasized, explanations lead to understanding; and understanding, even if it cannot lead to prediction in all cases, does lead to increased tolerance and, perhaps, sympathy for the individual who is the fulcrum poised between large group and small group, between work group and family group, between individual and individual.

Strain is a big factor in our society. Mental illness perhaps should not be so termed, but the symptoms of strain that are often diagnosed as mental illness are becoming increasingly common in all sectors of society. The stress of being an adolescent, of being a successful manager, of ceasing to be a successful manager, too often result in strain. The problem of society, not just of organizations, is the management of stress, that it does not become strain. Role theory is one way of looking at stress, at individuals under stress, at situations that cause stress.

Organizations and individuals need to do more to:

1 Compartmentalize roles appropriately, particularly between work and family. The involvement of the wife in the husband's work too often only creates role strain for her without relieving his. Holidays, respites after foreign travel, sacrosanct weekends, all are ways of compartmentalizing family from work but they can only be done with the organization's consent.

2 Prepare for role transition. More attention needs to be paid to ways of learning a new role, as opposed to a new set of techniques or tasks. Successful managers tend to change positions every two years. No specific time is allocated to role definition, role expectations, or role relationships. The mere act of changing position is stressful enough. Complicate it with fostered ambiguity and stress can easily become strain.

3 Encourage the second career as a way out of the role underload problem of the sideways-shunted executive. Often, an individual can no longer contribute to an organization in proportion to his status and salary expectations. There should therefore be no implication that he cannot contribute to another type of organization or another type of work. He should be encouraged to make the big role transition from a manager to adviser, or from organization man to lone wolf, or from businessman to local government official. The alternative is security, but often accompanied by a particularly denigrating form of role underload. This role underload of the older executive is becoming an important problem for society which only the co-operation of government and organizations can solve.

4 Remember that many of the problems in organizations arise from role strain, misconceptions about role, role underload, or bad communications because of false role expectations. Often, discussion of the problem in terms of role theory clarifies it out of existence. 'There is nothing so practical as a good theory,' said Kurt Lewin years ago.

So much of our time is spent in interactions, at home with our families or our friends, with colleagues at work, or strangers in the street, that it seems strange that we give ourselves or our children so little formal training in it. There is now developing a corpus of training methods in this area, but most of them focus on the operational end of interactions, the actual act of communication. Yet roles and the perceptions of roles underlie all interactions between individuals. More understanding of role perception and of the part that roles play in interactions would surely help to reduce the misunderstandings so common with all of us. This book is not the place for a complete discussion of all the aspects of individual interactions. There are suggestions in Part Three for further reading in this interesting area.

4 ━━ On Leadership

1 Introduction

Leadership as a topic has rather a dated air about it. It smacks of trench warfare and imperial administration. It implies setting one person up above another, raises spectres of élites and privileged classes. 'Why is leadership necessary?' asked a group of undergraduates. 'Surely a group of intelligent, well-meaning individuals can tackle any problem without the need for a leader?' Yet, call it chairman or co-ordinator, representative or organizer, there is a need in all organizations for individual linking-pins who will bind groups together and as members of other groups represent their groups elsewhere in the organization.

Anyone who has ever been responsible for organizing or co-ordinating the work of others, who has sought to get things done through other people, has encountered some of the problems of the management of groups. But the management of people is like driving a car or, perhaps, making love. Most of us do it at some time or other. Most of us do it at least adequately though perhaps we worry from time to time that we might do it better. But we are certainly not going to admit it openly, certainly not going to ask for lessons in it, hardly prepared to discuss it except in a jocular vein. For the management of people is something that all able-bodied men and women can take in their stride.

Or is it? Is leadership, for want of a better word, an innate character-istic? Are leaders born or made? Can anyone be a leader, or only the favoured few? Is there a particular trick to it or a particular style, something that, if we could learn it, would transform our lives? Are there models we should imitate, great ones we can learn from? Do you have to be popular to be effective? Or is it the other way round: is it impossible to be both well-liked and productive?

Assumptions about the nature of leadership have affected not only particular institutions and organizations, but the whole shape of the political system in individual countries, the design of the educational system and the management of the government. In Britain, for in-stance, the belief that leaders had certain basic characteristics which were given them by birth or early environment led to a caste of leaders with educational systems geared to developing those features thought most desirable in leaders. The Second World War was probably a milestone in a continuing trend in that it demonstrated that all sorts of people from all sorts of origins and educational backgrounds could be effective leaders. The re-designed selection procedure for officers in the army was a formal recognition of this. Since this war the whole issue of leadership has been thrown wide open, with consequences for education, for admission procedures to government service, for the management of industrial enterprises.

But the scene remains one of confusion. Can anyone be an effective leader? Or are the traditionalists right and it is bred into you? The search for the definitive answers to the leadership problem have prompted hundreds of studies and as many theories, many of them seeking a justification for their view of the proper nature of society. Theorists have speculated that the secret lay in the style of the leader, or in the nature of the task and the situation or indeed in the characteristics of his personality.

Let it be said at the outset that, like motivation, the search for the definitive solution to the leadership problem has proved to be another endless quest for the Holy Grail in organization theory. There is no secret trick. But, again, better understanding of the nature of the overall problem may lead to better solutions of individual situations. This is the aim of this chapter.

Approaches to the problem of leadership have usually fallen under one of three general headings: *trait theories*, *style theories* and *contingency theories*. Each of these seems to contain some elements of truth but has always in the final analysis failed to explain enough of the difference between effective and ineffective leadership to be generally useful in a variety of situations. The theories will be briefly discussed and reviewed. A more complex, but potentially more realistic, model for understanding leadership situations will then be suggested and its implications discussed.

2 Trait theories

2.1 The findings

These theories rest on the assumption that the individual is more important than the situation, that if we can identify the distinguishing characteristics of successful leaders we shall have the clue to the leadership problem, that if we cannot *make* good leaders we will at least be able to *select* good leaders. By 1950 there had been over 100 studies on this kind of basis. Unfortunately, when looked at *en masse* only 5 per cent of the traits identified were common throughout. In part, this diversity probably reflected the differing biases of the researchers who inevitably tailored their interviews and research instruments towards the particular qualities or traits that they expected to find. In part, however, the diversity suggests that good leaders can come from a wide variety of sources, that the traits that lead to success may differ according to the situation. Most studies single out the following traits:

Intelligence should be above average but not of genius level. Particularly good in solving complex and abstract problems;
Initiative. Independence and inventiveness, the capacity to perceive a need for action and the urge to do it. Appears to correlate quite well with age, i.e. drops off after 40;

Box 4.1   A leader's prayer

Dear Lord, help me to become the kind of leader my management would like to have me be. Give me the mysterious something which will enable me at all times satisfactorily to explain policies, rules, regulations and procedures to my workers even when they have never been explained to me.

Help me to teach and to train the uninterested and dim-witted without ever losing my patience or my temper.

Give me that love for my fellow men which passeth all understanding so that I may lead the recalcitrant, obstinate, no-good worker into the paths of righteousness by my own example, and by soft persuading remonstrance, instead of busting him on the nose.

Instil into my inner-being tranquillity and peace of mind that no longer will I wake from my restless sleep in the middle of the night crying out 'What has the boss got that I haven't got and how did he get it?'

Teach me to smile if it kills me.

Make me a better leader of men by helping develop larger and greater qualities of understanding, tolerance, sympathy, wisdom, perspective, equanimity, mind-reading and second sight.

And when, Dear Lord, Thou has helped me to achieve the high pinnacle my management has prescribed for me and when I shall have become the paragon of all supervisory virtues in this earthly world, Dear Lord, move over. Amen.

Self-assurance. Implies self-confidence, reasonably high self-ratings on competence and aspiration levels, and on perceived ultimate occupational level in society.

Recent studies in a large international company added another:
The helicopter factor. The ability to rise above the particulars of a situation and perceive it in its relations to the overall environment.

In addition most successful leaders appear to:

Have good health;
Be above average height or well below it;
Come from the upper socio-economic levels in society.

Other studies mention *enthusiasm*, *sociability*, *integrity*, *courage*, *imagination*, *decisiveness*, *determination*, *energy*, *faith*, even *virility* (Dueu).

2.2   The criticisms

In general, these theories have been criticized because:

Possession of all the traits becomes an impossible ideal (see Box 4.1);
There are too many exceptions, people who do not have the major traits but are notably successful as leaders;
If reduced to the useful minimum, the top three, they become at best necessary but not sufficient conditions, i.e. good leaders have these qualities but possession of them does not always make one a good leader;
The traits are so ill-defined as to be useless in practice.
There is, however, a danger that these very real disadvantages of trait theory may have led to its undeserved demotion in the leadership studies. In practice most managerial selection schemes work on some assumed, and often unspecified, trait basis, i.e. what traits are most effective or most necessary in what conditions.

To some degree the fade-out of trait theory in favour of style or contingency theory may be a function of a democratic culture. For the implied assumption behind these latter theories is that anyone can be an effective leader provided he or she behaves in the right way, or at least in the way appropriate to the situation, whereas trait theories seemed to imply an élite officer corps of managerial talent who had inherited or acquired the requisite characteristics.

3 Style theories

3.1

The assumption behind these theories is that employees will work harder (and therefore more effectively) for managers who employ given styles of leadership than they will for managers who employ other styles. The styles usually compared are the *authoritarian* and *democratic* dimensions. The major differences between these styles resides in the focus of power. In the extreme authoritarian style power resides with the leader; authority for decision-making, arbitration, control and reward or punishment is vested in the leader who alone exercises this authority. In the democratic style, on the other hand, these powers and responsibilities are shared with the group in some way or other. It is commonly assumed that people will produce more under democratic conditions than under authoritarian conditions. One would like to add 'other things being equal' but not all the studies or theories do add this qualifying factor.

One theoretical base for this belief is that participation in these areas of responsibility will tend to satisfy the self-actualization and esteem needs of the individual and will therefore release more effort. Another set of theories holds that participation affects one's need for stimulation and variety in one's work, and thereby releases more effort.

3.2 A classification

Several theories of leadership, indeed whole theories of management, have been based on this question of style, as it ranges from autocratic to democratic. The following table clusters them along this autocratic–democratic scale, although the authors would rightly claim that such a terminology oversimplified their propositions.

	Autocratic			*Democratic*
Harbison/Myers	autocratic	paternalistic	consultative	participative
Likert	system 1	system 2	system 3	system 4
Tannenbaum/ Schmidt	leader control	shared control	shared control	group control
Vroom	leader decides	consults	shares	delegates
Ohio State Studies	initiating structure			consideration
Hersey/Blanchard	telling	selling	participating	delegating

Box 4.2 Wishful thinking

Douglas McGregor, on leaving Antioch College, of which he had been President, said:

> I believed, for example, that a leader could operate successfully as a kind of adviser to his organization. I thought I could avoid being a 'boss' . . . I thought that maybe I could operate so that everyone would like me – that 'good human relations' would eliminate all discord and disagreement. I couldn't have been more wrong. It took a couple of years, but I finally began to realize that a leader cannot avoid the exercise of authority any more than he can avoid the responsibility for what happens to his organization.

Since the words 'authoritarian' and 'democratic' can have an emotive connotation, and since the other descriptions carry the overtones of their particular creators, we shall, in this book, when wishing to refer to these styles, generically talk of *structuring* and *supportive* styles.

3.3 The evidence of style theories

There is evidence that supportive styles of leadership:

Are related to subordinate satisfaction;
Are related to lower turnover and grievance rates;
Result in less inter-group conflict;
Are often the preferred styles of subordinates.

There are also many instances where supportive styles of leadership were found to be associated with higher-producing work groups. But:

1 On average, over all the studies, the productivity differential has only been 15 per cent – a figure well below what some theorists would lead one to expect.
2 It has been suggested that it could be more effective working that leads to (or permits) more supportive styles – i.e. the causal relationships might be the other way round than that supposed.
3 Experimental studies, where the style of leadership has been deliberately manipulated as an experimental variable, have failed to reproduce the evidence on improved productivity. Out of six available studies, four report no difference in productivity between the styles, one reports the structuring style to be more effective and one reports the supportive style to be more effective.
4 It has been shown that some people prefer to be directed and structured – in particular individuals with low needs for independence

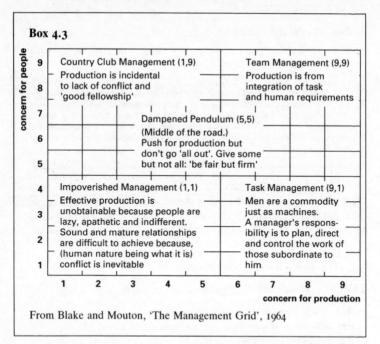

Box 4.3

concern for people

Country Club Management (1,9) Production is incidental to lack of conflict and 'good fellowship'	Team Management (9,9) Production is from integration of task and human requirements

Dampened Pendulum (5,5)
(Middle of the road.)
Push for production but
don't go 'all out'. Give some
but not all: 'be fair but firm'

Impoverished Management (1,1) Effective production is unobtainable because people are lazy, apathetic and indifferent. Sound and mature relationships are difficult to achieve because, (human nature being what it is) conflict is inevitable	Task Management (9,1) Men are a commodity just as machines. A manager's responsibility is to plan, direct and control the work of those subordinate to him

concern for production

From Blake and Mouton, 'The Management Grid', 1964

and in cultures where participation with the leader is not 'legitimate'.
5 In repetitive or routine work, a structured style of leadership leads to higher productivity in the short term, although usually accompanied by lower morale. (It is arguable, but unproven, that this lower morale will eventually lead to reduced productivity.)

3.4 The conclusion

The research findings suggest that style alone is not the answer to effective leadership, nor indeed would many of its principal prophets today maintain that it was. However, there are good indications that, where the psychological contract encourages it, a supportive style of management will lead to a higher degree of contentment and to greater involvement with the work group. This is not necessarily the cause of higher productivity but it is a good base to build on. Overall effectiveness, however, is clearly dependent on more than style alone. Hence, what are called *contingency* theories.

Box 4.4   Roles and styles

Hunt, in his researches into leadership style, found some interesting inconsistencies between roles and styles.

Personnel managers, for instance, were higher on the task-oriented dimension than on the human-relations dimension. On the other hand, welfare people, inductive officials, etc. scored higher on the consideration dimension, which may account for the criticism that they do not solve problems. First-line foremen often turn out to be human-relations oriented, but conceal it in the belief that it is weak and feminine.

Women, if successful as executives, proved to be more task-oriented. In one females-only organization, all the top executives preferred task-oriented roles. This produced endless struggles for power, resulting in much conflict and distress. The same was true of some hospitals, libraries and other organizations largely run by women. Do the human-relations-oriented women leave the workforce, or do such organizations promote only the more task-oriented (and therefore thought to be tougher) women? Nobody knows.

4 Contingency theories

4.1

Contingency theorists take more specific account of the other variables involved in any leadership situation, in particular the task and/or the work group and the position of the leader within that work group.

4.2 Fiedler's theory

Fiedler, in particular, concentrated upon (a) the relationship between the leader and the group, and (b) the structure of the task, as determinants in the choice of the most effective style of leadership. His conclusions are interesting. After looking at leadership situations in a number of organizations he found that a structuring style was most effective when the situation was either very favourable to the leader or very unfavourable. When the situation was only moderately favourable then the supportive style worked best. By 'situations favourable to the leader', Fiedler meant situations where:

(a) The leader was liked and trusted by the group;
(b) The task to be done was clearly laid down and well defined;

Box 4.5   The psychologically distant manager

Fiedler has shown that the leaders of more effective groups, when evaluating subordinates, indicate that they maintain greater psychological distance between themselves and their subordinates than do leaders of less effective groups. The explanation for this appears to be that a manager cannot properly control and discipline subordinates if he is too close to them emotionally: likewise if a manager is emotionally dependent on a subordinate.

An ingenious technique has been developed for measuring psychological distance. The manager is asked to rate his most preferred and least preferred subordinates on various psychological traits. The greater the difference between these two ratings, the more psychologically distant the manager was considered to be. Thus the psychologically distant manager (PD manager) rejects those with whom he cannot work easily while the psychologically closer (PC manager) is more tolerant of his subordinates, or he accepts or rejects subordinates on some criterion other than his ability to work with them. It has been suggested that the PD manager 'has many acquaintances, but few friends: he likes to be with others but he does not want to become emotionally dependent on them'.

Fiedler has shown in his study of the management of small consumer co-operatives that the PD manager was a 'task specialist'.

1 The PD manager tended to be considerably more role-oriented in his dealings with superiors and inferiors.
2 The PD manager saw himself as a professional administrator who held regular staff meetings with his inferiors.
3 The PD manager demanded and got considerable freedom from his superiors.

In contrast the PC manager was more of a 'human relations' specialist.

1 The PC manager saw his job primarily in terms of ensuring smooth interpersonal relations with his superiors and inferiors.
2 The PC manager had a strong trend to close informal ties with people. Some of the attitudes which Fiedler found characteristic of PC managers suggested a need of dominating and possessing people.
3 The PC manager held few formal meetings.

The PD leader is effective in achieving greater productivity from the group only when he is informally accepted by the members of the group. If this condition is not met, then the group will not 'listen to' him and he cannot influence their behaviour. In conclusion it can be stated, subject to the above qualifications, that PD managers are more efficient on task problems and that in contradistinction to PC managers they tend to formalize role relations.

Box 4.5 – *contd*

Fiedler illustrates this emphasis on the task and the formalizing of the role

. . . by the experience of one airforce officer in command of an air base who systematically varied his psychological distance from his chief subordinates. When he had very close relations with these officers, they seemed to feel secure and they did not worry overly about the efficiency of their units. As soon as he became more reserved and role-oriented, his sub-commanders began to worry whether anything had gone awry, they became less sure of their standing in the organization, and channelled their anxieties into paying more attention to their work. As a result, there was a noticeable increase in the efficiency of the base.

Summarized by Kelly in 'The organizational concept of leadership', *International Management*, 1970

(c) The power of the leader in respect to the group was high, i.e. the leader could reward and punish and had organizational backing.

Of these the leader-group relationship (a) was, in Fiedler's view, the most important. His findings are, in general, in agreement with much practical experience. When the task is clearly defined and the leader strong and well-respected he is expected to get on with the job and to be fairly directive. When the task is ambiguous and he is in a weak position *vis-à-vis* the group his best strategy is still to be directive or structuring – to involve the group would then be seen as total abdication of leadership. On the other hand an ambiguous task confronted by a respected leader calls for a more supportive approach, if he is to draw out from his group all the contributions they can make. Fiedler's general conclusion is that organizations could do much more to help the individual leader by either (a) structuring the task, or (b) improving the formal power *vis-à-vis* his group, or (c) changing the composition of the group in order to give the leader a more favourable climate to work in. He suggests that this approach is perhaps more practicable than hoping for the leader to adapt himself to changing circumstances.

Fiedler's approach to leadership is useful, not least because it reminds us that there are occasions when it pays to be distant and task-centred rather than democratic. His research has been criticized, however, on the grounds that he only examined a limited range of unusual groups – basketball teams, bomber crews, open-hearth steel furnace workers and members of small co-operatives – and that his data was not convincing enough to support his propositions. More importantly, Fiedler makes things too simple by restricting the problem to the nature of the task and the relationship between the leader and his subordinates. Most of life is more complicated than a game of basketball.

4.3   Vroom's decision tree model

Vroom rightly starts to deal with the complications by suggesting that a leader has five types of style to choose from, but then goes on to say that the right choice depends on answering, in order, seven different questions. The five styles are:

AI   You solve the problem or make the decision yourself, using information available to you at that time.

AII   You obtain the necessary information from your subordinate(s), then decide on the solution to the problem yourself.

CI   You share the problem with relevant subordinates *individually*, getting their ideas and suggestions. Then *you* make the decision.

CII   You share the problem with your subordinates *in a group*. Then *you* make the decision.

GII   You share the problem with your subordinates as a group. Then *together* you make the decision.

The seven questions, which could be set out like a decision tree, are:

1 Is one decision likely to be better than another? (If not, go AI)
2 Does the leader know enough to take it on his or her own? (If not, avoid AI)
3 Is the problem clear and structured? (If not, go CII or GII)
4 Must the subordinates accept the decision? (If not, then AI and AII are possible)
5 Would they accept *your* decision? (If not, then GII is preferable)
6 Do subordinates share your goals for the organization? (If not, then GII is risky)
7 Are subordinates likely to conflict with each other? (If yes, then CII is better)

This is a pleasingly rational model of decision-making and Vroom has found that it works well in helping managers to describe and plan their own decision-making processes. There is, however, some doubt that what they actually do conforms to what they say they do and, in practice, leadership is more than taking decisions with a group or for a group. Even Vroom's more complicated model is not complicated enough, it seems.

5 The 'best fit' approach

5.1 A description

In any situation that confronts a leader there are four sets of influencing factors that he or she must take into consideration:

The leader – his or her preferred style of operating and his personal characteristics;
The subordinates – their preferred style of leadership in the light of the circumstances;
The task – the job, its objectives and its technology.

These three factors and their fit will in their turn all depend to some extent on:

The environment – the organizational setting of the leader, the group and the importance of the task.

The 'best fit' approach maintains that there is no such thing as the 'right' style of leadership, but that leadership will be most effective when the requirements of the *leader*, the *subordinates* and the *task* fit together. This fit can be measured on a scale that runs from 'tight' to 'flexible'.

tight	flexible

There is no fixed measuring device for this scale – it is a low-definition subjective tool of analysis. The suggestion is that the three factors in any situation can be roughly placed along this scale. For instance:

tight	flexible

leader   _____
subordinates   _____
task   _____

In this situation you have a leader whose preferred style is fairly structuring, working with subordinates whose preference is to have more control over their work, on a task which is loosely defined with no tight time parameters. In this situation the task and the subordinates 'fit' but the leader is out on a limb.

In any situation such as this there will be a tendency for the three factors to move towards each other along the scale. If they remain too

Box 4.6   Bipods and tripods

There are two sorts of people in this world, says Alistair Mant, and one of them ought never to be promoted to high rank. One sort thinks of life, and success, in terms of his or her relationships with other people – the object being to control, dominate or seduce the other in the interest of personal survival. These are the bipods, or raiders.

The other sort are tripods or builders (ternary thinkers as opposed to binary thinkers). For them the question is not so much 'Shall I win?' but 'What's it for?'. For these people there is a third corner to all relationships – the task or the purpose. They can, says Mant, run personal risks in pursuit of some high purpose and can observe themselves in their relationships. They can, as it were, see the joke.

Mant argues that the raider or bipod mentality may thrive for a time but that this form of flawed leadership eventually self-destructs, while if you ask people for examples of great leaders in their own experience they will speak of teachers, managers, fathers (or, more likely, mothers) who were uncompromising in the pursuit of a task or a vision (the third corner).

'Transforming leadership' (the term used by James MacGregor Burns) is tripod thinking, while 'transactional leadership' is closer to the bipod mode. Similarly, Adorno's idea of the authoritarian personality fits the raider, not the builder. We need more builders and fewer raiders in our homes, schools, politics and businesses, but the British tradition fosters the raider, not the builder.

A. Mant, *Leaders We Deserve*, 1984

far apart the group will cease to function as a group or the task will not get done. In the situation described above a powerful leader will often pull the subordinates and the task towards him as far as he can. In the process he may breach the psychological contract with his subordinates and impair the optimum performance of the task. Alternatively he may adjust his style to the requirements of the other two factors. Whether he can do this without losing credibility will depend on the organizational setting – the environment. Before analysing any further the way this scale works let us look in more detail at the three factors.

5.2   The three factors

The leader. For the leader tight or flexible can be interpreted as structuring or supportive. The preferred place on the scale will depend on:

1 His or her value system. To what degree does he feel that subordinates should be involved in planning, deciding, controlling? How does he *in general* define a leader's job? How much importance *in general* does he give to organizational efficiency, subordinate satisfaction, personal success?

2 His or her confidence in subordinates. If she feels that they are technically competent and can be trusted she is more likely to give them control over the work.

3 His or her habitual style. Though most people hope that they can be flexible they usually have a way of operating in which they feel most comfortable – this becomes their habitual style.

4 His or her assessment of his personal contribution. If he feels that his contribution to the group is vital he will tend to want to be more structuring and controlling.

5 His or her need for certainty. A leader who relinquishes control of a situation reduces the predictability of the outcome. If she has a high need for predictability, a low tolerance for ambiguity, she will tend towards the 'tight' end of the scale. Similarly, a low risk-taker will be less willing to relinquish control.

Box 4.7   Culture's creatures?

Machiavelli, writing in Italy in the early sixteenth century, described a theory of leadership akin to manipulation. It was based on the assumption that leaders have, and should have, much more power than their followers (a large Power Distance Culture). Thomas More, writing in England at the same time, described a Utopia based on consensus, where ideally power is distributed more equally (a small Power Distance Culture). Leadership theories in the sixteenth century were, therefore, heavily culture-biased.

They still are, argues Hofstede. His research suggests that Italy still is more comfortable with large Power Distances. So are France, Mexico and Brazil. Denmark, Sweden, Austria, Israel and New Zealand, on the other hand, prefer much smaller Power Distances and so would look for a consensus type of leadership. Britain, the United States, Canada and the Netherlands are in the middle, which might explain the more ambivalent contingency-type theories which emanate from these countries.

Leadership is also about followership. You can only be the sort of leader your followers are comfortable with. What works in Scandinavia may well look weak and wet in Mexico.

G. Hofstede, *Culture's Consequences* (Abridged Edition), Sage Publications, 1984.

6 Degree of stress. Stress and tension will usually lead to a tighter style.

7 Age. Older people seem to be more structuring.

These forces in the leader will often conflict with each other. However, the net result will be to place the leader somewhere along the tight–flexible continuum in relation to a particular group. This will be a personal starting point in considering any particular task or objective. The degree to which anyone is able to move from that point on the scale will be considered shortly.

The subordinates. Their preference for a particular type of leadership (structuring or supportive) will be influenced by:

1 Their estimate of their own intelligence and competence. The more competent and professional they feel the more control they will normally want.

2 Their psychological contract with that group and that leader. Does the contract specify involvement or is it a satisficing contract?

3 Their interest in the problem and their view of its importance. They will not want lots of involvement in trivia.

4 Their tolerance for ambiguity or their need for structure.

5 The past experience of the group. Have they been used to involvement? Are they used to working together and do they have respect for each other's competence? New, inexperienced or distrustful people tend to need structuring leadership at the start.

6 Cultural factors. Younger people, more highly educated and perhaps more permissively reared, tend to want more involvement. Democratic norms in most societies reinforce this tendency. People in creative situations (R and D, and marketing) tend to want more responsibility for their own work.

The task. Should it be programmed and structured or should it be left open-ended? This will depend on:

1 The kind of task. Is it decision-making or implementing? Does it require initiative or obedience? Is it a routine administrative function? Is it creative (e.g. R and D), or problem-solving (e.g. consultancy), or pioneering (e.g. new product marketing)? In general if it is a problem with an open-ended solution it will tend towards the flexible end of the scale. Closed or finite problems tend towards the tight end.

2 The time-scale. Participation takes time. Short time-horizons drive one towards the tight end of the scale.

3 The complexity. This can go either way. Technical or conceptual complexity will usually push the task towards the flexible or open-ended portion of the scale. Organizational complexity will push it to the structuring or tight end.

4 Do mistakes matter? (a) In a creative or problem-solving task the more brains the better – but such involvement will take time. A more structured approach may be less perfect or less creative. Does a 60 per cent solution matter? Or is it desirable? (b) In an executive or controlling function tight controls may be necessary to prevent any possibility of error, e.g. in the manufacture of manned space rockets.

5 The importance of the task. Unimportant tasks do not merit time or attention, i.e. should be tightly structured.

5.3   Analysis of the 'fit'

For any given situation the three factors should be plotted very roughly along the scale tight–flexible. In practice this will normally be done by the leader himself, and one must recognize that his analysis is likely to be biased. The aim of all analysis is to remove bias and substitute objectivity. Clearly the more objective the leader can be, the more useful will be the analysis.

In many situations there will not be a perfect fit. To some degree one can generalize about the nature of the misfits:

1 In many middle-management situations the comparative youth and high educational level of both manager and managed pushes their preferred styles towards the supportive or flexible end. But in many such situations the task requirements, as they are normally defined, are for structure and tight control mechanisms.

2 Top management, on the other hand, is inclined by age and by middle-management task experience towards the tight end of the scale, but is confronted by open-ended problem-solving tasks which need a more flexible approach.

3 Sales executives, developed in a job with a fairly high degree of structure and control, and promoted to posts of marketing responsibility with numbers of staff marketing experts reporting to them, often find the new and more 'flexible' requirements of task and subordinates a big challenge to their habitual style.

4 The effect of technology and computers is often to tighten up the job in order to achieve better predictability. This can be at variance with any wish for more flexibility on the part of men or management.

5.4   Achieving the best fit

Confronted with a lack of fit the leader must consider which of the three factors to adjust in order to achieve a fit. Theoretically, it is easiest for him to alter his own style – particularly if the other two factors already have a degree of fit between themselves. This explains why there is emphasis on *leadership style* in literature on the subject.

However, although the leader's style is theoretically the easiest to alter in the short term, there are often long-term benefits to be achieved from re-designing or re-defining the task (e.g. job-enlargement) or from developing the work group.

5.5   The environment

The fourth element, the *environment*, must now be considered. The leader, the subordinates and the task do not occur in a vacuum. The setting of the situation will have a big bearing on the degree of freedom which the leader has to adjust any of the three factors. There are six key aspects of the environment:

The power position of the leader in the total organization;
The relationship of the leader to the group;
The organizational norms;
The structure and technology of the organization;
The variety of tasks;
The variety of subordinates.

These aspects of the environment can best be considered in pairs:

The power position of the leader in the organization;
The relationship of the leader and the group.

These two elements – two of those considered by Fiedler – are best regarded as conditioning the freedom of the leader to adjust his style and the task. Variability in leadership style can lead to unpredictability and to lack of confidence, credibility and trust in the subordinates unless the leader is already trusted and respected by them. Power based on expertise and achievement gives the leader more freedom than purely legal power. Most organizational tasks are not isolated tasks – they have some impact on other parts of the organization. The re-definition of any task, in terms of time-span, complexity, scope or implication will therefore require the ability of the leader to negotiate this re-definition with the affected parts of the organization. Hollander coined the phrase 'idiosyncrasy credit' to explain a leader's degree of freedom. If the leader has piled up lots of credits with the group (for conformity in the past, for success, for status) he or she can spend them on deviant behaviour. If, on the other hand, there is no credit then there is nothing to lose by doing the unexpected or unwanted and everything to gain if he makes it work. It is the leader in the middle, with middle status with the group, who has to be careful and conform to the group:

The organizational norms;
The structure and technology of the organization.

A leader is never completely free in an organization to behave as he or she would want to behave. There are organizational requirements, such as hours of work, reports and returns; and organizational norms, such as methods of reward and punishment, mode of address to subordinates. Neil Rackham and his colleagues, for example, discovered that in the US division of one corporation effective leaders were expected to be critical of their subordinates, whereas in the UK there was no such expectation. Conformity to these organizational norms is to some degree required of all managers and supervisors, particularly those low in position power in the organization. Organizations also have formal structures and procedures. Not only does this mean that work cannot easily be re-defined in isolation but re-definition of work may involve a change in the structure of the organization. Decentralized or project-type organizations allow more scope for individual managers to re-define their style and task but decentralized organizations are not possible in certain technologies (e.g. process manufacturing):

Variety of tasks;
Variety of subordinates.

Most managers find that the task of achieving a best fit is complicated by two further factors:

(a) They have a wide variety of tasks to perform, ranging from complex long-range assignments, through more intangible tasks such as building a team or developing subordinates, to the day-today routine. The best fit for each task may well be different. To manage variety through adaptability requires a very good relationship with the group but,
(b) the membership of work groups is constantly changing, partly because the actual work group may be re-defined for differing purposes (one committee for this, another for that) and partly because individuals move in and out of groups as their lives and careers progress.

Given this complexity, it is understandable if managers give up the attempt to find a best fit and merely impose their habitual style upon the task and the subordinates.

The emphasis in the literature of management theory upon the importance of group relationships is at least partially justified in that an individual leader's ability to adapt is very largely governed by his relationship with his group. Given the changing nature of that group a leader needs to allocate a considerable amount of energy to building the required relationship to start with.

Box 4.8   The three circles

John Adair has perfected a very successful model of leadership training in Britain based on the three overlapping circles that are involved in any leadership situation:

He emphasizes the importance of distinguishing the *individual* from the *group*. There will seldom, if ever, be a perfect match between the needs of the individual, the group and the task. The leader's job is to be aware of the tension and to manage it. To do this he needs a *functional* approach which has eight elements:

Defining the task;	Evaluating;
Planning;	Motivating;
Briefing;	Organizing;
Controlling;	Setting an example.

The training is organized around precept and practice in each of these eight areas. Style, as Adair points out, is more than and different from the business of taking decisions, which is relatively straightforward.

See J. Adair, *Effective Leadership*, 1983

Thus, one set of studies of leadership in schools (by Nias) uses three scales, not one: *Initiating Structure*, *Consideration* and *Decision-*

Centralization. Teachers, it appeared, wanted from their heads a lot of the first and second and relatively little of the third. In other words, for the best-fit diagram to be useful in any particular situation the leader had first to build up a more general image and style which allowed room for manoeuvre.

'Positive' heads, as opposed to 'passive' or 'Bourbon' (autocratic) heads, demonstrated a high level of personal and professional commitment, gave support and encouragement to individuals, had clear aims for the institution which were open to limited negotiation and were able to create a sense of cohesion for the school as a whole. Teachers, it seemed, wanted to be led, not left to their own devices. 'Passive' heads left too much alone, being low on Initiating Structure and Decision-Centralization and not very high on Consideration. They would find themselves in a double-bind on the diagram because, Fiedler would say, their only hope was to move to a more structuring approach but their personality would preclude that. 'Bourbon' heads were too autocratic and too low on consideration; they would therefore find it hard to move away from the tight structuring style because there would be little trust in their staff or by their staff.

A head, therefore, like any leader, has to shape the environment as well as being shaped by it. Leadership is not exercised in a vacuum. First set the stage, then act on it.

6 A new synthesis

6.1

Recent years have seen a renewed interest in leadership as opposed to management, perhaps because 'great neccesities call forth great leaders' as Abigail Adams wrote to Thomas Jefferson in 1790, perhaps because we have gradually come to realize that people prefer to be led rather than managed. Warren Bennis and Bert Nanus interviewed 90 leaders, some in business, some in public service, some in the arts or in sport, in order to arrive at their new synthesis of leadership.

'Managers are people who do things right and leaders are people who do the right thing' was their principle conclusion, echoing Peter Drucker thirty years before. They were impressed by the way their interviewees were concerned with the purpose and direction of the organizations which they headed, rather than with the nuts and bolts.

Trait theory got short shrift. Almost all were white males, it is true, but the authors felt this was more to do with the legacy of sexism and racism in the American corporate world than with any underlying truth about leaders. Apart from that common fact, and the surprising one that almost all were still married to their first spouse and were indefatigably enthusiastic about marriage, there were no common traits. They were right-brained and left-brained, tall and short, fat and thin, assertive and retiring, of multiple styles (including one who confessed to 'participative fascism').

6.2

Out of the interviews Bennis and Nanus distilled four themes or necessary areas of competence, which they call strategies and which can be summarized as: vision, communication, trust and self-knowledge. These strategies do not presume to tell you how to achieve a perfect fit in any particular situation. They are best regarded as the necessary conditions for any freedom of action. Without them, or some approximation of them, no aspiring leader will stand much of a chance. We can examine each in turn.

Vision. The vision which these leaders conveyed seemed to bring about a confidence on the part of the employees, a confidence which gave them a belief that they could actually deliver the dream. They recalled the character in Shaw's *Man and Superman*, said Bennis and Nanus: 'This is the true joy in life, the being used for a purpose recognized by yourself as a mighty one; the being a force of nature instead of a feverish selfish little clod of ailments and grievances complaining that the world will not devote itself to making you happy.'

Communication. It is, however, of no use having a dream if that dream is not shared by everyone else. It is best if everyone else has a part in the shaping of the dream, leaving it to the leader to articulate it and to capture it in some way so that it steals into the imaginations of the people. Some of the leaders did it with words, some with visual models, some just by living and breathing their vision in contact with their people.

Trust. By trust is meant consistency and integrity, the feeling that a person and an organization can be relied upon to do what they say, come what may. Admiral Rickover called it 'courageous patience'. Theodore Friend III, past President of Swathmore College, put it well when he said, 'Leadership requires that one knows where one is taking oneself; from the being that has been to the one that wishes to be, despite ambiguities, and against the odds that inhere in ideals.' Can others trust you to be you?

Self-knowledge. The 90 leaders were not self-worshippers but they knew their worth, and their weaknesses. They build on their strengths and compensate for their weaknesses and they consciously look for the fit between who they are and what the organization needs. No man and no woman can do everything everywhere. What they were universally good at was getting others to feel good at what they were doing, to be proud in *their* self-knowledge. Self-knowledge and the 'emotional wisdom' it brings allow one to trust others to do what they are good at, to do without the constant approval of others, to accept people as they are instead of judging them.

A leader, we can say in summary, is someone who is able to develop and communicate a vision which gives meaning to the work of others. It is a task too important to be left only to those at the top of organizations. Leaders are needed at all levels and in all situations. Interestingly, the Japanese language has no word for 'leadership', the leader being thought of as inseparate from the group. In fact, anyone who wants to get something done with or through other people can and should learn the lessons of leadership. We are all leaders at one time or another.

7 Summary

This chapter has reviewed the main theories on leadership and suggested a more integrative way of looking at the subject.

The approaches reviewed were *trait theories*, *style theories* and *contingency theories*. The approach suggested was an extension of the contingency theories called *best fit approach*. This approach requires that the style preferences of the *leader, subordinates*, and the demands of the *task* be ranged along a scale from *tight* (or structured) to *flexible* (or supportive).

The suggestion is that for effective performance the requirements of the three factors have to 'fit' together on the scale. The way the fit is achieved, i.e. which factors will adapt or be adapted, will depend on *the environment* (or organization setting) which includes:

The power or position of the leader;
The relationship with his group;
The organizational norms;
The structure and technology;
The variety of tasks;
The variety of subordinates.

Leaders need to develop vision, communication, trust and self-knowledge in order to do this. The leadership of groups or divisions is a vital part of organizational effectiveness but results in role complexity, incompatibility, conflict, ambiguity, and therefore stress. To help manage this complexity there are things that:

> Organizations need to know and understand;
> Organizations need to *do*;
> Individuals need to *do*;
> Individuals *and* organizations need to *do*.

These *desiderata* are spelt out in the next section.

8   General conclusions on leadership

8.1   The desiderata

The modern trend in organization theory has been to play down the importance of the individual and the group leader in favour of things like structure, control systems and climate. Later chapters in this book will however suggest that trends in these areas are beginning to high-light once again the importance of the individual as an 'integrator' or a 'linking-pin' or a 'catalyst'.

Whatever words are used, the leadership of groups within organizations is always going to be a vital ingredient in the effectiveness of organizations. The discussion in this chapter should have made it apparent that the role of leader is a complex one, riddled with ambiguity, incompatibility and conflict. The analytical model should make the complexity more understandable though it will not always make it more resolvable. For that to happen:

1 Senior managers need to develop a better understanding of the complexity of the role of group or divisional manager. Lack of understanding can lead to stereotyping which in turn can lead to a unified set of models for leaders in the organization, often based on narrow 'trait' definitions. Better understanding of the complexity and variety of leadership situations should lead to better differentiation between situations and leadership requirements.

2 Senior managers need to help individual leaders to reduce the complexity of their roles by:
  (a) Clearer role definitions;
  (b) Creating less variety in the composition of the work groups;
  (c) Allowing more freedom to individuals to pursue a style different

from the norm. One of the hardest tasks of management is to allow your subordinates to behave in a different style from yourself;

(d) Judging effectiveness by ends not means, i.e. by performance and not by style;

(e) Giving an individual time to produce results, i.e. not moving him every eighteen months.

3 Individuals need to learn to:

(a) Develop and communicate a clear vision of the task, so that a consensus of purpose develops in the group;

(b) Allow others to influence that vision, so that they are committed to it;

(c) Build up the trust and respect of their group so that they have the essential conditions to allow them to adapt their style to the contingency requirements;

(d) Remember that successful performance of their ambassadorial role is essential if they are to have freedom to behave as they think best within their group;

(e) Remember that they represent the organization to their subordinates and should practise all the precepts enjoined on the senior managers (above).

4 Individuals and organizations should bear in mind that the individual who meets the above requirements will tend to:

(a) Have high tolerance for ambiguity and be good at handling open-ended problems;

(b) Be good at differentiating – between people and between situations;

(c) Have a clear self-concept which will tend to go with self-confidence;

(d) Have a high reservoir of the 'E' factors, in particular, energy;

(e) Be prepared to set moderately high standards for himself and his co-workers and to give and receive feedback on performance.

8.2 The differentiated trait approach

All this adds up to what might be called a differentiated trait approach to leadership. For although the personality and style cults have been overthrown in favour of a more complex model, all experience tells us that there are, nevertheless, individuals who are in general better leaders than others. Research is beginning to suggest that it is those who have the characteristics listed in the previous paragraph, because those are the kind of people who can handle the complex model described in this chapter.

In particular situations, particular characteristics or particular styles will be effective because they will be appropriate. In that sense almost everyone can be an effective leader by finding the circumstances that suit him. Organizations can also do far more to fit the job to the man and so make better use of their available talent.

But organizations will always have a need for the 'manager', the leader who is effective in a variety of situations. They need criteria for selecting them. The criteria listed above will provide a starting-point. They have affinities with the early traits of intelligence, integrity and helicopter factor – but are capable of more precise definition and measurement and can be related to the requirements of particular situations. The criteria will be altered or added to in each organization depending on its culture (see Chapter 7) and its particular leadership requirements. In one part of one organization, Rackham and his colleagues found that the desired characteristics included:

Checking that people understood communications;
Giving specific objectives;
Admitting when things are not going well.

8.3 In conclusion

How can individuals improve their leadership abilities? How can organizations help them to do so? This will be discussed in more detail in a later chapter. The characteristics listed in 8.1 cannot be taught in the classroom. To some extent they will be there, or not be there, by the time the individual reaches maturity and joins the organization. Early environment and education clearly have a lot to do with them. The individual and the organization can, however, build on what is already there. The only effective way of doing this is to:

Place the individual in situations, real or artificial, where the principal characteristics will be tested;
Help him or her to understand how these characteristics could be improved, by particular examples.

This will involve the organization in:

Devising 'leadership learning' situations, even if this distorts the short-term efficiency of the organization structure;
Paying more attention to the 'coaching role' in organizations. It is unrealistic to leave this to the immediate superior since the 'coaching role' and the 'leader role' are not easy ones to combine. Under pressure

Box 4.9 Six good leaders

Maccoby studied six successful leaders in very different types of organizations on both sides of the Atlantic, ranging from a foreman in Tennessee to a factory manager in Scotland, and from a union leader to a Congressman. They included a woman government official and a Swedish chief executive. The six were both different and similar!

They all shared certain traits – intelligence, ambition, will and optimism. All were persuasive communicators. Although they came from very different backgrounds, they shared a critical attitude to authority. Each of them had also taken time off from the tiring managerial tasks of getting the job done to question whether the mission of their organization served society and individual employees. They were pragmatists, not ideologues, but some of them were also quite clear that they would not sacrifice people for power. Bluestone (the union leader), for example, was unwilling to sacrifice friendship to compete for the union presidency, while Reaves (in Scotland) would not sacrifice his family to become a national leader.

They don't try to control everyone, observed Maccoby. They spend more time developing consensus than controlling things or dealing with mistakes. They defend basic values of human dignity, equity and liberty, including the right to be heard, even when the majority is opposed. They don't feel they have to win every contest, but approach conflict strategically, prepared for retreat when necessary, though without losing sight of long-term goals.

M. Maccoby, *The Leader*, 1981

Ten good schools

Her Majesty's Inspectorate of Schools in Britain examined ten secondary schools of different types, all reckoned to be successful by a broad range of criteria. They concluded:

'What they all have in common is effective leadership and a climate conducive for growth . . . Emphasis is laid on consultation, team work and participation but, without exception, the most important single factor in the success of these schools is the quality of leadership of the head. Without exception, the heads have qualities of imagination and vision, tempered by realism, which have enabled them to sum up not only their present situation but also attainable future goals. They appreciate the need for specific educational aims, both social and intellectual, and have the capacity to communicate these to staff, pupils and parents, to win their assent and to put their own policies into practice. Their sympathetic understanding of staff and pupils, their accessibility, good humour and sense of proportion, and their dedication to their task has won them the respect of parents, teachers and taught.'

Ten Good Schools, 1977

the coaching role is too easily forgotten or postponed in favour of the decision-making role. Someone other than the immediate superior can often be more objective and more helpful to a junior struggling in a leadership situation. Perhaps this 'uncle role' needs to be more formally recognized and legitimized in organizations.

5 → On Power and Influence

1 Introduction

Motivation theory, role theory, leadership theory are all ways of describing why people behave as they do and how it is that others can set them to behave as they do. It is time now to look at this problem in a more general way, at the overall problem of power and influence.

Power and influence make up the fine texture of organizations, and indeed of all interactions. Influence is the process whereby A seeks to modify the attitudes or behaviour of B. Power is that which enables him to do it. Organizations can be looked at as a fine weave of influence patterns whereby individuals or groups seek to influence others to think or act in particular ways. If we are to understand organizations we must understand the nature of power and influence for they are the means by which the people of the organization are linked to its purpose. Yet they are unfashionable words, words that we shun in daily discourse. Perhaps because they imply levels, one person over another. Yet we recognize that hierarchies are inevitable in groups or societies of any size at all. Perhaps because power and influence in some way implies the infringement of some individual's freedom over his or her actions. But if so then only the ostrich among us can survive modern organizational life with his ideals of individual freedom intact. Complete individual freedom is the perquisite of the hermit and the recluse; today perhaps only the solitary artist or poet, the tramp or the hippie can enjoy that luxury. For part of any psychological contract with any group, family, firm or society is an exchange of some individual freedom in return for the rewards of belonging. All interactions, Homans would maintain, involve an exchange of something for something in return. But how much individual freedom should one give up? And how defined, in what areas? Who shall influence me, and whom shall I influence? Which methods will be tolerated, and which will not? What ways are there of resisting influence, what of gaining it? These questions lie bedded in the true reality of organizational life. Anyone who would wish to understand organizations must try to deal with them.

The power to influence is something that most people would like more of, in some respect, even if they do not want the responsibility that may go with it. Thus, many research studies show that individuals in organizations would like more influence over their work. There is also some evidence that the person who feels they exercise influence gives more of themselves to the job, takes more interest, is more involved. The responsibility which goes with influence creates a stake in success or failure – even to the extent of illness. (More managers tend to have psychosomatic disorders than workers.) Likert has shown that groups where individuals feel they each have more influence tend to be more productive.

I have distinguished between power and influence. Not everyone does so in ordinary life; nor do all the theorists. This often causes confusion, which is partly due to the fact that power, in English, is a noun which does not, as in French, have a verb to go with it, whereas influence is both a noun and a verb. For clarity, I shall use influence to mean the *use* of power (its verbal form), keeping power to mean the *resource* behind it. *Authority* is another word which can add to the confusion. Authority is used when the power is legitimate and has some recognized official backing. To say that someone has influence is therefore, in my thinking, a shorthand way of saying the power to influence. To say that someone has authority is a shorthand way of recognizing and accepting his or her power source.

If A is to influence B then A must first have some understanding of B, of B's motivation calculus, of the psychological contract, of the role. Only then can he or she know what things are likely to influence B. These we have already explored in the early chapters. A must then understand what methods of influence are available in that situation, and the sources of power that underlie them. This is the immediate concern of this chapter. The particular exercise of influence that is involved in the formal leadership of groups was discussed in Chapter 4. But formal leadership is only one aspect of individual influence, only one expression of an influence system in an organization. Individuals, in any role, in any organization, have some power, some capacity to exert influence. When we speak of argument or persuasion, threats or blandishments, love or hate, we are talking of individual influence. When we talk of group pressure or conformity, socialization or propaganda, education or development, we are talking of organizational or group influence.

The study of influence and power has proved to be for social scientists 'a bottomless swamp' (Dahl). There are many piecemeal studies of various bits of the field – it is hard to pull them together into any coherent picture. This chapter will attempt to do just that. First we shall describe various *sources of power* which underlie the *methods of influence*. The use of any particular method of influence will involve *implications* about the individuals involved, the situation and the response mechanisms. We shall end by looking at the *messages for the manager* in all of this.

2   Power as a source of influence

2.1

There have been various categorizations of power in social or organizational settings. The one used here is a variety of that proposed by French and Raven. The possible sources of individual power which give one the ability to influence others are physical power, resource power, position power, expert power and personal power.

Before describing these particular sources of power there are some general considerations which we shall need to bear in mind throughout the discussion.

1   The relativity of power. If A's power source has no importance for B then that source of power is ineffective in that situation: A will have no ability to influence B. The group that overawes one person with its prestige and renown looks ludicrous to another. The guns that silence one will only stimulate another. Bribes will sway some but repulse others. The effective amount of power that anyone has will constantly ebb and flow as the constituency in which it is exercised changes its membership.

2   The balance of power. Most influence situations, most relationships, come to that, are balanced on a power equation. Power is seldom one-sided. Even the prisoner can hit back. The power to disrupt, for instance, or 'negative power' as it is termed later in this chapter, is always available in some form to everyone. Power seems most blatant and most extreme when the power equation is most unbalanced. It follows that the possession of a power source does not automatically mean that you can influence someone. It depends on what power he can put into the balance, remembering always that one type of power can offset another. Money has been known to overrule expertise.

3 The domain of power. Few sources of power are universally valid
over all constituencies. Many of the arguments and haggles about
power in organizations are to do with the domain of a particular
power source. Individuals wish to extend the scope of their own
power, to limit the scope of others' power. When we speak of
someone's power or influence as legitimate we mean that the domain
has been prescribed, the conditions under which and over whom it
can be exercised have been laid down. As a professor of sociology
put it once: 'If I try to influence the views of my students about
Marx, I may succeed. If I try to influence their choice of partner I
will fail. It is not my legitimate domain.'

2.2 Physical power

This category of power is self-explanatory. It is the power of superior
force. The bully or the big man has it. The tyrant or the commander
of the army has it. In many developing nations physical power is ultimately more important than the will of a majority of the people.
Prisons and the enforcement of law rest ultimately on physical power.
For, of course, in order to be effective as a basis for influence physical
power does not have to be used. Its existence, or the belief in its
existence, is enough.

In few work organizations is physical power the source of any individual's influence. Ultimately no organization, save those supposed
guardians of public safety, the prisons and some mental hospitals, have
the right to detain an individual by force. Some schools may claim the
right, a few pupils question their headmaster's physical power, but
most adult organizations are in essence organizations which the individual is *physically* free to leave.

This is not to deny, however, that in individual transactions the
threat of physical coercion may not seem temporarily a very potent
source of influence. Bullies are not confined to schools. Picket lines
have often held a distinct element of coercion in their attitudes. The
physical presence of a dictatorial boss can often seem like coercion
to his or her quavering subordinates. Whilst physical power is less
respectable in our society than all other power sources there are signs
that it is increasingly becoming the power of last resort when the other
sources appear ineffective or too closely balanced against opposing
sources. Ulster, lock-outs, mass demonstrations are all examples of
this phenomenon.

Box 5.1   Fear is real.

In the office in which I work there are five people of whom I am afraid. Each of these five people is afraid of four people (excluding overlaps), for a total of twenty, and each of these twenty people is afraid of six people, making a total of one hundred and twenty people who are feared by at least one person. Each of these one hundred and twenty people is afraid of the other one hundred and nineteen, and all those one hundred and forty-five people are afraid of the twelve men at the top who helped found and build the company and now own and direct it.

J. Heller, *Something Happened*, 1975

2.3   Resource power

Possession of valued resources is a useful basis for influence. Reward power is another term for it, preferred by French and Raven. It is the power source implicit in most calculative contracts. For resource power to be effective (a) there must be control of the resources, and (b) those resources must be desired by the potential recipient. (These are rather obvious conditions but ones not always remembered.) For instance, in union negotiations if the union negotiator does not have control (i.e. cannot commit or withdraw the labour of his members), or if his resources are not desired by the employers (i.e. there are other sources of labour) then he will have very reduced power. The union movement's attempts to create labour monopolies are simply an effort to increase their resource power. Governments' attempts to match this with the ultimate threat of legal enforcement of physical power is an interesting but perhaps unresolvable conflict between two types of power, the resource power of organized labour and society's ultimate sanction of physical imprisonment. A manager often has resource power to the extent that she can give promotion or pay increases to her subordinates. If the subordinate does not want promotion the manager may find herself in the position of the harassed mother whose bribe of ice-cream is met with the rejoinder. 'I don't like ice-cream today!' The codification of pay, the bureaucratization of promotion – as in teaching institutions, civil service departments, hospitals – is an effective reduction in the power of the individual manager since it reduces her control over these desired resources.

Resources do not have to be material. They can consist, for instance, of grants of status, the equivalent of a key to the executive washroom. Belonging, the admission to a select group, is another valued resource to many people. But one must beware of overrating the attractions to others of the things one values oneself. A friend's attempt, in undergraduate days, to form an exclusive dining-club foundered when no one else saw it as exclusive. The kind of exclusivity over which he had control was not valued by anyone else. Power is always relative to the constituency in which it is exercised. Resource power is not usually popular. People do not like to be reminded that they can, in effect, be bought. Paternalistic organizations are sometimes surprised when their occasional bountiful distributions receive only grudging thanks. Maybe without meaning to, they are seen to be needlessly re-emphasizing their power base.

2.4 Position power

This has been called 'legal' or 'legitimate power'. It is the power that comes as a result of the role or the position in the organization. The occupancy of a role entitles one to all the rights of that role in that organization. The manager is by right allowed to order people to do so-and-so. The inspector is by right allowed to inspect other people's work. When theorists distinguish between power and authority, position power is usually equated with authority as being legitimized power, or power residing in the position rather than in the individual.

The value of position power as a source of power depends ultimately on the value placed on the guarantor of the position. Position power has to be ultimately underwritten by either physical power or resource power. If the occupant of a particular role either (a) does not receive backing from the organization, or (b) the organization is not seen as controlling any desired or coercive resources, then the occupant of the position will find that his influence attempts will fail, because his power source is invalid. The occupant of a position, it should be made clear, does not himself have to have resource power, but the organization guaranteeing or establishing that position has to have it. The secretary of a voluntary organization, a post which is unpaid and of not very high status, will have position power but only to a limited degree. Once the guaranteeing power source is withdrawn the position power is minimal or illegitimate or both. The ambassador of a deposed government turns into a dispossessed citizen. The chairman's secretary is just another person when the chairman is deposed.

Position power gives to the occupant potential control over some *invisible assets*. Principally these are:

1 *Information*. A flow of information often belongs as of right to a 'position' in the organization. If it does not already belong it can often be originated as a necessary input to that position. This can be horizontal information, i.e. information, often of a technical nature, from the same level of the organization: vertical information, from above or from below but potentially trapped in the particular 'position' and to be dispersed with the agreement of the occupant. Information, above all else in life, seems to display the essential features of synergy. The whole is so often much more meaningful than the sum of individual parts. An informational jig-saw, even though all the pieces are separately available, is nothing until put together. A 'position' can be, or can be made to be, simply by function of its position, a junction-box for information.

Box 5.2   Bureaucracy

1 A division of labour in which authority and responsibility is clearly defined for each member, and is officially sanctioned.
2 Offices or positions are organized into a hierarchy of authority resulting in a chain of command.
3 All organizational members are to be selected on the basis of technical qualifications through formal examinations or by virtue of training and education.
4 Officials are to be appointed, not elected.
5 Administrators work for fixed salaries and are career officers.
6 The administrative official does not own the administered unit but is a salaried official.
7 The administrator is subject to strict rules, discipline, and controls regarding the offical duties.

Max Weber, *The Theory of Social and Economic Organization*, 1947

---

2 *Right of access*. A position gives its occupant the right of access to a variety of networks. Some networks are of course informal, or professional, and membership depends on 'expert' or 'personal' power. But many organizational networks are initially recruited from the occupants of specified positions. Most committee memberships, for instance, are *ex officio*. This right of access not only leads to more information, the other invisible asset, but also lends propinquity. It is hard to apply influence without access to the bodies to be influenced. The right of access to individuals and to networks is an indispensable invisible asset.

3 *The right to organize*. As will be seen later under the discussion of

ecology as a method of influence, the way in which work is organized, the physical and social environments, the flow of communication, the right to decide, these factors are all potent ways of influencing behaviour. The occupant of a position has this right should he choose to exercise it and regard it as a hidden asset.

It is not, therefore, without reason that titles and places on organigrams are so valued in organizations. Status has only a small part to do with it. Official positions in bureaucracies carry with them these hidden assets. Organizations that like to do away with organigrams and formal position descriptions have usually very good reasons for doing so. It must be recognized, however, that they are eliminating one potent type of power within the organization. The fact that the assets accruing to a position are unspoken of and therefore largely invisible should not detract from their potency. Indeed some writers (e.g. Pettigrew) regard them as principal power resources. I feel it easier to classify them as potential assets that stem from position power. The word 'asset' is used because assets are still potentially productive whether or not they are activated. The invisible assets of position power do not, of course, have to be activated to make them exist.

2.5 Expert power

Expert power is the power that is vested in someone because of their acknowledged expertise. It is, for many, the least obnoxious of the sources of power. In a meritocratic tradition people do not resent being influenced by those whom they regard as the experts. It is, furthermore, a power base that requires no sanctions. The specialist departments of an organization, if acknowledged to be expert, will find their suggestions or instructions readily implemented. Only if their expertise is questioned will they have to fall back on other sources of power to implement their wishes. Too often the personnel departments of organizations are forced to rely on position or resource power when their expert power proves to be unrecognized. For expert power is hedged about by one major qualification; it can only be given by those over whom it will be exercised. This is not to say that you cannot claim expert power for yourself in some field, and have your claim recognized. But until that claim is recognized, explicitly or implicitly, the power will not really be yours. Because this power source is the most socially acceptable it is also the most sought after and will bring out many spurious claimants. Their bluff, if bluff it is, may well work, but if discovered the dethroned expert will find that she has created a credibility gap that may well contaminate future attempts to claim expertise for herself.

Expert power is comparative – anyone is an expert who knows more than anyone else around. This works both ways. It means that even a small differential in expertise can give one person great power over their fellows if that expertise happens to be in great demand. But it also means that he or she will lose all his power to another arrival if that other has even a small degree of further expertise. In the country of the blind the one-eyed man is king – until he with two eyes comes along.

2.6   Personal power

Sometimes called *charisma*, sometimes popularity, sometimes sociometrically central. This power resides in the person and in their personality. It can be enhanced by position or by expert status, so that a Prime Minister loses a lot of charisma on leaving office, and the sports star fades when dropped from the team. For charisma is brittle. It is elusive, is fanned by success and by self-confidence and can evaporate in defeat. Like expert power, personal power only comes from those who will be exposed to it, from beneath it in a sense. Because it is tied to the individual rather than to a position, a role or a block of resources, personal power is much sought after. Many a manager will attribute his degree of influence to his charisma rather than to his position, only to be disillusioned when, having been removed from his position, he finds that no one invites him to meetings, consults him or seeks him out.

2.7   Negative power

It is necessary at this stage to point out that all of these sorts of power can be used both legitimately and illegitimately. If used in the agreed manner in the agreed constituency, i.e. in its appropriate *domain*, the power is regarded as legitimate. If used contrary to accepted practice or outside the domain the power is regarded as disruptive and illegitimate. We shall call this the *negative* use of power.

Negative power is the capacity to stop things happening, to delay them, to distort or disrupt them. The clerk who sorts the incoming mail has little power to initiate, but can misdirect, mislay or destroy important documents. The power to block or distort, or negative power, is quite out of proportion to the position. On a higher level, staff people in organizations tend to be used as expert filters. Filters have a lot of latent negative power: they can cease to filter, or filter arbitrarily. All subordinates are, in a sense, gate-keepers to their bosses. They screen out information and activities, they do completed staff work and operate under management by exception. All this means that the boss only sees what they want him to see. They have a high degree of latent negative power.

Box 5.3   The case of the missing factory

Jim was only 29 but he was the envy of many of his friends. His job, in the Head Office of a large international organization, carried the title of Manufacturing Co-Ordinator – Mediterranean. Under 'Mediterranean' fell all the countries that bordered that sea, including France and Italy, all of them with their own companies, reporting to Head Office in London, and most of them with their own manufacturing facilities.

What Jim did not tell his friends outside the organization was that he was not permitted to visit any of these countries and that his formal job description defined his authorities as 'Approval of incidental expenses up to a limit of £10.' Jim, in fact, in spite of his grand title, was essentially a post-box in the Head Office organization, with the processing of and occasional analysis of, incoming manufacturing problems and proposals from the Mediterranean countries. Decisions were taken from above him in the organization and he was never involved, rarely consulted.

One day, when life had been particularly tedious and unexciting, Jim received from the Italian company a proposal for a large new integrated factory in southern Italy. He decided to test his powers. Without consulting anyone he sent back the proposal to the Italian company asking for further details and raising some questions. In due course they replied. He queried some of their responses and asked for their comments on possible political implications. In all, it was six months before Jim felt obliged to pass on the factory proposal to those above him, but with the proposal went six months' worth of supplementary information. Jim had thoroughly enjoyed exercising his role as filter.

Negative power has its attractions, and sometimes its uses when positive power is abused by dictators or cliques.

Negative power is latent; it does not operate all the time. It operates at times of low morale, irritation, stress, or frustration at the failure of other influence attempts. The disgruntled bus driver on a rainy evening who allows no more passengers on to a half-full bus is activating his negative power out of resentment against his employers or the world or his wife. Successful, high morale organizations see little negative power. Discontented, low-utilization (e.g. role underload) organizations bring out negative power. The use of negative power breeds lack of trust by the superior for the subordinate. The superior then sets up checking procedures and alternative information channels to thwart the use of negative power. This is seen by the subordinates as job diminution and further provocation to activate their negative power!

In one of its aspects negative power is the ability to filter or distort information, instructions, or requests from one part of the organization to another. At an extreme it is the ability given to even the meanest of employees to throw a wrench into the assembly line or to fuse the computer. It is this power latent in all positions that allows individuals and groups of individuals to exert influence laterally and upwards in organizations. The distortions that result from the exercise of negative power have much to do with the politics of organizations, to be discussed in Chapter 10.

3 Methods of influence

3.1

These bases of power allow one to use one or more methods of influence. These methods of influence can be usefully divided into two classes: *the overt* and *the unseen*. Although attention has been paid to the sources of power by social scientists not much description has been recorded of the influence methods, particularly the unseen ones. A rough table will relate the methods of influence to the sources of power.

Power source:	physical	resource	position	expert	personal
Influence					
(overt):	force	exchange	rules and procedures		persuasion
(unseen):	ecology	magnetism			

These will now need to be described in their turn.

3.2 Force

This is the crudest of the methods. It derives from physical power or, occasionally, from resource power. A applies force, or the *threat* of force, to influence B to do what he wants him to do. Physical bullying, hold-ups, armed raids, are examples of force. Whole systems, such as some prisons or concentration camps, are based on force as a method of influence. Individual instances of force are found in business or government organizations but they are rare, are usually related to a particular individual, and tend to be short-lived. The supervisor who threatens physical force, the boss who loses his temper, the strike leader who hints at violence in the picket lines, are all relying on force. But though the immediate effects are usually very satisfactory to A, who is doing the influencing, the longer-term fall-out is sufficiently damaging to make it a tactic of last resort in situations of any permanency. In other words, if you are not going to see the person again, and are big enough, bullying will get you what you want. Economic force, or the threat of economic force, is a little more common. It is found in some union situations, or, with individuals, when one person is totally dependent on another. Sometimes concealed as exchange influence, the effects of economic force are the same as for physical force, effective and short-lived.

3.3   Rules and procedures

A vast amount of influence in our society, from childhood to old age, is exerted through *rules* and *procedures*. A can influence B to do something by laying down a rule that the something must be done by all people in B's position. It need not necessarily be an influence attempt on B specifically, but on all people in B's position (e.g. nobody may smoke in the factory). Alternatively it is used as an indirect way of influencing B personally by implying that it is a genuine, all-embracing, rule and not A trying to impose his or her will on B. If A is going to use rules and procedures A must have:

The perceived right to institute these rules and procedures;
The means and will to enforce them, i.e. the appropriate power base.

Without these two provisos the influence attempt will fail, as many parents of adolescents have found. Rules and regulations therefore derive largely from position power, backed by resource power. Experts, however, in functional organizations, can well give expression to their wishes through a series of rules or required procedures. Provided that the power source is adequate this is a very acceptable method of influence.

Michel Crozier has argued, and demonstrated in a study of some French organizations, that the way to increase one's power in an organization is to circumscribe your opponent with rules and regulations whilst retaining the maximum degree of uncertainty relating to your own position. This is using rules and procedures to play politics.

Their usage does not, however, always have to be so blatantly political. Provided that the appropriate power base exists, rules are a very efficient way of getting B to do X. In the majority of cases B is not going to make an issue out of following a procedure. Few people revel in constant petty decisions. It is usually called inefficiency. Rules and procedures are one very sensible way of reducing the number of one-off decisions. Rules protect liberty as well as restrict it. Rules sanction behaviour as well as prohibiting it. Rules are in themselves non-evaluative. They are a convenient way of influencing behaviour.

3.4 Exchange

Call it bargaining, negotiating – even cajoling or bribing in some situations. A agrees with B to give her something in return for desired behaviour. Sweets to a child, tips to the dustman, promotion to the executive are obvious examples. Less obvious, but perhaps more common, are friendship and favour, inclusion in a group, approval and status. Exchange methods can follow from any power source, depending on what is offered. But resource and position are the most frequent bases.

If exchange methods are going to work A has to offer something that B desires, and the payment has to be worth the effort or expenditure. Obvious perhaps, but too often the exchange is only implicit, not explicit, and the expectations of B are unreal and she is destined to be disappointed. Homans and other exchange theorists would argue that all influence can be regarded as an exchange transaction. Homans suggests that in every transaction there are rewards and costs. A gives something (maybe help) to B. In return B gives gratitude or respect. Ideally both parties make a profit, i.e. both parties give something they can well afford (advice or respect) and get that which they desire more (respect or advice).

Exchange methods are very often self-cancelling; like incentive theories or motivation. Once the reward for certain desired behaviour has been paid that transaction has been completed. The new bargain then often becomes 'A will withdraw the reward if B does not continue the behaviour'. This is still an exchange method of influence but one that is much less pleasing to B who may see it either as rules and procedures or, ultimately, as economic force.

Exchange methods, therefore, if based on correct assumptions about the individual to be influenced and if made explicit, can be very effective in the short term. They do, however, carry some longer-term implications, since the 'rewards' get progressively less desired by the recipient as he gets more used to them. Thus, again like incentive schemes, the exchange gets more and more highly priced until, ultimately, a bargain may be impossible.

3.5 Persuasion

The least value-laden of the methods of influence – this method relies supposedly on logic, the power of argument and the evidence of the facts. It is the preferred method of influence of most people and is usually the method of first resort. However, in practice, it nearly always gets contaminated by one of the other methods. A manager who genuinely attempts to reason with a subordinate may not be heard as persuading but as telling, i.e. using rules and procedures as a method of influence.

The arguments advanced in any cause gain most of their validity and much of their weight from their source. Therefore the evaluation of the source by the recipient is a vital part of any assessment of persuasion as a method of influence. Expert or personal power, acknowledged, it will be recalled, by the recipient, are the foundations for this method. Like all other methods, it is only as strong as its sources.

These four – force, exchange, rules and persuasion – are the most obvious, or overt, methods used to get another to do something. Many of the leadership issues can be explained by the typology thus far. A leader whose power is based only on position will be wise to maintain a psychological distance from his or her subordinates and to adopt a fairly formal style based on rules and regulations. Democratically elected leaders, or those appointed with the support of their group, can assume that they have some degree of expert power and can therefore safely resort to persuasion, or participation, methods of leadership. Dictatorial styles will be effective, even if not enjoyed, when the leader owns the outfit or has effective control over the allocation of rewards, i.e. has resource power. Good teachers, with recognized expert power, can afford to be more liberal and relaxed than bad teachers who have to rely on rules upheld by the authority of their position.

But there remain two ways of influencing people which are not normally discussed under the heading of influence because they are, in a way, unseen and unperceived. Nevertheless they are very effective and the first in particular, *ecology*, is a method available to, often neglected by, and sometimes abused by, every manager.

3.6 Ecology

Ecology is the study of the relationship between an environment and its organisms. As politicians have also discovered, we cannot afford to neglect the ecology of the organization, or the relationship of the environment to individual behaviour or attitudes. Behaviour and attitudes occur within an environment, a physical, a psychological, a sociological environment. That environment has its effects upon them. For instance, in the physical environment we know that:

Noise tends to impair performance on complicated tasks;
Variety relieves monotony, provides stimulation and contributes to improved performance;
Seating patterns tend to affect interaction patterns;
Open-plan offices are popular and improve communications when the work is routine;
Segregation prohibits communication;
Dangerous surroundings increase tension and lower productivity.

In the psychological and sociological environments, we know for instance that:

Small groups are easier to participate in than large groups;
Specific, challenging but attainable targets tend to produce commitments irrespective of their specific content (people can get committed to morally unacceptable tasks for this reason);
Increased interaction leads to increased sentiments – either favourable or hostile;
Participation increases commitment if the individual considers participation worthwhile and legitimate.

All behaviour takes place in an environment. To ignore the influence of the environment is implicitly to accept constraints and conditions, to take a negative decision about influence. To adjust the environment in order to remove constraints or facilitate some aspect of behaviour is indirect influence. The understanding of ecology is necessary to an understanding of behaviour. The use of ecology is a powerful means of influencing behaviour, or at the very least, of allowing other methods of influence to work. To call ecology 'manipulation' is to libel it. It is powerful because often unrealized; only if abused does it become manipulation. This book in a sense is a guide to the ecology of organizations. The design of work, the work, the structure of reward and control systems, the structure of the organization, the management of groups and the control of conflict, are all ways of managing the environment in order to influence behaviour. Let us never forget that although the environment is all around us, it is not unalterable, that to change it is to influence people, that ecology is potent, the more so because it is often unnoticed.

This idea of ecology, or environmental control, as a method of influence is unusual. It is more normal to think of influence as a direct interaction between A and B, with A and B being either groups or individuals. Most behaviour, however, in organizations is conditioned more by the way things and people are organized than by the more obvious forms of influence. Much of this we know is not deliberate conditioning. People do not create large committees in order deliberately to cause frustration. Assembly-lines were not designed to cause apathy. Autonomous groups in R and D laboratories were not designed as a deliberate attempt to promote commitment. At least not usually! The environment is often created for other reasons and is accepted by most of us as one of those so-called 'facts of life'. It is not, however, unalterable. One can change behaviour by changing the environment, changing the way in which things are done as well as the physical and social atmosphere. The practitioners of OD (organization development) talk of improving the 'climate' of organizations. They refer to the human climate – one aspect of the environment. Chapter 7 describes the different cultures of organizations and how these cultures encourage certain types of behaviour.

The suggestion of this chapter is that attention to the way things are done, ecology, is one way of eliciting desired behaviour from individuals. To a very large extent, ecology consists in seeing that environmental aspects *do not prevent or obstruct normal behaviour*. Participation takes time. If you want it you must allocate the time. Mini-jobs promote apathy. If you do not want apathy you must enlarge the jobs. If you want innovative behaviour, set selection criteria that capture innovative people. Conflicting objectives bring conflicting groups. If you wish to remove a principal cause of conflict the responsibilities must be so re-arranged that objectives do not conflict. On an opposing tack, responsibility is only effective if all the information is available. If you wish to curtail someone's responsibility the easiest method is to cut off information.

The concept of ecology is similar in many senses to what two famous writers on organizations, March and Simon, have called the 'vocabulary' of the organization. By this they mean things like the structure of communication rules and regulations, standard programmes (e.g. for stock control or material purchasing), selection and promotion criteria. This 'vocabulary' forms the premises for decision-making and is, they claim, easier to change than the process of decision-making itself.

In short, ecology sets the conditions for behaviour. Inattention to ecology will make things difficult if not impossible. Similarly ecology can be used to create impossible conditions for other people, if you are so minded. Before you plant an azalea you check that the soil and climatic conditions are suitable. Similarly the manager in an organiz- ation will check the environment before he acts. If unsuitable for his purpose he will alter it, using, in general, those hidden assets of pos- ition power, the right to organize, the right of access, and information.

But just as the weather is only a subject for conversation in poor climates, so ecology is often only mentioned when it does not work:

'The fact that the division was spread over seven counties accounts for the lack of co-ordination';
'Putting two groups on the same site with no indication of overall ranking was bound to result in conflict';
'Separate car-parks for production and marketing certainly created a "them" and "us" feeling from the first day at the new site';
'With a committee of fifteen when only two were needed, of course there was frustration'.

It is a pity if ecological considerations are only taken into account after the event rather than before. The size of the group, the facilities, the time available, the method of decision-taking, are all within the scope of the manager to change, no matter how weak his power base.

3.7 Magnetism

The invisible but felt pull of a stronger force, *magnetism*, is the applica- tion of personal power. We have all felt, at some time, the perhaps illogical, often inexplicable, attraction of an individual, the desire to work with and for them whenever they call. Not easily measurable by social scientists and therefore more frequently mentioned in novels than in textbooks, this way of influencing people cannot be ignored. Since it depends on personal, or sometimes expert, power, it is very much, like beauty, in the eye of the beholder. Most open to abuse, because perhaps it has no obvious mechanism, it is the favourite method of demagogues, some salesmen, guerrilla leaders and faith healers.

Magnetism, however, has its other aspects. We are often influenced by someone not so much because of their personality but rather because we trust or respect them. Such a person does not have to persuade us, or to give us rules. We will follow them and be pulled towards them, be- cause we are convinced of their ability, or of their principles, or of their loyalty to us. This pulling power, this magnetism of trust can stem from expert power at least as frequently as from personal power, for we will trust those whom we dislike if we respect their competence.

Empathy, the feeling of being pulled towards someone because you share the same views or convictions, because you suffer with them or rejoice with them, is another manifestation of magnetism. In its strongest form, that of love, it can influence people to abandon rationality. Love, though not unknown, is infrequently found in organizational relationships. But the other aspects of magnetism, the unseen drawing-power of one individual, are found all the time. Trust, respect, charm, infectious enthusiasm, these attributes all allow us to influence people without apparently imposing on them. The invisibility of magnetism is a major attraction as is its attachment to one individual. Each of us in some way is a magnet to someone, but the magnetism is unique, special to ourselves.

Box 5.4   Women and power

Historically, women in management have found their opportunities in routine, low-profile jobs, in staff positions or in supervisory jobs managing stuck subordinates. In these roles they have few favours to trade, are not in a position to take the kinds of risks which build credibility and cannot develop their own team by pushing bright subordinates. They are, by comparison with men, powerless.

The behaviour of other managers can also contribute to the powerlessness of the woman manager in a number of informal ways:

by overprotecting her; putting her in a safe job, not giving her enough rope to prove herself (it's a jungle, why send her into it?);
by overprotecting themselves; fearful that others would be held responsible for her failure, that their judgement would be on the line, they hold her back;
by witholding support; by being too ready to accept criticism of her from others, by allowing her to be bypassed;
by excluding her from the informal cliques or drinking and eating groups to which her male peers belong.

As a consquence of these, often well-intentioned, actions women in management jobs tend to hug power to themselves and to be authoritarian in style. This is a natural response to felt powerlessness; it is not, as some assume, a characteristic of women managers.

From Kanter, 'Power Failure in Management Circuits', *Harvard Business Review*, July–August 1979

All the aspects of magnetism stem from particular sources of power, usually personal or expert power. Magnetism is therefore only as effective as its sources, to increase it we must work on those sources, to maintain it we must be careful to nourish those sources. Trust, for instance, is easily fractured by one false step, and hard to mend – like a pane of glass.

4 Implications

4.1

Where does this leave us? What are the major lessons to be learnt from this categorization of methods of influence and sources of power?

4.2 The choice of method

Anyone contemplating, or involved in, a process of influence needs to reflect upon the source of their power, and thence the range of methods of influence that it suggests. In particular they need to remember that the source of power, and the method of influence, will depend as much on the individual recipient and their perceptions as on the person applying the influence. The perception of the individual will be very largely coloured by the nature of the psychological contract with that group.

In a coercive environment, expert power is of little avail. Calculative contracts are good for those whose power is based on resources or position. In a co-operative environment expert or charismatic power works best and position power is less effective. Thus in a voluntary organization (co-operative) the secretary is useful but has little influence. In consultancy firms (usually co-operative), expertise is valued more than length of service. In universities (co-operative) the experts, the faculty, have a lot of influence. The administrators with only position power have little influence. Hospital administrators might sympathize, as they see their position power outflanked by the expert power of the consultant.

A prophet is without honour in his own country, the expert often without influence in her own family because her power base has changed. The prophet has exchanged expert power for nothing, the expert position power and expert power for resource power (money and affection). Professional people, one has noticed, often have very undisciplined children. Whether it be educationally sound or not is one matter, the reason for it often lies in the nature of influence. In their working lives professional people are used to relying on expert power, or using persuasion as their preferred method of influence and finding it effective. In the family situation they have no expert power. Reasoning and argument seem not to prevail. They are reluctant to invoke physical power, resource power, or parental position power and, therefore, find themselves without influence and baffled by their recalcitrant families.

There are two general considerations underlying the choice of a method of influence:

1 *Credibility*. The relativity of power has already been stressed. Your power source, under normal circumstances, is only as good as it is believed to be. This applies totally to expert and personal power. It applies partially to the other sources. If you have to demonstrate your resource power you have probably already failed to use its latent ability to influence. Credibility comes from many sources: a record of prior success, the reports of respected colleagues. A lot of credibility credits can stem from one's observed behaviour, e.g. a willingness to see what is important or salient in the situation for the other party, or evidence that your objectives are consistent with theirs, or a low-key, low-threat approach. These will all enhance your credibility.

   In any situation one should ask oneself how many credibility credits one has with that particular constituency and to what power sources do they pertain, remembering always that what works in one constituency may not work in another. The Nobel Prize-winner may have little credibility in the factory, however influential he may be in the laboratory.

2 *Multiplex or Uniplex*. A relationship which has only one strand in it is usually weaker than a multi-strand one. The lawyer who only sees his or her client in a formal legal situation can only relate to him in that role. If he is a friend as well, or a colleague in another venture, the relationship will be harder to break. Similarly an influence attempt backed by more than one sort of power is likely to be harder to resist. The specialist who relies only on expert credentials without establishing any personal rapport will find any attempts at persuasion that much more difficult.

4.3   The individual response to influence

The recipient of an influence attempt can always reject it, ignore it or rebel. But if we accept it, we have in some way to justify to ourselves the fact that we have been influenced. We have to reduce the disson-

ance between what we are now doing and what we would, uninflu-
enced, be doing. The individual recipient of influence responds to
influence assuming it is effective, in psychologically different ways.
There are three psychological mechanisms for adjusting to influence:

Compliance;
Identification;
Internalization.

1 *Compliance*. The recipient agrees to the influence attempt because
   it is worth his while to do so. Force, rules and procedure and some
   exchange methods will usually result in compliance.
   The implication of compliance is that the individual is doing what
   he is doing because he has to do it. The onus for seeing that he does
   what he is supposed to do remains with the initiator of influence.
2 *Identification*. The recipient adopts the idea of proposal because he
   admires or identifies with the source, the initiator of influence.
3 *Internalization*. The recipient adopts the idea or proposal as his own,
   he internalizes it so that it becomes one of his possessions.

Each mechanism carries some consequences in its train. The outcome
of influence cannot be predicted without some understanding of the
likely response mechanism at the other end.

Compliance. If you have the necessary power source, you can usually
make sure that your attempt at influence is accepted. It will be accepted
because the recipient acknowledges your power, but it will be accepted
grudgingly since the act of acceptance is seen as a denial of his choice.
If the influence is received freely, then the psychological adjustment
mechanism will be either identification or internalization. Compliance
always implies 'has to'. It may well be that the individual would have
accepted the influence willingly if he had had the choice; it is the
implicit denial of that choice from the outset that produces the grudging
nature of the acceptance. Compliance therefore has its advantages for
the person with power. It is reliable in the short term (if his assessment
of his power source is correct), and it is usually quick. The impatient
father enforcing his instructions with 'because I say so' is going to get
his way and soon, but with compliance rather than internalization.
The manager who uses his position to enforce his preferences on a
subordinate will be obeyed, but probably reluctantly. For the costs of
compliance as a way of responding to influence are clear enough.
Firstly, the order or request will be carried out grudgingly, with less
than full commitment. Secondly, some mechanism must be available
to back up the influence, if necessary. Influence attempts which assume

compliant responses need maintenance. Those attempts which rely on identification or internalization are self-maintaining – if they succeed. Compliance and trust do not go together, compliance and checking do. Internalization and identification imply choice on the part of the recipient, the right to reject as well as to accept. Compliance carries no such implication. Often a manager will start off by using persuasion or some form of magnetism in an attempt to influence and hope for a free and accepting response. When his attempt is rejected he will fall back on position or resource power and ensure that his views are adopted. The result will be compliance, meaning lowered commitment and no guarantee that what he wants to happen will continue to happen unless he enforces it.

In many parts of organizations, choice, or the right to reject an idea or request, cannot be admitted without the possibility of chaos. Fair enough, but the inevitable outcome will be compliant responses to orders, rules and requests, meaning lowered commitment and the need for maintenance or checking.

Identification. This is the most pleasurable to the person exerting influence. It is nice to be identified with, to exert magnetism, or even to have your group or its task exert magnetism. But such magnetism has to be maintained; it can too easily disappear. More importantly, identification makes the recipient of influence dependent on the source of magnetism. Dependency is nice but it carries responsibilities and costs. The source of magnetism becomes indispensable, thus reducing flexibility. The dependent person is also more inclined to obey than to initiate (charismatic leaders are often surrounded by followers rather than by other leaders). Identification, therefore, while attractive to the individual exerting influence, is not usually favoured by the organization. Commando leaders, in organizations, while often very effective, tend to be regarded as a glamorous nuisance because their magnetism has resulted in identification and thus reduced flexibility. They have made themselves indispensable to the effective performance of their group.

Identification with a group or a task carries the same problems. It is a very effective form of commitment, but change the group or the salience of the task, and the commitment will vanish. Identification does not maintain itself. Initial enthusiasm for a project can evaporate. The magnetism will need constant re-charging.

Internalization. This is the form of commitment most desired by organizations. It is commitment that is self-maintaining and independent of the original source of influence. But it is the hardest to obtain and takes the longest time. In addition, if internalization is truly desired, then no pressure must be put on the individual to accept influence. He must be totally free to argue about it and even to reject it if he is to regard it as his own. If he is *forced* to accept it, his response, whatever he may say, will really be one of compliance or identification. If the source of influence is respected or liked, the individual will respond out of goodwill for that source (identification); if the source is not respected but can enforce the influence, the response will be compliance. Since organizations cannot always spare the time for full discussion or easily tolerate individuals independently rejecting influence, it is not common to find internalization responses except at the highest levels.

Internalization also means that the individual recipient of influence adopts the idea, the change in attitude or the new behaviour, as his own. Fine. He will act on it without pressure. The change will be self-maintaining to a high degree. But he will also tend to believe that the change was his idea and no one else's. He will in a sense deny that influence took place. This matters not at all in terms of the desired result, but if you are the person exerting influence it is remarkably hard to let the recipient take all the credit for himself. The successful psychotherapist is the one whose patients all believe they cured themselves – they internalized the therapy and it thereby became truly an integral part of them. Consultants suffer much from the dilemma of the psychotherapist – the problem of internalization. If they wish the client to use the right solution with full and lasting commitment then they must let him believe it is *his* solution. But in that case they won't get the credit – or the goodwill. Commitment through identification is more profitable for consultants, and staff experts. The report is stamped with their name and they lend their prestige to support it. Internalization is as hard for a boss to endure as it is for a consultant, but it's better for the organization.

Internalization, then, is the most lasting. Identification is the most pleasant. Compliance is the quickest. But each has its costs.

Interestingly, ecology, being indirect or unnoticed, is a method of influence that requires no response mechanism from the recipient. Should he, however, suspect that he is being deliberately manipulated, should ecology be uncovered, then he is likely to see ecology as concealed force and to respond with the compliance mechanism. But most ecological mechanisms are not seen as deliberate manipulations. Groups have to be organized in some way, meetings chaired, offices sited, tasks defined. To ignore ecology is stupid, to boast about it is folly.

Box 5.5   Patterns of influence

An international study of the methods of influence used by 360 managers in three countries (USA, Australia and Britain) threw up seven strategies of behaviour.

Reason
Friendliness
Coalition
Bargaining
Assertiveness
Higher authority
Sanctions

There were some common principles determining the choice of strategies:

(a) The greater the power (resource or position) of the manager, the greater variety of strategies he or she could and did employ.
(b) The managers used a battery of strategies (Assertiveness, Friendliness, Bargaining and Higher authority) on their subordinates but relied mostly on Reason in dealing with their superiors (because their power base was smaller).
(c) The greater the power distance between manager and subordinate the more likely was the manager to be directive, using Assertiveness more often when other methods failed.
(d) If the expectations of success were high the managers preferred to use Reason.

The authors summarized their results as follows:

Assertiveness is frequently used when
• Objectives are to benefit the *organization*
• Expectations for success are *low*
• Organizational power is *high*

Reason is frequently used when
• Objectives are to benefit the *organization*
• Expectations for success are *high*
• Organizational power is *high*

Friendliness is frequently used when
• Objectives are to benefit the *person*
• Expectations for success are *low*
• Organizational power is *low*

Kipnis *et al.*, 'Patterns of Managerial Influence', *Organizational Dynamics*, 1984

Box 5.5 describes one of the few studies of the way in which managers actually use influence. In the language of this chapter it is clear that they try to use persuasion whenever possible, resulting in internalization, and fall back on their position and resource power (and compliance) if they need to and have lots of it, or personal power (and identification) if they have nothing else.

Box 5.6 Dissonance theory

'I love you and I respect you,' my daughter wrote to me once, 'but what you are asking me to do with my life is not acceptable.' She was expressing her feeling of dissonance or lack of harmony between two conflicting messages. She could either live with the dissonance or reduce it by bringing one or other of the messages into line. I, of course, hoped that her love and respect for me would influence her to change her proposed career. The other possibility, however, was that she would abandon her love and respect in order to pursue her own choices. Influence attempts often fall foul of dissonance theory as the well-meaning manager finds that those constructive bits of feedback lead to comments like 'silly old fool' or 'interfering idiot', that behaviour is not changed while the managerial authority is diminished.

Dissonance theory leads to unexpected results. The more you pay for something or the more you endure for something the higher you value it (otherwise you have to live with the conclusion that you are an idiot). Thus, after buying an expensive car or a house in an exclusive area we look out for every sign that we did right, even if the signs are only advertisements. Similarly, dissonance theory suggests that all training course evaluations will be favourable – if you stayed the course and hated it you were either a prisoner or a coward, and so, rather than admit to that, you look for the good points in the course.

As we grow older and more mature we seem to be able to cope with higher levels of dissonance. We can admire people and disagree with them, accept that we are social cowards or even wrong. Managers would, however, be foolish to assume such maturity in all around them. They should not push their power base too far or expect people to change their minds or their decisions just because reason or logic says they should – that would mean admitting to themselves that they had been unreasonable and illogical. It is psychologically easier for them to trivialize the issue or the person raising it.

5   **Messages for the manager**

5.1

Your role, and the role relationships between you and those you wish to influence, will tend to determine the methods of influence open to you. The most that you can do is to be honest in your predictions, to understand, for instance, that whatever you may pretend it is actually exchange or ecology methods which you are using, methods which will result in compliance or at best identification, which are not self-maintaining states. A meeting that ends with the chairman saying 'So I take it that we are all agreed?' (expecting the answer 'Yes') is seldom an example of a completed influence attempt which will be self-maintaining. The 'false consensus' is an influence attempt that failed, usually because the chairman thought he was using persuasion when in fact he was using the dynamics of the meeting, i.e. ecology backed by his position power, to obtain an unreal agreement. When ecology is uncovered, as when individuals leaving the meeting are heard to comment 'I didn't like to say it in there, but I cannot see how this scheme will work in view of . . .', then ecology uncovered becomes manipulation, results in compliance, and compliance only works when the initiator uses his coercive or resource power. So it will be that, unless the chairman demands implementation, the first meeting will be followed by a second meeting which will pretend that the conclusion of the first meeting never happened.

As the formal leader in the group, your estimate of your source of power in relation to your group will affect your positioning of your leadership behaviour on the tight–flexible continuum. Similarly your group's assessment of the proper source of power for your role will condition their preferred position on that continuum. Participative management implies expert power sources, influence by persuasion, and response by internalization. Great if it works. But as we have seen the likelihood of this method of influence working properly in the hustle and bustle of organizational life is very unlikely. In situations where resource power is evenly spread, where there are no time pressures, where individuals are free to refuse influence, where there is respect for expert power, then participative management might be expected to flourish and authoritarian (rules and procedures) management to fail. Where does this happen? Sometimes in universities, occasionally in R and D laboratories, often in the advisory units (e.g. corporate planning, investment analysis, market analysis) of functional areas. Hardly on the assembly line, in the accounting office or the typing pool as their work is normally organized.

Persuasive influence, expert power, are more compatible with contemporary feelings about the essential rights of the individual, about society as a contractual system, about freedom to say 'No' in all situations. They are more compatible with rising standards of education, with the changing role of women – from 'female' to 'person'. They will tend to move the preferred management style of subordinates well down towards the flexible end – more control to the subordinates, i.e. more freedom to reject influence. But this form of influence, this source of power, is not obviously compatible with the emerging forms of the giant corporation, is not compatible with the task requirements of most managerial roles in the organizations of today, or of tomorrow.

We have therefore another way of looking at the organizational dilemma of today. How to select and implement an appropriate source of power that will reflect the trends in society and still get the work done? Nor is this a purely idealistic dilemma – how to be rich but good – it is a very practical problem of the short-term long-term variety. The psychological contract, the preferred method of influence, the ultimate source of power, are hygiene factors. If they are not right, then individuals will leave the organization, good individuals will not join the organization. Turnover will go up, talent will go down. You may get this year's task done with rules and procedures but you may not be around next year to get any task done. Do we then have to think of re-designing the tasks and structures of our corporations, accepting lower economic returns perhaps, raising output prices perhaps, in order to take account of changing values on influence and power? Is the assembly-line doomed? Not because it is inefficient in the normal sense, but because the assumptions it makes about influence and the sources of power are no longer acceptable in our society? Must we de-systemize our work, break up the large units, decentralize our control system even if it costs more in order to realign the structure in line with new conceptions of power and influence?

These and other issues, including the use and, too often, the misuse of power and influence in the everyday work of organizations will be examined in Part Two in Chapters 9 and 10.

6 ━► On the Workings of Groups

1 Introduction

If a camel is a horse put together by a committee, why then do people
spend so much of their lives in groups? On average, managers spend
50 per cent of their working day in one sort of group or another. Senior
managers can spend 80 per cent.

There are more myths, more stereotypes, about groups and committees than about most subjects in organizations. There are the individu-
alists, to whom groups and committees are an encumbrance and a
nuisance. There are the team people, who want participation and involvement by all concerned. Does it matter? Are groups a fashion or
a necessity?

What is a 'group' anyway? They vary from the formal – a work group,
a project team, a committee, a board – to the informal – the *ad hoc*
meeting or discussion, the luncheon group, the clique, the cabal. They
are permanent or temporary. They are liked by their members or regarded as a waste of time. They can be a most effective device for blocking
and obstructing new ideas, or the best way of putting them into practice.

What is the truth about groups? Is there any better understanding
that we can gain about this universal phenomenon? Is there a diagnostic
framework that we can apply to the workings of groups which will
allow us to understand more fully this part of organizational life?

In this chapter we shall look first at *the purposes of groups* – what
they are used for, and by whom, what they are good at and when. We
shall then consider *the determinants of group effectiveness* and conclude
with some *conclusions and implications*.

2 The purposes of groups

2.1

We shall first need to define the types of group rather more precisely.
A group, first of all, is any collection of people who perceive themselves

to be a group. If this seems to be dodging the issue, reflect a minute. A dozen individuals in a pub by random chance are not a group, although they may be interacting (talking), have a common objective (drink and socialization), and be aware of each other. (These are some other definitions of groups.) But put those same people in an emergency situation, let them be trapped by fire in the saloon bar, then that random collection of people will become a group, will start to have some collective identity, because they will start to perceive themselves as a group, with another sort of objective and with needs for other sorts of interaction. All of us, at some time, must have experienced the formation of a group from random individuals, when danger seems to threaten, when the bus is marooned by snow, when the yacht loses its rudder, even in power cuts when one is trapped in the lift. Then we suddenly perceive ourselves to be members of a group. Common objectives, defined membership criteria, predetermined hierarchies, these are not enough without this self-perception by the members. So you will find that when the numbers get too large the members, perceiving themselves to be no longer a group but a crowd or an association, will start reforming into smaller collections. So it is that a name, even a jocular name, for the group becomes an important part of acquiring a perceived identity. Put random collections of people into groups – for instance on a management training programme – and they will, if they wish to be a group and it is important for them to be a group, start to find a name, or a private territorial sign, or a ritual, which will give them an independent identity. If they do not do this, it often means that membership of such a group is not important to them, that they are happy to remain a random collection of individuals.

2.2   The organizational purposes

Organizations use groups, or teams and committees for the following major purposes:

1 For the distribution of work. To bring together a set of skills, talents, responsibilities, and allocate to them their particular duties.
2 For the management and control of work. To allow work to be organized and controlled by appropriate individuals with responsibility for a certain range of work.
3 For problem-solving and decision-taking. To bring together a set of skills, talents and responsibilities so that the solution to any problem will have all available capacities applied to it.

Box 6.1

I once facetiously described a rowing eight as a typical British group – eight people going backwards without talking to each other, steered by the one person who was too small to see where they were going. I was sternly rebuked by an oarsman in the audience. 'They are the perfect example of a good team,' he said 'they would not have the confidence to pull at the oar so strongly without either talking or seeing if they did not have complete trust in each other and in the little person at the rudder.' I stood rebuked.

My son, educated in the best British tradition of individual achievement, had always scorned groups and teams as an unnecessary impediment to his personal goals – 'they waste so much time,' he complained. Then he joined a drama college where he would work and study full-time for three years with 24 others. Together they would perform a multitude of plays, each playing a wide variety of parts. He quickly realized that for him to be successful the whole play had to be successful, that he was as dependent on the skills and resources of his companions as they were on his. His whole demeanour changed. Now the group was his passion and his chief priority. He would help, support, befriend them and learn from them in any way he could, he would hear no ill of them, no trouble was too much for them, for his and their success were inextricably intertwined.

I told him that he had discovered one of the key reasons for Japanese success in manufacturing.

4 For information processing. To pass on decisions or information to those who need to know.

5 For information and idea collection. To gather ideas, information or suggestions.

6 For testing and ratifying decisions. To test the validity of a decision taken outside the group, or to ratify such a decision.

7 For co-ordination and liaison. To co-ordinate problems and tasks between functions or divisions.

8 For increased commitment and involvement. To allow and encourage individuals to get involved in the plans and activities of the organization.

9 For negotiation or conflict resolution. To resolve a dispute or argument between levels, divisions or functions.

10 For inquest or inquiry into the past.

Some of these functions may well be combined. Some will overlap. It should become clear from the discussion in this chapter that groups will behave differently and will need to be organized differently, managed differently, for each of these functions. Some of the major difficulties with groups arise because the same group is expected simultaneously to perform two different functions. A management meeting, for instance, which starts as a negotiation between functions will not proceed very satisfactorily to a discussion of the long-term plan of the organization. This does not mean that the same collection of individuals cannot perform two or more different functions. But they need to see themselves as a different group in order to do so. Thus the functions need to be separated by time, or place, or title. There is more sense than might appear in the comedian's stereotype of the small town functionaries who flit from committee to committee where all the participants are the same, and only the name of the committee changes.

2.3   The individuals' purposes

Individuals use groups for one or more of the following purposes:

1 A means of satisfying their social or affiliation needs; to belong to something or to share in something.
2 A means of establishing a self-concept. Most people find it easier to define themselves in terms of their relationship to others, as members of a role set with a role in that set.
3 A means of gaining help and support to carry out their particular objectives, which may or may not be the same as the organization's objectives.
4 A means of sharing and helping in a common activity or purpose which may be making a product, or carrying out a job, or having fun, or giving help, or creating something.

Again these purposes often overlap. They may also conflict. As many studies have shown, the social functions of work groups can get in the way of the productive functions. Rate-setting is the use of a group to set standards, achieve objectives, which may be contrary to the organization's objectives. The individual who is satisfying his affiliation needs through membership of that group must pay the price of conformity or be expelled.

The famous Hawthorne Studies in the Western Electric Company of Chicago demonstrated above all that the membership of a group is important to most individuals and that the norms and objectives of the group will have a very large say in the norms and objectives of the individual who belongs to it (Box 6.2).

The optimum, of course, is to see that the objectives and purposes of the individual, the group and the organization all coincide.

2.4   Group effectiveness

In general, can we say anything about groups and the things they are good at? There are some things:

1 They are necessary in order to provide a psychological home for the individual. They are essential to organization effectiveness in that they provide the cells within the honeycomb. If they weren't required for the organization of work they would be formed by the individuals. (See Box 6.1.) Individuals will usually look to the work group, as a place of first resort, to satisfy their needs. Only if this fails will they turn elsewhere.

2 Groups produce less ideas, in total, than the individuals of those groups working separately. So much for the stereotype of brainstorming! But groups, though producing less ideas in total, produce better ideas in the sense that they are better evaluated, more thought through. A group will often produce a better solution to a quiz than the best individual in the group, since it can add the missing bits to the best performer. As we shall see, size and the organization of the group are factors that can stop this happening.

3 Groups, rather surprisingly, take riskier decisions than the individuals comprising them would have done if they had been acting independently. Nobody is quite sure of the reason for this but it is either that:

Groups give a sense of shared responsibility; or risk-taking, within limits, being 'a good thing', we tend to behave more adventurously in groups than in private, where we do not have to live up to any public standard.

3   The determinants of group effectiveness

3.1

As with most features of organizations, the answer to the question 'what makes an effective group?' is 'it depends'. In the first place, it depends on the answer to the question 'effective for whom?' We have to remember that productivity and member satisfaction are two possible outcomes of group activity which may or may not be in double harness.

A point however worth stressing: although satisfaction does not necessarily lead to productivity, productivity can often lead to satisfaction. The pride and sense of achievement that comes from being a member of an effective group can lead to satisfaction if the individual values the group and the work that it is doing. This has been called a sense of competence, and 'competence motivation'.

We shall divide the determinants of group effectiveness as follows:

the givens   the group   the task   the environment
the intervening factors   leadership style, processes and procedures, motivation
the outcomes   productivity, member satisfaction.

The implication behind this division is that there are some aspects of the situation which will affect the outcome but which are 'given'. They can be altered in the long or medium term but in the short term they are constraints within which the group has to operate. The intervening factors are determinants of effectiveness which can be changed in the immediate present. The division is not absolute. Aspects of the group or of the task can often be altered in the short term, can become intervening factors. No one should assume that 'the givens' are given for all time. The successful manager is the one who constantly appraises and challenges the constraints. The management of the 'givens' is one example of influence through ecology – and a very important example of it. As a starting-point for analysis let us accept the ecology as fixed for the medium term.

3.2 The group

Under this heading we shall briefly examine *size, member characteristics, individual objectives* and *stage of development*.

Size. There are two, fairly obvious, conflicting tendencies in group size: (a) the larger the group, the greater the diversity of talent, skills and knowledge and (b) the larger the group, the less chance of an individual participating.

In fact, under (b), participation does not diminish uniformly. Some people talk more easily than others in groups; individuals have different thresholds of participation. One man finds no difficulty in speaking in a group of twenty strangers, another will find a group of ten too large unless he knows them well, or has some official role in the group. Studies have shown that those who participate most in a group are perceived as having the most influence. This means that as a group gets larger the influence pattern will get distorted in favour of those with low thresholds of participation. This distribution of

Box 6.2   The Hawthorne studies

In the late 1920s a group of girls who assembled telephone equipment were the subjects of a series of studies undertaken to determine the effect on their output of working conditions, length of the working day, number and length of rest pauses, and other factors relating to the 'non-human' environment. The girls, especially chosen for the study, were placed in a special room under one supervisor and were carefully observed.

As the experimenters began to vary the conditions of work, they found that, with each major change, there was a substantial increase in production. Being good experimenters, they decided, when all the conditions to be varied had been tested, to return the girls to their original poorly lit work benches for a long working day without rest pauses and other amenities. To the astonishment of the researchers, output rose again, to a level higher than it had been even under the best of the experimental conditions.

At this point, the researchers were forced to look for factors other than those which had been deliberately manipulated in the experiment. For one thing, it was quite evident that the girls developed very high morale during the experiment and became extremely motivated to work hard and well. The reasons for this high morale were found to be several:

1 The girls felt special because they had been singled out for a research role; this selection showed that management thought them to be important.
2 The girls developed good relationships with one another and with their supervisor because they had considerable freedom to develop their own pace of work and to divide the work among themselves in a manner most comfortable for them.
3 The social contact and easy relations among the girls made the work generally more pleasant.

A new kind of hypothesis was formulated out of this preliminary research. The hypothesis was that motivation to work, productivity and quality of work are all related to the nature of the social relations among the workers and between the workers and their boss. In order to investigate this more systematically, a new group was selected. This group consisted of fourteen men: some wired banks of equipment which others then soldered, and which two inspectors examined before labelling it 'finished'. The men were put into a special room where they could be observed around the clock by a trained observer who sat in the corner of the room. At first the men were suspicious of the outsider, but as time wore on and nothing special happened as a result of his presence, they

Box 6.2 – *contd*

relaxed and fell into their 'normal' working routines. The observer discovered a number of very interesting things about the work group in the bank-wiring room.

Result 1. Though the group keenly felt its own identity as a total group, there were nevertheless two cliques within it, roughly corresponding to those in the front of the room and those at the back. The men in front felt themselves to be of higher status and they thought that the equipment they were wiring was more difficult than that of the back group. Each clique included most of the wiremen, soldermen and inspectors in that part of the room, but there were some persons who did not belong to either clique. The two cliques each had their own special games and habits, and there was a good deal of competition and mutual ribbing between them.

Result 2. The group as a whole had some 'norms', certain ideas of what was a proper and fair way for things to be. Several of these norms concerned the production rate of the group and could best be described by the concept of 'a fair day's work for a fair day's pay'. In other words, the group had established a norm of how much production was 'fair', namely 6,000 units, a figure which satisfied management but well below what the men could have produced had fatigue been the only limiting factor. Related to this basic norm were two others: 'one must not be a rate-buster', which meant that no member should produce at a rate too high relative to that of the others in the group, and 'one must not be a chiseller', which meant that one must not produce too little relative to the others. Being a deviant in either direction elicited kidding rebukes, social pressure to get back into line, and social ostracism if the person did not respond to the pressure. In that the men were colluding to produce at a level below their capacity, these norms taken together amounted to what has come to be called 'restriction of output'.

The other key norm which affected working relationships concerned the inspectors and the supervisor of the group. In effect, the norm stated that 'those in authority must not act officious or take advantage of their authority position'. The men attempted to uphold the assumption that inspectors were no better than anybody else and that, if they attempted to take advantage of their role or if they acted officiously, they were violating group norms. One inspector did feel superior and showed it. The men were able to play tricks on him with the equipment, to ostracize him, and to put social pressure of such an extent on him that he asked to be transferred to another group. The other inspector and the group supervisor were 'part of the gang' and were accepted for this reason.

Box 6.2 – *contd*

Result 3. The observer discovered that the group did not follow company policy on a number of key issues. For example, it was forbidden to trade jobs because each job had been rated carefully to require a certain skill level. Nevertheless, the wiremen often asked soldermen to take over wiring while they soldered. In this way, they relieved monotony and kept up social contacts with others in the room. At the end of each day, each man was required to report the amount of work he had done. Actually the supervisor was supposed to report for all the men, but he had learned that the men wished to do their own reporting and decided to let them do it. What the men actually reported was a relatively standard figure for each day, in spite of large variations in actual output. This practice produced a 'straight line output', a standard figure for each day. Actually, however, the output within the group varied greatly as a function of how tired the men were, their morale on any particular day, and many other circumstances. The men did not cheat in the sense of reporting more than they had done. Rather, they would under-report some days, thus saving up extra units to list on another day when they had actually under-produced.

Result 4. The men varied markedly in their individual production rates. An attempt was made to account for these differences by means of dexterity tests given to the men. Dexterity test results did not correlate with output, however. An intelligence measure was then tried with similar lack of success. What finally turned out to be the key to output rates was the social membership in the cliques. The members of the high-status clique were uniformly higher producers than the members of the low-status clique. But the very highest and very lowest producers were the social isolates, who did not belong to either group. Evidently the individual output was most closely related to the social membership of the workers, not to their innate ability.

The output rates were actually one of the major bones of contention between the two cliques because of the pay system: each man got a base rate plus a percentage of the group bonus based on the total production. The high-status clique felt that the low-status one was chiselling and nagged them about it. The low-status group felt insulted to be looked down upon and realized that the best way to get back at the others was through low production. Thus, the two groups were caught in a self-defeating cycle which further depressed the production rate for the group as a whole.

From the original researches of Roethlisberger and Dickson, *Management and the Worker*. Summarized by Schein, *Organizational Psychology*, 1965 influence may not be in accordance with the distribution of knowledge or experience. The 'neglected resource' is a common feature of groups; the retiring expert whose views are never heard or never noticed because his participation level is so low.

The size of the group is therefore a trade-off. For best participation, for highest all-round involvement, a size of between five and seven seems to be optimum. However, in order to achieve the requisite breadth of knowledge or the requisite representation, the required size may be considerably larger. If that is so then the leader or chairman must be particularly aware of the participation–influence problem.

In work groups, size tends to be related to cohesiveness, which in turn is positively related to member satisfaction. Large workgroups tend to have more absenteeism and lower morale. Large in this context, however, seems to be twenty or over.

Member characteristics. First and most obviously, the members must have the requisite skills and abilities to do the job. So must the leader. But other things are known about the mix of characteristics and personalities.

People who are similar in their attitudes, values and beliefs tend to form stable enduring groups. Homogeneity tends in general to promote satisfaction. Heterogeneous groups tend to exhibit more conflict, but most studies do show them to be more productive than the homogeneous groups. However, as one might expect, these groups were heterogeneous only in certain specific characteristics. One study pinpointed radicalism, adventuresomeness and character integration as the variables which should vary amongst group members. Variety in sensitivity, suspiciousness and aggressiveness impeded productivity. Variety but compatibility was the conclusion of another study, i.e. too many potential leaders was bad, groups with a mixture of assertive and dependent people were effective, for they had variety, but variety which could be organized.

Study of the teams playing a year-long business game at Carnegie Institute of Technology has shown that those groups where there was the greatest differentiation of influence among team members were highest in morale and also performed best. That is, teams whose players saw themselves as all about equally influential were less satisfied and made less profits than teams whose players agreed that some particular individuals were a good deal more influential than others. Belbin's study is reported in Box 6.3.

There have been many studies concerned with compatibility in groups. It was found that compatibility became more crucial as the task became more complex. With simple routine tasks characteristics of the individuals could be as heterogeneous as you liked. Not so with complex tasks where interaction between group members is required. Compatibility can be achieved in various ways. An assertive leader with dependent followers makes for a compatible group. When the individuals all rate highly on warmth and affection it will contribute to compatibility. One common thread stands out. The need for consensus on a focal person, or leader. Two potential leaders do not make for compatibility in a group.

Box 6.3 Belbin's teams

Belbin has made a long study of the best mix of characteristics in a team, based originally on research into teams of managers involved in a management simulation as part of a training course. His first surprise was the Apollo syndrome – the discovery that a team composed of the brightest did not turn out to be the best.

He ended up with a list of eight roles that are needed for a fully effective group:

The Chairman. He* is the one who presides over the team and co-ordinates its efforts. He need be in no sense brilliant or creative, but would rather be called disciplined, focused and balanced. He talks and listens well, is a good judge of people and of things: a man who works through others.

The Shaper. The shaper is highly strung, outgoing and dominant. He is the task leader and in the absence of the chairman would leap into that role, even though he might not do it any too well. His strength lies in his drive and in his passion for the task, but he can be over-sensitive, irritable and impatient. He is needed as the spur to action.

The Plant. Unlike the shaper, the plant is introverted but is intellectually dominant. He is the source of original ideas and proposals, being the most imaginative as well as the most intelligent member of the team. He can, however, be careless of details and may resent criticism. He needs to be drawn out or he will switch off.

The Monitor-Evaluator. The monitor-evaluator is also intelligent, but it is an analytic rather than a creative intelligence. His contribution is the careful dissection of ideas and the ability to see the flaw in an argument. He is often less involved than the others, tucked away with his data, aloof from the team, but necessary as a quality check. He is dependable but can be tactless and cold.

*He emphasizes that 'he' means humankind, i.e. both genders.

Box 6.3 – *contd*

The Resource-Investigator. This is the popular member of the team, extrovert, sociable and relaxed. He it is who brings new contacts, ideas and developments to the group, the salesman, diplomat or liaison officer. He is not himself original or a driver, and therefore needs the team to pick up his contributions.

The Company Worker. The company worker is the practical organizer. He it is who turns ideas into manageable tasks. Schedules, charts and plans are his thing. Methodical, trustworthy and efficient, he is not excited by visions and can be unexciting himself. He does not lead, but is adept at administering.

The Team Worker. The team worker holds the team together in another way, by being supportive to others, by listening, encouraging, harmonizing and understanding. Likeable and popular but uncompetitive, he is the sort of person you do not notice when he's there but miss when he isn't.

The Finisher. Without the finisher the team might never meet its deadlines. He it is who checks the details, worries about schedules and chivvies the others with his sense of urgency. His relentless follow-through is important but not always popular.

Too many of one type in a team means a lack of balance; too few roles and some tasks do not get done. In a small team, therefore, one person may have to perform more than one role. The full set is most important where rapid change is involved in the workforce, the technology, the market-place or the product. More stable groups can often get by without the full set of roles.

R. M. Belbin, *Management Teams*, 1981

Individual objectives and roles. It is only common sense to assert that if all members of a group have the same objectives the group will tend to be that much more effective. Nevertheless most people bring hidden agendas to groups. These hidden agendas are a set of personal objectives, which often may have nothing to do with the declared objectives of the group. Hidden agendas can include:

Protecting the interests of one's sub-group;
Impressing one's boss;
Scoring off an opponent;
Making a particular alliance;
Covering up past errors.

In most group situations it is not possible to satisfy all the individual and group objectives simultaneously. There has to be a trade-off. In order to achieve the best combined result each individual has to (a) take a risk, (b) accept a less than optimum outcome for himself. Only in certain conditions will this happen:

If the participants can agree on a common objective;
If they trust each other.

These conditions will normally only happen if:

The individuals are given a chance to communicate about objectives;
The individuals are allowed to prove that trust is justified by putting it to the test in some other instance.

The exception is:

When there is a 'common enemy' – an objective so obviously common to each that it makes clear sense to make the trade-off.

In most ordinary organization situations the exception does not apply. Unless, therefore, the individuals in a group make specific efforts to agree on common objectives and to prove a level of trust, they will tend to promote their own interests at the expense of the group. Naturally they will not normally do this to the extent of destroying the group or ensuring their own eviction from it – they will only promote their self-interest up to a point, a point where the group's performance 'passes', e.g. is not over budget.

Times of emergency, of crisis and mutual peril, tend to make us all sink our differences. Then it is that the 'common enemy' is dominant, groups become much more cohesive and productive. It is a pity that we have to rely on outside events to produce this change in the individual calculus. It might not have to be so if more attention were paid to the collective purpose and more time devoted to improving the trust relationship.

Groups, however, can be *too* cohesive; they can become so important to each member that the goals of the individuals are inseparable from the goals of the group. Religious sects, campaigning groups, some military and para-military groups, sports teams and pop groups provide the most visible examples of these all-absorbing groups; but they can be found at the top and in the middle of more conventional organizations. These ultra-cohesive groups can be dangerous because in the organizational context the group must serve the organization, not itself. In its absorption with itself, its own members and its own priorities, it can blind itself to what is going on around it. Blinkered, it can forge ahead down quite the wrong road. Janis, in Box 6.4, describes this phenomenon of group-think. To avoid it one needs the mix of roles in Box 6.3 as well as a judicious intrusion of outside comment to keep the group open.

In each group to which we belong we will have one or more roles. We may choose them or we may be cast in them. The choice and the casting is almost always unconscious, accidental and the result of circumstances (who else is in the group, one's previous reputation, one's early behaviour in the group). The role, however, be it a conscious or unconscious one, always influences the way in which people see and hear us as well as the way we behave. We need at least to know what roles we are playing, even if we had no say in choosing them.

Box 6.4 Group-think

'How could we have been so stupid?' asked President John F. Kennedy, after he and a group of close advisers had blundered into the Bay of Pigs invasion.

Stupidity was certainly not the explanation. The group who made the decision was one of the greatest collections of intellectual talent in the history of American government. Irving Janis describes the blunder as a result of 'group-think'.

Group-think occurs when too high a price is placed on the harmony and morale of the group, so that loyalty to the group's previous policies, or to the group consensus, overrides the conscience of each member. 'Concurrence-seeking' drives out the realistic appraisal of alternatives. No bickering or conflict is allowed to spoil the cosy 'we-feeling' of the group. Thus it is that even the cleverest, most high-minded and well-intentioned of people can get into a blind spot. Janis identifies eight symptoms:

1 Invulnerability. Cohesive groups become over-optimistic and can take extraordinary risks without realizing the dangers, mainly because there is no discordant warning voice.
2 Rationale. Cohesive groups are quick to find rationalizations to explain away evidence that does not fit their policies.
3 Morality. There is a tendency to be blind to the moral or ethical implications of a policy. 'How could so many good men be wicked?' is the feeling.
4 Stereotypes. Victims of group-think quickly get into the habit of stereotyping their enemies or other people and do not notice discordant evidence.

Box 6.4 – *contd*

5 Pressure. If anyone starts to voice doubts the group exerts subtle pressures to keep him quiet: he is allowed to express doubts but not to press them.

6 Self-censorship. Members of the group are careful not to discuss their feelings or their doubts outside the group, in order not to disturb the group cosiness.

7 Unanimity. Unanimity is important so, once a decision has been reached, any divergent views are carefully screened out in people's minds.

8 Mindguards. Victims of group-think set themselves up as bodyguards to the decision. 'He needs all the support we can give him.' The doctrine of collective responsibility is invoked to stifle dissent outside the group.

The result of group-think is that the group looks at too few alternatives, is insensitive to the risks in its favourite strategy, finds it hard to rethink a strategy that is failing and becomes very selective in the sort of facts it sees and asks for.

Group-think is unfortunately most rife at the top and centre of organizations where the need for 'keeping things close' seems more important. Such groups must actively encourage self-criticism, the search for more alternatives, the introduction of outside ideas and evaluation wherever possible, and a positive response to conflicting evidence. One way of avoiding group-think in the boardroom is the growing use of non-executive directors, for small groups can get *too* cohesive to be effective.

Kennedy learnt his lesson. The Missile Crisis was handled differently, with a more diffuse group, more outside ideas, more testing of alternatives and more sensitivity to conflicting data.

I. L. Janis, *Victims of Group-Think*, 1972

Belbin, in Box 6.3, gave one set of roles. Chapter 3 provided another (p. 89). There is, however, a further set of questions that each individual would be wise to think about as he joins a group:

1 Who am I in this group? What is my occupational role here? What are the role expectations of me? Am I here to listen or to lead? Am I a representative or present in my own right? Who is judging me on my role performance?

2 What is the influence pattern? Who has the power? What kind of power is it? Do I want to change the influence pattern? If so, how do I do it?

3 What are my needs and objectives? Are they in line with the group?

Should they be? What do I do about them if they are not? If one of these needs is to be liked and accepted, how important is that for me?

When people put groups together, they select individuals mostly on the basis of their official function in the organization (e.g. someone from finance, someone from personnel, someone from operations). Seldom do they think in advance of the other functions, the ways we behave, which have a profound effect on the success of the group. The bag of agendas that individuals bring to the group, the roles they choose or are cast in, and the network of forces influencing them, are at least as important as their knowledge of the problem.

Stage of development. Groups mature and develop. Like individuals they have a fairly clearly defined growth cycle. This has been categorized as having four successive stages:

1 *Forming.* The group is not yet a group but a set of individuals. This stage is characterized by talk about the purpose of the group. The definition and the title of the group, its composition, leadership pattern, and life-span. At this stage, too, each individual tends to want to establish his personal identity within the group, make some individual impression.
2 *Storming.* Most groups go through a conflict stage when the preliminary, and often false, consensus on purposes, on leadership and other roles, on norms of work and behaviour, is challenged and re-established. At this stage a lot of personal agendas are revealed and a certain amount of inter-personal hostility is generated. If successfully handled this period of storming leads to a new and more realistic setting of objectives, procedures and norms. This stage is particularly important for testing the norms of trust in the group.
3 *Norming.* The group needs to establish norms and practices. When and how it should work, how it should take decisions, what type of behaviour, what level of work, what degree of openness, trust and confidence is appropriate. At this stage there will be a lot of tentative experimentation by individuals to test the temperature of the group and to measure the appropriate level of commitment.
4 *Performing.* Only when the three previous stages have been successfully completed will the group be at full maturity and be able to be fully and sensibly productive. Some kind of performance will be achieved at all stages of development but it is likely to be impeded by the other processes of growth and by individual agendas. In many periodic committees the leadership issue, or the objective and

purpose of the group, are recurring topics that crop up in every meeting in some form or other, seriously hindering the true work of the group.

When the task is very important, when the individuals are highly committed to the group, or when individual and group objectives are identical then these stages may become almost perfunctory. Certainly the group will 'grow up', will mature very rapidly and reach its optimum performance level. More often the issues are not dealt with specifically and the group's maturing process is driven underground, particularly the 'storming' stage. When this occurs you have the backstage covert politicking, the hidden agendas, the abuse of negative power. In other words, the storming, not culturally acceptable in the open, goes on all the same but often in a much more disruptive manner, concealed under the heading of *performance*, but subverting that performance.

Box 6.5   For 'self' or for 'group'

Fouriezos, Hutt and Guetzhow studied the effects of low 'group task motivation' upon group productivity in the seventy-two conference groups in the Conference Research Project of the University of Michigan. The groups were rated on the extent to which the members expressed self-oriented needs, i.e. motives resulting in behaviour 'not necessarily directed towards a group's goals, or . . . a solution of group's problems' but 'primarily toward the satisfaction of the need itself, regardless of the effect on attainment of the group goal'. The experimenters found that the amount of such self-orientated behaviour correlated negatively with measures of member satisfaction. In other words, groups in which there was a high frequency of self-orientated behaviour were relatively dissatisfied with the meeting as a whole, with the decisions arrived at, with the procedures used to reach decisions, and with the chairmanship. These 'self-oriented' groups were also high in the amount of conflict they exhibited.

Finally, measures of productivity showed significant inverse relations with amount of self-oriented behaviour. For example, groups rated high on such behaviour tended to complete fewer items on the agenda, although their meetings lasted longer.

Abridged from Fouriezos, Hutt and Guetzhow, 'Measurement of self-oriented needs in discussion groups', *J. Abnormal Soc. Psych.*

Whether a particular group needs to be fully mature to do its job will, of course, depend on the importance of that job. In many instances the cost of developing a group to maturity, in sheer time, the displacement of other priorities, the displacement of other groups in importance to the individuals, will not be worth the increased gain in effectiveness. But in many instances – the start-up of a new operation for the top management team, or a new group resulting from a re-organization – it is worth spending time specifically to build a group. Many organizations now recognize the benefits in doing this. There are known techniques built around the theories of Group Dynamics which can help. Essentially these techniques help the group to analyse and improve its 'process', as opposed to its work on particular tasks, and to hasten its maturity by focusing specifically on each of the stages of development. Process consultation, T-groups, Coverdale training are some of these techniques.

3.3 The task

The 'givens' that must be looked at under the heading of the *task* are *nature of the task*, *criteria for effectiveness*, *salience of the task* and *clarity of the task*. The implications of these are straightforward, but they must not be ignored.

The nature of the task. The types of task for which groups or committees are used have been listed in 2.2. Obviously, the type of task will affect the kind of group you can have. Information dissemination permits a larger group size than problem-solving. Task allocation allows a structured approach, idea formulation needs a more supportive style. The point was made in 2.2 that to confuse two tasks in the one group is inadvisable. In particular this is so when the change in tasks involves a change in role for individuals. For instance in work allocation or in an inquest situation the individual will be wearing a departmental, ambassadorial hat. For problem-solving or creativity he or she is expected to don overall company apparel and to forget departmental-politics. The switch in roles is not easy. The departmental hat will stay on. The creativity discussion will bog down in departmental quibbles. The individual will be castigated as narrow-minded and short-sighted. The group will be ineffective. Essentially it was a different group. The people were the same but the roles were different. A different group needs a different identity – fixed by title, place or time. Agendas or meetings could usefully be split by type of task, rather than all items lumped together in the order they were received by the secretary.

The criteria for effectiveness. In addition to the type of task, one has to consider the *urgency* with which results are required. Pressures of time or competition legitimize more structured forms of working, allow less freedom to develop a group or to deal with individual needs. As a result, the work will often be less accurate, or worse in terms of possible quality. One needs therefore to reflect upon the required *standards*. How, in short, is the effectiveness of the result to be measured? In quantity? In quality? In speed? In cost? In profit? The criteria for assessing performance is going to be a big determining factor on the way the group can operate as well as on what is meant by effectiveness at the end of the day.

Salience of the task. This aspect has already intruded into the discussion of individual objectives. The more important the task to the individuals the more committed they are going to be to the group, the less concerned about their own objectives.

The more important the task to the organization the more attention it is likely to pay to the group's performance. If this attention takes the form of setting high expectations on effectiveness this will tend to increase the salience of the task for the individuals. If, however, the increased attention is accompanied by increased monitoring or controls then the implication is of lack of trust and confidence in the group. The group will then experience the pressure of control rather than the pressure of expectation. Pressure by control is demotivating. It is also expensive.

In general, the more salient the task is, the more you can demand of the group. But salience that leads to increased control will only cause strain within the group and within individuals.

Clarity of the task. The less ambiguous the task the more structured the leadership can be. A precise, detailed and compartmentalized task implies no requirements in the way of homogeneity or compatibility. A precise task will assist the group through the forming and norming stages of development.

But not all tasks can or should be described so precisely. Ambiguous, open-ended assignments or objectives increase complexity, bring increased demands for compatibility, for time, for supportive leadership. Ambiguity increases stress, and therefore has implications for the kind of individuals required in the group and particularly in the leadership roles.

3.4   The environment

All groups work within an environment, usually the environment of the total organization. The achievement imposes certain conditions or constraints on the way they operate. The principal 'givens' in this area are *the norms and expectations*, *the leader position*, *inter-group relations* and *the physical location*.

Norms and expectations. The degree of salience that the task has for the organization, and the implications of that for the work group, has already been discussed (3.3).

In addition, however, every organization has some norms about ways of working, style of meeting, methods of reporting and co-ordinating. It is not always possible for a group or a committee to avoid conforming to these norms whether or not they are the most appropriate in their circumstances.

Leader position. The power position of the leader has been discussed in the chapter on leadership. The view taken there was that the more powerful the leader in the organization as a whole, the greater the freedom to be flexible in style.

It is also true that a powerful leader has a positive effect on the morale of the work group. People like working under a respected chief. Just as civil servants appreciate a Minister who is effective in cabinet, so in all organizations the leader who is effective in the ambassadorial role will do most to help, not only the ultimate effectiveness of the group, but also its internal *esprit de corps*. A leader who cannot give effect to, cannot sell, the product of the group or the committee is often sufficient grounds for the group members to turn the group into a social or casual group, rejecting the task goals as unrealistic.

Research studies support these common-sense conclusions. Studies have shown that in high-producing groups the leader is seen by subordinates as possessing more influence with superiors than the leader of the low-producing groups.

Inter-group relations. The standing of the group or the committee as a whole will affect its productivity and its morale. The degree to which the group is accepted as important, as helpful, as co-operative to the overall goals of the organization; the influence wielded by the group with key figures in the organization; the degree to which it is perceived to influence events in the organization or outside; these factors are all important. No one wants to spend whole mornings in committees whose conclusions will never be noticed, or will be overruled.

The ambassadorial role of the leader has a big bearing on this. But so does the status of the individual members. The marginal group, the low-status group, the unnoticed group, is under a big temptation to activate its latent *negative power*.

Membership of a group which appears to make no difference to anyone will cause dissonance for most individuals. There are two possible ways for someone to resolve that dissonance, and bring their wishes into accord with reality:

1 They can reduce the importance of the group to themselves. They can cease attending, or cease contributing.
2 They can activate the negative power of the group, its blocking or nuisance value, so that more people notice it. Its salience in the organization is then increased, if not its popularity.

This irritation factor in committees will always tend to arise if the committee is low in *centrality* in the organization, is not perceived to be useful or necessary or high in status by other groups.

The physical location. The simplest of the 'givens' but one very often ignored. There are certain specific aspects of the physical location of the group and the members of the group that must be considered:

1 Physical proximity increases interaction. One study showed that a flight of stairs interposed between the offices of members of one group reduced interaction of all types by 30 per cent.
2 Interaction normally increases co-operative feelings. In the exceptional instances, where interaction leads to increasing dislike, divorce ensues and interaction ceases. Studies in a housing project showed that people whose doorways faced each other were more likely to become friends than others.
3 Physical barriers can prevent groups from forming. Assembly-lines inhibit the formation of social groups at work. This is a drawback to workers and one reason for their forming other groups, e.g. strike committees, purely social groups, etc. Concentration camps and prisons use the technique of isolation very effectively to prevent the formation of groups and to deprive the individual of a psychological home.
4 The location of a meeting gives out signals. The Managing Director's office reinforces his role. If it is off-site, in a hotel in the country, the signal is that people can forget their representative role for the time being, and be themselves, be individuals.
5 Shared facilities, even shared discomfort, does much to help group identity. Luncheon and coffee facilities, meeting places and conference rooms can be used deliberately for this purpose. The 'Nissen Hut' experience, groups crowded uncomfortably together, will often produce high cohesion. An isolated location, where all facilities have to be shared, will tend to create involvement in the group.

3.5   The intervening factors

These are the aspects of group work that can be changed or adapted in the short term, taking account of the 'givens', to improve group productivity or member satisfaction. They fall under the headings of:

Leadership style;
Process and procedure;
Motivation.

Leadership style. This has already been discussed in Chapter 4. The 'best fit' approach, the need to adapt the style to the task, the requirements of the subordinates, and the natural preference of the leader should have been underlined by the foregoing discussion.

Process and procedures. For any group to be effective there is a set of processes or functions that has to be done by some person or persons in the group at some time or other. It is the ultimate responsibility of the leader to see that they are done – his choice of style will determine whether he does them, or whether the processes are shared out amongst other individuals. In certain types of group it would be quite appropriate for all the members at some point to perform each of these functions.

The processes or functions are usually grouped under two broad headings – *task functions* and *maintenance functions* – and comprise the following:

task	*maintenance*
initiating	encouraging
information seeking	compromising
diagnosing	peace-keeping
opinion-seeking	clarifying, summarizing
evaluating	standard-setting
decision-managing	

Task functions. Particularly in any problem-solving situation all the listed processes ought to happen. Furthermore, they ought to happen in the order in which they are listed. Too often group discussions leap from initiating through rudimentary opinion-seeking to evaluation. The chairman states the problem, a solution is proposed, it is evaluated and a decision taken. The separation of information from opinion, of diagnosis from evaluation, greatly improves the quality of the solution. Evaluation is, at its heart, a comparative process. It compares one

Box 6.6   The ineffective management committee

The organization was having trouble getting its top management committee to act as a *management* group. It was composed of the senior divisional and functional managers. The MD complained that they could only think in departmental terms and in the short term. He could not get them to take a long-term, company-wide view. He attributed this to their personal incapacities. Investigation revealed that:

1 The committee meetings usually started with some form of 'inquest' which forced the managers into departmental roles. They found it hard to exchange these roles for company ones for the next item, which was usually of a different 'type'.
2 Decision was by authority rule. Discussion therefore was peripheral and mainly concerned to pinpoint departmental pitfalls.
3 The agenda was lengthy, the time available was short. Interjections therefore had to be short and factual. Philosophical discussions were not encouraged.
4 The offices of the departmental managers were all in the centres of their departments. This enhanced their ambassadorial or departmental role.
5 The meetings were run on a 'wheel' basis – thus accentuating the power of the chairman and providing the basis for authority rule.
6 Two of the members of the group were not trusted or respected by their colleagues. Everyone, including the two, was aware of this but the formality of the proceedings prevented its coming into the open.

Changes were made:

1 The committee was re-organized and re-named to exclude the two 'unrespected' members.
2 The offices of the others were then all situated on the fifth floor away from their departments. This not only changed their view of the role but also cut down their day-to-day interaction ('interference' said subordinates) with their departments.
3 The agendas were shortened, and the items divided by type.
4 The meeting times were lengthened.
5 The smaller number permitted the interaction pattern to change from the wheel to all-channel. The decision mechanism changed to consensus.

All agreed that the committee worked much more effectively and more like a management group. Levels of mutual trust went up. The MD's appraisals of his managers were revised – upwards.

solution with other available solutions. To be well done it is therefore important that all solutions are known before any are evaluated. The stages of opinion-seeking, or idea generation, and evaluation should be separated. A mechanism for recording these ideas is also important – a blackboard, or large sheet of paper, some public recording device so that all members have available to them all possibilities before evaluation starts.

It has been shown in experimental studies that groups who attack a problem systematically perform better than groups who 'muddle through' or 'evolve'. The decision-making procedure is also of great importance. Will it be:

Decision by authority;
Decision by majority;
Decision by consensus;
Decision by minority;
Decision by no response?

The last two are usually only negative. That is, an idea is suggested: either no one responds and it is dropped, or a minority bloc exercises its veto. Most group decisions are negative decisions and as such often pass unnoticed as decisions. If ideas are evaluated separately it can easily happen that each idea receives a veto or negative decision, the meeting then becoming totally unfruitful and very dispiriting to all present.

The kind of task procedure to adopt and in particular the decision-making process are two of the things that the group has to make up its mind on in the 'norming' stage of its development. The leader, by virtue of position power, has great influence over choice of procedure (ecology), although he or she does not have to perform all of the functions themselves.

Maintenance functions. Effective groups, be they problem-solving or producing, need maintenance. There are neglected resources in groups, they need encouraging; there are often opposing factions, they must be helped to compromise, to resolve or manage their conflict; individuals too often do not listen in groups, each man intent on preparing his own contribution; someone must clarify and summarize so that there is a common awareness of all that has happened. Lastly, the performance of the group will be vastly influenced by the kind of standards that it is aiming at. Someone has to set those standards and have them adopted by the group. Groups without standards will satisfice at the lowest level. Standards without groups, not accepted by the group as realistic for them, are meaningless.

Again, the leader does not have to perform all these functions himself, but they need doing. Groups in which these tasks and maintenance functions were observed to happen have been entitled co-operative groups. They were found, in one study by Deutsch, in comparison with 'competitive' groups to:

1 Be more productive in quantity.
2 Produce higher quality.
3 Have a stronger push to complete the task.
4 Have a greater division of labour and better co-ordination.
5 Experience fewer difficulties in communication.
6 Show more friendliness in the discussions.
7 Experience greater satisfaction with the group and its products.

Interaction pattern. The other factor that the group itself can control, and the leader can influence, is the interaction pattern, the pattern of communication between members. Is it, for instance, a *wheel*, *circle* or *web*? (See Figure 9.)

Well-known sets of experiments have been done by numbers of social scientists to demonstrate the relative merits of these communication patterns in small groups. The main conclusions are not unexpected:

1 The wheel is always the quickest to reach a solution or conclusion, the circle is the slowest. This finding is true as long as the people at the periphery of the wheel accept the authority of the person in the centre. If they do not, then the wheel effectively becomes a web.

wheel   circle   web

Figure 9

2 In complex open-ended problems the web is the most likely to reach the best solution, the ability of the person at the centre of the wheel determining the outcome of that pattern. The wheel is usually inflexible if the task changes.

3 The level of satisfaction for individuals is lowest in the circle, fairly high in the web and mixed in the wheel, with the central figure usually expressing great satisfaction and the outlying figures feeling isolated.

One might suppose, although the research did not test this, that feelings of satisfaction in the web group would depend on the importance of the task. No one wants involvement in a trivial 'Mickey Mouse' assignment. Similarly, not all individuals react positively to being the central figure in the wheel – even in experimental situations people have been known to collapse and withdraw under the overload of communication.

Under pressure of time or competition the web system either restructured itself into a wheel – or disintegrated. In general, then, wheels are good for speedy results where quality is not vital, but morale may be low for all but the leader. Circles are always bad, no coordination. Web systems are participative and involving and good for quality, but they take time and do not stand up under pressure. These conclusions can be seen at work in numberless committees where often, *pace* Parkinson, the wrong system is used for the wrong task – allchannel for the trivia of the parking lot, wheels for the big merger decision.

Motivation. This topic has been discussed in general in Chapter 2. As regards motivation in group settings, certain aspects need to be stressed:

1 Motivation is more than satisfaction. Satisfaction is one of the possible outcomes of groups. Lack of satisfaction will lead to absenteeism and turnover of members. But a satisfied group is not necessarily a productive group, although it helps. Satisfaction is a necessary but not sufficient condition of productivity. An individual will be satisfied in a group, will value membership of that group if:

(a) He or she likes the other members and is liked by them (friendship); or
(b) He or she approves of the purpose and work of the group (task); or
(c) He or she wishes to be associated with the standing of the group in the organization (status).

One or all of these will lead to satisfaction, depending on the psychological contract of the individual with that group and the particular needs subsumed in that contract. You can therefore have a satisfied and productive group in which condition (a) does not apply, in which the members do not particularly like each other.

2 Knowledge of expected results, or standard setting, is crucial if the motivation calculus of individuals is to operate. Hence the importance of realistic standards, of standards accepted by the group, of standards sufficiently high to give them a feeling of achievement when attained. Hence also the importance of knowing the results, of feedback. Both of these items are essential to the motivation of groups. Both are too frequently neglected.

3 Motivation by involvement will only work if the group and the task are important enough to the individual to justify his or her acceptance of additional responsibility. Otherwise it will be involvement by order – rules and procedures based on coercive or resource power and requiring control and maintenance mechanisms to make it work. One cannot assume that, because someone is nominated to a committee, that person will do any more than attend its meetings.

Box 6.7   Group blockages

John Hunt has usefully listed the most commonly found behaviours which can inhibit and block the work of groups. Some of these are:

Restricting information – a group member knows the answer but is not telling, for a variety of possible reasons;
Lying – deliberate distortion of the facts in order to preserve a position in the group;
Paring – breaking into sub-groups rather than solving the problem together;
Fighting – win-lose conflicts within the group;
Flight – withdrawal, sometimes physical such as leaving the room, sometimes psychological or symbolic, sulking, sleeping, doodling, telephoning;
Noise – speaking to be heard rather than to contribute.
Suppressing emotion – demanding logic and rationality when emotions may be part of the problem or the solution.

It can be salutary to check one's own behaviour in a group against this list.

See further, Hunt, *Managing People at Work*, 1987

Perhaps, however, the most important aspect of motivation in groups is the establishment of a 'common enemy', discussed in 3.1. Hopefully, the task assigned to the group will be sufficiently salient and clear to all members that it will automatically become a common enemy. But this cannot be assumed. The leader, particularly, may see the task as much more important than the other members. If the individuals put their own agendas in front of the task the productivity and morale will decline and the whole group will be much more difficult to manage. The leader therefore needs to do all he or she can either to:

Re-define the task so that it becomes a common enemy; or
Raise the individual's expectations of the task so that it dwarfs their individual needs.

A solution sometimes adopted, lacking a task of sufficient interest, is to make the building of a group the key task. This is:

(a) Difficult, without an external task;
(b) Counter to organizational interests since a group will be created whose primary goal will be its own satisfaction and survival.

4 Summary and conclusions

4.1 The summary

The complete model for the analysis of groups now looks like this:

	The group	The task	The environment
	size	nature	norms and expectations
the givens	member characteristics	criteria for effectiveness	leader position
	individual objectives	salience of task	inter-group relations
	stage of development	clarity of task	
which all affect the intervening actors		choice of leadership style	
		processes and procedures	
		motivation	
which determine the outcomes		productivity	
		member satisfaction	

Are there any general conclusions that we can reach; or additional points to make?

4.2   The 'group' ideology

Groups fit well with a democratic culture, with representative systems of government. Participation and involvement go well with assumptions of man as an independent individual. Committees similarly are democratic and representative, but they are extraordinarily difficult things to operate effectively. The model presented in this chapter should help to give an understanding of many of the reasons. In addition, we must remember that:

1 Groups can be used by individuals, and by organizations, to diffuse, and even to lose, responsibility.
2 Committees are often better ways of 'recognizing' problems than 'solving' problems. A 'committee to investigate X' is a recognition of 'X' but that does not necessarily mean that it is the best way to solve 'X'. Committees are often, like Royal Commissions, a way of simultaneously accepting the importance of a problem but deferring its solution.
3 The conforming power of groups was demonstrated in Chapter 3. Even strong individuals can be reduced to impotence by a group. But weak individuals can be bolstered – it all depends on the norms of the group and its collective motivation and standards.

The problem is this: if groups or committees are convened or constructed for an inappropriate task, or with impossible constraints; if they are badly led or have ineffective procedures; if they have the wrong people, too many people, too little power or meet too infrequently; if, in short, any one part of the model is badly out of line, frustration will set in and dissonance will be created. The result will either be an activation of *negative power* or a badly attended non-effective group, wasting people, time and space. The chances of this happening are, in fact, very high. If 50 per cent of managerial time is spent in groups, the cost of wasted time begins to look colossal, let alone the damage done by the use of negative power.

This is why the study of groups, the improvement of the work of groups and committees, merits a deal of attention. It may at least prevent the establishment of another committee to improve the workings of committees! Most attention, by theorists and trainers, has focused on the intervening factors. All the courses on leadership, on supervisory style, on effective membership of groups, on participation as motivation, have been dealing with this part of the model. Undoubtedly much can be done in this area.

But the thrust of this chapter has been to emphasize the more basic ecological conditions – the *givens*. No leadership style, no process, no motivation principle, can work in an impossible situation. More attention needs to be paid to the *givens*. If it were, the conclusion might be that no group was necessary in a particular situation, or at least that it would be bound to be ineffective so let no one waste their energies.

Groups there must be. Individuals must be co-ordinated and their skills and abilities meshed and merged. But let us not be mesmerized. Let us realize that a proper understanding of groups will demonstrate how difficult they are to manage. Let us pay more attention to their creation and be more realistic about their outcomes.

7 → On the Cultures of Organizations

1 Introduction

1.1

The chief delight of Europe is the variety it offers of climate and culture. One of the more pleasurable ways of ending a long English winter is to drive south along the highways of the continent, to watch spring and its blossoms come to meet you up the road, and to linger awhile in the sun, adapting to another culture with different traditions, habits, ways of organizing work and of ordering daily life. Anyone who has spent any time in another country will appreciate how values, beliefs and cherished philosophies affect the way society is organized. They will appreciate too how these values and beliefs are shaped by history and tradition, by the climate, the kinds of work people do, the size of the country and its prosperity.

So too, anyone who has spent time with any variety of organizations, or worked in more than two or three, will have been struck by the differing atmospheres, the differing ways of doing things, the differing levels of energy, of individual freedom, of kinds of personality. For organizations are as different and varied as the nations and societies of the world. They have differing cultures – sets of values and norms and beliefs – reflected in different structures and systems. And the cultures are affected by the events of the past and by the climate of the present, by the technology of the type of work, by their aims and the kind of people that work in them.

Should this variety be so? After decades of management theory should the mix of type and structure be so great? Is there not one optimum span of control, one best way of describing jobs, appraising people, controlling people, of budgeting, forecasting and planning? The contention of this chapter is 'No'; that the cultures of organizations rightly differ, that cultures are affected by a variety of factors, that these diverse cultures are reflected in diverse structures and systems. Indeed it will be argued that many of the ills of organizations stem from imposing an inappropriate structure on a particular culture, or from expecting a particular culture to thrive in an inappropriate climate. Vines don't grow where the sunshine doesn't fall in the right proportions with the rain – nor has anyone yet found a more effective technology for tending the vines than the human hand.

Earlier management theory, in its search for universal formulae or cure-all remedies, did a great disservice in seeking to disseminate a common organizational culture. Fortunately organizations, unhearing or unheeding, were unaffected. More modern theories of organization are increasingly persuaded of the wisdom of the appropriate, of the match of people to systems, to task and environment, of inter-relations between all four, of what has come to be called the *institutional* approach to management theory. This is a word sufficiently vague to cover all manner of specific approaches but it tends to connote inter-relationships, feedback mechanisms, and appropriateness of fit. The institutional approach to describing organizations is not the same as systems theory but it shares with it a concern for linkages and appropriateness. It is, in its interest in the appropriate, akin to those approaches to organizing described generally as *contingency theories*.

1.2

This chapter will first examine four varieties of *organization cultures* which are each reflected in a structure and a set of systems. It will then consider the *influencing factors* on these cultures. Finally it will look at the *implications for organization design*.

2 The cultures

2.1

Roger Harrison, in a stimulating paper referred to in Part Three, has written of 'organization ideologies'. The word 'cultures' is preferred here because it conveys more of the feeling of a pervasive way of life, or set of norms. In organizations there are deep-set beliefs about the way work should be organized, the way authority should be exercised, people rewarded, people controlled. What are the degrees of formalization required? How much planning and how far ahead? What combination of obedience and initiative is looked for in subordinates? Do work hours matter, or dress, or personal eccentricities? What about expense accounts, and secretaries, stock options and incentives? Do committees control, or individuals? Are there rules and procedures or only results? These are all parts of the culture of an organization. This culture often takes visible form in its building, its offices, its shops or branches. The kinds of people it employs, the length and height of their career aspirations, their status in society, degree of mobility, level of education, will all be reflections of the culture. The mammoth teaching hospital has a culture manifestly different from a merchant bank, which is different again from an automobile plant. They look and feel different. They will require different kinds of people, will appeal to different kinds. They have different ways of working. They are different cultures. Even within organizations cultures will differ. The R and D laboratory in the fields of the countryside will have a different atmosphere to the director's floor in the central office. The invoicing department would not be mistaken for the market research department, or the factory for the sales division.

Box 7.1   Two cultures

Schein describes two very different organizations:

Organization A operates on the assumption that:
- ideas come ultimately from individuals
- people are responsible, motivated and capable of governing themselves
- nevertheless, in practice, truth can only be arrived at by fighting things out in groups
- such fighting is possible because members of the organization see themselves as a family who will take care of each other.

It is therefore safe to fight and be competitive.

Organization B operates on the assumption that:
- truth comes ultimately from older, wider and higher-status members
- people are capable of loyalty and discipline in carrying out directions
- relationships are basically lineal and vertical
- each person has a niche in the organization that cannot be invaded
- the organization is responsible for taking care of its members.

In Organization A there are open office landscapes, few closed doors, people milling about, intense conversations and arguments and a general air of informality.

In Organization B there is a hush in the air. Everyone is in an office with closed doors, nothing is done except by appointment and prearranged agenda. When people of different ranks are present there is real deference and obedience. An air of formality permeates everything.

Neither is wrong – they are just different.

From Schein, 'Coming to a New Awareness of Organizational Culture', *Sloan Management Review*, 1984

There is a growing literature on the culture of organizations, for it has come to be realized that the customs and traditions of a place are a powerful way of influencing behaviour (ecologically).

Strong pervasive cultures turn organizations into cohesive tribes with distinctly clannish feelings. The values and traditions of the tribe are re-inforced by its private language, its catch-phrases and its tales of past heroes and dramas. The way of life is enshrined in rituals so that rule books and manuals are almost unnecessary; custom and tradition pro-vide the answers. Japanese firms have their company songs – as do some American companies – while many a school or voluntary organization is proud to trumpet its values and belief in itself through its literature and speeches. Experience suggests that a strong culture makes a strong organization, but does it matter what sort of culture is involved?

Yes, it does. Not all cultures suit all purposes or people. Cultures are founded and built over the years by the dominant groups in an organization. What suits them and the organization at one stage is not necessarily appropriate for ever – strong though that culture may be. There seem to be four main types of culture which (following Harrison) are called *power*, *role*, *task* and *person*. It must be emphasized that each can be a good and effective culture; but people are often culturally blink-ered, thinking that ways that worked well in one place are bound to be successful everywhere. This is not the case.

2.2 The power culture

A power culture is frequently found in small entrepreneurial organiza-tions, traditionally in the robber-baron companies of nineteenth-century America, occasionally in today's trade unions, and in some property, trading and finance companies. Its structure is best pictured as a *web*:

If this culture had a patron god it would be Zeus, the all-powerful head of the gods of ancient Greece who ruled by whim and impulse, by thunderbolt and shower of gold from Mount Olympus.

This culture depends on a central power source, with rays of power and influence spreading out from that central figure. They are connected by functional or specialist strings but the power rings are the centres of activity and influence.

The organization depends on trust and empathy for its effectiveness and on telepathy and personal conversation for communication. If the centre chooses the right people, who can think in the same way as it thinks, they can be left to get on with the job. There are few rules and procedures, little bureaucracy. Control is exercised by the centre largely through the selection of key individuals, by occasional forays from the centre or summonses to the centre. It is a political organization in that decisions are taken very largely on the outcome of a balance of influence rather than on procedural or purely logical grounds.

These cultures, and organizations based on them, are proud and strong. They have the ability to move quickly and can react well to threat or danger. Whether they do move or whether they move in the right direction will, however, depend on the person or persons in the centre; for the quality of these individuals is of paramount importance in those organizations and the succession issue is the key to their continued success. Individuals employed in them will prosper and be satisfied to the extent that they are power-orientated, politically minded, risk-taking, and rate security as a minor element in their psychological contract. Resource power is the major power base in this culture with some elements of personal power in the centre.

Size is a problem for power cultures. The web can break if it seeks to link too many activities; indeed the only way the web organization can grow and remain a web is by spawning other organizations, other spiders. Organizations which have done this (most noticeably GEC in the UK) continue to grow but are careful to give maximum independence to the individual heads of the linked organizations (which incidentally do not have to have a power culture) usually keeping finance as the one string that binds them to the central web.

These cultures put a lot of faith in the individual, little in committees. They judge by results and are tolerant of means. Often seen as tough or abrasive, though successful they may well suffer from low morale and high turnover in the middle layers as individuals fail or opt out of the competitive atmosphere. And it must be remembered that these cultures can be as bad as they can be effective. Many of the family businesses that stagnated and were eventually annexed in Britain after the Second World War were power cultures that had died in the centre. A web without a spider has no strength.

2.3   The role culture

The role culture is often stereotyped as bureaucracy. But bureaucracy has come to acquire a pejorative note in common parlance, so 'role' will be used here. The accompanying structure to a role culture can be pictured as a *Greek temple*.

Its patron god is Apollo, the god of reason; for this culture works by logic and by rationality. The role organization rests its strength in its pillars, its functions or specialities. These pillars are strong in their own right; the finance department, the purchasing department, the production facility may be internationally renowned for their efficiency. The work of the pillars, and the interaction between the pillars, is controlled by:

Procedures for roles, e.g. job descriptions, authority definitions;
Procedures for communications, e.g. required sets of copies of memoranda;
Rules for settlement of disputes, e.g. appeal to the lowest crossover points.

They are co-ordinated at the top by a narrow band of senior management, the pediment. It is assumed that this should be the only personal co-ordination needed, for if the separate pillars do their job, as laid down by the rules and procedures, the ultimate result will be as planned.

In this culture the role, or job description, is often more important than the individual who fills it. Individuals are selected for satisfactory performance of a role, and the role is usually so described that a range of individuals could fill it. Performance over and above the role prescription is not required, and indeed can be disruptive at times. Position power is the major power source in this culture, personal power is frowned upon and expert power tolerated only in its proper place. Rules and procedures are the major methods of influence. The efficiency of this culture depends on the rationality of the allocation of work and responsibility rather than on the individual personalities.

The role organization will succeed as long as it can operate in a stable environment. When next year is like this year, so that this year's tested rules will work next year, then the outcome will be good. Where the organization can control its environment, by monopoly or oligopoly, where the market is stable or predictable or controllable, or where the product-life is a long one, then rules and procedures and programmed work will be successful. So the civil service (a monopoly in a sense), the automobile and oil industries (long product life-cycles and perhaps some oligopoly situations), life insurance companies and retail banking (long product life-cycles), are usually role cultures and successful ones. Small newcomers to this field, however, may well not have a role culture since their aims will not be stability and predictability, but survival and growth.

But Greek temples are insecure when the ground shakes. Role cultures are slow to perceive the need for change and slow to change even if the need is seen. If the market, the product needs or the competitive environment changes, the role culture is likely to continue to forge straight ahead confident in its ability to shape the future in its own image. Then collapse, or replacement of the pediment by new management, or take-over, is usually necessary. Many large organizations found themselves in this position in the changing conditions of the 1960s.

Role cultures offer security and predictability to the individual. They offer a predictable rate of climb up a pillar. They offer the chance to acquire specialist expertise without risk. They tend to reward the satisficer, the person concerned with doing his job up to a standard. But come disaster – collapse or take-over – and the security of the role culture may be found to be built too much on the organization and too little on the individual's capacities. The role culture is frustrating for the individual who is power-orientated or wants control over his or her work; who is eagerly ambitious or more interested in results than method. Such a person will only be content in the pediment.

The role organization will be found where economies of scale are more important than flexibility or where technical expertise and depth of specialization are more important than product innovation or product cost. Organizations used to operating in a sellers' market until the mid 1950s, or with the state as their only customer, were quite properly operating in a role culture since there was a high premium on product reliability and few penalties for cost or lack of product innovation.

Box 7.2   The seven S diagram

This diagram appears in *The Art of Japanese Management* written by Richard Pascale and Tony Athos and also in *In Search of Excellence* written by Tom Peters and Bob Waterman. That is no accident. All four authors were members of a McKinsey team charged with finding a powerful model to analyse organizations to compete with the Cows, Stars and Dogs of the Boston Consulting Group. The two books came out almost simultaneously and both have been very influential.

In later versions superordinate goals sometimes became shared values. Athos finds that the main conflicts come between the advocates of the 'cold triangle' (strategy, structure and systems) and those who favour the 'warm square' or the 'soft S's of superordinate goals, staff, skills and style. This is one of the 'dilemmas' which Charles Hampden-Turner discusses so helpfully in his book, *Corporate Culture*.

2.4   The task culture

The task culture is job or project orientated. Its accompanying structure can be best represented as a *net*, with some of the strands of the net thicker and stronger than the others. Much of the power and influence lies at the interstices of the net, at the knots. The so-called 'matrix organization' is one structural form of the task culture.

The task culture has no totally appropriate presiding deity, although Athena, the warrior goddess and champion of the commando leader Odysseus, fits the role best, for the whole emphasis of the task culture is on getting the job done. To this end the culture seeks to bring together the appropriate resources, the right people at the right level of the organization, and to let them get on with it. Influence is based more on expert power than on position or personal power, although these sources have their effect. Influence is also more widely dispersed than in other cultures, and each individual tends to think he has more of it. It is a team culture, where the outcome, the result, the product, of the team's work tends to be the common enemy obliterating individual objectives and most status and style differences. The task culture utilizes the unifying power of the group to improve efficiency and to identify the individual with the objective of the organization.

This culture is extremely adaptable. Groups, project teams, or task forces are formed for a specific purpose and can be reformed, abandoned or continued. The net organization works quickly since each group ideally contains within it all the decision-making powers required. Individuals find in this culture a high degree of control over their work, judgement by results, easy working relationships within the group with mutual respect based upon capacity rather than age or status.

The task culture therefore is appropriate where flexibility and sensitivity to the market or environment are important. You will find the task culture where the market is competitive, where the product life is short, where speed of reaction is important. But the task culture finds it hard to produce economies of scale or great depth of expertise. You cannot organize a large factory as a flexible group; although the technical person in the group may be clever and talented she will, by virtue of having to work on various problems in various groups, be less specialized than her counterpart in a role culture. The task culture therefore thrives where speed of reaction, integration, sensitivity and creativity are more important than depth of specialization. The product groups of marketing departments, the general management consultancies, the merger, take-over and new venture sections of merchant banks, the account groups of advertising agencies – these are all places where the task culture might be expected to flourish.

Control in these organizations is difficult. Essentially control is re-tained by the top management by means of allocation of projects, people and resources. Vital projects are given to good people with no restrictions on time, space or materials. But little day-to-day control can be exerted over the methods of working or the procedures without violating the norms of the culture. These cultures therefore tend to flourish when the climate is agreeable, when the product is all-important and the customer always right, and when resources are avail-able for all who can justify using them. Top management then feels able to relax day-to-day control and concentrate on resource allocation decisions and the hiring and placing of key people.

However, when resources are not available to all who can justify their needs for them, when money and people have to be rationed, top management begins to feel the need to control methods as well as results. Alternatively team leaders begin to compete, using political influence, for available resources. In either case, morale in the work-groups declines and the job becomes less satisfying in itself, so that individuals begin to change their psychological contract and to reveal their individual objectives. This new state of affairs necessitates rules and procedures or exchange methods of influence, and the use of position or resource power by the managers to get the work done. In short, the task culture tends to change to a role or power culture when resources are limited or the total organization is unsuccessful. It is a difficult culture to control and inherently unstable by itself.

The task culture is the one preferred, as a personal choice to work in, by most managers, certainly at the middle and junior levels. It is the culture which most of the behavioural theories of organizations point towards with its emphasis on groups, expert power, rewards for results, merging individual and group objectives. It is the culture most in tune with current ideologies of change and adaptation, individual freedom and low status differentials. But, as will be seen, it is not always the appropriate culture for the climate and the technology. If organizations do not all embrace this culture it may be that they are not just out-of-date and old-fashioned – but right.

2.5 The person culture

The fourth culture is an unusual one. It will not be found pervading many organizations, yet many individuals will cling to some of its values. In this culture the individual is the central point. If there is a structure or an organization it exists only to serve and assist the indi-viduals within it. If a group of individuals decide that it is in their own interests to band together in order the better to follow their own bents, to do their own thing, and that an office, a space, some equipment or even clerical and secretarial assistance would help, then the resulting organization would have a person culture. It would exist only for the people in it without any super-ordinate objective. Barristers' chambers, architects' partnerships, hippy communes, social groups, families, some small consultancy firms, often have this 'person' orientation. Its structure is as minimal as possible, a *cluster* is the best word for it, or perhaps a galaxy of individual stars:

Dionysus is its patron deity, the god of the self-oriented individual, the first existentialist.

Clearly, not many organizations can exist with this sort of culture, since organizations tend to have objectives over and above the collective objectives of those who comprise them. Furthermore control mechanisms, or even management hierarchies, are impossible in these cultures except by mutual consent. The psychological contract states that the organization is subordinate to the individual and depends on the individual for its existence. The individual can leave the organization but the organization seldom has the power to evict the individual. Influence is shared and the power-base, if needed, is usually expert; that is, individuals do what they are good at and are listened to on appropriate topics.

The change in the culture of the modern family from a power or role culture more common in Victorian times with a clear power structure and apportionments of tasks and responsibilities, to a person culture with shared influence and roles apportioned according to expertise, is becoming one of the sociological features of our society. The kibbutz, the commune, the co-operative, are all striving after the person culture in organizational form. On the whole, only their original creators achieve any success. Too soon the organization achieves its own identity and begins to impose on its individuals. It becomes, at best, a task culture, but often a power or a role culture.

But although it would be rare to find an organization where the personal culture predominated, you will often encounter individuals whose personal preference is for this type of culture but who find themselves operating in a more typical organization. The stereotype of the professor is of a person-oriented man operating in a role culture. He does what he has to, teaches when he must, in order to retain his position in that organization. But essentially he regards the organization as a base on which he can build his own career, carry out his own interests, all of which may indirectly add interest to the organization though that would not be the point in doing them. Specialists in organizations – computer people in business organizations, consultants in hospitals, architects in city government – often feel little allegiance to the organization but regard it rather as a place to do their thing with some accruing benefit to the main employer.

Individuals with this orientation are not easy to manage. There is little influence that can be brought to bear on them. Being specialists alternative employment is often easy to obtain, or they have protected themselves by tenure, so that resource power has no potency. Position power not backed up by resource power achieves nothing. Expert power they are unlikely to acknowledge. Coercive power is not usually available, only personal power is left and such individuals are not easily impressed by personality.

3 The influencing factors

3.1

The cultures have been described in impressionistic and imprecise ways. They have not been rigorously defined. A culture cannot be precisely defined, for it is something that is perceived, something felt. However, a self-analysis questionnaire in Box 7.7 will fill out the descriptions in more detail. It will also allow you to identify the prevailing culture in your organization as well as your own personal cultural preference. A fit between the two should lead to a fulfilled psychological contract, to satisfaction at work.

3.2   The factors

The impressionistic descriptions pointed to some of the factors which would influence a choice of culture and structure for an organization. These factors now need to be looked at in rather more detail. The principal ones are:

History and ownership;
Size;
Technology;
Goals and objectives;
The environment;
The people.

3.3   History and ownership

The age of the company, its ownership and its history will affect its culture in the following ways:

Centralized ownership will lead towards a power culture with more control of the resources. Diffused ownership allows diffused influence based on alternative sources of power. Family firms, or founder-dominated organizations, will tend to be power cultures.

New organizations need either to be aggressive and independent (power) or flexible, adaptable and sensitive (task). They are often a combination of the two. Explicit repudiation of role cultures and of the systems, procedures and jargons that accompany role cultures, often emanate from new organizations:

1 Mergers often mean an aggressive organization moving into a static organization – a power culture superimposed on a Greek temple.
2 A new generation of managers often heralds its arrival by a change of culture. 'Systems instead of politics' equals 'role replaces power'; 'efficiency not bureaucracy' means 'task instead of role'.

3.4   Size

Size of organization has often proved to be the single most important variable in influencing a choice of structure or of culture. It is clear that, on the whole:

Large organizations are more formalized;
Large organizations tend to develop specialized groups which need systematic co-ordination.

In general, size pushes the organization towards a role culture. Specific actions, spinning-off subsidiaries, or radical decentralization may allow the core organization to develop a different culture. A web linking a series of temples is quite conceivable. Size, however, does not in itself bring low morale:

> Large organizations are seen by their members as offering more potential and being more friendly places;
> Large organizations are thought to be more efficient but more authoritarian by their employees.

3.5 Technology

Ever since the Tavistock theorists coined the phrase 'socio-technical system' and Joan Woodward in Essex demonstrated that the technology of production was a major determinant in the organization of efficient firms, it has been clear that the kind of technology will have an effect on the culture and the structure.

Trist and Bamforth of the Tavistock Institute in London demonstrated that changing a technology from small group work to three-shift working had a disruptive effect on the relationships of the men during the job, and thus on productivity. The design of the organization must therefore take into account the nature of the work as well as its people.

Joan Woodward classified a range of manufacturing firms in Essex into *unit* (or small batch), *mass* (or large batch), and *process*. She discovered that the length of the line of command, the span of control of the chief executive, the percentage of turnover devoted to wages and salaries, the ratio of managers to others, of graduates to non-graduates and indirect to direct labour, all increased as the technology involved moved along the line from unit to process. However, mass production was more formalized and mechanistic than the other two. She demonstrated that those organizations whose structures were in line with the norm for their technology were the most effective.

Perrow suggested that the continuum in technology was really from routine to non-routine. He is interested in the impact of technology on systems of co-ordination, control, on degree of inter-dependence, on individual influence and power, on goals and motivation. He puts forward a complex scheme for linking these factors to technology.

These studies, and others, in general demonstrated that technology was important. They do not all, however, obviously point towards one or other of the cultures, but:

1 Routine, programmable operations are more suitable to a role culture than any of the others.
2 High-cost, expensive technologies, where the cost of breakdown is high, tend to encourage close monitoring and supervision and require depth of expertise. Both are more appropriate in a role culture.
3 Technologies where there are clear economies of scale by mass production of heavy capital investment tend to encourage large size and thence role cultures.
4 Non-continuous discrete operations, the one-off job, unit production – these technologies are suited to power or task cultures.
5 Rapidly changing technologies require a task or power culture to be dealt with effectively.
6 Tasks with a high degree of interdependence call for systematized co-ordination and suggest a role culture. In markets where co-ordination and uniformity are more important than adaptability a role culture will therefore be appropriate.

Technological considerations do not always push in the same way. High-cost, rapidly changing technologies will leave the culture ambivalent between role and task. So will a need for swift reaction but high co-ordination. In general, however, the tendency towards increasing automation and high investment in technologies of work is pushing cultures towards a role orientation.

3.6   Goals and objectives

The objectives of an enterprise are seldom as clear-cut as they seem. It is too simple to claim that a business firm pursues profitability. How hard does it pursue it? Over what time-span? With what degree of risk? What constraints does it accept in the way of pressures on people, ethics, level of debt? It is sometimes conceptually simpler to regard profit as a necessary factor in achieving the other corporate objectives such as survival, rate of growth, market share, reputation, increased share value, standard of excellence, good place to work, source of employment, strategic necessity, national prestige. The level of profit required to pursue any combination of these objectives will vary. Strategic necessity, for instance, requires minimal profit generation, whereas increased share value requires a high profit ratio.

The objectives of hospitals, schools and local government are often a mixture of service to a community and maintenance of standards, within the limits however of constrained resources. How do these goals affect the culture and structure?

Quality of product goals are more easily monitored in a role organization;

Growth goals are more appropriate to a power or a task culture;

Place to work, centre of employment, strategic necessity point towards role cultures;

Goals not only influence cultures, they are influenced by them. An organization's goals can change over a period of time as its culture changes.

These tendencies are only tendencies. A role culture can achieve growth. A power culture can have strategic necessity as its goal. Goals and objectives are only one of the influencing factors. Too often to be helpful the real goals of an organization are undeclared, even to the top manager himself. A leading banker once said, 'There are only a handful of people in Britain interested in making money. The rest are interested in making things for money.' He was suggesting that most organizations are wedded to their technology or product or industry, that success is defined for them within those constraints. Role cultures for instance are reliable cultures. They are not cultures in a hurry. They take pride in their process whereas power cultures take pride in their results. The difference in goals may seem semantic but it can be decisive.

3.7 The environment

The environment includes:

The economic environment;
The market;
The competitive scene;
The geographical and societal environment.

The nature of an environment within which an organization works is often taken for granted by those who work within it but it can be crucially important in determining the culture.

Some of the major points are:

1 Different nationalities prefer different organizational cultures. This should not be any surprise but it is only recently that organizational studies have been able to spell out the differences in any detail. See Box 7.3 for the most important of these studies.

2 Change in the environment requires a culture that is sensitive,

adaptable and quick to respond. A task culture is most suited to coping with changes in the market or the product. Burns and Stalker discovered that firms with what they called an 'organismic' or 'organic' structure responded more effectively to changes in the technology than firms with a mechanistic structure. Organic and mechanistic correspond to the task and role cultures.

3 Diversity in the environment requires a diversified structure. Diversity inclines towards a task culture. Standardization inclines towards a role culture. Thus pure functional organizations with, for instance, one sales department, are usually found in firms with undiversified markets and products with a long life-cycle. They will usually have a role culture.

Box 7.3   National cultures

For many years Hofstede collected opinion surveys from employees of IBM in over forty different countries. From this data he was able to put together an impressive analysis of the cultural differences between nationalities. He ended up with four dimensions:

1 Power distance. The dimension measures the equality of power distribution between boss and subordinate. High power distance means that in that culture bosses have much more power than their subordinates. Dictatorships (and Belgium and France) prefer high power distance.

2 Uncertainty avoidance. High uncertainty avoidance indicates that the culture likes to try to control the future. It is associated with dogmatism and authoritarianism, with traditionalism and superstition. The new democracies (Austria, Ireland, Italy, Japan) were higher on this scale than the old democracies (Canada, Great Britain, the Netherlands, USA).

3 Individualism. Individualism is the opposite of collectivism. Venezuela, Colombia and Pakistan are the most collective in their preferred behaviour, while the Anglo-Saxon bloc is strangely individualistic. Where individualism is low, people expect more help from family, friends and organizations and give them more commitment in exchange.

4 Masculinity. Masculinity is connected with ambition, the desire to achieve and to earn more, whereas its opposite, femininity, is more concerned with inter-personal relationships, the environment and a sense of service. Masculinity prefers quantity of things to quality of life, with men almost always preferring the quantity alternatives.

Mant has pulled out eight countries to demonstrate Hofstede's cultural differences in the chart opposite:

Box 7.3 – *contd*

individualistic			collectivist
low power distance			high power distance
low uncertainty avoidance			high uncertainty avoidance
feminine			masculine

Anglo-Saxon bloc (USA, UK, Australia) ──────────
Scandinavian bloc (Sweden, Denmark, Norway) ─ ─ ─ ─ ·
Germany ·······························
Japan ─ · ─ · ─ · ─ · ─ · ─ · ─ · ─ · ─ · ─ · ─ ·

The chart shows that the Japanese are far more collective, but also much more cautious, authoritarian and materialistic than the Scandinavians and the Anglo-Saxons. It makes for an effective wealth-producing state but one in which few of the individualistic Anglo-Saxons or the more feminine Scandinavians might want to live. Looking at this chart it is hard to see how Japanese management methods could work in Britain, America or Scandinavia.

See further: Hofstede, *Culture's Consequences*, 1980; and Mant, *Leaders We Deserve*, 1983

If the important difference is that between the products, then a product organization is suggested. Only in this way will individual products get differentiated attention. If the important difference is between geographical regions, then a regional organization may be appropriate. If the difference is type of distribution, or customer classification, then that should be your structure. When the difference is a mix of all four, or of two or three, the organization will tend to reflect this. Which structure is subordinate to which may change with time, as for instance regional differences tend to blur and products become more important.

Threat or danger in the environment are best countered by power cultures. Mergers and take-overs, nationalization or economic disaster are examples of threats and dangers. Those organizations which are web-like, with a strong figure at the centre, will be most likely to be successful in these circumstances. Successful field generals in time of war tend to be power-orientated. Merger battles are often decided by personalities. For power cultures can move swiftly and decisively, are aggressive rather than adaptive, strong rather than flexible.

Box 7.4   The case of the invisible job

Jim went straight from university into a large and prestigious manufacturing organization. There could, he felt, be no better preparation for a managerial career than an apprenticeship in such a successful and renowned corporation. In his eight years there he did a variety of jobs in a variety of functions and learnt much about the way they ran their business. In particular he schooled himself in methods of investment appraisal, procedures for job evaluation and description, organization design and management development. He was impressed by the budgeting and authority system and by the meticulous standardization of procedures which applied to much of their large business.

Jim was reasonably successful. But circumstances changed and he felt that he would like to move to a smaller but more vigorous organization. One such, a financial organization with funds to invest in new ventures, was looking for a man to analyse new investment opportunities. Jim applied and was quickly accepted. Confident in his mastery of all the proper techniques and procedures, he reported for work.

The office they had provided for him was elegant. His secretary delightful. He was assigned to the management luncheon room and introduced to the directors that he had not already met. Everyone was extremely charming and pleased to see him. At the end of his first day, Jim felt very satisfied with his decision to join. The second and third days, however, were less pleasant. Nothing happened. Nothing at all. Jim looked for a formal description of his job but it appeared not to exist. He decided to write one, and by way of preparation asked his boss, a director, for an organization chart. It seemed that there was no such thing. Asked to sketch one his boss put down a list of all the directors and under them a list of all the other executives. There seemed to be no proper system of departments, no formal allocation of duties. It was unclear, even, who approved investment decisions and whether Jim himself had authority to initiate any investment or even to spend money on searches and surveys.

Bewildered, at lunch at the end of the week he confessed his mystification to one of the directors and said that he had still been given no work to do and was very unsure of what he was supposed to be doing. 'Why,' said the director, 'you should be out there somewhere, talking to people, getting on aeroplanes, making contacts, getting information. We want ideas, suggestions, projects from you.'

Gradually, Jim grew to understand that there were no rules and procedures, that one had to proceed intuitively, to know by instinct what the directors would approve, what they would shrink from; that he was trusted completely and expected to do what was necessary, spend what was necessary, to get them into profitable new ventures.

Box 7.4 – *contd*

At home, however, he pondered over his collections of procedures, his books of techniques, his manuals and tables. 'Do they know of these things and for some reason have rejected them,' he wondered, 'or should I try to introduce them?'

3.8   The people

It has already been stressed that different cultures call for differing psychological contracts, that certain types of people will be happy and successful in one culture, not in another. A match between organization, culture and an individual's psychological contract should lead to a satisfied individual. Satisfaction, we know, does not imply productivity but it is a good place to start from. The studies in job satisfaction do not differentiate between cultures or between individual expectation so that the statements above cannot as yet be demonstrated to be true, but they represent a plausible hypothesis. Leading on from there, some further hypotheses can be advanced:

1 Individuals with a low tolerance for ambiguity will prefer the tighter role prescriptions of the role culture.
2 High needs for security will be better met in the role culture.
3 A need to establish one's identity at work will be appropriate in a power or task culture. In a role culture it will be seen as a 'person' orientation and thought disruptive.
4 The impact of individual skills and talents will be more marked in power and task cultures than in role. Hence greater care needs to be paid to the selection and appraisal of individuals in these cultures.
5 Low-calibre people resources – in the sense of intelligence or inter-personal skills – would push an organization towards a role culture, where jobs can be defined down to the level of manpower available.

In general, the availability of people with the right orientations will be significant element in the freedom that an organization has to move towards a particular culture. The individual orientations of the key people in an organization will have a large say in determining what the dominant culture is, irrespective of what it should be. You decide, in large part, on your culture when you decide on your people.

Box 7.5   Maccoby's corporate types

Maccoby made a socio-psychoanalytic study of 250 corporate managers in American organizations. He came up with four character types which can be found in different combinations.

1 The Jungle Fighter. The jungle fighter needs power. He sees life as a battle for survival in which winners destroy losers. At his best he is a lion, protective towards his 'family' and ruthless to his competitors. However, his domineering attitude upsets independent subordinates and his obsession with defence can create unnecessary enemies.
2 The Company Man. This kind of person is oriented to the institution, concerned with the human side of the company and committed to maintaining corporate integrity. He can turn into a senseless careerist, obsessed with organizational politics, but at his best he can sustain an atmosphere of discipline and service. He is perhaps too conservative to lead an innovative organization.
3 The Gamesman. The gamesman likes to take calculated risks and is fascinated by techniques, new methods and problems. He thrives on competition and can communicate his enthusiasm to his group. He is a team player who looks for glory rather than riches. At extremes he can live in a fantasy world, finding games and competitions where none need exist.
4 The Craftsman. The craftsman is an individualist interested in making something. Self-contained and exacting, he can become uncooperative at times. He is a good master to apprentices but a poor member of a team. He leads by ordering subordinates to do what he decides upon.

Maccoby, *The Gamesman*, 1976

A type for each culture?

3.9   Conclusion

Any one organization, examining itself in the light of these influencing factors, will find itself pushed towards at least two and perhaps three of the cultures. Often an organization will find that the forces in the environment push it towards a power culture, that its size and technology push it towards role, and the personal inclinations of the middle managers incline it to a task orientation. How is it to decide? Which of the factors should be determining when all influence it but in differing directions?

4 Implications for organization design

4.1

Organizations gradually change their dominant cultures. Most start as power cultures: the founder sees the organization as an extension of himself, only necessary because he cannot do everything on his own. Time and success lead to growth and to the specialization and formalization of activities. These are often the first signs of organizational maturity – of an organization, in other words, that is no longer dependent on its founder. They are also the hallmarks of a role culture. Once cultural change begins, the structure of the organization, the planning and control of its work and the making of many of its decisions will no longer be the same. It often proves to be a difficult stage for the founder and the founding group, who have to adjust to the formalization of their power and the delegation of much direct decision-making. Some find it such a disturbing change that they leave, for few people are equally at home in all cultures.

The next cultural shift comes when the role culture is confronted with the need for greater flexibility. The market may start to change more quickly, or to move in different directions. The technology may develop, with all that entails for new work procedures, new manning levels and new skills. More often, the sheer growth of the organization compounds its complexity. At this stage, formalization and specialization are no longer sufficient to control the diversity of its problems and the organization has to face the fact that it needs a range of different cultures. The leadership may seek to retain the clear set of values (the tradition of service, excellence or hard work) that was the essence of the original company, but the more stylistic parts of the culture must be allowed to change to fit the requirements of each part of the organization.

One way to approach the problem of finding the appropriate cultural diversity is to look at the type of activity which primarily characterizes each part of the organization. There are four principal activity types:

Steady state;
Innovation;
Crisis;
Policy.

Steady state implies all those activities which can be programmed in some way, are routine as opposed to non-routine.

The steady state often accounts for 80 per cent of an organization's personnel. It includes the infrastructure of the organization – the accounting system, the secretarial system, the office services section. It includes, usually, most of the production component of the organization. Most sales activities would come under the steady state category, but not the marketing activity.

Innovation includes all activities directed to changing the things that the organization does or the way it does it. R and D of course, but also parts of marketing, the development side of production, corporate planning, organization and methods departments, perhaps parts of the finance department.

Crisis. All organizations have to deal with the unexpected. No one part of the organization will have a monopoly of crises or breakdowns, although the part of the organization that interfaces with the environment is more likely to have to cope with the unexpected. Marketing, parts of production, middle management are the sectors most exposed.

Policy. The overall guidance and direction of activities must not be neglected. The setting of priorities, the establishment of standards, the direction and allocation of resources, the initiation of action, these are activities which form a category of their own, although there is some degree of overlap with the other sets.

Some parts of the formal structure of the company will fall neatly into one of these categories, e.g. R and D or office services. Others, such as marketing, may have a mixture of categories. Usually each department will find the bulk of its activities in one or other set. That bulk will tend to determine the main focus and culture that is appropriate to it, as shown in Figure 10.

The suggestion is that, if the appropriate culture prevails where that set of activities prevails, then that part of the organization will be more effective. The suggestion is that organizations should differentiate their cultures and structures according to the dominant kind of activity in that department, division or section. R and D, for instance, should be organized differently from the accounting department. The innovative part of marketing can be expected to be more informal, more task-orientated than the assembly-line. The management of crisis should override committees, rules and procedures, and rely on political support for initiative. The management of steady state activities should properly be concerned with rules, procedures, regulations and formal controls. Apply these to the innovation arms of the organization and they will suffocate.

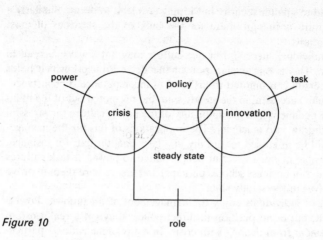

Figure 10

Box 7.6

Mintzberg distinguishes seven types of organization:

> The entrepreneurial;
> The machine;
> The professional;
> The innovative;
> The missionary;

which loosely match the four cultures described here, if the professional is seen as the up-market form of the role culture. To these Mintzberg adds:

> The diversified – the organization which is divided into self-contained units
> The political – a law unto itself.

He sees these types as mostly coexisting in any large organization and exerting their own pulls on the organization. The challenge is to bind them together without losing their necessary differences.

See H. Mintzberg, *Mintzberg on Management*, 1989

4.2 Implications of differentiation

One culture should not be allowed to swamp the organization. Too often organizations wish to bring everything into the steady state. This may lead to greater security but it may also lead to decay. Similarly a task culture is inappropriate for the bulk of the activities of most organizations.

An individual successful in one culture may not always succeed in another. This is one explanation of the Peter Principle which holds that a person is promoted to his level of incompetence. For instance, individuals successful in the steady state but promoted out of the pillar into the pediment find the ambiguity of the power culture too stressful and withdraw into inactivity. The implications of this for the management will be discussed more fully in a later chapter but, for instance, is it sensible or fair to recruit people suited to power or task cultures (graduates of business schools perhaps) and first require them to prove themselves in the steady state?

A lot of individuals enjoy the management of breakdown. Power-oriented, but in no position to direct policy, they get a real sense of achievement from dealing with crisis. In many organizations, particularly small ones, activities which should be programmed, routinized, systematized, are in fact dealt with on an *ad hoc* crisis basis because that is the individual's preferred culture. Anyone who has dealt with a jobbing builder, or a small manufacturer, or even the local store, may have found them superb in an emergency but very fallible on routine. It is pleasant to be busy. A deteriorating steady state produces lots of business.

Differentiation can easily lead to fragmentation. The R and D laboratory can become buried in the countryside, forgotten by all; the corporate planning department can be highly respected outside the company, deliver papers at learned congresses, and be ignored within. The steady state can churn out products not needed by the market, the chief executive sign contracts that no one can fulfil. When representatives of two cultures meet they will find that their priorities, their time scales, their styles of working will all be different. Yet the cultures must work together. For differentiation to be successful there must be integration.

4.3 Integration

The greater the differentiation the greater the potential for conflict. The sales executive, involved in the day-to-day management of breakdown, is going to find the long-term problematical perspectives of the research scientist irritating and irrelevant to his current preoccupations. The production controller will be loath to interrupt his schedules in order to help the crisis of the sales people. These and myriad other potential sources of conflict must be managed if a differentiated environment is not going to tear itself apart or fail to communicate at all. There is a whole range of integrative devices.

Direct managerial supervison. The most obvious form of integration, it is limited by the fact that one person can only integrate so many (hence the idea of span of control), by the time it takes and by the implication which it carries that the individuals cannot do the job completely themselves.

Appeal to the hierarchy. An addition to direct supervision, this method carries supervision up to the lowest crossover point between the reporting lines of the two sections which need to be integrated. Costly and time-consuming.

Rules and procedures. The standardization of work processes and routines which ensures that everyone does what they are supposed to do. Works well in the steady state where work can be routinized.

Standardization of skills. The training given to particular groups e.g. in medicine, ensures that everyone in that speciality will go about a task in the same way – an up-market version of rules and procedures.

Co-ordinators. Groups or individuals given the responsibility for liaison but not for managerial control. Sometimes essential in the short-term they can, by their very existence, perpetuate the problem.

Mutual adjustment. Informal communication between the different parties, usually two individuals.

Clustering. A type of reorganization which puts all the 'differences' into one unit. Expensive on the face of it, but effective where the task and the specialities required are clear. An account group in an advertising agency is one example of a cluster.

Integration should not be left to chance because the chances are that it will not happen but will instead become highly politicized.

4.4   Does it work?

The sections on differentiation of culture and integration have been very prescriptive. Is there any evidence to support the thesis? There is:

1 A series of studies by Lawrence and Lorsch (referred to in more detail in Part Three) looked at the distinguishing features of high-

Box 7.7   Differences in 'climate' characteristics in high-performing organizations

Characteristics	Akron (a manufacturing plant)	Stockton (a research laboratory)
1 structural orientation	perceptions of tightly controlled behaviour and a high degree of structure	perceptions of a low degree of structure
2 distribution of influence	perceptions of low total influence, concentrated at upper levels in the organization	perceptions of high total influence, more evenly spread out among all levels
3 character of superior-subordinate relations	low freedom vis-à-vis superiors to choose and handle jobs, directive type of supervision	high freedom vis-à-vis superiors to choose and handle projects, participatory type of supervision
4 character of colleague relations	perceptions of many similarities among colleagues, high degree of co-ordination of colleague effort	perceptions of many differences among colleagues, relatively low degree of co-ordination of colleague effort
5 time orientation	short-term	long-term
6 goal orientation	manufacturing	scientific
7 top executive's 'managerial style'	more concerned with task than people	more concerned with task than people

From Morse and Lorsch, 'Beyond theory Y', *Harvard Business Review*, 1970 performing organizations in three environments. The organizations were in the plastics, food and container industries. The industries ranged in the degree of their diversity from plastics (the most diverse and the most dynamic), through food to containers (a relatively stable and homogeneous environment) and sufficient integrative devices to manage that differentiation. Thus, by their measurements, the plastics organization was almost twice as highly differentiated as the container organization, with the whole array of possible integration devices, from rules and procedures through to a co-ordinating department. By differentiation was meant that individual parts of the organization would have:

(a) Differing time-horizons (long or short);
(b) Differing orientations to the market (customer needs or product quality);
(c) Differing inter-personal styles;
(d) Differing degrees of formality in the structure.

Thus in a differentiated organization the sales director and the research director will be fundamentally concerned with differing problems, over widely differing time horizons – the sales director worrying about specific rebates, the scientist about performance characteristics of a new product. But they would also have differing styles of management and habits of work, different 'cultures'.

2 Morse and Lorsch, in a study similar to the preceding one, looked at the comparison between successful and unsuccessful organizations in two widely different technologies – a manufacturing plant and a research laboratory. They found that the style of management in the successful laboratory differed markedly from that employed in the less successful laboratory – but it also was the opposite of the style practised in the successful factory. Vice versa, the style of the successful factory approximated to that of the less successful laboratory.

In the more open-ended, long time-horizon environment of the *laboratory* a supportive style worked best, with minimum rules and procedures and a lot of individual and group initiative (a task culture). In the successful *factory*, however, a tight structured approach not only worked best but was appreciated by the employees who, in that situation, wanted to know what they had to do, by when, for whom (a role culture).

3 Joan Woodward showed that the more effective organizations were the ones that had a structure which seemed appropriate to the technology.

4 Peters and Waterman, in an analysis of excellent American companies, advocate simultaneous tight–loose properties. They talk of flexible organization structures, jealous champions, teams, and entrepreneurial networks (task cultures with a mix of power and person characters), but they also found a set of tight properties in their companies. These included concise paperwork, quick feedback and a predominant discipline (role culture). They see companies developing three pillars – a stability pillar, an entrepreneurial pillar and a breaking-habits pillar – not dissimilar to the model in Figure 10. The problem is to hold the pillars together, which requires a value-led culture that starts from the top. Zeus, it seems, still has a role.

5 Charles Hampden-Turner has drawn on a number of corporate case-studies around the world to show how a good corporate culture can be used to mediate the inevitable dilemmas, i.e. to integrate the necessary differentiation. British Airways in the 1980s was a case in point. How it might reconcile the need for economic efficiency – 'lean and mean' – with the caring collective image – 'fat and happy' – which it wanted to present to its customers, was just one of the dilemmas. Both images are needed, and both pressures need to recognize the importance of the other. It was a new appreciation of what British Airways stood for, of 'how things are done around here', that helped to move it towards a 'lean but happy' blend.

6 Anecdotal experience would suggest that different ways of running organizations can be effective. This cannot all be attributed to luck or the genius of the managing director. We also know that if they do not change their culture when the environment changes they will cease to be successful. British industrial history is strewn with firms that grew to success in the days of imperial protection and sellers' markets, pride in their product and a pure role culture. Oftentimes a marketing department did not even exist, sometimes not even a sales division. Confronted by change and threat they seemed fossilized in the past – like the Greek temples at Paestum in Italy, the world passed by and left them isolated in the marshes.

5 Summary

Each organization, each part of an organization, has a culture, and a structure and systems appropriate to that culture. Individuals will each have a preferred culture.

Cultures	*Structures*
power	web
role	temple
task	net
person	cluster

The choice of the appropriate structure will be determined by:

History and ownership;
Size;
Technology;
Goals and objectives;
The environment;
The people.

Within each organization the activities can be divided roughly into four sets:

Steady state;
Innovation;
Breakdown;
Policy.

Each of these sets has its appropriate culture, structure and systems. Organizations that are *differentiated* in their cultures and who control that differentiation by *integration* are likely to be more successful.

The management of differentiated organizations is not easy. Part Two will be mainly concerned with drawing attention to some of the problems. The problem is aggravated by the tendency of many management theorists and writers to remain rooted in their preferred culture. For instance:

1 Classical management theory was talking about role cultures – the management of the steady state.
2 Modern management thinkers concentrate on the task culture and have found their favourite organizations among the project-based companies of the US aerospace industry and the innovative ends of more traditional organizations.

Box 7.8   What kind of organization?

To be done by individuals (40 minutes) and the scores collated in groups.

1 What kind of organization do you belong to? What set of values, styles of behaviour, characterize it?
2 What kind of organization would you *like* to belong to?

Please complete this questionnaire:

(a) For yourself, your own values and beliefs;
(b) For your own organization.

Rank each statement in order of salience. Put '1' against the statement which best represents the dominant view in your organization, '2' for the next closest. Then go back and do the same for your own beliefs.

    At the end, please add up the scores for the first statement under each heading, the scores for the second statement, and so on (e.g. a score of 15 for the first statement would mean that it had ranked top in all categories).

    The group should then analyse its combined results.

(a) Ask each individual to note which set of statements had the lowest score for himself; for his organization.
(b) Complete the following matrix for the group

numbers of individuals with lowest score for statements

	number 1	number 2	number 3	number 4
self				
organization				

(c) The four sets of statements describe the four cultures described in the text. If statement number 1 has the lowest total score for any individual that would suggest that culture number 1 is his preferred culture. The numbering of the statements corresponds to the order in which the cultures are listed in the text.
(d) How dominant a cultural preference is in the life of an individual or an organization will be represented by the *difference* between the total scores for the four sets of cultures. A score of 15 would imply that the corresponding culture was totally dominant.
(e) A perfect match between an individual's preferences and his organization's cultures would suggest a perfectly fitting pscychological contract. Most people will not have a perfect match. The group may like to explore the reasons for the differences *after* they have read the text.

Box 7.8 – *contd*

Own ranking	Organ-ization's ranking	
1 *A good boss*		
. . . . .	. . . . .	is strong, decisive and firm but fair. He or she is protective, generous and indulgent to loyal subordinates.
. . . . .	. . . . .	is impersonal and correct, avoiding the exercise of personal authority for personal own advantage. A good boss demands from subordinates only that which is required by the formal system.
. . . . .	. . . . .	is egalitarian and influenceable in matters concerning the task. He or she uses their authority to obtain the resources needed to get on with the job.
. . . . .	. . . . .	is concerned and responsive to the personal needs and values of others. He or she uses their position to provide satisfying and growth stimulating work opportunities for subordinates.
2 *A good subordinate*		
. . . . .	. . . . .	is compliant, hard-working and loyal to the interests of the superior.
. . . . .	. . . . .	is responsible and reliable, meeting the duties and responsibilities of the job and avoiding actions which might surprise or embarrass a superior.
. . . . .	. . . . .	is self-motivated to contribute his or her best to the task and is open with ideas and suggestions, but is nevertheless willing to give the lead to others when they show greater expertise or ability.
. . . . .	. . . . .	is vitally interested in the development of personal potentialities and is open to learning and receiving help. He or she also respects the needs and values of others and is willing to give help and contribute to their development.

Box 7.8 – *contd*

Own ranking	Organization's ranking	

3 *A good member of the organization gives first priority to*

. . . .	. . . .	the personal demands of the boss.
. . . .	. . . .	the duties, resposibilities and requirements of their own role, and the customary standards of personal behaviour.
. . . .	. . . .	the requirements of the task for skill, ability, energy and material resources.
. . . .	. . . .	the personal needs of the individual involved.

4 *People who do well in the organization*

. . . .	. . . .	are shrewd and competitive with a strong drive for power.
. . . .	. . . .	are conscientious and responsible with a strong sense of loyalty to the organization.
. . . .	. . . .	are technically competent and effective, with a strong commitment to getting the job done.
. . . .	. . . .	are effective and competent in personal relationships, with a strong commitment to the growth and development of people.

5 *The organization treats the individual*

. . . .	. . . .	as though his or her time and energy were at the disposal of the persons higher in the hierarchy.
. . . .	. . . .	as though his or her time and energy were available through a contract having rights and responsibilities on both sides.
. . . .	. . . .	as a co-worker who has committed his or her skills and abilities to the common cause.
. . . .	. . . .	as an interesting and worthwhile person in their own right.

Box 7.8 – *contd*

Own ranking	Organ- ization's ranking	

6 *People are controlled and influenced by*

. . . . .	. . . . .	the personal exercise of economic and political power (rewards and punishments).
. . . . .	. . . . .	impersonal exercise of economic and political power to enforce procedures and standards of performance.
. . . . .	. . . . .	communication and discussion of task requirements leading to appropriate action motivated by personal commitment to goal achievement.
. . . . .	. . . . .	intrinsic interest and enjoyment in the activities to be done; and/or concern and caring for needs of other persons involved.

7 *It is legitimate for one person to control another's activities*

. . . . .	. . . . .	if that person has more authority and power in the organization.
. . . . .	. . . . .	if the role prescribes that they are responsible for directing the other.
. . . . .	. . . . .	if he or she has more knowledge relevant to the task at hand.
. . . . .	. . . . .	if the other accepts that the first person's help or instruction can contribute to the other's learning and growth.

8 *The basis of task assignment is*

. . . . .	. . . . .	the personal needs and judgement of those in authority.
. . . . .	. . . . .	the formal divisions of functions and responsibility in the system.
. . . . .	. . . . .	the resource and expertise requirements of the job to be done.
. . . . .	. . . . .	the personal wishes and needs for learning and growth of the individual organization members.

Box 7.8 – *contd*

Own ranking	Organ- ization's ranking	

9 *Work is performed out of*

		hope of reward, fear of punishment or personal loyalty towards a powerful individual.
. . . .	. . . .	a respect for contractual obligations backed up by sanctions and personal loyalty towards the organization or system.
. . . .	. . . .	satisfaction in excellence of work and achievement and/or personal commitment to the task or goal.
. . . .	. . . .	enjoyment of the activity for its own sake and concern and respect for the needs and values of the other persons involved.

10 *People work together*

		when they are required to by higher authority or believe they can use each other for personal advantage.
. . . .	. . . .	when co-ordination and exchange are specified by the formal system.
. . . .	. . . .	when their joint contribution is needed to progress the task.
. . . .	. . . .	when the collaboration is personally satisfying, stimulating or challenging.

11 *Competition*

. . . .	. . . .	is for personal power and advantages.
. . . .	. . . .	is for high-status position in the formal system.
. . . .	. . . .	is for excellence of contribution to the task.
. . . .	. . . .	is for attention to one's own personal needs.

12 *Conflict*

		is controlled by the intervention of higher authority and often fostered by them to maintain their own power.
. . . .	. . . .	

Box 7.8 – *contd*

Own ranking	Organization's ranking	
. . . . .	. . . .	is suppressed by reference to rules, procedures and definitions of responsibility.
. . . . .	. . . .	is resolved through full discussion of the merits of the work issues involved.
. . . . .	. . . .	is resolved by open and deep discussion of personal needs and values involved.

13 *Decisions*

. . . . .	. . . .	are made by the person with the higher power and authority.
. . . . .	. . . .	are made by the person whose job description carries the responsibility.
. . . . .	. . . .	are made by the persons with most knowledge and expertise about the problem.
. . . . .	. . . .	are made by the persons most personally involved and affected by the outcome.

14 *The appropriate control and communication structure*

. . . . .	. . . .	Command flows from the top down in a simple pyramid so that anyone who is higher in the pyramid has authority over anyone who is lower. Information flows up through the chain of command.
. . . . .	. . . .	Directives flow from the top down and information flows upwards within functional pyramids which meet at the top. The authority and responsibility of a role is limited to the roles beneath it in its own pyramid. Cross-functional exchange is constricted.
. . . . .	. . . .	Information about task requirements and problems flows from the centre of task activity upwards and outwards, with those closest to the task determining resources and support needed from the rest of the organization. A co-ordinating function may set priorities and overall resource levels based on information from all task centres. The structure should shift with the nature and location of the tasks.

Box 7.8 – *contd*

Own ranking	Organization's ranking	
		Information and influence flow from person to person, based on relationships which are voluntarily entered into for purposes of work, learning, mutual support and enjoyment, and shared values. A co-ordinating function may establish overall levels of contribution needed for maintenance of the organization. These tasks are assigned by mutual agreement.

15 *The environment is responded to as though it were*

. . . .	. . . .	a competitive jungle in which all are against all and those who do not exploit others are themselves exploited.
. . . .	. . . .	an orderly and rational system in which competition is limited by law and conflicts yield to negotiation and compromise.
. . . .	. . . .	a complex of imperfect forms and systems which are to be re-shaped and improved by the achievements of the organization.
. . . .	. . . .	a complex of potential threats and support. It is to be manipulated by the organization to extract nourishment from it, pull its teeth and use it as a play and work space for the enjoyment and growth of members.

Adapted from a questionnaire compiled by Dr Roger Harrison

3 Journalists, historians, and biographers have found the power cultures, centred around a key figure or figures, easier to focus on, more tempting to describe.

4 Sociologists, religious and youth leaders, have been concerned with the clash between the organization and the individual with a 'person' orientation.

It is left to the manager to handle all four cultures, to differentiate and to integrate within his own organization. What this means for the structure and the systems of the organization will be discussed in more detail in Part Two.

Part Two

The Concepts in Application

→ Introduction to Part Two

Part One will have introduced the reader to a bewildering and no doubt sometimes baffling array of concepts, sets of categories, pieces of jargon. The immediate relevance to the problems of his own organization may not have been immediately obvious. God, it has been said, did not see fit to divide up the world to accord with the faculties of universities. Nor did he fashion the problems of organizations to fall neatly under one of the chapter headings of Part One. The purpose of the chapters in Part One was to provide a language. Without a language we are reduced to pointing to particular objects. A child cannot apply experience learnt in one situation to another situation unless the situations are identical or unless he has perceived the linking concept. He may, for instance, have discovered that the electric fire should not be touched. But the lesson will have to be learnt anew for the gas cooker in the kitchen, unless he can comprehend the concept of heat, and thence proceed to the generalization 'all hot things can hurt'. To do this, he needs the ability to think in classes and concepts. He also needs a language that will give some names to the classes and concepts. What the language is may not be material. The Chinese and the American can both appreciate heat although the names for it are different. They will not be able to talk about it across their cultures, but it will be understood within them.

So it is with organizational understanding. Learning by experience, left to itself, can be a painful and a tedious process. It is also inefficient. Unless the present situation matches a past one in all respects the experience of the past may be inappropriate learning for the present. To interpret experience, to learn from others' experience as well as one's own, we need linking concepts and a language. But to be understood language must be used. Jargon is 'someone else's language'. To turn jargon into one's own language we need to use it.

If Part One was the dictionary or the grammar, Part Two is an attempt to show how this language can be used to help with better understanding of the problems that are encountered in all organizations. Problems in organizations come in all shapes and sizes. They are not always clearly labelled. They spring from a telephone call from an irate client or customer, a sudden slump in the output record, a dispute in the factory. The type of problem varies with the level of management, with the nature of the job.

There are many possible ways of classifying managerial problems. One could do it by type of organization (manufacturing, service, educational or governmental, for instance), or by function (production, marketing, personnel) or by type of problem (mergers, redundancy, unions or technological change). While each of these schemes would be useful to some, others would feel excluded. I decided on a broader classification because I was not attempting to provide a comprehensive handbook but an explanation of how the language and concepts of Part One get translated into actual organizational behaviour.

Every organization has to come to practical decisions about:

1 The people in the organization: who they should be, how they should be treated, paid and developed.
2 The work of the organization: what it should be, how it should be structured and designed.
3 The politics of the organization: why they exist, how they are useful and necessary for change.

While researching these chapters, I have been very conscious of the way in which the dilemmas in each area remain unchanged while the solutions have a much more transitory air about them as yet another 'flavour of the month' gets tried out by organizations as they twist and turn in their efforts to control the multiplicity of variables that affect their work. There will never be a perfect remedy for all seasons. It will always be the task of the manager to understand what is going on, to judge the interplay of forces and to choose the best available compromise in a changing and imperfect world. I therefore added two further short chapters to emphasize these points:

4 The job of the manager: what it is, what it involves, how it can best be understood.
5 The future of organizations: how they are likely to change in shape, size and nature in the years ahead, as technology, values and the nature of work change.

Part Two is not, therefore, a set of recommended practices. It is not a managerial cookbook but an exploration of the art and problems of cooking given what we know of the materials and the processes. There will be references to some current practical handbooks in Part Three but I remain persuaded of the truth of Kurt Lewin's remark that there is nothing so practical as a good theory.

There is little or nothing in Part Two about those traditional features of the manager's art such as accounting, finance or marketing. Nothing is said directly about strategy, information systems, or mergers and acquisitions. Even industrial relations scarcely get a mention. These topics are important. They matter to schools, hospitals and police forces, even to voluntary agencies, just as much as they do to commercial enterprises. Were there space enough and were I knowledgeable enough in all of them there would be a chapter on each because an understanding of people and why they do as they do is as essential to the proper design of a management cost control system as it is to a people appraisal system.

The book, however, has to end somewhere. I have therefore concentrated on the more directly organizational practicalities in order to show how the principles of Part One get carried through into policy and practice. I have to leave it to the intelligent reader to do the same for the other practicalities. I would add only one general warning – do not assume that numbers mean the same to all people, or that all men and all women are to be persuaded by the logic of a system or a case or, finally, that the strategy, systems and technology of an organization are, or ever can be, independent of the people who live in it.

Facts are facts. Data is data. Not so, unfortunately. It all depends on where you are standing.

1. Estimated sales are the basis for many an organization's plans for everything else. But sales estimates come from the sales force and if those sales estimates are going to be used as the rod to beat the backs of the sales people at the end of the year they will keep them as low as they reasonably can.

2. On the other hand if those selfsame sales estimates are going to be the basis for the allocation of new resources or the reorganization of the sales division there will be some who will push them as high as they reasonably can.

3. Measured against last year the sales may look good. Measured against a competitor they can look awful. Choosing the basis for comparison is crucial. Percentages always beg a crucial question 'percentages of what?' Too often the answer depends on what the author of the number wants to prove.

4. Sales estimates for financial planning should, arguably, be pessimistic ('if the worst happens') but for facilities planning should be optimistic ('if we could sell this much . . .'). Which does the chief executive believe?

8 ➤ On the People of Organizations and their Development

1 Introduction

It is fashionable to speak of the human assets of organizations. It is also useful, for it reminds us that although people only appear as costs in the formal accounts, they are assets in the sense that they are, or should be, a productive resource; a resource that needs maintenance and proper utilization, that has a finite life, and an output greater than its cost. But it is interesting to reflect on the implications of the ways in which we put human assets into accounts. Salaries and benefits are really regarded as maintenance expenses – something to be kept as low as possible as long as the machine does not break down. There is no capital cost and therefore no need for depreciation. Indeed, the return on investment of most companies would look very strange if their human assets were capitalized at, say, ten times their annual maintenance cost, and depreciated over twenty years. Perhaps one day, industrial and administrative organizations will start behaving like football clubs and charge realistic transfer fees for their key people assets. It is, in fact, instructive to ponder on the implications of looking at one's employees as players in a football team. For in a football club, the players truthfully are human assets. They have a productive capacity, an earning power, that is potentially far greater than their cost. That cost has both a capital and a maintenance element. Rewards are proportionate to group performance, the asset has a finite life. There is no question of the organization assuming responsibility for the asset beyond the limits of its useful life, nor is there any stigma in the declaration that the asset has grown too old to be worth maintaining. The care and attention and protection given to key assets by leading clubs is of a different order of people maintenance than any known in industry. Training and development become vital, for if you can increase the productive potential of the asset, in a short time you not only have greater productivity, but also an appreciated asset in terms of capital value.

But, of course, in spite of all the fine words, most organizations do not regard their people as assets in anything like the sense that football clubs do. The implications of doing so are a bit threatening. Would anyone buy you for ten times your annual salary? Is your increasing maintenance cost justified by your increased earning power, or only by the fact that you are perhaps a fully depreciated asset? Does one value people assets at cost or at resale value? If the latter, would their value increase *exponentially*, as real estate can, or in a ⌒ shaped curve, like football players? Would the asset belong completely to the organization, or would it have powers of self-determination?

In another sense, however, the application of economic and financial terminology to the management of people has given rise to a whole corpus of methods, systems and procedures for the maintenance, control and utilization planning of these assets. A whole new profession, the management of human resources, has sprung from this conception of the people of organizations as a collection of assets that must be managed in the same way as the other, non-human, assets of the corporation. This conception of the management of people as assets, unattended by the financial or psychological corollaries of that conception, is full of implications for the individual, for the organization and, perhaps, for society. It has given rise to diametrically opposed views on the role of the personnel department; 'the personnel function will assume a more important role in the management of the business' (Frank Fischer) or 'fire the personnel department' (Robert Townsend).

It is all this that justifies a separate chapter on the people of organizations in a book that, in a sense, is all about people and organizations. We shall consider: *the management of human assets*; *the development of the individual*; followed by a *summary and discussion*.

2 The management of human assets

2.1

There is a battery of mechanisms in this field, a treasure-house of procedures and forms. Many a large corporation will be proud to talk to you of its manpower planning models, its managerial inventories, its replacement charts and appraisal procedures, its job specifications and training schedules. If some of the terminology occasionally smacks of the world of production, so some of the procedures occasionally, not always, seem to reflect a deep desire that humans might become as predictable and manageable as, perhaps, a very sophisticated machine tool! We shall not attempt to describe all these methods and procedures here. The latest models are well documented in a variety of books and journals, some of which are listed in Part Three.

Box 8.1 How effectively does your organization manage its human resources?

Can you or anyone else in your company answer the questions listed below?

Number	Question
1	How much money was spent last year to recruit and select people?
2	Was this expenditure worth the cost?
3	Does your organization have data on standard costs of recruitment, selection, and placement which are needed to prepare manpower budgets and to control personnel costs?
4	Was the actual cost incurred last year less than, equal to, or greater than standard personnel acquisition and placement costs?
5	How much money was spent last year to train and develop people?
6	What was the return on your investment in training and development?
7	How does this return compare with alternative investment opportunities?
8	How much human capital was lost last year as a result of turnover?
9	How much does it cost to replace a key man?
10	What is the opportunity cost of losing young, high-potential managers, accountants, engineers, etc.?
11	What is the total value of your company's human assets?
12	Is it appreciating, remaining constant, or being depleted?
13	Does your company really (I mean *really*) reward managers for increasing the value of their subordinates to the firm?
14	Do your compensation and other motivation-reward systems reflect an individual's present value to the firm?
15	Does your organization consider its investment in human resources when evaluating capital budgeting proposals requiring the allocation of people?
16	Does your firm assess the effects of corporate strategies upon its human resources in *quantitative* terms?

Adapted from Flamholtz, 'Should Your Organization Attempt to Value its Human Resources?', *California Management Review*, 1971

Every organization, as soon as it gets to any size (perhaps 1,000 people), begins to feel a need to systematize its management of human assets. Perhaps the pay scales have got way out of line, with apparently similar-level jobs paying very different amounts; perhaps there is a feeling that there are a lot of neglected skills in the organization that other departments could utilize if they were aware that they existed. Perhaps individuals have complained that they don't know where they stand or what their future is; perhaps the unions have requested standardized benefits and procedures. Whatever the historical origins, some kind of central organization, normally named a personnel department, is formed to put some system into the haphazardry. The systems that they adopt are often modelled on the world of production, because that is the world with the best potential for order and system.

These systems and procedures, often very desirable in themselves, do not always work as well as they should. Often there are unintended consequences. There are three areas of particular difficulty:

Appraisal schemes;
Career planning;
Compensation systems.

We shall examine the problems caused by these three systems, and then seek to draw some general conclusions about the management of human assets.

2.2 Appraisal schemes

These schemes usually have some or all of the following objectives:

(a) To provide a data base for the organization's inventory of people, skills and potential;
(b) To provide a mechanism for the proper assessment of performance by an individual so that he may be appropriately rewarded;
(c) To provide the individual with feedback on performance and personal strengths and weaknesses;
(d) To help the individual and subordinates to plan personal and job objectives and ways of achieving them.

All of these are desirable objectives, and forms can be devised which will, on paper, provide for the implementation of all four simultaneously. Unfortunately, as many organizations have discovered the hard way, the four are not psychologically compatible, and some of them, (c) and (d), extremely difficult to do well, even in isolation. Some of the reasons for this are:

1 No individual is going to admit to deficiencies of any significance on a form which will provide data for future job assignment decisions. Yet, unless we genuinely accept deficiencies, we will have no commitment to dealing with them. *(a) is incompatible with (c) and (d)*. This suggests that any piece of paper dealing with (c) and (d) should not be copied and should remain in the possession of the individual concerned. If anyone else retains the document, this part of the appraisal system will be seen as a control mechanism not a development mechanism.

2 The appraisal interview has little effect on performance improvement. Criticism arouses defensive mechanisms and does not improve performance. In fact, in a famous study in GE individuals actually performed worse, twelve weeks later, on those aspects of their job for which they had received most criticism. In that same study the majority of individuals left with a lower estimation of their performance than when they went in. This lowering in self-esteem results in attempts to justify the past, refute the accusations, or reduce the salience of job and superior. Praise is ineffective unless close in time to the behaviour. General commendation is discounted as politeness. *(c) does not help towards (d) but will in fact tend to render it useless*.

3 Salary is a separate issue. Studies have shown that most individuals in large organizations do not believe that their salary is directly related to performance, but rather to such overall factors as length of service, seniority and qualifications. In the GE study, those individuals receiving lower appraisals did not, in fact, receive lower *increments*. But the salary issue does tend to dominate the interview and colour the receptivity of the subordinate. *(b) is important but unconnected*.

4 The superior's previous relationship with the subordinate will affect the interview. When the subordinate does more of the talking, it was found in the GE study that commitment to improvement was higher but this only occurred when this was the style of all their previous interactions. The personal concerns of the superior will colour the interview. Nervousness and tension will tend to make him dominate the session and thus make it unproductive. The interview is difficult, but few managers receive any training in it.

5 An assessment of performance is not necessarily the best basis for deciding on promotions. But it is notoriously hard for a superior to judge the potential of a subordinate for any job higher or different than his own. In fact, in one study, 52 per cent of employees felt that the assessment form had no influence on promotions. In many

organizations they are useful only for low-range jobs; for other jobs they are part of the ratifying not the selection procedure. *(a) is not very effective.*

Box 8.2 The self-concept and appraisal in the classroom

The school classroom has provided ample scope for studies of the effects of appraisal on performance. The results must give anyone pause for thought although they are understandable if they are seen as a natural consequence of the individual's desire to protect his or her self-worth.

(a) Success is accepted as being due to one's own efforts, whereas failure is ascribed to factors outside one's control ('the test was unfair').

(b) The unusual is ascribed to fortune, good or bad. The usually successful student writes off the occasional poor performance as bad luck but the usually poor student will likewise ascribe the occasional success to luck.

(c) Teachers reinforce the luck theory. If a usually successful student flunks a test they ignore it and if a usually poor student does well they discount it as a fluke.

(d) Effort is good but ability is better. Students do all they can to protect their concept of basic ability. 'I didn't try' is a more legitimate excuse than 'I wasn't able'. In extreme cases a student will deliberately do no work in a weak area so that the true nature of his or her ability is never known. There is even a name for it – attribution theory.

Are we any different when we are older?

See further: Rogers, *A Social Psychology of Schooling*, 1982

The traditional appraisal procedure is not, therefore, very effective, in large part, because the superior is expected to be, at the same time, judge and counsellor. This form of role conflict is unacceptable, one has to be one or the other. From studies at GE and other places, there is now a consensus of recommendations:

1 All the four objectives should be fulfilled by different means, at different times, and often by different people.
2 Criticism only improves performance when:
   (a) it is given with genuine liking for the other person;
   (b) it is related to specific instances;
   (c) the subordinate trusts and respects the superior.
3 Improved performance results when:
   (a) Goal-setting, not criticism, is used. The goals are specific, jointly set and reasonable;

(b) The manager is regarded as helpful, facilitating, receptive to ideas and able to plan;
(c) Evaluation of performance is initiated by subordinates, and as a prelude to further goal-setting, not appraisal.

But, as we shall see, even these rather broad conclusions are not the whole answer.

Box 8.3   Reinforcement – the Skinner way

B. F. Skinner was the main proponent of reinforcement as a way of influencing behaviour, so much so that his name has become almost a synonym for manipulation (which may be a backhanded way of saying it works too well). He has five simple rules for giving positive reinforcement to individuals as a way of encouraging them to do more of the same:

1 Be specific, with as much information as possible. Speak of specific achievements, not all-round standards.
2 Be immediate, give the bonus or the pat-on-the-back today, not at the annual appraisal.
3 Make the targets achievable; small, frequent wins are more reinforcing than one big one.
4 Remember the intangible; the attention of one's superior may be more important than any bonus.
5 Keep it unpredictable, because the unexpected bit of praise counts for more than the counted-on commendation.

Skinner, *Beyond Freedom and Dignity*, 1973

2.3   Career planning

Many organizations have elaborate schemes for planning the career progression of all, or some proportion of, their managerial cadre. This is done with the laudable objectives of (a) providing each individual with a satisfactory career, and (b) ensuring that the organization makes optimum use of its managerial resources. To do this, they rely on either the formal data of assessment forms, or on the informal data of subjective impressions, or on a mixture of both. Many of these schemes do not work as well as in logic they might. For instance:

1 In one organization, after ten years, only 10 per cent of the managers in the scheme were in the positions planned for them ten years before, while 35 per cent had left the organization altogether.

2 Many individuals believe that they have not had the opportunities they wanted and merited – hence they feel frustration. The individual is very dependent on the opinions and influence of his superior.

3 Most systems make it possible for divisional managers to hold good people at the expense of the total organization and of the individual careers.

4 In spite of centralized systems, it is usually possible for individual managers to promote from within their own department or their own range of acquaintances, possibly neglecting better people, and devaluing the system.

5 Assessment of potential is usually judged only in relation to past performance and present experience. Thus, a chemist is seldom considered for a planning job, or a production expert for a sales appointment. The trapped specialist, recruited for her professional skills in her youth and thereby labelled for life, is becoming a more common feature of organizations.

6 Failure can be damaging. Poor performance in any assignment, even a training one, can become a permanent stigma, as it gets written into the record.

7 The individual sees the organization as taking responsibility for his career and his necessary development. He ceases then to develop himself or to think creatively about his future. He becomes dependent on the organization and can well become unsuited for the independent, creative entrepreneurial roles of senior management.

To remedy these defects, the following experiments have been tried:

(a) The personnel department initiates all appointments. This strengthens the system but weakens the superior–subordinate bond. Very seldom is the personnel department strong enough to enforce this expedient except at middle and lower levels.

(b) Appraisal forms are destroyed after three years or so, thus obliterating the past and allowing a man a clean slate. Alternatively, assignments of a training nature are evaluated on a different form, recording what he learnt rather than how he performed.

(c) Open, rather than closed, systems of appointment are adopted. Anyone of a certain status can apply for any job and is evaluated and interviewed as if he were an outside applicant. This too often becomes a superficial formality concealing an informal closed system. For it to work, there is needed:

Adequate information to all in the organization about job opportunities and possible career paths;

A counselling service to help individuals evaluate their strengths and
weaknesses;
Time spent on proper evaluation of unknown individuals' potential.
(d) Complete open systems are unusual, but variations include:
'Hunting licences' for frustrated individuals to apply for other jobs
in other parts of the organization;
Rules prohibiting superiors from blocking the transfer of an individual who wants to leave.

However, in spite of all these corrective devices, it remains true that
career planning in many organizations is not a development process so
much as a weeding-out process. Career development becomes a human
hurdle race, the hurdles being different appointments or different
levels of authority. Those who clear a hurdle can progress to the next,
until there are no more. This sort of system meets the organization's
objective, for it ensures the survival of the fittest. Only the strong
survive to the end, but the drawbacks are considerable, for the organization as well as for the individual. For example:

1 There are a lot of hurdles. There tend to be many hurdles on the
way to the top. The young cannot get there unless they are allowed
to by-pass some hurdles. Rigid hurdle systems tend to have old
managements, and high departure rates from younger levels.
2 There is no retrieval mechanism. Many good horses fall at the first
hurdle. There is often no remounting mechanism, no way of catching
up. Another reason for high departure rates.
3 The intervals are too short. It is in everyone's interest to get over
the hurdles as quickly as possible and go on to the next. Indeed,
promotion is the favourite form of reward in most organizations. As
a result, most successful managers seldom do a job for more than
two years until they reach very senior levels. A good rule of thumb
in these organizations is 'the faster you move, the more successful'.
This practice leads to short time-horizons in each job. Furthermore,
it has been demonstrated that in periods up to two years, the most
effective form of leadership is highly structuring and authoritarian.
As Chapter 4 discussed, it is very probable that this style of leadership eventually generates low morale, high turnover and compliance
responses to influence. These long-term costs will not, however, be
personally experienced by the fast-moving manager who can carry a
structural style to the top, effective in the short-term and uncontami-
nated by its trail of delayed damage. Fast promotion rates can therefore encourage a structuring and potentially damaging style of
management throughout the organization.

The hurdle philosophy, carried to extremes, could result in the creation of quite unnecessary levels in the organization, put there to provide promotional opportunities (perhaps twenty for the high-flying twenty-year-old). This is not only absurd but expensive. Organizations have become flatter and have recognized, increasingly, that they need courses for horses as well as vice versa: they need a mix of abilities and have to devise appropriate career paths for them (Box 8.4). It is no use expecting the life-time bureaucrat to turn entrepreneur when he reaches the top. If the organization needs entrepreneurs it must create entrepreneurial pockets for them all the way up. The idea of the rounded person who had experienced, and survived, all parts of the organization, all too often meant someone who had no edges left to cut with.

Box 8.4   Career anchors

Schein studied forty-four male graduates of the MIT Sloan School of Management over the first twelve years of their working lives.

He conceptualized their careers as a process of finding a 'career anchor' which becomes a guiding focus in their lives, giving them a self-image built around their needs, motives, talents and values. In his particular group he identified five career anchors:

1 Technical/functional competence: the career is organized around a set of technical or functional skills, which can often be used in a range of organizations.
2 Managerial competence: the career is built upon the ascent of an organizational ladder of increasingly senior management positions.
3 Creativity: the purpose of the career is to create new things, be they products, businesses or services. Such people are entrepreneurs.
4 Security or stability: the point of the career is to provide stability and security for the individual and his family.
5 Autonomy: The career is organized around the search for an occupation, such as teaching, writing or consulting, which allows the individual to determine his own work-hours and life-style.

Other career anchors such as service to others, power, or political ideology would be possible. The concept has also been used to explain the different orientations of policemen.

Would some career anchors fit more neatly into one of the four cultures than others?

From Schein, *Organizational Psychology*, 1980

2.4   Compensation systems

Money as a motivator was briefly discussed in Chapter 2. Let us briefly review some of those conclusions:

1 Pay is a useful incentive because it is instrumental in satisfying a wide range of needs, although it never appears itself in any need hierarchy.
2 If pay is to be effective in the motivation calculus, the individual must see that it will satisfy some important needs and also that expenditure of 'E' will lead to more pay.
3 Pay is comparative. The absolute level is unimportant as soon as physiological–economic needs are satisfied. It is the level relative to past or future expectations, to peers or to other opportunities.
4 Pay increases that do not immediately follow on improved perform-ance are not seen as connected with results but rather with such things as seniority, experience and qualifications.
5 Pay does not work as an incentive if it only occurs at the cost of satisfying other needs, e.g. social respect, family life, etc.
6 Managers who do see their pay as totally dependent on results tend to be the most effective and the most highly motivated, as judged by themselves and by their superiors.

Theoretically, therefore, pay should be a very convenient motivating agent. It is simple. It can be calibrated. It is all-embracing. It does not lead to organizational complexities in the way that promotion does. It leaves the individual with control. It is effective if tied closely to results. It is uncluttered. Why, then, do relatively few organizations deliber-ately use pay as a motivator? For, with few exceptions, organizations tend to use pay as compensation rather than as incentive. The percep-tions of most managers that they are not rewarded for particular results but for seniority and experience is, on the whole, an accurate percep-tion. Seniority is the reward for success and pay follows seniority. They are not treated as two separate forms of reward. Seldom do you find a boss earning less than a subordinate.

The reason seems to be (there is no hard evidence) that if pay is the principal reward and incentive mechanism, there are going to have to be large differentials in levels of pay. If the differentials are not large, pay will not work as an incentive, since pay is comparative. Organiza-tions have to justify these differentials. This is only easy to do when pay is attached rigidly to results which are both unambiguous and attached to one individual. Thus, pay is the principal reward mech-anism for insurance salesmen – where, incidentally, it works extremely well. But where success must be judged more subjectively, or where it is hard to isolate an individual's contribution, the organization shrinks from the responsibility of assessing and justifying differentials. Top management of small to medium firms is another instance where results can be measured and can be attributed to a small number of individuals. It is not therefore unusual to find some variety of profit-related pay schemes for the top management of these organizations.

In their worry over differentials, organizations:

(a) Foster secrecy about pay levels. This has proved to be self-defeating. Several studies have shown that lacking firm facts, individuals make estimates of the pay of peers and superiors. These estimates always make the differentials wider than in fact they are. People always suspect that they are more badly paid than they actually are, in comparison to their peers.

(b) Pursue rules for equity. Equity usually means paying a rate for the job, rather than paying the man or paying his results. Under conditions of liquidity, the rate for the job should be assessed as objectively as possible, for equity must be seen to be equity. Jacques' time-span of discretion, job definition and evaluation systems, competitor's rates for similar jobs, job grade levels related to salary grade – these are some of the methods used in the pursuit of equity.

The implications of the pursuit of equity in pay are:

1 The incentive and reward properties of pay are discarded. Pay becomes merely fair compensation, just one part of the psychological contract.

2 Other methods of reward and incentive have to be devised. The usual one is seniority or promotion.

3 Most individuals require some reward or recognition of effort at least every two years, hence the tendency towards frequent job changes and the cluttering effects on organizational structure already remarked on under career planning.

4 Promotion as a reward for performance leads to Dr Peter's principle – people get promoted to the level of their incompetence, since they are promoted on the basis of performance in the job below rather than potential for the job above.

5 If seniority and status are rejected as rewards along with pay, the reward for effort will have to come from some form of job satisfaction. This might appear the cheapest and most desirable form of reward, but studies show that job satisfaction on its own does not last very long as a reward. If not followed by some more tangible or

visible symbol of success, only very charismatic tasks will continue to motivate. Praise, as has already been mentioned, is not an adequate reward in itself.

6 Without job satisfaction or any other form of reward mechanism, satisficing behaviour will become the norm. Individuals will perform well enough to get the compensation they are entitled to under whatever rules for equity apply.

7 The pursuit of equity in pay begins to use up much of the energy that should desirably go into the task. It is interesting to observe how many union arguments in labour negotiations are today based on considerations of equity, whilst managements are still talking of productivity. Yet productivity as a basis for negotiations is essentially results-related pay, something that most managements long ago abhorred.

Box 8.5   Contribution pay

Rosabeth Moss Kanter lists the five dilemmas of merit pay.

1 To reward the individual or the group contribution.
2 To reward the whole company or the unit's performance.
3 To make the distribution subjective (management judgement) or objective (specific targets).
4 To make the amounts relative to base pay or to the value of contributions.
5 To have one system for the whole company or several.

She concludes that the pay-cheque of the future may well have five elements.

1 A base salary.
2 An individual merit component.
3 A group or division component.
4 A company profit or gain-share element.
5 A one-off, one-shot bonus or award.

From Kanter, *When Giants Learn to Dance*, 1988

2.5   The conclusions

Where does this leave us? The three principal mechanisms for the management of human resources have been seen to have many unintended consequences. These consequences all tend to divert energy from the legitimate objectives of the organization. Are the mechanisms then unnecessary? Should they be abandoned and the personnel apparatus reduced to a girl and filing-cabinet as Robert Townsend would have it in *Up the Organization*? Or are they the right mechanisms, but often badly administered?

As a start to answering this question let us recall the diagrammatic representation of the organization in Chapter 7, reproduced in Figure 11.

The reader will recall that each of these divisions of activity had its appropriate 'culture', as follows:

Steady state – role
Innovation – task
Policy and crisis – power.

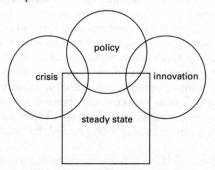

Figure 11

It does seem that the management of human assets has to take into account the dominant cultures. The centralized, formalized systems and procedures are appropriate to a role culture – to the steady-state activities of the organization. In this culture, jobs are precisely defined, career progression is up the pillars of the temple, performance in the lower job is the best predictor of performance in the next job in the pillar, performance over and above the job definition is not required, can indeed be injurious to the other procedures and jobs, security of tenure is part of the psychological contract, and influence by rules and regulations is the accepted norm. Centrally managed career plans, formalized appraisals, job-related compensation are all appropriate and fitting to role cultures and steady-state activities.

Obviously the procedures still have to be well administered. Appraisal interviews, for example, need to be well conducted and cannot achieve the four objectives simultaneously. But the major disadvantages of the normal systems and procedures only show up when they are applied to task or power cultures. In a power culture, individuals are developed in a way that amounts to apprenticeship. The new man is expected to learn from his seniors and to model his behaviour on theirs. Apprentice-masters, the senior managers, choose their own apprentices and their own successors from amongst these apprentices. The relationship between manager and subordinate is crucial, assessment is highly personal and subjective, with promotions depending on personal or political 'fit'. It would be very unusual to find any of the more formal systems of people management being seriously used in power cultures.

In a task culture, results are important, and rewards must be related to results. Status and position power, promotion not being highly valued, is not an adequate reward mechanism. Flexibility and the match of resources to tasks are important, meaning that open systems of career planning are required and are wanted by both individuals and managers. There is big emphasis on goals and objectives; individuals want and expect feedback on performance with pay tied to group results. In a task culture, therefore, there will be systems and procedures, but they will be at the 'open' or 'liberal' end of the scale. They will not be centrally controlled, although there may be a control source of advice and expertise, but will be administered by local managers. Individual differentials will be important within groups but not between groups, where total group differentials will be what matters.

It will be clear, then, that most organizations will need to adopt a differentiated approach to the management of human assets. The formalized, centralized systems will apply to the bulk of the organization, the steady state. At the top, or in the emergency activities, they are inappropriate, and, in most organizations, are ignored – rightly. In the innovative parts, marketing, R and D, some parts of finance or corporate planning, the individual manager should have much more discretion to override or not use the formal systems or the equity procedures. Unfortunately, most organizations try to reduce everything to the steady state, instead of looking at the problems of differentiation. Some of the principal problems are:

Can one organization tolerate different methods of compensation, selection and promotion?
How best does one select and develop the integrators or co-ordinators?
How to develop a career planning system which fits a person to a culture, rather than a person to a job?
Should an individual progress through all four divisions of activity, or remain in one culture throughout a career?

The answers to these questions are not fully known, partly because the problems have not been looked at in this way before. But they do suggest some practical implications:

1 Separate the innovative areas from the steady state. In the innovative areas, reward ideas, creativity and inter-personal skills – often the prerogative of the young. Do not require them, necessarily, to move into the steady state but to remain innovative, progress to policy or to leave. In the steady state, reward reliability, specialist skill, accuracy, knowledge and experience.
2 Confine life-time careers to the steady state, but use fixed-term contracts at higher salary rates for the innovative and policy areas. This way, the organization will reward the role-orientated man with security and financial sufficiency, and the task- or power-orientated man with money and independence whilst providing that pressure for results to which he is likely to respond. In this way, the young and creative can be paid more than their counterparts in the steady state, but the higher pay will be accompanied by a higher risk element.
3 In order to give individuals early experience of the policy or breakdown areas, and to train them in co-ordination skills, it may pay the organization to distort its structure, to create more small relatively decentralized units than strict reason would call for.

3 The development of the individual

3.1

Plato felt that education and learning should continue until the age of 40. Many would now feel that he put too early a date on its closure. Learning and development have become a life-long task.

Individuals do change over time. They acquire new knowledge or technical skills. They become more balanced, or more risk-taking. They find new capacities within themselves, or learn to interact with each other more productively. They learn to cope with stress, or to help others to do so. The problem of managing development within organizations is to understand how one may hasten and channel this process of learning and discovery. There are three major methods of individual learning:

Formal education and training;
Group learning;
Assignment or planned experience.

We shall look at each of these in turn to examine their strengths and their problems.

3.2 Formal education and training

Management education and training is big business. The category includes all formal in-company 'courses', varying from one day to one month. It includes the off-site programmes of consulting firms, independent institutes, business schools and universities. In spite of the proliferation of formal training programmes, there is a fairly common feeling that few of them live up to the high aspirations of their descriptive or promotional literature. What evaluation there has been tends to support the generally disappointing outcome. Why this lack of success? There are four principal reasons:

1 For learning to occur, the individual must want to learn. This, the oldest, most fundamental and most obvious tenet of learning theory, is often ignored. If an individual is not interested in the topic, believes that he has no need of it, or has no faith in the ability of the course to teach it him, then it is unlikely that learning will occur 'in spite of himself'. For him to want to learn, the topic must usually be closely related to a part of his work that he feels important, and the medium for the learning, the teacher or teaching institution, must have expert authority in the would-be student's eyes. A machinist on piece-rate, faced with the installation of a vital new machine tool next week, will clamour to attend a training course put on by the manufacturers. All students should be volunteers, or at least willing accomplices. Assignment by the organization to a programme only tangentially relevant to the individual's existing work – e.g. 'The mysteries of the computer, a background course for the salesman' – will arouse in the individual feelings of compliance. She may attend, but she will not learn. If the course is high-prestige, or expensive, an executive development programme at a foreign business school, she may see her nomination as a sign of high favour by the organization and be delighted to attend. But not to learn, for the implicit message was that she was pretty good already. This has been named the 'accolade effect'.

2 Learning takes place within a context. When we learn something, be it out of a book or from experience, it is put into a frame of reference in our minds. This is a psychological context. There is the more obvious physical context. Things learnt in one country are not always remembered or felt relevant in another. Just as we don't always

recognize friends out of context, so ideas or facts out of context are still there, are still lodged in our minds, but they may never get used. So the learning by rote of some financial formulae may be achieved at an off-site course with a high degree of accuracy. But studied and learnt in isolation, they will not readily be used by the individual back in his organization. So much of formal learning takes place in a 'cultural island', unrelated to the particular physical or psychological frames of reference of the individual. Much of that hard-earned learning is not shipped out from the cultural island to the world of work. Thus, evaluation studies have found high scores on content learning at the end of the programme but little evidence of any application.

Box 8.6 Intelligence has many faces

Why has intelligence been so narrowly defined? Recent work in America has given academic weight to what is only common sense, namely that intelligence (or ability) has at least seven different forms which do not necessarily correlate with each other. In concentrating on analytic intelligence as measured by IQ tests, we have down-graded the rest. The other six are:

Spatial intelligence, of the sort that the creative artist or the creative scientist has; the ability to see patterns in things and to connect the unconnected.

Musical intelligence, clearly seen in musical prodigies, but also in the pop groups of the young who may not necessarily score highly on analytic intelligence tests.

Physical intelligence, more naturally called ability, perhaps, but obvious in sportspeople, dancers and athletes.

Practical intelligence, of the sort that enables someone to fix a motor-cycle whilst failing engineering examinations.

Intra-personal intelligence, the ability to know oneself and to be sensitive to one's inner being, evidenced in much poetry and literature.

Inter-personal intelligence, the ability to co-operate with and work through others, essential for managers and leaders.

See further: Gardner, *Frames of Mind*, 1983

---

3 Learning, if it is to last, must be 'owned'. Rote learning, or the memorizing of other people's learning, does not last unless it is immediately and continuously applied. Discovery learning, where the student uncovers the answer or the truth for herself, lasts longer

– but again it must be used in the near future, and found useful, 'reinforced'. If learning is not by discovery or is not used and found useful, the individual will not internalize the learning, will not own it. That which is not owned is not maintained and is soon forgotten. The most brilliant lecture on mathematical techniques will make no impact on a group who, though sitting enthralled, will never need to use such techniques. A month later, they will recall the brilliance of the exposition but none of the content. Nichols, amongst others, has shown that on average, only 50 per cent of a lecture can be recalled by the audience at its end, a figure that drops to 25 per cent after two weeks – a statistic not very popular with lecturers!

4 People are different. That is obvious, of course, but we tend to forget it in the seminar room, regarding people as varying only along the scale from bright to dull. In practice, there are many scales (see Box 8.6) and people learn in different ways. The creative person will learn best if allowed to create, the practically gifted will have a hard time listening: how can inter-personal skills be more than talked

---

Box 8.7   Self-enlightenment

The Japanese have only a few small business schools. How then, I inquired, do their managers learn the key concepts of business, the things like accounting and marketing which it is not easy to learn on-the-job. Self-enlightenment was the answer they gave.

This turned out not to be some ancient Buddhist practice but a neat euphemism for correspondence courses! Young Japanese executives are required to learn the language and concepts of business in their own time, although at corporate expense, through forms of distance learning. The habit, once acquired, goes on. Managers in Japan read a lot. They know that it is their own responsibility to keep up with their field, just as doctors do, or architects, or any professional group.

In the USA they have their own phrase 'individual initiative and corporate support'. There are tuition support schemes in many corporations which provide money for a range of approved courses in local colleges and universities.

Business Week magazine defined the implicit new contract of employment this way: 'hereinafter, the employee will assume full responsibility for his own career – for keeping his qualifications up to date, for getting himself moved to the next position at the right time, for salting away funds for retirement, and most daunting of all, for achieving job satisfaction. The company, while making no promises, will endeavor to provide a conducive environment, economic exigencies permitting.' (*Business Week*, October 1987).

about in a classroom setting? If people differ, so do the problems with which they are faced: how many of the problems of organizations are actually going to be handled better after being talked about in a formal learning situation?

The assignments to regular programmes on 'communications', 'man-management' or 'personal development' may keep the training centre full and give the individual a much-needed break but, in many cases, any real learning will be fortuitous and fortunate.

3.3 Group learning

The realization that an individual's interactions with others were crucial to his effectiveness in an organization led to a concentration on the development of his inter-personal or interactive skills. Conceptual learning or formal knowledge, it was clear, was not going to do very much on its own in this field. A whole corpus of development methods grew up which sought to apply to interactions the three principles of learning outlined in the previous section. The most well-known of these methods was the T-group, which almost became a generic term for the whole genus of these methods. The methods vary in the degree of structure and in the amount of control exercised by the teacher. But they all have these elements in common:

Learning takes place in a group context, and is applied in that context during the programme;
The individual, early in the programme, receives feedback indicating his learning needs;
Activities and behaviour directly related to working on those needs is organized or occurs;
The individual has an opportunity to try out revised behaviour, or new skills, in the same context in which he learnt them.

There is little doubt that these methods, properly handled, can be very effective in developing skills in group interactions and in building more effective groups (their use for this latter purpose is mentioned in Chapter 6). There does, however, seem to be some evidence for thinking that the context is crucial, that is, the learning is anchored to a large extent in the group in which it is learnt. The individual does not carry much of the changed behaviour over to a new group. He or she has learnt how to be a more effective member of the learning group, but has not generalized from this experience. To some extent, this is logical behaviour, since each group is a different blend of people, task and environment, with different requirements of its individuals.

To be properly effective, therefore, the learning group should be the actual work group, so that the context of learning and application is the same and continuous. This, however, creates new problems:

1 The effectiveness of the group as a context for learning will depend very largely on the previous history of the group. Very authoritarian-structured groups will not easily learn another mode of interaction, no matter how well the training is handled. Not all leaders of groups can accept feedback about their behaviour, not all subordinates can give it. The climate of the work group carries over into the learning group and can contaminate it.

2 Ultimately, the individual will leave that work group, and may leave the learning behind. To a degree, the longer anyone practises changed behaviour, the more likely that behaviour is to become part of them, independent and irrespective of the context. But, realistically, group learning is group development more than it is individual development.

The use of groups for learning, group dynamics, has given birth to a host of variations on the original T-group. Groups are used for individual discovery and therapy (encounter groups), to study the development and growth of a group personality, to look at pair relationships (marriage groups), and to provide a shared and often almost psychedelic experience. None of these are necessarily bad or wrong in themselves, but some of them are not as well administered or controlled as they ought to be, nor do they have much place in the planned development of the individual in the organization.

Group learning is not, however, confined to the learning of interactive skills or personal discovery. Fruitful use is beginning to be made of task-orientated learning groups.

Called project groups, or some similar name, they utilize the supportive interactive nature of group work to encourage more specific forms of learning related to problems or skills. Focusing on a particular task or problem, often in her own organization, the individual learns something about group processes and her own inter-personal skills, whilst simultaneously acquiring some particular skill or knowledge, usually set in her own organizational context. These methods, properly designed, can cope with the relevance, contextual and application problems of learning and can help to spread some common philosophies and experiences across the organization. Action Learning, pioneered by Revans in revolt against the formal learning programmes of the business schools, is the best-known model. It is widely used in

Britain and Europe, but the principles have increasingly infiltrated formal learning programmes at all levels.

3.4   Assignment or planned experience

This is the most common form of individual development in organizations and potentially the most effective. But to get personal learning from experience, certain things have to happen:

1 The individual must be able to generalize from particular incidents. He must be able to explain why things worked the way they did. A set of experiences, no matter how successful, does not necessarily give learning unless the lessons are conceptualized. Everyone has encountered the great manager with a string of success stories who is hard put to it to explain his success. It is easier to learn from failure than from success. Success only means that the total formula worked, but which parts of it were crucial and why, which were universally valid, which particular to the situation, remain unknown until tested.

2 The individual must have some idea of what she needs to learn from each assignment and how it will help her in her development. This assumes a degree of knowledge about ourselves, our strengths and weaknesses, our goals and our ambitions, which is rare in most of us. For the ancient Greeks, 'Know thyself' was one of the key prescriptions for success, inscribed above the temple of Zeus at Delphi.

3 The individual must receive information about his performance, and the standards expected of him, not only in terms of results, but in terms of his particular learning needs, as they relate to knowledge and skills or to behaviour. This kind of feedback is particularly difficult to give and to receive. It requires, as with normal appraisals:

(a) To be given with genuine regard for the individual;
(b) To be related to specific instances and to needs previously listed by the individual;
(c) To have a lot of time spent on it – quarter-hour interviews get nowhere.

As suggested in the section on appraisals, there is good evidence for suggesting that this type of feedback for learning should be separated from performance appraisal, and perhaps given by persons other than the superior – often people in a diagonal or lateral relationship, where the role of judge will not overlay the role of helper.

4 The organization must tolerate mistakes and failures as long as they produce learning and as long as the long-term value of the learning outweighs the costs of the mistakes. One advantage of, and reason for, the continued success of many fast-growing companies has been that mistakes get 'rolled over' by growth. There is greater tolerance for genuine mistakes, more learning and a bigger stock of developed managerial talent to sustain the growth record. In this way, growth breeds growth. A hurdle system of development, where a fallen hurdle means career failure, will not encourage experimentation or the testing of hypotheses about ideas or behaviour. It will breed caution and conservatism, and rule out the entrepreneurial spirit that the organization will say it needs.

5 The organization must make its expectations clear. One study of new graduate recruits has shown that those for whom the organization initially set the highest standards were the most successful after a few years.

We know, from the classroom, that if a teacher thinks the students are clever and able they will become clever and able. Research findings have verified this. If an organization believes that its managers can perform effectively, they will perform effectively if allowed to do so. High expectations, if properly communicated, can create a self-fulfilling prophecy. In Chapter 3, this was called the 'halo effect of role perception'.

There are two forms of learning from experience – learning from the

---

Box 8.8 Horizontal fast-tracks

The big Japanese companies practise what they call 'slow-burn development'. The new recruit to executive ranks could not expect to reach the first rung of the managerial ladder, 'kacho', for thirteen or fourteen years. 'That is a long time,' I remarked to one Personnel Manager, 'is there not a fast-track for the best and the brightest?' 'Indeed there is,' he replied, 'but it is horizontal not vertical.' What he meant was that the competent and fast-learning recruits were passed more swiftly than others through the different departments of the company, doing different jobs, working for different bosses, although always under the attentive eyes of one mentor, who coached a group of these beginners. 'That way,' he explained 'we see in what areas they shine, we give them the chance to work under different people, with different people, on different tasks.' It is not foreordained at the age of 22 what you will be good at.

situation and learning from the person or modelling. Most planned assignments work on the former basis. An individual is asked to learn from a variety of job or task situations. There is, however, some reason to think that we can learn a lot, all through our lives, by modelling ourselves after chosen individuals, by identification. Apart from some 'personal assistant' schemes, few organizations have tried systematically to develop characteristics and behaviour in an individual by attaching him to suitable models. Fitting people to people might well be a more effective strategy for development than fitting people to tasks. It is easier to learn by modelling than by conceptualizing experience.

3.5   Some conclusions

Once again, development strategies for the individual would seem to depend on the culture. Formal training systems are appropriate to the role cultures and the steady-state parts of organization. The job requirements can be defined fairly accurately in terms of skills, knowledge and abilities. Training requirements for each job at each level can therefore be decided upon and provided in a fairly systematic way. The most effective schemes of formal training are indeed those which grow out of very detailed and specific job definitions.

In power cultures, however, the policy and breakdown parts of organizations, learning will be by experience or modelling and will usually be initiated by the individual. Individuals who learn fastest in power cultures are those who have most clearly defined goals and career paths for themselves. Such people are often organizationally mobile, changing their organizations and even industries or occupations in order to develop their knowledge and skills. The use of the personal assistant role, or ADC in the Army, is a typically power culture way of educating the next generation, by a form of imposed modelling.

In task cultures or the innovative ends of organizations, the group and the interactive skills of individuals are key factors. Although other forms of skill training and personal learning from experience are required, the various types of group learning will flourish most successfully in these cultures. It is no accident that just as the norms, values and practices of a task culture are most in accord with the precepts of the 'liberal' theorists on organization, so group learning is their preferred method of development. Group learning will, however, be rejected by power cultures, along with most formal training schemes, as time-wasting and irrelevant, and by role cultures as threatening and too culturally laden. Zeus figures only turn up for the dinners on formal courses, to show themselves and to spot talent.

4 Summary and discussion

4.1

We have considered the methods involved in *management of human assets*, and in particular *appraisal systems*, *career planning* and *compensation systems*.

We considered the common problems and some remedies, and suggested that a culturally differentiated approach was needed but had not been systematically applied in any organization. We looked at *development of the individual*, and in particular *formal education and training*, *group learning*, *assignment and planned experience*, and examined the advantages and drawbacks of each, again suggesting that some methods were more appropriate to some cultures than to others.

4.2

But in looking at the people of organizations there remain some major questions not yet fully covered. These are strategic macro-issues, questions of policy and judgement not easily resolvable by logic or scientific fact. But they need to be raised, even if they cannot be answered.

Should you grow your own timber? Many organizations work on the assumption that they must provide their future manpower needs from their own resources. To continue the agricultural metaphor they create plantations, weed out the weaker growths, transplant and nurture the stronger saplings, plan and plant according to their estimate of future needs. Let us review briefly some of the implications of this philosophy:

(a) It necessitates a manpower plan, including estimates of future manpower needs at all levels, worked back over time to intake requirements for particular years.
(b) It needs progression plans, ineptly called development plans, for bringing forward, and weeding out, the required numbers and calibres for the various levels.
(c) It needs the mechanisms and procedures to implement these plans, the whole battery of appraisal schemes, replacement charts, development plans.
(d) It can easily result in a surplus inventory of potential at the lower

levels as the organization overstocks to take care of errors in forecasts, fall-outs, or failure to develop the potential properly. This overstocking at the bottom results in people being overpaid for the work they do, low morale and high rates of departure.

(e) It can result in an overstocking at the older levels of middle management. Organizations feel that they owe continued employment to the individual who has passed his optimum level. Although socially well-motivated, this policy can lead to a cluttered organization, as individuals make work to justify their employment, and to low morale, when individuals feel themselves the recipients of organizational charity. A charity which leads to insecurity and dependency, neither of them very pleasant sensations.

Items (d) and (e) are invisible costs, but when added to the other more measurable items, they amount to a very costly policy. Is it justified? To answer this, one must compare the cost of an alternative policy, e.g. hiring individuals on specific-term contracts, or for specific jobs or ranges of jobs. This would involve:

(a) Higher selection and recruitment costs;
(b) Probably higher salary and wage rates, since the organization, in order to attract people, or renew existing contracts, would have to pay at least the full market rate;
(c) Letting go larger numbers of middle managers, or reducing their salaries in line with reduced jobs;
(d) Inadequate staffing of key jobs, if particular individuals were not available in the market at that time.

Modification of this approach would include drastically curtailing recruitment of people in their early twenties and a lowering of the normal retirement age to fifty.

These philosophies are more appropriate to power and task cultures. Wholesale adoption by organizations would require a radical change in society's attitude to work and career progression. The norms would have to become that:

(a) one could, over a period of time, work for more than one organization;
(b) that earnings do not have to progress monotonically until retirement but can peak in the middle;
(c) that times of work should pay for times of not working.

Interestingly, these norms are currently found at the very top and bottom of the social orders, but not in the spreading middle.

Whether organizations should or should not grow their own timber is a question that only they can answer. But a comparison of the alternative costs would be useful data.

Should you develop the organization or the individual? Attempts by organizations to improve effectiveness by changing individuals have too often resulted in:

(a) Little or no changed behaviour in the individual;
(b) A perception by the individual that the organization is seeking control over his or her life – resulting in the responses of compliance or rebellion;
(c) The loss of the investment when an individual leaves the organization.

A different approach was to improve the effectiveness of the organization by changing some aspects of the organization and the way it did its work. This would have its effect on the individual since the overall approach of Organization Development, as it grew to be called (OD for short), was to find ways of integrating the goals and values of the individual with those of the organization. OD endeavours to change the culture of the organization so that this integration becomes possible.

The main worth of the OD approach lies in its willingness to attack the problems of the organization directly, rather than through the agency of particular individuals. A combination of appropriate methods of individual development combined with the OD approach to the problem areas of the organization would seem to be the happy compromise which meets the needs of the organization and its individuals.

Are the goals and values of the individual compatible with those of the organizations? It has been said that the work of 90 per cent of the people is boring for 90 per cent of the time. The practitioners of OD and many of the theorists of the Human Relations school, whilst conceding that this is so, would deny that it need be so. Who is right? Let us at least admit that the 90 per cent figure can be considerably reduced. More people can be given more interesting work with more relevance to their own development and maturity. But let it at the same time be recognized that investment in work, identifying with the organization, can carry its costs.

Involvement consumes energy. Not everybody's psychological

Box 8.9   The back-firing appraisal scheme

After much research, thought and consultation, the new personnel manager had evolved a comprehensive appraisal and review scheme. The organization had recently got to the size (1,000 employees) where some systematic way of cataloguing their resources in terms of individuals was required, together with a less haphazard way of developing and rewarding people. This was a generally recognized need in an organization where pay differentials, promotion and management development opportunities had hitherto been opportunistic, haphazard and subjectively determined.

The new appraisal scheme was very well thought out. It provided for a proper job definition, a regular performance review initiated by the individual but carried through with his superior, required that the superior's comments be seen and signed as accepted by the subordinate, a space for the identification of development needs, the likely potential of the individual, and even for his suggestions as to the way in which the organization could help him to do his work better. The original of this comprehensive document was kept by the manager, with copies for the subordinate and for the personnel files.

Indirectly seeking feedback on the reception of his system, three months later, the personnel manager was surprised to hear the following comments reported:

I filled it in as accurately as I could, but imagine my horror when the director in charge of my function – not my line boss, and at least three levels above me, told me three weeks later when discussing a possible new appointment for me, that he fully agreed with my assessment of my weaknesses. And I thought the document was private to me and my boss! Honesty just does not pay!

Just how gullible do they think we are – trying to get our signatures to our shortcomings? Obviously it's a way of preparing the ground for the next redundancy operation. They had a lawsuit arising out of the last one.

More paper, more forms. I called all my people in together, told them that we had to do this, but that I didn't want to interfere with the normal work of the department. I said that I would fill in my comments on each of their forms, let them take them home overnight, and bring them back signed on the following day. It all seemed to work OK. We had no problems.

I'm sure they mean well, but do they really expect us to put down the truth?

---

contract would put all their 'E' into one bucket. A lot of people prefer what might be called a portfolio approach to life with proportions of 'E' allocated to different activities. Perhaps for the richness and diversity of our society, it is as well that individuals tend to have more than one commitment.

One way of looking at this question is to examine the match between the organization's culture and the cultural preferences of the individuals. Individuals with a power or task orientation are likely to find role cultures frustrating and inhibiting. Individuals with role orientations will be insecure and threatened in a power or task culture. People with person orientations will tend to shun organization altogether unless they can use their facilities with minimum cost. The organization and the individual could be regarded as integrated if the cultural aspects of psychological contract matched. The organizations usually regarded as integrated in this sense are the successful task cultures. The more successful aerospace firms in the US, some consultancy organizations, some Research and Development departments are the examples often cited. But the power cultures of entrepreneurial firms, the financial merchant firms, the pediments of large organizations are also capable of high integration with the individual. So are parts of the Civil Service, and the steady states of many organizations where the role culture predominates. For if the truth be told, even though never revealed in questionnaires, 90 per cent of the work-force may well be role-orientated, may like to be bored 90 per cent of the time, even if it is not fashionable to say so!

This being so, are organizations justified then in the processes of socialization which they nearly all apply to their new recruits? Socialization is a way of binding them to the organization and at the

---

Box 8.10   Socialization in the Roman Empire

Antony Jay has observed that, paradoxically, the Roman Empire grew so large and survived so long *because* there was no railway, car, aircraft, radio, paper or telephone. 'Above all no telephone. And therefore you could not maintain any illusion of direct control over a general or a provincial governor, you could not feel at the back of your mind that you could ring him up, or he could ring you, if a situation cropped up that was too much for him, or that you could fly over and sort things out if they started to get into a mess. You appointed him, you watched his chariot and baggage train disappear over the hill in a cloud of dust and that was that . . . There was, therefore, no question of appointing a man who was not fully trained, or not quite up to the job: you knew that everything depended on his being the best man for the job before he set off. And so you took great care in selecting him. But more than that you made sure that he knew all about Rome and Roman government and the Roman army before he went.'

Jay, *Management and Machiavelli*, 1970

same time making them more amenable to the preferred ways of influence.

Role cultures tend to use schooling, power cultures co-option and, occasionally, mortification; task cultures favour apprenticeship. The typical larger organization will run induction and training courses for the bulk of its individuals, but the professionally trained recruit to the innovative groups will be put under care and guidance for the early months. At higher levels, co-option to the clubs of power becomes important and the aspiring individual learns to adapt his attitudes and behaviour to accord with the norms of the club.

Socialization is efficient and effective. Socialization is a way of binding people into the organization. Strong organizations have strong cultures, as we observed in Chapter 7 (and Box 8.10). But there can be problems for the individualist, for the creative thinker who does not want to be homogenized, and even for the committed careerist who has other interests. One of the big questions which organizations have to face is the extent of their ownership of the individual. Do they have the right to dominate a person's life? Is it a deliberate contract or does it creep up on one gradually once it becomes clear that the way to advancement is immersion? There is some evidence (see Box 8.11) that successful managers may have to choose between success in the organization and fulfilment in the home. Organizations might have to resist the blandishments of too dominant a culture if they want to keep some of the special talents which they may need to ensure their long-term future.

Box 8.11   Must success cost so much?

'I suppose like everyone else I've always wanted to be the company president. But the price that one has to pay is too high. I've seen those guys up on the sixth floor, and the stress that they are under. God help them – I certainly don't envy them any longer. So I made a decision a few years back to pay more attention to my family, and I don't regret it, I suppose you could say that I've matured, become more realistic about my chances, if you like.'

Reported in Evans and Bartolomé, *Must Success Cost So Much?*, 1980

On the other hand, there is the Japanese example of the culturally dominant organization and its interpretation in America as the Theory

Z organization (Box 8.12) which suggests that Douglas McGregor may have been right when he said: 'Effective performance results when conditions are created such that the members of the organization can achieve their own goals best by directing their efforts toward the success of the enterprise'.

For my own part, I would want to shun any grandiose conclusion. Individuals are different, so are organizations. There can and should be no one grand design or theory, but rather a plethora of possibilities from which to choose. The Theory Z organization may suit some, but others will find a power culture more to their taste perhaps, and the power culture will thrive where a Theory Z corporation could not cope. The variety is the challenge and the delight but it behoves organizations to understand the differences just as it behoves those who manage them or work in them to understand the organizations.

Box 8.12   Theory Z organizations

William Ouchi argues that some American corporations have successfully adapted Japanese methods to their own cultures. He calls these firms Theory Z organizations. They have the following key characteristics:

1 Long-term employment
2 Slow evaluation and promotion
3 Moderately specialized careers
4 Consensual decision-making
5 Individual responsibility
6 Implicit, informal control (but with explicit measures)
7 Holistic concern for the employee.

A survey by Ouchi and Johnson in the electronics industry showed that corporate prestige, managerial ability and reported corporate earnings were all closely associated with the Z-ness of the organization.

Ouchi, *Theory Z*, 1981

---

9 → On the Work of the Organization – and its Design

1 Introduction

It is not granted to everyone to design an organization. Yet most managers have dabbled with the organizational drawing-board from time to time, whether it be a wistful tampering with the organigram, re-definitions of authorities and responsibilities, the layout of the factory or the office, or the degree of delegation to a group or an individual.

Most organizations are not designed, they grow. Indeed, there are several studies which draw on biological analogies to describe organization phenomena. But not all organizations adapt equally well to the environment within which they grow. Many, like the dinosaur of great size but little brain, remain unchanged in a changing world. Others, 30 per cent in one study in Poughkeepsie, New York, die in the first year of their life. The law of the survival of the fittest is as inexorable for organizations as it is in nature.

For survival, for continual growth and development, in organizations as with individuals, it helps to know what you would like to be before you try to become it. Analysis of the ideal, of what should be, when compared with the reality of what is, may be disillusioning, but it is the proper starting point for improvement and for planned change.

In this chapter we shall examine some of the problems involved in *the design of the structure*, *the management of diversity* and *the design of the job*, followed by *summary and implications*.

2 The design of the structure

2.1

'Structure' includes the allocation of formal responsibilities, the typical organization chart. It also covers the linking mechanisms between the roles, the co-ordinating structures of the organization, if any are

Box 9.1   If organizing goes wrong

Child has compiled a depressing but impressive list of the things that can be wrong if the work of the organization is not properly designed and structured. Here is just part of his list:

1 Motivation and morale may be depressed because:
   (a) Decisions appear to be inconsistent and arbitrary in the absence of standardized rules.
   (b) People believe that they have little responsibility, opportunity for achievement and recognition of their worth because of insufficient delegation.
   (c) There is a lack of clarity as to what is expected of people and how their performance is assessed.
2 Decision-making may be delayed and lacking in quality because:
   (a) Necessary information is not transmitted on time to the appropriate people.
   (b) Decision-makers are overloaded due to insufficient delegation.
   (c) There are no adequate procedures for evaluating the results of similar decisions in the past.
3 There may be conflict and a lack of co-ordination because:
   (a) There are conflicting goals between projects or departments.
   (b) Mechanisms for liaison have not been laid down.
   (c) The people involved in operations are not involved in the planning.
4 Costs may be rising rapidly because:
   (a) The organization has a long hierarchy with a high ration of 'chiefs' to 'indians'.
   (b) There is an excess of procedures and paperwork.

For the complete list see Child, *Organization: A Guide to Problems and Practice*, 1984

needed. The basic forms make up what might be called the skeleton of the organization. They need to be joined by muscles, nerves and flesh if they are going to work, but the decision on the underlying bone structure is a first priority. How do organizations decide on the appropriate structure – is there a best form, or is there perhaps an inevitable progression as companies get older or larger?

In Chapter 7 the view was put forward that the effective organization was that which had an appropriate structure and culture. 'Appropriate' would be determined by a variety of forces, the technology, the market, the size of the organization, its people. The problem now is to make this conceptual doctrine of 'appropriateness' operational in designing an organization's structure.

In pursuing an optimal structure, organizations have normally followed an implicit re-formulation of Occam's Razor – 'As simple as you can, as complex as you must'. Or, to put it another way, the designer of organizational structures needs to tread a tight-rope stretched between the pressures for uniformity on the one hand and diversity on the other. Let us consider these pressures separately.

2.2 Uniformity

Uniformity implies standardization and common procedures centrally administered. The pressures for *uniformity* can include:

1 The cheapness of standardization. It costs less to produce and to process standard forms. Training for standard procedures is easier and cheaper. There are economies of scale in most standardized operations, e.g. a central computer or legal department *vis-à-vis* separate installations in each unit.
2 The need for interchangeability. Many operations, e.g. airlines, banks, postal services have operations which require that they use common procedures so that interactions within the organization and between organizations can be carried out according to standard procedures.
3 The need for control of process. Some organizations need to monitor the on-going process of their organizations, as opposed to monitoring the results. Organizations in which one unit is dependent on the output of another, e.g. process industries, vertically integrated organizations, need a uniform system so that fluctuations in the requirements of one unit can be reflected in the operations of another. Any interdependence of operations will result in a pressure for some uniformity of method.
4 The need for a standard product. Many organizations need uniformity of output from a variety of sources. Multiple stores (e.g. Marks and Spencer and Tesco), branch banking or airline offices are some examples of market-induced needs for uniformity. Organizations with more than one production facility for the same product, or organizations producing to a legal standard e.g. the pharmaceutical industry, have a production-induced need for uniformity.
5 The need for specialization. By pooling all the requirements for maintenance, or for electronics engineers, the organization can build up a competence core in that field and can offer career paths to specialists. But a competence core is only possible if there is some uniformity in the organization. The haphazard employment of specialists becomes too costly, so rules are set for their use.

6 The desire for central control. The requirement of senior management that they 'know what is going on' is a push towards uniformity or control of the process rather than the results. Standardization permits the centre to be fed with a vast amount of information in a digestible form and in approximately real time. This allows the centre to monitor the daily process of the business, to be the only pool of all relevant information, and to intervene should the occasion demand it. This requirement by senior management for central control can well be a desire rather than a need imposed by the situation.

The stereotype of the French educational system – that at any given hour on any given day, the French Minister of Education could state with complete certainty what every child in any level was doing throughout the country – is an example of a system where all the needs for uniformity were felt and fully responded to. Uniformity would clearly reduce the costs of production of teaching materials, would permit the freer interchangeability of children from one location to another, would regulate the flow from one part of the system to another (e.g. into the university system) and would give a guaranteed value to any certificate of education so that employers would know what they were buying. Uniformity is the hallmark of the steady state. Where the requirements for uniformity are high, a role culture will tend to predominate, carrying with it all the other aspects of that culture in addition to its penchant for rule and procedures.

2.3 Diversity

The other set of pressures in any organization will be for *diversity*. These pressures include:

1 *Regional diversity*. An organization may operate in more than one geographical area. But it may or may not regard these areas as 'different' for its own particular purposes. What is 'Europe' or 'South America' to one organization will be twenty different areas to another. Surrey may differ from Kent for some organizations, but both be defined as Southern England for others.

2 *Market diversity*. Markets can be defined in regional terms (France, or Yorkshire), in socio-economic terms (suburban, middle-class), by end-use (agricultural, industrial), by customer activity (Government, construction industry) or even by their social habits (television viewers, pub-goers). The number of market categories and the degree to which they differ are important aspects of diversity.

Box 9.2   Examples of the basic managerial structures

types of managerial structure	chart	degree of formalization	degree of centralization
entrepreneurial		informal	centralized
functional		formal	centralized
by product line decentralized by geographical area		formal	decentralized

From Weinshall, 'Application of two conceptual schemes of organizational behaviour in case study and general organizational research', Ashridge Management College, 1971

3 *Product diversity*. How wide is the mix of outputs, be they soap powders or medical services? Can they all be treated as one, or does each product have its own peculiarities in terms of market, image, need for servicing, quality, etc. A large number of products does not necessarily imply diversity, twenty different sizes of screw can still be regarded, conceptually, as one product. It is the degree of difference between them that is the diversity that matters.

4 *Technological diversity*. Is the organization based on one technology, or a variety of them? If a variety, are the differences between them significant? In high-technology organizations, differences are often crucial, as technical knowledge and skills become more hardly acquired and more narrowly focused. Low technologies permit wider ranges of expertise and shorter learning periods. Diversity in high technology therefore is more pressing than in a low-technology organization (e.g. insurance, local government, many service industries).

5 *Goal diversity*. Does the organization have one set of goals, to which all divisions and departments subscribe, or do the goals vary? How much does the variety matter? For instance, the sales manager's concern with customer service and the problems of today could be far removed from the worries of the research director about the materials required. The personnel department's aims for the welfare

---

Box 9.3   Bees or flies?

Karl Weick describes an experiment by Gordon Sin:

. . . If you place in a bottle half a dozen bees and the same number of flies, and lay the bottle down horizontally, with its base to the window, you will find that the bees will persist, till they die of exhaustion or hunger, in their endeavour to discover an issue through the glass; while the flies, in less than two minutes, will all have sallied forth through the neck on the opposite side . . . It is their (the bees) love of light, it is their very intelligence, that is their undoing in this experiment. They evidently imagine that the issue from every prison must be there where the light shines clearest; and they act in accordance, and persist in too logical action . . . Whereas the feather-brained flies, careless of logic as of the enigma of crystal, disregarding the call of the light, flutter wildly hither and thither, and meeting here the good fortune that often waits on the simple, who find salvation there where the wiser will perish, necessarily end by discovering the friendly opening that restores their liberty to them.

Quoted by Peters and Waterman in *In Search of Excellence*, 1983 of the people may conflict or may be in line with the production department's desire for large-scale automation.

This internal goal diversity is the crux of what Lawrence and Lorsch have called differentiation. They have shown that this internal differentiation is more appropriate, and more common, when the market environment or the technology is changing more rapidly. Plastics is a faster-growing and faster-changing industry than containers, and therefore more internal goal diversity would be expected in a plastics firm than a container firm.

6 *The identity of diversity.* Individuals find it easier to identify with smaller groups than with large organizations. Buried deep in a functional specialization of a large complex, it is hard to feel committed to the aims of the total organization. The goals of the specialization are the important ones, even though they may at times be suboptimal for the whole. Smaller groupings, in which the specialists are parcelled out, may cost more, but it makes it easier to establish a 'common enemy'; and makes it easier for the individual to identify with a collection of activities, rather than just one. Metaphorically, the individual seeks for a village even in the midst of a town, a territory small enough to feel that he or she is a significant part of it.

7 *The pull for disaggregated control.* Just as the centre feels a need to hold all the strings in its grasp, so the managers on the periphery feel a need to have more control over the resources that they are required to organize and administer. To be an area manager when in fact all the resources in the area are functionally controlled from head office reduces the role of the manager to that of reporter or public relations representative. Justifiably or not, the groups on the periphery can be expected to strive for a redistribution of control over resource. If power without responsibility be harlotry, responsibility without power is masochism.

8 *The need to experiment.* More and more organizations are finding that the ways to the future cannot often be systematically planned. New products, techniques and methods do not always succumb to logic even if backed up by massive resources. There is therefore a growing respectability for more experimentation and for more free-form types of structure (see Boxes 9.3 and 9.4).

Conglomerates are the extreme business example of diversity. Untrammelled by uniformity or central control, diversity can be highly exciting – but sometimes ruinous, as several conglomerates have proved. Governments with departments ranging from police and fire brigades to licensing and tax assessments are another example of diversity. The advance of technology in all areas of life, the apparent increase in the rate of change of the environment, the pressures for the agglomeration of activities tend to increase the pressures for diversity. Weinshall has argued that organizations tend to progress from an entrepreneurial structure to a multi-structure as the size or scope of their decision making process (DMP) expands. Scope of DMP appears to be approximately equivalent to diversity. Increasing diversity leads ultimately, then, to a multi-structure organization. Stopford, examining a number of multi-national firms, demonstrated that there was a progression from firms with low product diversification and low technology, which had a functional structure, to firms with high product diversification, high technology, and high geographical diversification which had what he termed a grid structure. Again, diversity is associated with complexity of structure.

2.4 The implications

Organizations are always pulled by those two forces of uniformity and diversity. By nature they would prefer uniformity. That way lies predictability and efficiency. If the status quo could be the way forward, organizations would be happy. In practice, of course, only monopolies can rejoice in that luxury and then only for a time, for even essentials like coal and transport monopolies can find themselves overtaken by new competitors if they do not change. Nevertheless, organizations (as a first step) are inclined to manage the environment rather than respond to it and in that way to limit diversity and reduce uncertainty. They have evolved a number of methods, first listed and analysed by Thompson. These include:

1 Buffering – keeping high stocks of raw materials or finished products shelters the organization from price fluctuations (but can be expensive).
2 Smoothing – using pricing to smooth out peak requirements and troughs, in transport, seasonal products, telephones etc. Rationing is a tougher variant of smoothing.
3 Forecasting – anticipating changes to minimize the unsettling effects of diversity.
4 Contracting – sub-contracting on short-term contracts is a way of exporting uncertainty.
5 Co-opting – putting your banker on the board or buying your

Box 9.4 The new organizational metaphors

Adhocracy: Alvin Toffler's word, built on theoretically by Mintzberg, the adhocracy is a challenging array of projects, task groups, committees, and freelance individuals. In Toffler's words, 'adhocracies now change their internal shape with a frequency and a rashness that makes the head swim. Titles change from week to week. Jobs are transformed. Responsibilities shift. Vast organizational structures are taken apart, bottled together in new forms, then re-arranged again.'

Tents: Hedberg contrasts organizational 'tents' and 'palaces'. Tents have 'ambiguous authority structures, unclear objectives, and contradictory assignments (which) can legitimate controversies and challenge traditions . . . Incoherence and indecision can foster exploration, self-evaluation, and learning.'

Technology of foolishness: March writes: 'organizations need to supplement the technology of reason with the technology of foolishness. Individuals and organizations need ways of doing things for which they have no good reason. Not always. Not usually. But sometimes. They need to act before they think.'

Loosely-coupled: Weick argues for constant experiment in organizations and says that 'retrospective sense making' is the key to success, by choosing from a large number of experiments, only possible if the organization is loosely coupled.

Market-place: Williamson, in a difficult but important book, *Markets and Hierarchies*, argues that the 'transaction costs' of a centrally planned hierarchical organization are often higher than one thinks. Using an internal market-place to sort out preferences, or contracting to outsiders, may result in duplication but it will save in transaction costs and often produce the better answer.

Champions, Bootlegging, Skunk works, Cabals, Shadow organizations: are words used by Peters and Waterman to describe what they found in the more successful American businesses.

Networks: Nancy Foy sees networks as crucial to organizational success and coins a 'law' that 'the effectiveness of a network is inversely proportional to its formality'. It needs a spider, not a chairman; a list of members, not a set of by-laws; groups, not committees; and a phone number rather than a building.

Clusters: Mills sees the effective organization being made up of large numbers of self-contained 'clusters' which may be called projects, business units, task forces etc., co-ordinated by a central cluster which administers the business as a whole.

competitor or customer is one way of controlling a bit of the environment.

6 Coalescing – reducing uncertainty by mergers or price-fixing agreements with competitors, or long-term agreements with suppliers and customers.

In spite of such attempts to iron out diversity, organizations will never reach that state of perfect equilibrium for which they search. The result is a seemingly endless process of oscillation between the pressures and measures for uniformity and those for diversity, from centralization to decentralization and back again, rather as one used to adjust the bathroom shower. In fact, as Chapter 7 sought to demonstrate, organizations need a blend of uniformity and diversity. Unfortunately, the pressures for tight control and uniformity are often at their height in hard times, when organizations most need to be creative and experimental. It is never easy to find the optimum blend.

The first two questions that the designer of the organization must ask are:

How much diversity?
What kind of diversity?

There is no objective statistical way of answering these questions. Each member of the organization, his view coloured by his role, will have a different answer. But at least a systematic approach would help. To examine each of the pressures for uniformity and diversity, to ask to what extent this pressure must be recognized or can be ignored, to rank order, to put in order of priority the pressures that apply, and to repeat this exercise with the senior members of management would be one way of starting the analysis.

It is unlikely that any organization with more than 1,000 employees, more than one category of product or service, more than one type of client, will not come out of such an analysis with the recognition of some pressures for diversity. The problem remains of recognizing these pressures in the design of both structure and culture.

The matrix organization arose in the aerospace industry out of a need to combine customer needs and priorities within the organizational requirements for economies of scale, long production runs and the development of specialist skills. A product-based organization, with the functions as its servants, would have sacrificed considerations of scale and predictability to meeting customer needs. In the long run this would tend to drive up the product costs. A production-based organization would find it difficult to adapt to the needs of individual markets or customers and would run the danger of losing its outlets, irrespective of the quality of its products. This tendency to place production priorities over customer needs often shows up in a failure to meet completion targets, or at best, necessitates long delivery dates. This need to balance the demands of uniformity and diversity results in the creation of product or customer groups, with representatives drawn from each of the functions. The pressures for diversity are channelled through to the functions by their representatives or the product groups.

A decentralized organization, with functional replicas of the central office under regional managers, is a recognition of the importance of the pressure for regional diversity. Regional organization under product organizations recognizes another priority of pressures. Decentralization schemes where the only central department is finance implies that this is the only form of uniformity that is crucial in comparison with the pressures for diversity. In US corporations, where the home market is relatively homogeneous, distinctions between products are more important and decentralization by product division the common pattern. In Europe, regional differences used to be recognized in the structures of multi-national corporations. Increasingly, as Europe comes to be regarded as one market, the regional organization becomes overlaid by a product organization (e.g. Unilever). Weinshall's 'multi-structure' shows how both forms of decentralization can be, and often should be, contained within one organization along with the entrepreneurial (power culture?) and functional (role culture?) organizations at the centre (See Box 9.2).

A differentiated organization, in the sense in which Lawrence and Lorsch use the term, an organization in which the goals, time-horizons and working practices of different parts of the organization differ widely, is appropriate to a changing technology or changing market. Combine these pressures with those for diversity of product or region and you should end up with a decentralized differentiated organization. Combine them, however, with pressures for a uniform product and interchangeability and you might find differentiation and centralization. The clearing banks in Britain face strong pressures for standardization, their procedures precisely similar to permit daily monitoring and interchangeability. But they are today facing a changing market, increased competition, pressures to diversify and to utilize new technologies. The answer lies in differentiation without decentralization. The spread of marketing departments, merchant-banking offshoots, development sections, all with personnel, systems and styles different from those traditional to the clearing banks, is a sign that the organizations are responding appropriately.

Decentralization is in vogue. The head of one consultancy firm was heard to say, 'This firm stands fast on the bedrock principle of decentralization.' Theorists, idealists and practitioners all advocate it. They often rely on the argument that the individual manager is more committed in a decentralized organization with his own command. This, it is held, will release motivational 'E' that will more than offset any diseconomies of scale or loss of central control. This argument is too simplistic. A decentralized organization is often a more satisfying form of environment to work in, it is true. The need to identify with a group, to control the means to one's own destiny are better satisfied with decentralization. But satisfaction does not necessarily lead to productivity and organizations that decentralize for these purposes alone may well be disappointed at the outcome. For decentralization is a response to the pressures for diversity. Only if these pressures are stronger than those for uniformity will it be effective. A sense of identity and control of resources are only two of the pressures that need to be considered. Differentiation is another response to other pressures for diversity. It is a response too often neglected. Decentralization without differentiation may well only lead to uniformity with complications. For a structural allocation in itself solves few problems; the sinews, nerves and muscles must change with the skeleton. Otherwise, role-oriented people, used to rules and regulations, unused to initiative, may find themselves heading up decentralized groups, expected to be entrepreneurial after a life of obedience, possessed of expert power without time to acquire it, leaders of groups instead of perusers of papers. It is one thing to prescribe the appropriate diversity, decentralization and differentiation, it is another to manage it.

Organizations, as they grow, come up against the uniformity/diversity problem again and again. Greiner has summed up the dilemmas of growth in a classic diagram (Box 9.5) which describes a sequence of crises as the organization lurches from too much central control and uniformity to too much diversity and too little co-ordination. The loose formations described in Box 9.4 may be very creative but, unless their creations are caught and harnessed (often into a very traditional role culture), they will remain expensive organizational frills.

Box 9.5   The pains of success

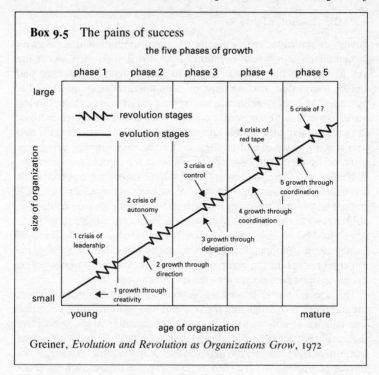

Greiner, *Evolution and Revolution as Organizations Grow*, 1972

3   The management of diversity

3.1

Having decided on the right degree and the right form of diversity, the designer of organizations must proceed to staff them and link them with integrating and co-ordinating mechanisms. Excessive diversity in the structure will therefore be unnecessarily costly, cluttering up the organization with unnecessary co-ordinating mechanisms. Lawrence and Lorsch, in their oft-quoted study, found that organizations which had more integrating devices than required were less effective and often more frustrating to work in. The most pertinent issues in the management of diversity appear to be *distribution of power*, *match of culture and structure* and the increasingly important issue of the *outside diversity*.

3.2   Distribution of power

Power, or the capacity to influence, is not something that appears on formal charts, but a consideration of the distribution of power is the key to the effective implementation of the structure. Lawrence and Lorsch found that in their most differentiated industry, plastics, the perceived amount of influence was spread very evenly among the top six levels in the hierarchy. By comparison, in the container industry (an environment more stable and uniform), influence was concentrated to a much greater extent to the top, middle management being represented by their divisional chiefs. In the more diverse environments of plastics and food, the research and sales divisions were perceived to have more influence than production. In our terminology, the task culture was found more appropriate in a changing environment.

Interpreting the findings of Lawrence and Lorsch, increasing diversity should be accompanied by increased influence at middle levels of management. With diversity, top management cannot expect to be in possession of all the relevant information or technical knowledge; decisions must be delegated to those who can take them.

This accords with the norms of a task culture. Power resides where the technical knowledge and the relevant information are to be found. The balance of power swings toward the innovation areas, away from the steady state as the diversity increases, with the promise that the integrative mechanisms, the departments or individuals responsible for linking co-ordination, are seen as retaining at least as much influence as any of the functional, product or regional divisions.

On the other hand, in a more stable, predictable environment where the pressures of uniformity outweigh those of diversity, most situations can be foreseen, and most expertize is channelled into the execution of pre-determined tasks. Unforeseen situations can be resolved at the top of the organization because there alone, in the pediment, will all the information be available. Since, too, the technology is not so fast-changing, the skills available in the pediment will still be relevant to the problems of the pillars. Ability to influence at the middle levels will therefore be confined to the specifics of each man's task and will be, in total, considerably less than the influence exerted at the top.

Lawrence and Lorsch found that in one organization in the container industry (relatively uniform), top management had endeavoured to lower the decision-making levels and increase the power of the middle levels of management. This was the low-performing organization and it seemed that the norms, praiseworthy in task culture, were inappropriate and ineffective in the role culture of a steady state.

Box 9.6 'Informating'

Shoshana Zuboff studied the introduction of a computerized technology in eight organizations between 1981–6.

She describes how this technology can be used to increase the 'automaticity' of the work, reducing skill levels and centralizing power. But she also shows how it can, more productively, be used to 'informate' the organization. In this case the organization uses the new technology to increase the intellectual level of work at virtually every level, spreading information and the ability to make decisions based on that information more widely. The result is to challenge the distinction between manual and mental work, between the managers and the managed.

Power, in the informated organization, is inevitably much more widely spread.

Zuboff, *In the Age of the Smart Machine*, 1989

Zuboff found that 'informated' organizations (see Box 9.6) inevitably spread power more widely along with the information.

The distribution of power finds its most practical expression in the shape of the organization and in its spans of control. Tall, thin organizations keep power in the centre and at the top. At its extreme this results in a one-over-one organization which can really only be justified if the one on top (often the chairman) is preoccupied with the world outside the organization.

Such organizations permit little discretion but risk few mistakes. The top remains responsible and in charge. The British Civil Service has, in the past, epitomized this tradition. Shorter and flatter organizations, while they increase discretionary power in the middle and lower levels and encourage diversity, also disperse power and control. Organizations where risk is unacceptable, where there is the need for a lot of co-ordination or where there is, for whatever reason, a reluctance to delegate, will keep spans of control small and the number of levels high. Box 9.7 sums up the pressures and the findings. Too often, however, the outcome is not dictated by reason but by more earthy considerations; the need to keep an artificial number of levels in order to meet the status requirements of older managers, or the inability of senior managers to co-ordinate and control more than three or four subordinates. The idea of six or seven subordinates as a 'normal' span of control has perhaps crept into our subconscious definition of a manager's role. The world is in fact more interesting and can cope with spans from one to over 100 *depending on the circumstances*.

Box 9.7   Tall or flat?

- The bigger the organization the more levels you need *unless* you increase the spans of control.

- Tall structures and narrow spans restrict responsibility. The Fulton Committee identified departments in the British Civil Service with nine levels and spans of control of two or three.

- Most organizations need only five levels to do the work, the biggest may need seven (say Rowbottom and Bills). Extra levels are more to do with power and overstaffing than efficiency.

- No manager should supervise the work of more than six subordinates whose work interlocks (said Urwick in 1956).

- Sears Roebuck deliberately increased the span of control of store managers so that they would be forced to delegate, which was effective if the work did not interlock.

- Joan Woodward found that hierarchies in general became taller and narrower as technologies moved from unit manufacture to process production, but spans of control at middle-management level were biggest in mass production, where work should be more routine.

- One Japanese bank has over 100 managers reporting to an area manager, but their work does not overlap.

Staff and line is the other hoary old organizational divide, with the staff in theory providing advice and the line having the decision-making responsibility and power. In practice it never worked out like that, and today too many organizations tie themselves into knots trying to work out who is line and who is staff instead of focusing on where different types of decisions should be taken and by whom. In a modern organization, no one is purely operational or purely advisory but everyone is some mix of both, depending on the situation. It would be better for organizations if they dropped the terminology altogether.

3.3   Match of culture and structure

A differentiated organization, it will be recalled from Chapter 7, is one in which the tasks of policy, innovations, crisis and uniformity, or steady-state activities, are carried out by different organizational forms and cultures. In a diverse environment, in a rapidly changing environment, the parts of the organization which interface with the environment, will appropriately be the flexible, power-equalized, task cultures. Appropriately they will be the driving forces of the organization and hold the greater balance of power. In organizational terms, the developmental end of marketing, of production, of research, of personnel and finance will tend to be task cultures. To separate them from the steady-state portions of those same functions they are often given a separate title, frequently including the word 'development', e.g. product development, production development, organization development. In more uniform environments, where there is less pressure for diversity, such departments, if they exist at all, are normally without power and just molluscs attached to the pillars of the temple. Start-up situations, the opening of a new plant, the development of a new market area, or a new product line, the first year of a merger situation, can also be the occasions when diversity should be acknowledged by the creation of a task culture, specifically separated from the requirements of the steady state. These situations are often recognized by the creation of a project team or a task force.

These are the structural forms of task cultures. But although beloved of many theorists and idealists, task cultures appear to be extremely difficult to manage well, particularly when surrounded by other cultures. Perhaps it is that organizations have more experience with the management of steady-state activities, perhaps that, when it comes down to hard reality, people are more role-oriented, more fond of the steady state than they are prepared to admit. The project team or task force, set up for a specific job with a finite end, is perhaps the purest example of a task culture. We might therefore expect to find the problems of adjusting culture to structure at their height in this sort of organization, particularly if it is super-imposed onto a functional or role-orientated organization. Corning Glass, in a deliberate and systematic application of the findings of Lawrence and Lorsch, set up, in one division, a series of project teams to help manage the pressures of diversity. In the process they experienced 'many problems associated with the clash between values and behaviours of bureaucracy and those of project teams'. Allen Hundert of their Organizational Research and Development department categorized their conclusions on the management of project teams after two and a half years' experience under four headings:

1 *Team formation*. Project teams are a waste of resources when a task can be handled effectively through the existing structure. The task should have a beginning and an obvious end so that members can

perceive their progress towards a goal (the 'common enemy'?). If the task has minor impact, little complexity and low priority, it is unlikely that the permanent organization will allocate adequate resources to it. The new team must be protected from the surrounding bureaucratic organization. Clear definition of the scope of the task, allocation of fully competent people who do not need to check back for confirmation, commitment by the interested managers of the permanent organization, all help to give this protection. Team members need to be technically competent but also inter-personally competent, so that the team can work effectively as a group from its earliest days.

2 *External problems*. The individual members can encounter problems with their peers, colleagues or superiors in the permanent organization. The manager in the functional organization may try to control the actions of his or her representatives on the team so that his or her own functional interests are preserved, but the goals of the team distorted. This is really a violation of the formation conditions.

3 *Internal problems*. An early problem is usually that of role clarity. The role of integrator is most confusing for people who are members of project teams for the first time, since that has never been a legitimate role in typical bureaucracies. In addition, problems of trust and confidence inevitably arise. Long-ingrained attitudes and behaviours of inter-departmental competition must be dealt with openly so that these barriers to progress can be avoided. One other internal problem has to do with the need for changing membership. It has to be understood and accepted that, when an individual's skills are no longer needed, he should leave.

4 *Performance evaluation*. When a team member knows that he will be measured according to total team results, his behaviour will be supportive of group goals rather than the sub-goal of his function. A lot, however, depends on how the team defines its task. If a team decides its goal is fruitless, then to admit that, on adequate evidence, must be considered success. Too often, only successful implementation of a possible idea is recognized as achievement, with the result that a lot of effort goes into what all those concerned know to be unlikely to achieve success.

In the matrix organization, the project team is permanently cemented into the structural skeleton in the form of a product, or regional grouping composed of representatives from the mainstream structure. The cultural clash in a matrix organization will be similar to that experienced by project teams.

To some extent, these kinds of problems will be encountered by any task culture operating in a large organization where the steady state is likely to be traditionally dominant, and the more permanent feature of the organization. We must also remember, however, that even in the best organization there are crises, and the need for the management of breakdown. Here we have seen that a power culture, with norms as distinct from the role culture as those of any project group, will appropriately dominate. Those at the top, too, concerned with policy and the future, with the overall design and climate of the organization, are likely to operate in a different culture. The structural recognition of the policy sector is normally an executive or management committee of some form.

Less often is there any structural recognition of the crisis activities. Sometimes, when the crisis is extreme, an emergency task force is created, e.g. to deal with a threatened strike. More often, breakdown is part of the everyday life of most line managers. Herein lies the rub, for the manager finds that in one role he has to combine two or more activities, perhaps steady state with breakdown – a frequent combination for a works manager. The cultural norms of role and power appropriate to these two activities are incompatible. We shall consider the problems of the manager in dealing with this cultural role incompatibility in Chapter 11. Here we are concerned with the organizational mechanisms for handling a mix of different cultures, the integrating mechanisms.

3.4   The external diversity

'If you want to control it, own it' was the old watchword. Today that gets expensive. If your business is making cakes, do you need to run a transport business and a printing firm as well, or could you let someone else do that for you? If you are contemplating entering the market in Eastern Europe are you better off doing it on your own, or could a partner with local knowledge add some value?

The discussion in this chapter, so far, has concentrated on the structure *within* the organization. Increasingly, however, much of the work is now done outside the organization by people associated with it but not owned or employed by it. These are the new alliances, although, in fact, they have been part of the tradition of many industries for many years and are only now becoming widespread. Publishing, for example, has always relied on outsiders to write the books, on independent retailers to sell them and, usually, on independent printers to print them and has not been averse to joint publications in risky ventures.

The old alliances, with suppliers, consultants, advisers, retailers and agents, were, however, contractual alliances. There is now a new set of strategic alliances with other businesses or organizations who would in the past have been seen as competitors and kept at arm's length. The network of alliances in the motor industry is a good example, where competitors in one market become allies in another, with Volvo linking arms with Renault to produce trucks but competing with its cars.

These alliances are not easy to manage – one study by McKinsey showed that 70 per cent of joint ventures or formal alliances are disbanded or fall short of expectations. None the less, alliances are a favourite way of handling diversity and of sharing the risks of uncertainty. No organization today is an 'island entire unto itself ', to borrow John Donne's phrase about man. Every organization is now a network of other organizations. No discussion of structure can therefore rest content with the inside or the organization.

Box 9.8   The network firm

In 1990 Lithonia Lighting, in Georgia USA, was the world's largest supplier of lighting equipment, but its competitors were catching up fast. Lithonia took a radical re-look at its organization and realized the factory was not, as they assumed, the real hub of the organization; that place belonged to their agents, who were not even employed by them, but who generated all their business. A plan emerged to create a network which would make the agents more efficient and more profitable and break down the barriers between specifiers, suppliers, agents and Lithonia's own factories to the benefit of all.

Computers now link specifiers, agents and factories. Computer-aided design systems allow products to be tailor-made. Distributors can check stock on-line with warehouses and factories and the computers route components for each order direct to the relevant factory. Suppliers are being brought into the network so that stocks can be dramatically reduced if not eliminated.

Lead times on orders were cut from nine days to less than one. Sales and profits doubled over six years. Agents profited too and this bonded them to Lithonia. If, and it can be a big 'if ', the computer systems work as they should, everyone's lives are made easier and everyone does well.

Lithonia has put its diversity outside but manages it from inside.

Reported in *The Economist*, 6 October 1990

Alliances come in three types:

1 *Stakeholder alliances*. These are contractual relationships between
  different parties in the total chain of value-adding. They principally
  involve suppliers of both goods and services. Hitherto these suppliers
  were just that – suppliers. More and more, however, companies are
  seeing them as partners in order to get greater benefit from the
  relationship. Arm's-length trading results in satisfying behaviour,
  acceptable quality at minimum cost. Partnership relationships allow
  the partners to move beyond and above the benchmarks to their
  mutual benefit. The Vice-President of TRW Safety Systems
  summed it up well: 'We want better quality. We want their help in
  reducing our inventories. We want help and ideas about how we can
  improve our final products.'

  Alliances with customers are also possible. Manufacturers are no
  longer just selling the product but are providing the services that go
  with it, moving into their customers' premises to help them make
  their products work for them. It is, after all, only the flip side of the
  supplier contract. Every supplier has a customer contract, helping
  them to manage inventories, rethink product lines and innovate.

  Alliances with employees is another way of thinking about industrial relations, and a potentially more fruitful one than the old adver-
  sarial stance. Single union agreements for new plants are, in effect,
  an alliance to make the best out of the work for both parties.

2 *Consortia alliances*. These are alliances between a group of organizations in the same field who want a common service but are not able
  or willing to do it themselves. Trade Associations are the oldest and
  the loosest of the alliances but are often of limited value. At the
  other end of the scale are the pre-competitive research alliances of
  some high-technology companies who pool their resources for basic
  research. In 1985 there were over 40 of these research consortia in
  the United States. There are also selling consortia, insurance consortia and consortia of the sort that back research projects at universities or business schools.

3 *Joint ventures*. These are the newest and the most prolific of alliances. Over 800 new joint ventures were started in Europe in the
  first half of 1989, and the pace shows no sign of slackening. New
  markets, e.g. in Eastern Europe, or new technologies e.g. advanced
  aluminium designs, are the main spurs to those alliances, encouraging alluminium firms, for example, to ally themselves with motor
  manufacturers to develop the aluminium car. Typically, technology
  allies itself with the market, as when Pepsi Cola's pizza-making skills

linked up with Whitbread's knowledge of the British food and drink market to form Pizza Hut in the UK.

Alliances are a way of organizing work, and diversity *outside* the company. They are, however, partnerships of equals not relationships of masters and servants. The distinction is important.

Box 9.9   Corporate marriages

Richard Walker and Andrew Tank have categorized alliances as 'marriages'.

The conventional couple. She stays home; he goes to the office (or vice versa) . . . or in corporate terms, each of the alliance partners performs a separate but complimentary task.

The career couple. She goes out to work; so does he. Both companies compete but collaborate in certain areas. Air France and Lufthansa merged their service functions of reservations, maintenance and training but competed for customers and routes.

The odd couple. Opposite temperaments but a cause in common. A large US pharmaceutical manufacturer, American Cyanamid, linked up with Celltech in the UK who were researching monoclonal antibodies but needed backing.

Just good friends. A career couple who do not have the time or wish to get married. In corporate terms, competitors who set boundaries to their competition and collaborate within strict limits.

Shotgun weddings. Marriage happened because an outsider is threatening. The Belgian Bank Generale and the Dutch Amro started to merge to fend off takeover but pulled out before it was finalized when the takeover threat disappeared.

---

4   The design of the job

4.1

Even if the design of the total organization is beyond his grasp, every manager or supervisor has some responsibility for the design of the jobs under their control. The scope of the job, the degree of responsibility or control kept by the individual, their participation in discussions and decisions, the methods of supervision and control, are all issues that need to be considered. The issues usually come to the surface under the headings of *job enlargement*, *participation* and *delegation*. Each of these merits some discussion, to highlight some of the dilemmas and to lead to a better understanding of when and where they are appropriate.

4.2   Job enlargement

The theories and practices of job enlargement are in large part a reaction against what has been called the micro-division of labour, or the industrial engineering approach to work. They are also examples of deliberate attempts to implement some assumptions about the motivation to work. Let us first examine the rationale that underlies the micro-division of labour approaches:

1 If jobs are broken down into their smallest elements, unskilled people can do them with little training. Workers are therefore less indispensable as individuals and cannot dictate to management.
2 If jobs are broken down, and training times are low, the work-force is more interchangeable. If a worker is sick, gets fired or just does not show up, production will still continue.
3 The personnel department of one US automobile plant explained that a 70 per cent turnover on their assembly line did not bother them because they had so defined the jobs that anyone off the street could be taught a job in one and a half hours.
4 A high degree of mechanization means that the worker will not get physically tired, and can therefore work long shifts.
5 Standardization of jobs would seem to ensure better control of quality, particularly when allied to mechanical pacing, as on an assembly line. If a man is only doing one operation he is likely to become more expert in it, and do it better, than if he is required to carry out a variety of tasks.
6 If jobs are closely defined and machine-paced, production will be more predictable and more easily controlled by management. The supervisor is better able to control a number of simple and well-defined operations than a small number of complex tasks where the worker might be more knowledgeable than the supervisor.

On the other side of the coin, it has been argued and often demonstrated, that:

1 The micro-division of labour induces fatigue, boredom, distraction, accidents and anxieties. The indirect costs of these things are reflected in spoilage, absenteeism and staff turnover.

2 The true costs of monotony come in very high wages for low skill levels, high incidence of strikes and wastage.

3 Moderately complicated tasks resist interruption and generate psychological impulses towards their own completion.

4 People, unlike most machines, work more efficiently at a variable than at a constant rate.

5 When work is minutely subdivided the individual feels that the simplification of the work is some reflection on himself.

6 Minute sub-division inhibits the worker from identifying her contribution with the end product. She will not therefore take any autonomous action to correct obvious deficiencies.

7 Excessive specialization reduces the opportunity for social contact or team-work. Long periods of unrelieved social isolation are hard for most individuals to tolerate.

When variety is lacking, employees will often find ways of providing it. In automobile assembly-lines, the game of making anagrams out of the letters of the model name was well-established. In mass-production activities, individuals will break up the assignment into manageable segments (e.g. I will do 500 boxes and then have a break). Social groups, trivial games or rituals are used to break up the monotony. Spanners in the lines, wildcat strikes, unpredictable absenteeism, are often means of providing a necessary variety. A frequent problem for designers in mass-production industries is to make products assembly-line proof. In addition, it is claimed that a well-designed job should:

1 Allow the individual some scope for setting his own standards regarding quantity and quality.

2 Allow the individual to have some control over the ancillary and preparatory stages so that she does not have to suffer from others' mistakes.

3 Allow for interlocking tasks and job rotation where there is a necessary interdependence between jobs, or a high degree of personal stress, as with danger or noise or isolation.

4 Allow for scope for comments and recommendations by the worker on any re-design.

5 Provide for feedback on performance to the individual.

Based on these assumptions, company-wide schemes of job-enrichment have been instituted, and well documented, in a wide variety of organizations, including IBM, Philips, Volvo, Shell, to mention only the most well-known. Advantages claimed for these and other instances include in one analysis:

Increase in job satisfaction (22%);
Decrease in costs (22%);
Increase in quality of work (17%);
Increase in quantity of output (15%);
Decrease in monotony (14%);
Other (4%);
Not ascertained (8%).

Several organizations have experimented with the abandonment or partial abandonment of the assembly line, substituting for it assembly stations, where one employee, or a group of employees, assembles a whole or a substantial part of the product. An electronics firm, for instance, that manufactured measuring instruments on an assembly line turned over to unit production. Each worker was given a whole instrument to assemble. In many cases this represented a week's work for one employee. When she finished the assembly work, the employee tested the instrument, signed it and sent it to the customer. The employee was also personally responsible for correcting any problems that might cause the instrument to be sent back to the factory. It took about six months for the workers to learn the skills necessary to assemble the instruments. In the long term, production went up very slightly, but, more important from their point of view, quality was very high without the need for inspection and quality control experts, absenteeism and turnover went down to low levels, production flexibility was greatly increased and the job satisfaction of the employees was higher.

This is a rather dramatic instance of job enrichment, although it has been repeated, with similar results, in at least a score of other reported cases. Job enrichment does not have to be such a *volte-face* in working arrangements to achieve some of the results listed above.

What can we conclude about all this? Is job enrichment *de rigueur* for the modern company? There are some general conclusions, but also some caveats and distinctions, to be drawn:

1 Micro-division of labour can easily create a self-fulfilling prophecy. Monotony can lead to boredom, apathy and frustration so that the tight control and prescribed operations become necessary even if they were not so at the outset.
2 Organizations would, therefore, be well-advised to take the monotony out of jobs, for monotony is costly. To reduce people to extensions of machines cannot ultimately be right or profitable. A large proportion of the work-force will do much the same job for the whole of their working life. Even if they do not seek for self-actualization at work, they may at least expect variety.

Box 9.10   Turning people on to work

Pasmore, in 1984, reviewed all the studies of job-enrichment, along with those which concentrated on data feedback in which information is collected from employees regarding the state of the organization and is then used in collaborative problem-solving, and those studies which involved sociotechnical interventions, which adapt the technology of the organization and bend the way work is organized to meet the needs of employees. He concluded:

1 There is no guarantee that involving employees or increasing their motivation will lead to improved performance. Other variables have their effects, including the ability of the employee and the design of work.
2 Turning people on to work requires their involvement in decision-making regarding changes in the work itself.
3 Trying to change motivation or performance by changing one thing at a time usually changes nothing. To improve an organization's performance the whole organization needs to change.
4 Often, the major problem is not employee resistance but *managerial* resistance to creating the conditions needed to allow employees to achieve success.

Pasmore, in Kolb (ed.), *Organizational Psychology*, 1984

3 Even those who want their jobs enriched will expect to be rewarded with more than job satisfaction. Job enrichment is not a cheap way to greater productivity. Its pay-off will come in the less visible costs of morale, climate and working relationships.
4 Bavelas and Strauss told of a treatment in which women were given control of their own conveyor belt, resulting in a phenomenal production increase, and no loss of quality. This unique programme disintegrated, however, because the experimental group began to make much more money than the others. To avoid embarrassment management cancelled the 'learning bonus'. The assembly line reverted to its previous speed and within a month six of the eight women had left.
5 Not everyone is capable of doing an enlarged job. Selection systems based on minimum criteria for the unenlarged job may severely restrict the possibility of schemes for job enrichment. Under job enrichment, selection and placement generally come to assume more importance.
6 To increase responsibility, without decreasing the monotony, is an undesirable form of job enlargement. Automation has thrown up a

number of jobs which essentially consist in watching a dial but with high consequences if deviations are not acted upon. The burden of responsibility linked to the strain of monotony can be stressful.

7 Job enlargement is not a once-for-all process. It needs constant self-renewal. We humans are often stimulated by variety. We seek to reduce it to order and system; having done so, we get bored by the routine. Children having mastered a new game are bored with it. Airline pilots make demands for more precise regulations, only to find that systematization takes the fun out of the job.

In general, however, although there are pitfalls in any programme for job enrichment, the pressures are inexorable in the long term. The work role forms such a key part of the physical and psychological world of the average individual that we continually seek for more opportunities to realize part of our identity in our work. Rising levels of education can only hasten this trend. These inexorable pressures are beginning to have their effect on technology and may ultimately spell the end to the assembly line and mass production. For it has been suggested (Lawler) that in a continuum from unit, through mass, to process production or automation, the trends will be to move to one end or the other, as set out in Figure 12.

Figure 12

4.3 Participation

Participation is sometimes regarded as a form of job enlargement. At other times it is a way of gaining commitment by workers to some proposal on the grounds that, if you have been involved in discussing it, you will be more interested in its success. In part, it is the outcome of an almost cultural belief in the norms of democratic leadership. It is one of those 'good' words with which it is hard to disagree. Box 9.14 describes the work of an extremely participative group, an 'autonomous work group' as it has been labelled. Much of the discussion on leadership and the workings of groups in Part One has been to do with participation, participation in the job, that is, not participation in its broader sense of 'industrial democracy'.

As with many of the precepts of management, it is worth considering the consequences of doing the opposite, in this case of 'no participation'.

It is, for instance, psychologically true that people like to have some say in their own destiny, some control over the facts that affect them. To use the territorial metaphor, an individual likes to be master in his own house. If this wish is denied, if the landlord exercises his legal right to paint the wall some obnoxious colour, the tenant may be forced to accept the situation, but he will be less likely to protect those walls, to guard them from damage. In psychological terms, he will respond with compliance rather than identification or internalization.

The compliance mode of response, it will be recalled, requires continual maintenance and will usually elicit only satisficing behaviour, behaviour sufficient to fulfil the minimum requirements of the contract. 'No participation', therefore, in issues that concern an individual's psychological territory will lead to compliance at best, often, if the action is perceived as territorial violation, to non-compliance or covert rebellion. Nor must one forget the very practical point that the ideas and knowledge of the man directly involved may be very valuable – the tenant can know more about the house than the landlord.

A denial of participation to an individual, in decisions that he perceives as affecting him, can carry its costs. However, this does not imply that the opposite is always true, i.e. that 'participation is good'. The general criteria for the use of participation methods, summarized from Part One, are:

1 The invitation to participate must be genuine. Any feeling by subordinates that participation is but genuflection at the altar of democracy when the decision has already been taken will produce a 'compliance' response. An invitation to participate in a redundancy problem when he knows he will lose his job regardless of what he may contribute will only result in a credibility gap.
2 The problem must be worth the time and the effort in the eyes of all concerned. Participation takes time and consumes energies. If the issue or the task is trivial, or foreclosed, and everyone realizes it, participative methods will boomerang. Issues that do not affect the individuals concerned will not, on the whole, engage their interest. Similarly, if a work group does not have effective control of the factors determining its output, e.g. the speed of the line is

pre-set, or a prior shift sets up the machine, then participation within such reduced limits will seem meaningless.

3 The 'contract' must be clear. If the 'group' is asked for a decision then that decision must be accepted. If advice only is required then this should be stated.

4 The individuals concerned must have the skills and the information to enable them to participate effectively.

Box 9.11   The effects of participation – the classic studies

Bavelas worked with a group of women performing a sewing operation on a group incentive basis. He selected one group whose production averaged 74 units hourly. He asked them to set their own production goal. After considerable discussion, they agreed unanimously on a goal of 84 units hourly, which they exceeded within five days. A goal of 95, set at a later meeting, could not be met. The goal was then reduced to the relatively permanent level of 90 units. During the next several months, the group's output averaged about 87 units.[1]

At the Harwood Manufacturing Company, Virginia, in the 1940s, producing men's pyjamas, shorts and children's blouses, a controlled experiment on the introduction of changed working methods was conducted by Coch and French. Three types of group were formed – (i) a 'no-participation' group of eighteen hand-pressers, (ii) a 'participation through representation' group of thirteen pyjama folders, and (iii) a 'total participation' group of fifteen pyjama examiners. In each case the planning of the job-process change was handled in the manner indicated. The findings showed that 'total participation' groups re-learned their jobs most quickly; 'participation through representation' re-learned more slowly; and 'no-participation' groups generally failed to achieve their previous production standards.[2]

The Scanlon Plan is a formal attempt at worker-participation. Workers participate in this system by making suggestions and sequentially meeting to discuss and evaluate the ideas which could yield higher production. Departmental committees may put those ideas into action, as may lower-level supervisors. Higher level committees are instituted to evaluate plant-wide improvements. Savings are shared by all unit members where a change is made.[3]

Although there are exceptions, particularly with very large organizations, most evaluations have attested to the significant technical and economic advantages of Scanlon type schemes.

1 Quoted by Norman Marci in H. Miffin, *Psychology in Industry*, 1946
2 Described by Coch and French 'Overcoming resistance to change', *Human Relations*, 1948
3 The Scanlon Plan is described by Lesieur in *The Scanlon Plan*, 1958

5 Lastly, and perhaps most important, the manager must want participation and not indulge in it because he feels he ought to.

Given these conditions, participation will tend to result in increased
commitment from the individuals – a feeling of 'ownership' in the
process. That which one 'owns' one cares for, and invests in. Those
studies of particular applications of participation (some of them summarized in Box 9.11) that met the conditions produced increased contributions. Studies on participation as a general style of management
have been inconclusive – because, it is argued, the conditions listed
would only apply spasmodically, the style was not always the 'best fit'.

Box 9.12   The delegated letters

Jim, newly fired with enthusiasm for job enlargement, felt that he must
practise it on his only subordinate – his secretary. By the nature of his
work, Jim, a consultant, was usually in his office only in the morning of
every second day. During this period, he planned his activities, dictated
letters and signed those that had been typed during the previous two
days. It occurred to him that if he asked his secretary to sign the letters
in his place, (a) the letters would not have to wait two days for signature,
or up to five days if an alteration was required, (b) he would not have
to spend a considerable amount of time in the morning re-reading his
own dictation.

He therefore approached his secretary, Rosemary, with the suggestion
that once he had dictated the letters, she should type them, sign them
and send them off without any further reference to him. At first, Rosemary was a little reluctant – the thought of the increased responsibility,
no check on her mistakes, worried her. However, after thinking about
it, she agreed that it would add a more interesting element to her work
and would undoubtedly be more efficient.

The next day, Tuesday, Jim dictated his letters as usual. On Thursday
morning he was in the office again. This time the normal folder of letters
to be signed was not there awaiting him, and he felt an initial surge of
irritation at Rosemary's inefficiency until he remembered their agreement. He dictated Thursday's letters as usual, Rosemary made no comment about the new system and Jim decided to leave things alone for a
bit. But all that day, he felt strangely naked. Did Tuesday's letters get
done, he wondered, did they get typed accurately – one of them was
really rather important.

Late that evening, after the office had shut, he crept into Rosemary's
office, opened the files and checked the copies of the letters he had
dictated and she had signed.

Although participation in particular situations may always be appropriate, as a general approach to management it is best suited to 'task cultures'.

4.4   Delegation

Delegation is another of those 'good' words; one cannot, it is generally felt, have enough of it; managers, when questioned, feel they ought to do more of it and wish they got more of it from their superiors. What are the problems? Is there any better understanding that we can gain of this important part of job design?

The essence of the delegation problem lies in the trust-control dilemma. The dilemma is that in any one managerial situation, the sum of trust + control is always constant. The trust is the trust that the subordinate feels that the manager has in him. The control is the control that the manager has over the work of the subordinate. The implications of this constant sum are that:

(a) Any increase in the control exercised by the manager decreases the amount of trust perceived by the subordinate (control + x = trust − x);
(b) Any wish by the manager to increase her trust in her subordinate, i.e. to give him more responsibility, must be accompanied by a release of some control if it is to be believed (trust + x = control − x).

The dilemma is illustrated by the little story in Box 9.12. Control costs money, but trust is risky. This is another aspect of the dilemma. To monitor, check or control the work of the subordinate requires the time of the supervisor, along with the time and energy of those who compile figures and records for use in the control procedures. Furthermore, where a control mechanism exists, the tendency is for the subordinate to rely on it – i.e. to push things to the limit in the expectation that if he pushes them too far he will be pulled back. (For example, if there are limits on promotional expenses to be paid to sales agents, a salesman will be tempted to spend up to the limit rather than exercise his judgement on each case; a secretary will rely on her boss to do the final proof-reading of her letters; the subordinate will check his proposed course of action with his superior.) This tendency to rely on the control mechanism will help to perpetuate it as the superior finds that she has to use it, unaware that a self-fulfilling prophecy has been at work.

Trust, on the other hand, is cheap. Trust leaves the superior free to do other things; trust, if given and accepted, breeds responsibility and obviates the need for controls, as the controls become, in a sense, self-administered (the secretary refers the letters she is worried about to her boss, the salesman consults his manager in doubtful cases). But trust is risky, for the superior is held accountable for things that others did, even if they did them in ways she would not herself have chosen. Trust can be misplaced, trust can be abused. And since trust means the absence of superior-administered controls, trust can leave the superior feeling naked and a little lonely ('What are they all up to, I wonder'), like an anxious mother when the children are mysteriously quiet.

True delegation, effective delegation, is delegation with trust and with only the necessary minimum of controls. But trust is hard to give, for:

1 To give trust, the superior has to have confidence in the subordinate to do the job. This is easier if she has prior experience of his work and capacity, or if she has selected him herself – it is difficult with new or unknown subordinates.
2 Like a leap into the dark, trust must be given if it is to be received. This is not as trite as it may sound. If a superior wishes to get the benefits from trust, she must initiate the process, give trust and release control and then sit back and wait. If proved wrong, she can withdraw the trust and replace the controls. It is hard for the subordinate to initiate the process, although long acquaintance is often the basis for trust.
3 Trust is a fragile commodity. Like glass, once shattered, it is never the same again. The subordinate must always live up to the trust invested in him if that trust is to continue. The superior cannot withdraw the trust except by explicit agreement in specific circumstances.
4 Trust must be reciprocal. It is no good the superior trusting her subordinates if they do not trust her.

The proper amount of delegation, the proper blend of trust and control, will depend on the situation – the degree of risk, the skill and experience of the subordinates, the self-confidence of the superior, the pressures she feels from above. But delegation is made easier if:

1 The superior is allowed to select or at least approve her key subordinates, and they have some say in her appointment. (Sometimes found in task and power cultures, seldom in role cultures.)
2 The territory of trust is clearly defined for each individual, and is not violated. The individual must have full control within those limits.

(Unclear territorial boundaries lead to misapprehensions, e.g. 'I thought I had discretion to . . .')

3 There is control of ends, not means. Control of results, i.e. after the event, is not a violation of trust; control of means, i.e. during the event, can be. This implies that results can be determined and are known to the subordinate as well as to his superior.

In the light of this discussion of trust and control, it is possible to see why it is that management by objectives *should* work well but so often fails. Management by objectives at its best is:

(a) An agreed definition of the territory of trust;
(b) An agreed specification of desired results;
(c) A programme for action initiated by the subordinate.

Add to the considerations of trust and control what we know about the motivation calculus and the connection between objectives and performance, namely that:

1 The higher the objectives, the stronger the pull, provided that the individual feels they are attainable.
2 The more the individual is involved in setting the objectives, the more likely is he to feel they are his and to be committed to them.
3 If rewards are tied to performance against objectives, the individual will set the grade low in order to be sure of attaining the rewards.
4 In order to check that his calculus was right, he needs knowledge of results, i.e. feedback.

If any MBO scheme meets all these desiderata it becomes a useful mechanism for delegation and improving performance. If, however, it is used either:

(a) as a way of imposing targets on people;
(b) of controlling means rather than ends (e.g. hours at work, relationships with staff, method of organizing work);
(c) to award merit increments,

then the scheme will tend to be perceived as a control mechanism and as indicating low levels of trust. It may well result in *reduced* performance or at least in lower than optimum performance.

4.5   Autonomous work groups

Autonomous work groups are a practical application to a whole group of a blend of participation and delegation. The conditions of both will apply. When the conditions are met, the results can be dramatic, as demonstrated decades ago, in Britain, in the Durham Coal Mining Studies (Box 9.13). There is, however, some doubt as to how long the effects will last. The results obtained at Hawthorne, for instance, were not maintained. In another study, at Ahmadabad, there was a major change in managerial strategy after four years. It could be that the sense of experiencing a new way of working, of being the focus of managerial and research attention, may generate much of the improvement in morale and output (the Hawthorne effect). More likely, some of the conditions will cease to be met over time. For instance:

1 The ways of working and the standard outputs may become so standardized that participation in deciding on them is no longer sensible or the task is no longer complex enough to merit the investment of so much 'E'. Complexity is resolved by systematization and we then lose interest. (Participation, condition 2.)

2 The group leaders may not have the required skills to be representatives and co-ordinators rather than commanders. (Participation, condition 4.)

3 The contract is changed without explicit recognition of the fact, e.g. new constraints are placed on their work as the quality of raw material is changed, or customer requirements are tightened, or time limits and quality tolerances are raised without the group being consulted or involved. (Participation, conditions 3 and 5.)

4 The membership of the group may change and the newcomers have no wish to participate. (Participation, condition 5.)

5 The management may change and the new management have no real trust in the group's ability to set its own standards, and will in consequence start to check its procedures. (Delegation, condition 1.)

6 The group has one conspicuous failure. (Delegation, condition 3.)

7 Results are not made known to the group, or the task is re-defined so that clear measures of the group's performance are no longer possible. (Delegation, condition 7.)

The overall risk with autonomous work groups is that they will come to set norms and objectives that do not match those of the organization. The power of the group to determine the behaviour and attitudes of its individual members has already been seen, and although the reported studies always describe groups where there is a synchronization of group and organization goals, there is clearly a possibility that the groups might misappropriate the trust and the relaxation of control. The 'leap in the dark' element of delegation, the willingness to give

Box 9.13   The Durham studies

Eric Trist and his colleagues were able, in the Durham coal mines, to study the results of two different forms of work design in the same place and with the same technology over a period of two years. The first system was the conventional Longwall organization, a semi-mechanized system involving automatic coal-cutters and a conveyor-belt for loading the coal. A single face of up to 200 yards could be worked in place of the many short faces under the old hand-got system with groups of two or three men per shift. There were forty men divided over three shifts in the Longwall system. The men were assigned to a specific task group with liaison between the groups carried out by supervisors. Delays on one group or shift would then affect other groups and subsequent shifts. Each group was paid separately.

The second system, which Trist called the 'Composite system', incorporated many features of the old small-group hand-got methods. The men were multi-skilled and moved from role to role. The group accepted responsibility for the deployment of its members. There was also rotation over shifts, so that no man was pinned to a particular shift or task. Payment was on an overall output basis for the whole group of forty and divided up by them, usually in equal amounts.

The different outcomes were as follows:

	Conventional system	Composite system
productive achievement (% of coal face potential)	78.00	95.00
ancillary work at face (percentage hours per shift)	1.32	0.03
percentage of shifts with cycle lag	69.00	5.00
absenteeism (% of possible shifts)		
no reason given	4.3	0.4
sickness or other	8.9	4.6
accident	6.8	3.2
total	20.00	8.2

Reported in Trist, Murray, Pollock, *Organizational Choice*, 1963

away control and rely on trust, is much more difficult where groups rather than individuals are concerned. The stimulus of the initial complexity can wear off all too quickly and the participation become a chore rather than a challenge. Management then begins to introduce controls, trust is correspondingly withdrawn, and the experiment with autonomy breaks down.

Box 9.14 The autonomous group

The inside of the plant looked less like a factory than a warehouse full of machines and desks deposited haphazardly. Equipment, people and the odd potted plant seemed randomly scattered about the cavernous 10,000 square foot building. There was even a volley-ball net at one end.

Wendy Fox of the Boston Globe was describing her visit to a plant of 180 people producing printed circuit board modules on the 'team management' approach. Instead of working on a conventional assembly line there were ten teams of 18 people who were responsible for receiving the raw materials, assembling the boards and shipping the finished materials, organizing the work as they saw fit.

The workers set their own hours, planned their own schedules, checked their own work and took team responsibility for each board There were no time clocks, no security guards, no quality controllers and every employee had a key to the building.

The plant manager said that the new way of working had reduced the time needed to assemble one board by 40 per cent, had reduced scrap by half and had doubled the number of perfectly working modules.

But he added that the system is not for eveyone, 'It's threatening. We don't need as many people, and instead of getting better at what you're good at, you get better by adding to what you have.' Or, as one consultant put it less positively, 'it really isn't much of an enrichment if what you do is wash the spoons on Monday and the glassware on Tuesday.'

Reported in Morgan, *Creative Organization Theory*, 1989

5 Summary and implications

5.1

We have examined the *design of the structure* and recognized the need to achieve a balance between the pressures for uniformity of standardization, and those of diversity. As in Chapter 7, the general conclusion was that a structurally differentiated organization, sometimes but not always decentralized, would normally be required. The problems of the *management of diversity* were discussed, the need to fit culture to structure, to decide on the balance and location of power, and to manage the *outside diversity*. Within the scope of the individual manager was the *design of the job* and, in particular, the possibilities and problems of job enrichment, participation and delegation.

Box 9.15   Quality circles

Quality circles were invented in the United States in the 1950s as a practical example of a creative autonomous group. They were exported to Japan and re-imported to Europe and America thirty years later. It is estimated that one out of every nine Japanese workers is involved in a quality circle.

A quality circle is a *voluntary* group of workers with a shared area of responsibility. They meet together, usually weekly, in company time on company premises to discuss their quality problems. They analyse causes, suggest solutions and take appropriate action.

The process is not automatic. The groups usually have to be helped to learn how to do it. Communication skills, measurement techniques and problem-solving strategies need to be built into a learning programme for them.

Those companies that use them do so a lot. It would not be unusual to have over a hundred quality circles in a large organization.

Then, most importantly, the management has to take them seriously, to implement their recommendations or explain why not. To ignore a quality circle is to kill it.

5.2   Implications

Most of the particular implications have been spelt out in the individual sections. A couple of general reflections remain:

1 As organizations grow in size, as multi-nationals proliferate, the problems of integration multiply along with its costs, and so apparently do the felt pressures for uniformity. There is no clear evidence that bigness is best, although in some capital-intensive industries, bigness may be necessary. Most of the giants in size are well down in the profitability table. One wonders whether the pressures for uniformity are really there, whether diversity and differentiation might not be given a freer hand. Management sophistication can be too highly valued, as organizations take as much pride in their systems as in their results. Perversely, organization theory would suggest that more trust and less control, more diversity and less uniformity, more differentiation and less systematization might be the ways that organizations should move.

2 The long lists of conditions that attend success in the enlargement of jobs, in delegation, in the general area of making work more challenging and exciting, may well be enough to put off even the most determined idealist. This would be a pity. Although not all

people will seek to achieve their full self-concept through the medium of their work, yet most of us spend most of our conscious lives at work. If this work can be made more exciting, if the organization can simultaneously benefit in terms of reduced absenteeism and staff turnover, if the individual can earn more for increased productivity and the organization requires fewer people for more output, all must in the longer term benefit.

But, too often, the ideas of participation, job enrichment, delegation and autonomy raise false hopes in men and manager. Disillusionment can breed cynics on both sides. It is right that the difficulties, that the conditions for success, be understood. We must remember that we are pulled by the alternating desires for complexity and simplicity so that enriched jobs become reduced to simplicity and so become monotonous once more. There is no standing still, only a constant need to take two steps forward in case we have to take one back. But let anyone who finds this daunting at least concentrate on removing the negative aspects of work. The monotony, the stress, the unnecessary ambiguity, double-checking and concern with the means can be reduced to some extent in all activities. With them will go the costs of low morale, high staff turnover and absenteeism. Herzberg, in pursuit of optimum motivation, might call this working on the hygiene rather than the motivating factors. But many an organization needs to reflect that, even if they can't turn all their horses into champions, they can at least clean the stables out.

10 ► On Politics and Change

1 Introduction

1.1

Organizations are not machines, even though some of those running them would dearly like them to be so. They are communities of people, and therefore behave just like other communities. They compete amongst themselves for power and resources, there are differences of opinion and of values, conflicts of priorities and of goals. There are those who want to change things and those who would willingly settle for a quiet life. There are pressure groups and lobbies, cliques and cabals, rivalries and contests, clashes of personality and bonds of alliance.

It would be odd if it were not so, and foolish of anyone to pretend that in some ideal world those differences would not exist. Indeed, those differences are probably essential if the community is going to continue to adapt to the world around it, to change, in other words, and to go on changing or developing for ever. Change is a necessary condition of survival, be we individuals or organizations, and differences are a necessary ingredient in that change, that never-ending search for improvement. The challenge for the manager is to harness the energy and thrust of the differences so that the organization does not disintegrate but develops. Without politics we would never change and without change we would wither and die.

We should not be surprised, therefore, to find that dealing with differences takes up the largest single chunk of managerial time and energy and that it is not always well done at the end of it. Asked to describe their biggest problem over the last few weeks, the managers in one study did not list a decision but, in every case, a relationship that was not working or an interaction that had not gone well.

In another study it was found that:
(a) 87 per cent of middle managers felt that conflicts were very seldom coped with, and that, when they were, the attempts were inadequate;
(b) 65 per cent thought that the most important unsolved problem of

the organization was the inter-group rivalries, the lack of co-operation and poor communications;

(c) 53 per cent said that if they could alter one aspect of their superior's behaviour it would be to help them see the dog-eat-dog communications problems in middle-management.

These sorts of reply imply that differences have degenerated into conflict instead of into competition, into bad not good politics. The argument of this chapter will be that competition is useful and beneficial, conflict damaging and harmful. The trick must be to stop competition degenerating into conflict and to turn conflict, wherever possible, into competition. This is particularly difficult when the conflict is about power when it becomes politics. It is only after understanding the differences between good competition and damaging conflict that one can begin to channel the differences to create useful change.

To 'manage change' is wishful thinking, implying as it does that one not only knows where to go and how to get there but can persuade everyone else to travel there. To 'cultivate change' is something different, suggesting an attitude of growth, of channelling rather than controlling, of learning not instruction. A changing organization is one that uses differences to grow better, that treats politics as a bonus and people as individuals who are rightly different and usefully different.

This chapter will therefore look in turn at *competition* and *conflict*, at the *causes* and *tactics* of conflict turned politics, at the beneficial *strategies* for turning conflict into change and, finally, at the problems of *channelling change*, so that differences can be a positive advantage.

2   Competition

2.1   The positive features

(a) *Competition sets standards.* An economist in one East European government was once asked why they were building a second petro-chemical complex in their relatively small country when economies of scale in that industry would have suggested one larger complex. He replied that they had come to realize that it was often cheaper to suffer the diseconomies of smaller size, in order to arrive at appropriate standards for productivity and effectiveness by comparison with a competitor. Without competition such standards had to be set unilaterally by the central government. In a complex technology with no basis for comparison, this was not possible. By allowing competition, and basing their standards on the best performance, they obtained reliable standards and cut down the central bureaucracy, more than offsetting the lost economies of scale.

One of the most difficult tasks for any manager at any level is to set appropriate standards – for output, cost, effort, efficiency. A basis for comparison is needed. Without competition the only basis often available is last year's figures. Too often, these figures were not good enough in the first place; too often, there are too many reasons to discard them as bases for standards. Competition, even at the cost of distorting the rational structure, may be the economic thing to do.

(b) *Competition stimulates and channels energies.* Groups and teams benefit from competition. Within each competing group:

Members identify more closely with the group, forget their individual differences and accept a common objective;
The climate of the group becomes more task-centred with less concern for the individual's psychological needs;
The group becomes more highly structured, more 'organized';
The group demands more loyalty and support from its members, more purposeful activity.
The group is encouraged to be more creative and innovative.

Competition gives a common sense of purpose to a group which helps to channel their energies in a common direction; it may change their psychological contract by raising the salience of the group and the task, thereby releasing more effort and energy in total.

Competition can lend stimulation to both groups and individuals. Sport is more exciting when there is the challenge of competition. Competition can be a way of testing oneself, of discovering new sources of talent or energy. It is often at the heart of change, both social and personal, since it can be the spur to higher levels of activity. Ardrey regards competition and the common enemy of the environment as the very basis for fellowship and goodwill.

(c) *Competition sorts out.* This is the most obvious feature of competition. It sorts out the better from the worse. The whole system of market economics relies on competition to sort out the good producers from the bad, the efficient from the less efficient. More and more organizations are beginning to resemble market-places in which different suppliers or advisers compete for contracts. Even within the organization different teams or project groups may be asked to compete for new product ideas (see Box 10.5); that way the organization can feel more sure that it has the best idea and not just a satisfactory one.

2.2   The pre-condition

In every competition there are, at first glance, going to be more losers than winners. Were that to happen the benefits of setting standards, stimulating energy and sorting out the best would be more than offset by the disaffection of the losers. This need not happen. It all depends upon whether the competition is open or closed.

Box 10.1   Marathons or horse races

The popularity of the marathon in recent years may be due to the fact that, unlike a horse race, everyone who finishes feels a winner. Every runner is racing against themselves setting a new personal best. There are, indeed, overall winners and winners of particular categories. These overall winners set the ultimate standards and give credibility to the race but every marathon is truly a race which everyone wins, unlike a horse race, in which only the first three count and the rest are 'also-rans'. It is interesting, too, that the waiting public bet on the horses but support the marathon-runners with promises of donations to their charities, another open-ended competition.

Closed competition is sometimes called zero-sum competition. One person wins at the expense of the other. There is one contract up for tender, one bidder only can win. There is one cake for shares in which all parties are seeking, but one party can only increase his share at the expense of the others.

Open competition occurs when there is no finite amount, when there is competition but not out of a fixed amount. All parties can increase their gains, get more cake. If one party gets more cake than another it was not at the other's expense. There was enough cake, or even infinite cake, for all parties to garner as much as they were able.

Closed competition leads to bargains or what have been called 'distributive' relationships. Closed competition in organizations, e.g competition for fixed and finite resources, is more likely to degenerate into conflict than open competition, e.g. when money is available for all new investments that yield a given rate of return.

In most situations, looked at objectively, the competition *could* be open, the game *could* be looked at in such a way that ultimately there *could* be more cake for everyone. In most situations, however, the parties concerned seem determined to regard it as closed competition. Why is this?

Partly because to regard competition as open often requires a long time-horizon, and the assumption of collaborative rather than conflict behaviour from your competitors. In the short term the cake is fixed. To increase the cake means collaborating in the short term. Partly it happens because it is easier to see who has won in closed competition, and, to a lot of people, winning is more important than what is won.

In the end, it matters not whether the game is objectively and in reality, open or closed, infinite or zero-sum. What matters is the perception of the competing parties. This results in a chicken and egg situation. Open competition leads to healthy collaborative competition. But without collaborative attitudes to begin with, open competition is unlikely to occur. (The apparent self-defeating tactics of managements and unions in some labour negotiations can often be understood in this light.)

Open competition, therefore, can be used to channel energies, set standards, and to differentiate. Competition for resources and facilities need not degenerate into conflict. Competition for promotion, recognition or rewards need not become harmful conflict. But for competition to be fully productive, three conditions have to be met:

1 It has to be perceived as genuinely open, i.e. everyone can ultimately win, there is enough cake for all. (See Box 10.1.)
2 The rules and procedure for arbitration must be seen to be fair and adequate. No one is likely to be collaborative if the umpire is biased or the rules unknown.
3 The major determinants of success in the competition must be under the control of the competitors. They must have only themselves to blame if they fail.

If these conditions are not met, then the competition will be seen as closed, i.e. win-lose, or unfair, or both. In which case a competitor will either:

(a) Resort to the tactics of conflict if the prize is worth winning; or
(b) Withdraw, i.e. competition will not have generated more energy.

The benefits of competition will still tend to occur, but they will now carry with them the costs of conflict or of withdrawal. Desirably, the fruits of competition should be gathered without their costs.

It is reasonably difficult in most organizations to meet the conditions for fruitful competition. Only in a low-technology, diversified 'task' organization under conditions of rapid growth and plentiful resources are they likely to be met in full. In most organizations there are not unlimited resources or opportunities, nor can individual groups have full control over the variables that affect their success. For instance, the technology may dictate that they receive their input from another part of the organization at rates and prices which they cannot influence.

Competition, therefore, is very likely, left to itself, to produce conflict in organizational situations. Hence, the need for the managerial strategies outlined later which will at least contain the potential conflict and limit the costs of the benefits of competition.

Box 10.2   Zero-sum examinations

The examination system in British schools was norm-referenced for many years in most subjects. In essence this meant that each year the examiners took the middle student's score as the benchmark for the year and related the A, B, C and D grades to it. It was a well-intentioned attempt to be fair in subjects where it is hard to be precise as to what constitutes a pass. The effect, however, was to turn the examination into a closed competition in which a fixed percentage was bound to lose, even if everyone performs much better than the year before. It was not too surprising that many of the less able students felt that the cards were stacked against them and opted out. The move towards criterion-referenced examinations, with previously fixed levels, turns the system into a more open competition.

2.3 Competition for power

Competition for power merits separate discussion. When 'politics' is referred to in a pejorative sense it is often this form of competition that is in question. Is this form of competition healthy and productive, or is it disruptive, selfishly inspired and harmful? Should it be tolerated, encouraged or banned? The answer to these questions will depend upon the three conditions already listed, and upon the requirements of the situation.

Is the competition 'open'? Is the pool of power unlimited? This will depend on the type of power in question, and on the organizational situation. Usually, resource and position power are restricted. Only a few people can head up the pyramid, control the resources. Expert and personal power, however, are often available to all. It is open to everyone to increase their personal prestige or professionalism and thereby add to the pool of power in the organization. Only if this deprives others of their power would this situation become win–lose, become a closed competition.

Are the rules unambiguous? In role organizations the rules for achieving position power or even expert power are likely to be less ambiguous than in other cultures. In a power culture they are usually highly ambiguous.

Are the important variables controlled by the participants? Usually they are at the start. The game is to get more variables under one's control. Only in nepotistic versions of the power culture do some people – e.g. the owner's son – have an initial advantage.

Unless the organization is expanding very rapidly, or has a big managerial gap, the pool of power will be restricted. The competition, therefore, will be closed, not open. If, furthermore, the rules of competition are ambiguous, the competition is likely to generate conflict. The organization is now in a position where it will have to review the costs and benefits of the type of conflict.

Power competition is not usually going to be directly helpful to the tasks of the organization. The release of energies and the setting of standards in pursuit of internal power is not a desirable outcome in this case. In fact, it will tend to detract from the organization's business. The only remaining benefit of competition is that of 'sorting-out'. If it is important to the organization to differentiate widely between the performance of individuals or groups in selection or promotion, then it may be worth paying the cost of the tactics of conflict (to be described later). If wide differentiation is not important, if selection or promotion is based on performance to standard rather than going to the best, then cost-benefit analysis would suggest that conflict for power was not in the interests of the organization as a whole.

Politics is, however, a reality. Individuals have their own personal interests, or they have values or goals which they would like to have adopted by the organization. In all cultures there will be pressure groups and blocking groups, groups pursuing their joint interests and groups protecting theirs. Zaleznik has usefully distinguished between coalitions and collusions, collusions being essentially defensive, coalitions more positive. Since individuals will achieve little on their own, coalitions or collusions become essential if one's own viewpoint or interests or preferences are going to be advanced, or, at least, not ignored. The competition for power being essentially 'closed', an increase in the power of one group will mean a decrease in the power of others. Herein lie the seeds of conflict. Coalitions will provoke collusions in retaliation, energies will be devoted to the conflict, to surviving or winning rather than advancing the organization's goals. Since the bulk of power is at the top, it is there that coalitions are the most important. The manager who seeks to rule alone is playing a dangerous role. As Machiavelli pointed out, as many fallen giants of industry would acknowledge, unless supported by a coalition, the people at the top will become increasingly isolated. 'Uneasy lies the head that wears the crown.' Worrying about his own position he will trust no one, destroy dangerous coalitions by transferring key people, keep his possible rivals close to him and divided, become more arbitrary and authoritarian, behave in fact in a way not calculated to do best service to the organization, and may well legitimize the eventual palace revolution.

Competition for power nearly always turns into conflict.

Box 10.3   Organization politics

Mintzberg, in his comprehensive review of power and politics in organizations, has listed thirteen political games:

Games to resist authority:	the insurgency games – to sabotage the intentions of superiors.
Games to counter resistance:	the counter-insurgency games – more rules, regulations and punishments.
Games to build power bases:	the sponsorship game – hitching oneself to a useful *superior*, a star; the alliance game – finding useful *colleagues*; the empire game – building coalitions of *subordinates*; the budgeting game – getting control of *resources*; the expertise game – flaunting and feigning *expertise*; the lording game – flaunting one's *authority*.
Games to defeat rivals:	the line versus staff game – between units or functions.
Games to change the organization:	the strategic candidates game – informing on an opponent; the young Turks game – enclaves of key rebels.

Mintzberg argues that most of these games, when used in moderation, can have a healthy effect on keeping the organization on its toes. Carried too far, however, they turn the whole organization into a political cauldron and divert it from its main task.

H. Mintzberg, *Power In and Around Organizations*, 1983

3 Conflict

3.1 The symptoms

Before looking at the causes of conflict, we must recognize the symptoms. The symptoms of organizational conflict are:

1 Poor communications laterally and vertically. Decisions are taken on the wrong information. Group A is unaware that Group B is working on another part of the same problem. Two levels in the same division are moving in different directions on the same problem.
2 Inter-group hostility and jealousy. This usually comes out in statements beginning:
   'Department A is only concerned with keeping their lines straight . . .'
   'Division B are totally unaware that . . .'
   'If it wasn't for those people in X department . . .'
   'They never tell us anything . . .'
   'They expect us to know by intuition . . .'
   'They seem to have the MD's ear . . .'
3 Inter-personal friction. Relations between individuals, usually in different groups, deteriorate to icy formality or argument. Problems seem to get polarized around people and personalities.
4 Escalation of arbitration. More and more inter-group conflicts are passed up to the cross-over point for arbitration. The cross-over point becomes ever higher in the hierarchy as successive levels of superiors take up the defence of their interested parties. What started as a problem between clerks over a withdrawal of credit becomes a confrontation between the Directors of Finance and Marketing to be resolved by the Managing Director.
5 Proliferation of rules and regulations, norms and myths. It becomes more and more difficult to do anything without riding roughshod over somebody's regulations, somebody's established way of doing things, somebody's essential permission.
6 Low morale of the type expressed in frustration at inefficiency. 'We don't seem to be able to get anything moving . . .' 'It's no use trying to be imaginative around here . . .' 'You would think they didn't want anything to happen . . .'

Most of this frustration, under conditions of conflict, is directed at the higher levels of the organization.

These symptoms will be found at some time in almost every

organization. They arise as a direct result of the competition turning in to conflict. To treat the symptoms will be ineffective if the underlying disease is left untouched. A plaster on a boil will cover it up but if the boil is the result of a deeper ailment, another boil will pop up somewhere else.

Too often, organizations react to poor communications with more communications (meetings, house journals, circulation of documents, etc). If the underlying disease is untouched, the remedy will only complicate the issue and will ultimately be discarded (the graveyard of unwanted house journals was overcrowded long ago). If inter-personal friction is the dominant symptom, banging their heads together, sending them on T-groups, or removing them to other posts, will only have a short-term palliative effect. The underlying conflict will still be there and will show itself in some other way. The strategy for resolving conflict must be related to the disease, not the symptom. Diagnosis, therefore, differentiating between symptoms and cause, is the key to the proper management of conflict.

3.2   The causes

The causes of conflict have been listed and categorized in a variety of ways. Frustrated argument, escalated competition may be the immediate causes, but they all start from two underlying and fundamental issues:

Goals and ideologies;
Territory.

Goals and Ideologies. When two or more groups interact with differing goals, sets of priorities or standards, there is likely to be conflict. The higher the degree of interdependence of the units, the more crucial becomes the relationship of their objectives and ideologies. Ideology is a set of beliefs about the way to behave, about standards and values. Staff groups, for instance, have been shown to be strongly committed to preserving the integrity of control and rule systems, whereas line personnel want more flexibility and the freedom to override rules and regulations. Other ideological differences would be flexibility versus stability, organization goals or societal needs, short-run versus long-run. People and groups with a power orientation will have different goals and ideologies from those with a role orientation.

This friction, or occasionally clash, between goals and ideologies leading to conflict can arise when:

1 *Formal objectives diverge*, e.g. the sales/production dilemma. Typically, a sales department measures itself on sales turnover, gross deliveries, total output or some such index. The production department is primarily concerned with cost, expressed perhaps as variances against budget, or cost per unit sold. Sales are properly concerned with customer satisfaction. Production with optimum schedules. Sales therefore will feel it proper to press for special arrangements to meet a customer's special requirements. This may well involve uneconomic short runs, unscheduled overtime, disruption of work in the factory. In line with their objectives production will resist.

There is no answer which gives everyone all that they want. Each may need to give way a little for the greater good of all. Compromise has its own morality, but it is not easy. For the overall optimum to be achieved, there is needed

(a) Agreement on a super-ordinate objective (e.g. profit);
(b) Communication on alternative methods of achieving that objective;
(c) Trust in the other party;
(d) Likelihood of benefit to both parties.

Where these conditions do not exist there is the potential for conflicting objectives. Each party will then be perfectly justified in asserting its priorities. Like the brake and the accelerator working simultaneously, there will be much noise and little progress. (It is worth emphasizing that it is not enough to appeal to a super-ordinate goal – the interests of the organization, profitability, etc. – the goal must be accepted by both parties. There must also be an agreed method of deciding between alternatives and the necessary information to do so.)

2 *Role definitions diverge*. This can lead to conflicting objectives. Advisory functions often regard their function as being to produce new ideas, that being how they justify their existence. Executing functions, busy with day-to-day problems, are more interested in stability and the status quo. Thus it is that line functions acquire a reputation for conservatism while staff functions pride themselves on innovation. Auditing and advisory roles are often of a professional nature, e.g. quality control, accounting and legal positions. They have a professional code or a professional reference group which can provide another set of priorities in addition to the objectives of the organization. The medical department of a pharmaceutical firm

hovers uncertainly between its role as the public conscience of the organization and a servicing unit to the marketing department.

3 *The contractual relationship is unclear.* Co-ordination that is imposed will be regarded differently from co-ordination that is requested. Is the inspector helping the supervisor or is he the servant of the factory manager? Is the credit control section an aid to the sales department or the watchdog of the Finance Director? If the contract is unclear, it may be differently perceived by each party, leading to conflicting objectives. Diagonal relationships are prone to this type of ambiguity. Does the branch accountant work for the branch manager or the chief accountant? Is he a guest or a policeman or a member of the household? The view that each party takes of their allegiances and their relationships will affect their view of their priorities and their objectives.

4 *Roles are simultaneous.* A department may be both a service department and a co-ordinating department. In the former role they may act on the request of the individual department, in the latter at the behest of the managing director. It may not always be clear to the other actors which role is the current one. One role, moreover, may tend to contain the other. Can he who co-ordinated you yesterday service you today?

5 *There are concealed objectives.* The formal objectives of a unit or a group may conceal some more deeply felt objectives. Usually, these objectives will be for a larger share of resources or for greater influence in decision-making or for increased status. For instance:
(a) As Strauss showed in his interesting study of purchasing agents, professionals who feel they lack proper recognition start to activate their negative power.
(b) If a unit feels that its influence is not in proportion to the demands of the situation, it will start to work for more influence by activating its negative power. Lawrence and Lorsch showed that where the influence of each unit was consistent with competitive factors there was less conflict. Thus, in their more effective container firm where customer delivery and product quality were vital, sales and production were the most influential units. By contrast, in the food industry where market expertise and good science were essential, sales and research were the influential units.
(c) Seiler showed that in an organization where research had more prestige than engineering, which in turn ranked above production, there was no conflict if the initiation process followed this ranking.

But if a lower status unit, e.g. production, started to make demands on the others, there was conflict.

(d) Dalton and Strauss both demonstrated in separate studies that where a staff group felt asymmetry with a line group – e.g. the staff group had to understand all the problems of the line, get along with and justify their own existence, but not vice-versa – there is resentment and attempts to force the interaction to flow both ways.

The ways of avoiding or controlling these conflicts will be discussed later. We are currently concerned with diagnosis, not treatment. Any systematic diagnosis of conflict should start with an analysis of the real objectives and ideologies of both parties in their various roles. The diagnosis should also take a close look at the territorial situation, a phrase that has a metaphorical meaning as well as a literal one.

Territory. Robert Ardrey, in his book *The Territorial Imperative*, has put forward the proposition that a lot of animal behaviour is motivated by territory, the desire to possess, acquire, or preserve territory and territorial rights. In his intriguing and readable book he suggests that the territorial principle applies to societies as well as to animals. (See Box 10.4.) In the Ardrey tradition we shall here extend the principle of territory to the domain of organizations. But in this instance, territory will be interpreted psychologically rather than physically. An individual's psychological territory is his sphere of influence. Territory is only a metaphor, an analogy, but it is a useful one. Consider some further aspects of territory:

(a) Ownership of territory is conferred partly by deeds (organization charts, job descriptions) but partly by precedent, by squatting or staking a claim.

(b) The boundaries of the territory are set out in various ways. Physically, with screens, offices, separate buildings. Procedurally, through committee memberships, circulation lists. Socially, through dining groups, informal groupings, carpets and other status signs. The implications of the metaphor are:

Territory is prized by its inhabitants. They will not willingly relinquish it, nor allow it to get overcrowded;

Some territories are more prized than others;

Trespassing is frowned upon. You enter another's territory by invitation only;

One can seek to increase or improve one's own property even to the detriment of the neighbourhood as a whole.

Let us not push the metaphor too far, but pause to consider how territory can be the source of conflict in organizations.

Territorial violation. If in one's job, territory is either taken away or infringed upon by another group, there will be retaliation and conflict. When a head office department queries or overrules one of the branches, the branch is liable to see this as a violation of territory. If a specialist department starts to take decisions previously the prerogative of the line executive, it will be regarded as violation of territory.

Box 10.4   The territorial imperative

A territory is an area of space, whether of water or earth or air, which an animal or group of animals defends as an exclusive preserve. The word is also used to describe the inward compulsion in animate beings to possess and defend such a space. A territorial species of animals, therefore, is one in which all males, and sometimes females too, bear an inherent drive to gain and defend an exclusive property . . .

We may also say that in all territorial species, without exception, possession of a territory lends enhanced energy to the proprietor. Students of animal behaviour cannot agree as to why this should be, but the challenger is almost invariably defeated, the intruder expelled. In part, there seems some mysterious flow of energy and resolve which invests a proprietor on his home grounds. But likewise, so marked is the inhibition lying on the intruder, so evident his sense of trespass, we may be permitted to wonder if in all territorial species there does not exist more profound than simple learning, some universal recognition of territorial rights . . .

Man . . . is as much a territorial animal as is a mocking-bird singing in the clear California night . . . if we defend that title to our land or the sovereignty of our country, we do it for reasons no different, no less innate, no less ineradicable, than do lower animals. The dog barking at you from behind his master's fence acts from a motive indistinguishable from that of his master when the fence was built . . . Neither are men and dogs and mocking-birds uncommon creatures in the natural world. Ring-tailed lemurs and great-crested grebes, prairie dogs, robins, tigers, musk-rats, meadow warblers and Atlantic salmon, fence lizards, flat lizards, three-spined sticklebacks, nightingales and Norway rats, herring gulls and collicebus monkeys – all of us will give everything we have for a place of our own. Territory, in the evolving world of animals, is a force perhaps older than sex.

Adapted from Ardrey, *The Territorial Imperative*, 1967

If one group demands rather than asks for information belonging to another group, this can be seen as uninvited intrusion.

Departments such as Personnel suffer much from accusations of territorial violation. In order to do their job, they require information and seek to influence decisions such as promotion and transfer in the most well-protected territories of a manager – his people. The tactics resorted to in defence of territorial rights are roughly equivalent to putting a fence around the area. They will be discussed in more detail in a subsequent section.

Overcrowding. In a lot of situations there are too many people doing too few jobs. Metaphorically, there are too many animals in one patch of ground. One solution is to enlarge the patch. Within an organization, this can only be done at the expense of other groups. For those groups who interface with the environment, e.g. marketing, it is theoretically possible to capture territory from outside the organization, i.e. to expand the market coverage. This kind of approach must, however, be initiated and supported by the senior man in the group.

A key question to all newly promoted managers would be: 'Where do you get your personal territory from?' It is all too easy to take it from the current occupants, from one's subordinates. It requires a courageous manager to hand over the existing territory to her subordinates and to regard her job as the enlargement of the whole. The mechanisms for getting hold of territory are simple. The manager can choose from the following: she defines her sphere of interests, nominates particular problems or customers as her personal responsibility, decides that she must represent the group on particular committees, ensures that all incoming mail is seen and screened by her before distributing, re-writes the job definitions of her subordinates.

Overcrowding leads to frustration and energies devoted to protecting one's plot and, if possible, to increasing it. Overcrowding frequently follows structural re-organizations as individuals explore the territory involved in their new positions.

Territorial jealousy. Just as one herd looks covetously at the grazing grounds of another so do groups in organizations look at the territory of other groups or individuals. In particular:

(a) The overt status signs of office size, dining-rooms, cars, secretaries, etc. It is impossible to find a universally acceptable way of allocating these territorial desiderata. Though everyone agrees they are unimportant, they may often be the visible signs of cherished influence or status, and become important because of their symbolic value.

(b) Information jealousy, or the feeling that one would love to know what goes on behind that fence, is another common feature of organizations. All groups believe that they are excluded from information available to the group above them. Often this is true, but seldom to the extent that they believe. A manager coming out of a meeting with his peers that lasted three hours, may say to his subordinates that nothing of any interest took place. He may well be right, but he will probably not be believed. We long for the fruit in others' gardens until we have tasted it and found it sour.

(c) The in-group phenomenon. Groups are well-practised in the ways of improving the desirability of their territory. As Festinger, in his work on cognitive dissonance, pointed out, the harder it is to get something, the more we value it when we get it. The highest and most inaccessible mountain peaks are the ones most prized. The smaller and more exclusive the group, the more difficult the admission tests, the tougher the apprenticeship, the more we value membership. Those who get in become more cohesive, identify more with the group, protect its interests and its inviolability more determinedly. The effect of all this is to increase competition to enter the territory *per se* – the point and purpose of the territory or groups is almost immaterial. Dining clubs in British universities, fraternities in the USA, the one-time clubs of the British Empire, the Royal Enclosure at Ascot are all examples of public stamping grounds. In general, if you want to make your group desirable, make it difficult to get into.

'Territory' and 'Roles' are often two metaphors for describing the same phenomenon. Pick whichever is most appealing. Metaphors are merely an aid to diagnosis.

4 The tactics of conflict

4.1

Many of the tactics used by conflicting parties will be identical to the symptoms of conflict listed earlier. Several of the tactics are themselves the seeds of further conflict. In some analyses of conflict these tactics will therefore be found as causes. But they are not the prime cause, since they themselves have their roots in a more fundamental conflict. The principal tactics are listed below.

4.2   Information control

Information gives power. It is hard to argue with apparent facts even if you suspect they are wrong. The manager who keeps some vital data to himself which completely refutes the suggestions of his subordinates, the specialist department that refuses to distribute data before a vital meeting, the filters of 'confidential' and 'restricted', the levels of committees are all possible ways in which information is controlled in order to protect territory or objectives. Since differential information is itself a source of conflict in any discussion, this tactic tends to escalate conflict.

The 'gatekeeper' function of subordinate or specialist groups makes information control a very appealing tactic for increasing influence or enlarging territory. The manager confronted by an apparently open-and-shut proposal, based on details or technicalities with which he cannot be familiar, can often only accept the proposal or express his lack of confidence in the subordinates or specialists. He is in fact deprived of any real influence over that decision unless he asks for an outside opinion, and thereby runs the risk of destroying trust and morale. The use of information control has transferred the major influence on the decision to the 'gatekeeper'.

4.3   Information distortion

This is the misuse of information control. But it is not always deliberate. The perceptual bias that goes with any role can lead to unconscious distortion of information. The specialist, the craftsman, the engineer may be so concerned with quality or standard of performance that information on costs and benefits may be neglected or given only cursory attention. Proposals for new equipment in many organizations are frequently unaccompanied by any assessment of resulting benefits. The decision is therefore taken on cost and quality alone. There has been an unwitting distortion of the total pool of information required.

4.4   Rules and regulations

Groups, particularly specialist groups, who feel their influence neglected will seek to impose rules, regulations and official requirements on other groups. The proliferation of forms from a new division in a central office is often a use of this tactic to draw attention to their existence and their importance. Strauss's study of purchasing agents, already referred to, is a good example of this. Crozier, in his study of

French bureaucracies, demonstrates that to circumscribe others with rules whilst leaving yourself free is a recognized route to political ascendancy in organizations.

4.5   Networks

The answering tactic to rules and regulations is to establish informal contacts, liaisons, the friend in the dispatch department who will help one to by-pass formal procedures and give one advance information. At a higher level, the use of a 'friend at court', a protector with influence, is a further example of the use of an informal channel to protect one's interests. A collection of such informal channels may well become an informal clique, necessary in order to get the work done, as the clique sees it, in spite of the organization's rules. These cliques, though often formed from the best motives, can easily develop 'territories' of their own and become very protective of them. Informal alliances of whole departments against a common enemy have also been known.

4.6   Control of rewards

Line people will often retaliate against staff tactics by refusing promotion to a staff expert or rejecting his recommendations. The resources power of the line is usually superior to that of the staff and is brought into play if there is abuse of expert or position power by specialists.

4.7   Denigration or tale-telling

In conflict situations there will be a strong temptation to point out the flaws in the opposing group. This can go to the extent of duplicating some of the work of the opposition in order to detect its flaws.

4.8

The results of the persistent use of any of these tactics are:

(a) A 'hardening' of the conflict so that it perpetuates itself as each tactic is met with other tactics;
(b) The distortion and control of information, the checks and the barriers all working to promote hostility and suspicion;
(c) Collaboration degenerating into bargaining;
(d) The misapplication of individual and group energies.

5   The strategies for managing conflict

5.1

In order to limit the damage done by these tactics the purpose of any managerial strategy will be:

(a) To turn the conflict into fruitful competition or purposeful argument;
(b) If this is not possible, to control the conflict.

5.2   From conflict to competition

Fruitful competition is more likely to occur if:

1 There is a clear and shared purpose for the group or organization. Without a common goal individuals are, in effect, licensed to do the best for themselves within the rules. Management then has to start regulating the competition by adjusting the rules, i.e. it has to move to strategy (b). Too many captains of industry extol the benefits of an open market whilst running a centrally planned economy within the organization. The solution is to focus the group on a common task or to drench the organization in a common set of values. As we have seen (in Chapter 4), Mant believes that good leaders are builders rather than raiders, focusing their efforts with others on the 'third corner', the common task; while Peters and Waterman, in their analysis of excellence in American organizations, demonstrate that competition can flourish and be fruitful where the organization is sure of its purpose and its values (Box 10.5).

2 Information is available on progress towards the goal. It is little use to preach 'service to the customer', 'higher standards' or 'profitability' if the information system is all geared to controls rather than results, to time-keeping, costs and budgets instead of achievements. Individuals are realistic: they judge the real objects of the exercise by the type of feedback that comes their way. Schools which preach the development of the whole child but confine their information on performance to academic results will not find many staff competing to do more than academic teaching. The information must match the goal, even if it is soft information, such as encouraging production workers to meet the customers.

3 The system does not punish failure. In open competition, mass-marathon style, people or groups are competing with themselves as

much as with others. To do one's best is all that can be expected, even though some people's best may be better than others. Fruitful competition will encourage risk-taking and accept failure if it is the outcome of honest endeavour. The only fault is not to try at all. Where no one has to lose there is more likely to be trust, collaboration and mutual help – the sort of behaviour, indeed, that you find in good sports teams, but not too often in formal organizations.

Box 10.5   The organizational market-place

Peters and Waterman report that:

- 3M, Fluor, TI and Bechtel maintain markets for people wanting to be assigned to project teams
- Brands compete at Procter and Gamble
- Purposeful overlapping between divisions and product lines is found in Digital, HP, 3M, J and J and Wang
- Buyers and Fashion Co-ordinators compete for floor-space at Bloomingdales
- IBM encourages several groups to compete in solving the same problem.

They say that internal competition costs money in duplication but produces manifold benefits in commitment, innovation and hard results. Competition works, it seems, inside as well as outside the organization.

Peters and Waterman, *In Search of Excellence*, 1982

In a sense, this set of managerial strategies could be called 'control by ecology' in that it works by creating the environment for collaborative interaction. These conditions are rarely achieved, usually because we do not design the ecology carefully enough.

5.3   Control of conflict

It is not, however, always possible to arrange the ecology, to determine roles and relationships in such a way that collaboration can be ensured. Management is therefore forced to strategy (b), the control and regulation of conflict. This strategy is often the best short-term solution. Too often, the longer-term ecological strategy is then neglected or forgotten. Regulation of conflict in a sense recognizes and legitimizes conflict, and therefore perpetuates it. Regulation strategies include:

1 Arbitration. The use of the lowest cross-over point in the organiza-

tion to resolve conflicts. Only useful when the conflict is apparent and specific. Not very valuable in episodic or continual conflict.

2 Rules and procedures. These are often arrived at by negotiation, e.g. on credit procedure, or scheduling. They can easily become one of the bargaining elements and are seen as not a solution, but another constraint. They are useful when the conflict is recurrent and predictable, but should not be regarded as a permanent solution.

3 Co-ordinating Device ('boxing the problem'). A position is created on the organization chart to resolve the issue in conflict. The position often carries the name of the problem as its title – hence 'boxing the problem' – e.g. 'sales/production liaison', or 'new product co-ordination'. But Lawrence and Lorsch in their studies of integration showed that where this was overdoing the co-ordination, i.e. where the device resulted from spurious conflict rather than the need for

---

Box 10.6 Fending off the specialist

Pettigrew has listed some favoured devices used by the line executive to block the unwanted (by him) report of the specialist:

1 *Straight rejection*. The staff man and his report are dismissed without further consideration. Needs power and self-assurance on the part of the executive.

2 *'Bottom drawer it'*. The report is praised but then left unused. The specialist, grateful for the praise, may not press for utilization.

3 *Mobilizing political support*. The executive calls on support from colleagues with similar interests.

4 *The nitty-gritty tactic*. Minor objections to fact or interpretation are raised to discredit and delay implementation.

5 *The emotional tactic*. 'How can you do this to me' or . . . 'to my chaps'.

6 *But in the future* . . . The report is fine for today's conditions but unlikely to work in the (hypothetical) future.

7 *The invisible man tactic*. The executive is never available for discussion when wanted.

8 *Further investigation is required* . . . The report is sent back for further work on it.

9 *The scapegoat*. Someone else (e.g. Head Office) won't like it.

10 *Deflection*. The executive directs attention to the points where he has sufficient knowledge to contradict the specialist.

See further: Pettigrew. 'The influence process between specialists and executives', *Personnel Review*, 1974 co-ordination endemic in the situation, then this device merely complicated communication and increased conflict. Problem-solving groups have a vested interest in maintaining the problem they were set up to resolve. This device, therefore, is not good for episodic or occasional conflict, but it is useful where the conflicting pressures are going to be continual but are not so predictable that they can be handled by rules and regulations.

4 Confrontation. A technique much favoured by those who believe in 'openness' in organizational communications. This strategy will be effective if the issue can be clearly defined and is not a symptom of more underlying differences. It is an approach analogous to arbitration but to be preferred to it in that the solution will be 'owned' and 'internalized' by both groups rather than imposed on them by the arbitrator. Confrontation or inter-group meetings can do a lot to increase understanding of other people's point of view, but they cannot be a complete substitute for the ecological point of view. An interesting variation on confrontation is an approach known as *role negotiation*, recently developed by Harrison. In role negotiation, the conflicting parties negotiate and trade items of behaviour (e.g. I will stop doing X if you will stop doing Y). It does much to reduce the sores of conflict, particularly between individuals, although it may still leave the underlying disease untouched.

5 Separation. If interaction increases the depth of sentiments, separation should cool them. This strategy can work if interdependence is not anyway necessary because of the task. If it is, then the interaction will have to be managed somehow, either by a co-ordinating device, or rules and regulations. The strategy of separation works best if two groups are coincidentally interacting and conflicting, i.e. because they happen to be lodged in the same location. It also works if the true cause of the conflict is two incompatible individuals – incompatible in personality, or more often with relative status inappropriate to the situation. To separate the individuals, i.e. by transferring one, may then be a successful strategy. But inter-personal friction is more often the result of conflict than the cause of it. If this be so, then separation of the individuals will merely bring about a temporary lull in the situation, and two more conflicting personalities will soon arise.

6 Neglect. Not a desirable strategy, but one frequently adopted *faute de mieux*. To ignore conflict, often because the apparent cause is trivial, is to permit it to stabilize if not to perpetuate itself. Like weeds, neglected, it can stifle productive work.

6 Channelling change

6.1

Paradoxically, differences are essential to change. If there were no urge to compete and no need to disagree the organization would be either in a state of apathy or of complacency – both of them triggers of decline in a constantly changing world. Change no longer means more, or sometimes less, of the same. It usually means something completely different.

We are discovering the facts of discontinuous change in organizations just when scientists are coming to terms with the fact that there is no such thing as an equilibrium state in nature, everything is in flux, as Heraclitus pointed out more than two millennia ago. Furthermore, fossil evidence now suggests that evolution did not happen by slow and steady steps but by big jumps, discontinuous change, that took us abruptly from one state to another.

Even politics can be good news, therefore, in organizations if it is the means of upsetting the status quo when that status is no longer appropriate. But before things come to that pass, or before death looms to startle the organization into action (one of the few justifications for a hostile takeover bid) it is better to channel the differences to promote growth and positive change, remembering always that one can grow better without having to grow bigger (see Box 10.7).

The mechanisms for channelling change are easy to describe but difficult to do, as with most of this book.

Box 10.7 Bigger or better

There is a proper size for everything.

Biologists are fond of saying that a rat has everything it needs to be a rat. An elephant needs to be large, but it would not help a cockroach to be as large.

I met a vineyard owner in California. He was, he told me, trying to squeeze every cent of margin out of his product 'in order to develop my winery as fast as possible'. 'Do you plan to get very much bigger?' I asked. 'Oh, I don't want to grow bigger,' he replied, 'I want to grow better.' To do that, he needed better equipment, better vines, better people – not more.

6.2   Overarching goals

Conflict becomes competition if there is a common goal (see section 5.1). The goals, however, have to matter to the people involved and they have to promote open competition not closed competition. The 'bottom-line', for example, is not something which motivates many except the board who see it as a measure of the company's effectiveness. It is, or should be, a means to other ends and not an end in itself. Indeed, to turn a means into an end, or a requirement into a purpose, is a logical and often a moral error. We need profit in order to make or do something else and it is that 'something else' which should provide the common goal.

Goals, however, are of little relevance if you do not know when you have achieved them. Feedback loops need to be built into the organization so that everyone knows that a goal has been scored. Deming is the man who taught the Japanese that quality is what gives meaning to work and to organizations (see Box 10.8) but he also insisted that quality had to be measured or, if not measured, then recognized by those responsible for making it. In a marathon every runner wears a watch so that they can check their own progress – not so that others can check their progress; competition should be self-scored wherever possible.

Goals such as 'being number one' or 'the most successful company in our industry' fail the feedback test. They do not relate quickly enough, directly enough or measurably enough to the individual or the group. Such statements are worthy aspirations; they are not goals.

6.3   A climate of experiment

Stepping into the unknown is not something that can be completely pre-planned. Creativity and experiment are necessary. The best way to encourage these in an organization is to cultivate healthy, that is open, competition. Individuals and, more usually, teams or groups should be licensed to do all that they can to (a) improve what they are doing, (b) to think of new ways of doing it and (c) new things to do. Rosabeth Moss Kanter, in her study of changing organizations, talks of newstreams, as distinct from mainstreams, to describe the creative projects of large organizations. These newstreams, she concludes, are characterized by high uncertainty, high intensity and high autonomy. They do not suit everyone, but every organization needs its newstreams.

This climate of experiment that is necessary for change thrives in an atmosphere of curiosity, forgiveness and trust – three words with big political overtones.

1 *Curiosity*, the urge and the right to ask questions, to ask why and why not, is easily dismissed as impertinence by mainstream managers. Curiosity has to be respected.
2 *Forgiveness* recognizes that, in any experimental situation, some experiments will fail. Provided that people learn from the failures they must be forgiven. If they are punished the competition is closed not open, the risks of a mistake will be too great and no further experiments will be made. Because some experiments can be catastrophic if they fail ('he very nearly lent half our net worth to Brazil') most organizations seek to put limits on the size of the experiments permitted in the newstream.
3 *Trust* is the third requirement of a climate of experiment. If people and groups are to have the space to make experiments they have to be trusted. The selection of people for the newstream is crucially important. Since giving trust implies giving power this is a key political decision, to be taken by those in charge of the system as a whole.

It is easy to marginalize the newstream by violating any one of these three requirements. To do that would be to endanger the future of the corporation.

6.4 Sharing and privacy

Organizations, at their best, are full of paradoxes – 'both and . . .'. An organization devoted to change and improvement has no secrets but is a great respecter of territory. For any competition for ideas or initiatives to be truly open there has to be full and frank communication. The new technology helps because it is hard, now, to stop information, both hard and soft, running across the formal boundaries of authority. E-mail and voice-mail, like water, go everywhere, find every gap, seep where they cannot flow. They are a great aid to experiment and innovation.

At the same time we all need some territory to call our own. The project teams of the newstreams have their commando-type names, their own uniforms, usually an emblazoned T-shirt these days, and their own impenetrable jargon. This is natural, as we have seen earlier in this chapter. A sense of place and a sense of ownership of ideas and initiatives is necessary for our identity and commitment.

The boundaries around the territories must not be too great,

Box 10.8

Deming's Fourteen Points for the transformation of management:
1 Create constancy of purpose towards improvement of product and service.
2 Adopt the new philosophy. We are in a new economic age.
3 Cease reliance on mass inspection to achieve quality.
4 End the practice of awarding business on the basis of price tag.
5 Improve constantly the system of production and service.
6 Institute training on the job.
7 Institute leadership, to help people and machines do a better job.
8 Drive out fear.
9 Break down barriers between departments.
10 Eliminate exhortations and targets asking for zero defects.
11 Eliminate work standards. Substitute leadership. Eliminate management by objectives and numbers. Substitute leadership.
12 Remove barriers to a pride of workmanship e.g. annual reviews or merit ratings.
13 Institute a vigorous programme of education and self-improvement.
14 The transformation is everyone's job.

It could be called the preparation for a marathon!

Abridged from Aguayo, *Dr Deming, the man who taught the Japanese about quality*, 1990

however, or they get in the way of sharing. It is important that all should recognize that they are members of two states, their own home group and the larger organization. Organizations, recognizing this, try to find ways to encourage mutual congratulations among the groups, a kind of reciprocal boasting which simultaneously celebrates and shares it with others. Other organizations move people around between groups or encourage multiple membership of newstream groups to prevent group loyalty becoming counter-productive.

6.5   Implementing

It is one thing to get the sparks flying, another to turn them into a fire or, in organizational terms, to make the newstreams part of the mainstream when they work.

Newstream activity is nearly always a mix of the task and the person cultures, mainstream a mix of power and role. The two do not mix

---

Box 10.9

John Cleese and Robin Skynner have studied the characteristics of psychologically healthy families. It may be, suggests John Cleese, that organizations are no different. For example:

1 In very healthy families there is an unusual amount of consultation with the children, although the parents still take the decisions. If they feel that they have to take unpopular decisions the children will respect this.
2 There are no taboos or secrets in these families, with the result that their communication is exceptionally open and their understanding of each other and of the family objectives is astonishingly clear.
3 These psychologically healthy families have a deep separateness and a respect for individuality, allowing their members the highest possible degree of autonomy.

See further: J. Cleese 'People love to learn – so let them', *World Link Magazine*, 1991

---

easily; those who are happy in a climate of experimentation can feel imprisoned in the implementation stage.

Fortunately, few people are monoculturalists, worshippers of only one God. In the task culture there is often a Zeus masquerading as Dionysus, and an Apollo charmed for a time by the intellectual delights of Athena and the task culture. Charged with implementing its innovations in the mainstream the group may well have within itself the necessary key characters although they will probably not be the existing leaders or influential members.

Making the experimental group responsible for implementation is, however, only possible if the organization is already made up of mini-organizations and not patterned on the traditional pyramidal functional basis. This, fortunately perhaps, seems to be the way the organizations of the future are moving.

Richard Pascale sums up the formula of the successful organization as Fit, Split, Contend and Transcend, by which he means, firstly, that there has to be a good cultural fit, the organization cannot be just a holding company. That being so the organization should be divided up into the bits that others can do and the bits which are its core business and core competences. Then, to keep things moving, there needs to be contention, healthy competition, held together by a transcendent or overarching purpose. He cites General Electric,

Ford, Honda and General Motors as large-scale examples of the formula in practice.

It is not coincidental that all these large organizations had, at the time he was observing them, a power culture Zeus figure at the top even if, like Don Petersen at Ford, he clothed his powers in a modest mien. This is necessary, for only a power culture can override the tendency of the role culture which predominates in such large organizations to change things by changing the rules and procedures. You need power to change the balance of power. In the end politics, if we define it as the competition for power, is a necessary ingredient of a healthy organization – as long, that is, as the right side wins!

7 Summary and implications

7.1

This chapter started by looking at competition and conflict – topics often loosely described as 'politics' in organizations. It was suggested that competition was potentially good, provided it did not degenerate into conflict, particularly conflict for power, which is the narrower definition of politics, although there are circumstances where such conflict may be both necessary and useful, e.g. in order to change the balance of power in an unchanging organization.

The symptoms, causes and tactics of conflict were discussed along with a list of the strategies used to manage it – the point being that no living organization is, or should be, without the seeds of conflict so that to ignore it or to wish it away is folly.

Finally, we saw that competition, properly channelled, lies at the heart of change.

7.2 Implications

Differences are inevitable; differences are good. Change, too, is inevitable and should properly be seen as growth or learning. A good organization is always learning and always growing (better, not necessarily bigger). We should not wait until change is forced upon us, as individuals or as organizations because change then is hurried, unpleasant and often beyond our control. We should 'learn to love change' as the adage has it or, more positively perhaps, 'learn to keep moving'.

Such movement, always into an uncertain future, cannot be planned or prescribed from the top. No one, however clever, is omniscient. The movement has to come from within, from a proper understanding of things like competition and experiment, of territory and trust, of communication and healthy conflict. In that sense, every manager needs to think politically.

11 ➤ On Being a Manager

1 Introduction

It has never been easy to define what a manager is, or what he does. It is a useful concept, 'management', the missing 'x' which makes resources equal output. But the 'x', the exact qualities that are important, tends to shift from equation to equation. Definitions of the manager, or the manager's role, tend therefore to be so broad that they are meaningless, or so stereotyped that they become part of the background. 'Yes, of course', we say, and take no further notice.

At an opening session of a series of management seminars in one company I asked if there was any agreement on the essential part of a manager's job. With few dissentients they said that 'making decisions' was for them the vital part of the managerial function. We agreed, therefore, that for our next meeting in a week's time each of them would prepare a description of the most critical decision that he, as a manager, had taken that week. We would then analyse the way he had gone about it. The assumption here would be that if we could improve his decision-making capability we would improve his capacity as a manager. The next week a group of embarrassed managers faced each other. 'It was a strange week, last week, somehow I didn't seem to have any decisions to take,' said one. The others looked relieved. All said that they had found the same thing. Another managerial stereotype bites the dust! A manager, of course, does not just, or even mainly, 'take decisions'.

What does a manager do? In this chapter we shall first take a look at descriptions and definitions of *the manager's job*, then consider one particularly important part of the role, *the manager as GP*, before considering some particular *managerial dilemmas* and, last but not least, *the manager as a person*.

2 The manager's job

2.1

'He does one damn thing after another' was the comment by one observer of a field sales manager's day. *Brevity*, *variety* and *fragmentation* seem to be par for the course for most managers. A group of foremen studied by Guest actually averaged 583 incidents each day. Rosemary Stewart, studying 100 managers, found that in four weeks each of them had, on average, only nine periods of half-an-hour without interruption, which is less than one every other day. Mintzberg, studying chief executives, found what might be called the 'ten-minute itch': everything, even desk work and tours of the plant or office, seemed to get fitted into average bursts of around ten minutes except for scheduled meetings, although even these, on average, lasted only just over one hour.

Is the manager a masochist or is there something in the job of linch-pin which imposes this kind of life? A bit of both, seems to be the answer. Rosemary Stewart nicely describes the manager's job as made up of *constraints*, *choices* and *demands* (Box 11.1) and comments that while some jobs are mainly about doing what you have to do (meeting demands),

---

Box 11.1   The shape of a job

Jobs, says Rosemary Stewart, differ in the balance of constraints, demands and choices which they place on the individual, although the individual has some discretion in shifting the balance (by pushing back constraints, for example).

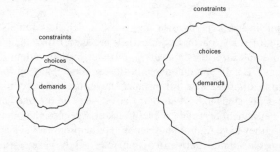

Differences in the demands, constraints and choices in two jobs

Demands include:	minimum criteria of performance;
	procedures that cannot be ignored.
Constraints include:	resource limitations;
	physical location;
	attitudes and expectations of others.
Choices include:	how the work is done;
	what work is done.

Stewart, *Choices for the Manager*, 1982

others are more about deciding what to do out of a vast array of options (making choices). The first is much easier. Mintzberg, after studying five chief executives, decided that they positively liked their hectic inter-active life because it kept them in touch with reality.

2.2 The roles of a manager

The problem, if it is a problem, is one of roles. Almost any manager has an array of roles to choose from. That can result in a feeling of role overload and stress, or it can be a licence to play all the parts in an ever-changing drama. Mintzberg has found ten roles for the manager:

Inter-personal roles	– Figurehead	(leading)
	Leader	
	Liaison	
Informational roles	– Monitor	(administrating)
	Disseminator	
	Spokesman	
Decisional roles	– Entrepreneur	(fixing)
	Disturbance handler	
	Resource allocator	
	Negotiator	

I have put in brackets my own, more colloquial, descriptions of the three sets of roles, partly because they are easier to remember but partly to emphasize that 'managing' *includes* leading, administrating and fixing. It is neither a synonym nor the opposite of any one of them. Professional organizations, for instance, never use the word 'manager' but find expressions like Senior Partner or Head on the one hand and Bursar, Permanent Secretary, Chief Clerk or Agent on the other. That is because they have traditionally separated the professional leadership role from the administrative or fixing roles. Only business uses the word 'management' and, in so doing, seeks to combine all the roles. Therein lies both the problem and the opportunity.

The mix of roles varies from job to job. Top jobs have a larger element of 'leading' roles, first line supervisory jobs more 'fixing', while middle-layer jobs are inevitably landed with the administering or informational roles – but every job has some of each. The size of the organization must also have some effect. The top jobs of small organizations are more mixed and there are more largely informational jobs in the bigger concerns (Box 11.2).

The balance of roles in a job will also change as the culture changes from one part of the organization to another. A role culture will have jobs with a larger informational content. The power cultures at foreman level will need more of the decisional roles in the jobs there, whilst at the top they will be the inter-personal roles.

Every job is different from every other job. This seems obvious, but the implications are hard to take on board. It means that the mix of the ten roles will be slightly different in every job. It means that to be successful in one job with one mix is no guarantee that one will be successful with the next. It means that to expect future leaders to start

---

Box 11.2   Selected comparisons of the work of chief executives of small and large organizations

	Small Companies 3 presidents 6 days of observation Choran Study	Large Organizations 5 chief executives 25 days of observation Mintzberg Study
Number of activities per day	77	22
Desk work sessions		
Number per day	22	7
Proportion of time	35%	22%
Average duration	6 min	15 min
Telephone calls		
Number per day	29	5
Proportion of time	17%	6%
Average duration	2 min	6 min
Scheduled meetings		
Number per day	3	4
Proportion of time	21%	59%
Average duration	27 min	68 min

Box 11.2 – *contd*

Unscheduled meetings

Number per day	19	4
Proportion of time	15%	10%
Average duration	3 min	12 min

Tours

Number per day	5	1
Proportion of time	12%	3%
Average duration	9 min	11 min

Proportion of activities lasting less than 9 min	90%	49%
Proportion lasting more than 60 min	0.02%	10%

Number of pieces of mail processed per day	17	36
Proportion of mail from		
Subordinates	54%	39%
Peers	2%	16%
Suppliers and associates	24%	8%

Proportion of time in verbal contact with		
Subordinates	56%	48%
Clients	7%	3%
Suppliers and associates	31%	17%
Peers and trade organizations	0.2%	11%
Directors and codirectors	0%	12%
Others	7%	8%

From Mintzberg, *The Nature of Managerial Work*, 1978

as outstanding fixers and end up as outstanding administrators may be hopelessly unrealistic. Organizations and individuals have yet to come to terms with the fact that 'manager' means too much and, as a result, can be a very confusing title to a job.

3   The manager as GP

3.1

The analogy of General Practitioner has been hauled in from the medical world to characterize one role that is not emphasized by Mintzberg but underlies all the other ten roles and is the real justification for this book. The manager, like the GP, is the first recipient of problems. However he may deal with them, whatever role he may choose to assume, he must first (just like a doctor) decide whether it is a problem and, if so, what sort of problem it is, before he proceeds to act. He must, in other words:

Identify the symptoms in any situation;
Diagnose the disease or cause of the trouble;
Decide how it might be dealt with – a strategy for health;
Start the treatment.

It is true that he may wish for expert help, or a second opinion, at any of these stages. Indeed, the good manager is often he who recognizes that he needs specialist help and is not averse to asking for it. But the *responsibility* for each of these stages lies with the local manager.

Like much that is true in life, this statement seems too obvious to be meaningful. Too many times, however:

1 The symptoms are treated instead of the disease – low morale is met by exhortation or a Christmas party, poor communications by briefing meetings or a house journal.
2 The prescription is the same whatever the disease – the equivalent of 'give him antibiotics' is often 're-structure the division' or 'send her on a course'. It is as true in management as it is said to be in medicine that when you select a consultant you select a treatment. That is not necessarily bad, as long as the correct diagnosis has already been made. *That* is the job of the manager on the spot.

3.2   The symptoms

What are these *symptoms*? In a managerial situation they will appear as problems. They may be such general things as low morale, inter-group bickering, inter-personal hostility. They may be particular instances such as a stock-out, a disastrous tender price, a faulty shipment. Managerial judgement is involved in deciding whether the problem is a one-off instance or a symptom of a deeper malaise. If, however, the instinctive managerial reaction to a problem is not 'Whose fault is it?' but 'What is wrong here?' it will be a reaction that errs on the right side. Organizations find it very easy to grow accustomed to their blemishes. Remarks like 'that is a characteristic of this industry' often mean 'we've had this squint for so long that it has become part of our identity'. The usefulness of outsiders in organizations, as consultants, directors or advisers, often consists mainly in pointing out that one does not necessarily have to have a squint. Similarly, managers in all parts of the organization do not *have* to treat their problems as endemic. If they regard them as symptoms and look for the underlying cause they may find it is something very responsive to treatment.

3.3   Diagnosis and treatment

If symptoms are problems, what corresponds to diagnosis and strategy?

Diagnosis is essentially the theme of this whole book. The first seven chapters outline the kinds of diagnostic interpretations that can be used to explain or understand an organizational situation. Diagnosis implies understanding and understanding implies that you can explain a particular instance by placing it in a general category. The first part of this book can be viewed as a list of categories. If the manager can see that a breakdown in procedures is an instance of an inappropriate culture in one part of the organization, then he has placed the particular instance in a general category. He has identified the cause of the symptom through his understanding of the general organization.

This stage of diagnosis is often instinctive. But instinct can be fallacious. It is useful to subject it at times to some discipline. To use the chapters of a book such as this as a diagnostic check-list – 'do any of these ideas explain the current situation?' – may not be so time-wasting or academic as it seems at first sight. For to leap from sight of symptom to application of treatment looks efficient but may be just habit.

Treatment is another matter. There will be times when no treatment can help – times, too, when the right treatment will cost too much in pain or people to make it possible. None the less, the doctor manager needs to be clear as to what should be done and what could be done. It is here that a checklist of options is a help and the best is probably the simplest, the seven S framework developed by Peters and Waterman and by Pascale and Athos when they all worked for McKinsey (see Box 7.2).

The seven S framework divides into hard and soft.

Box 11.3   Is there time for treatment?

The British subsidiary of the multinational giant was very performance-oriented. There were monthly targets, quarterly performance reviews, annual budgets, two-year plans and five-year forecasts. The visitor was impressed, both by the systems and by the performance. The systems had been instituted by the managing director when he arrived from the headquarters some eighteen months before. Indeed, most of the management team dated from his arrival and were very eager to make their mark. It was, they all felt, a very busy but very stimulating environment. Only one thing puzzled the visitor. What was going to be underneath those upward-sloping lines in the five-year forecast? 'Oh, they're projections,' said the marketing director, 'we don't have much time to worry about them. The future around here ends in eighteen months' time when the boss returns to HQ.'

Three years later the visitor was passing by once more. The activity was still impressive. The MD was new, so were most of the management team. The forecasts still pointed upward but it seemed to the visitor, from his memory of his last visit, that they did not start where the others left off. The earlier forecasts had been thrown away as 'unrealistic', 'drawn up by the previous management'. Only the personnel manager was left of the previous team. He was very busy. 'Lots of activity at the moment,' he said, 'new faces and new structures. The MD believes in action – and returns. He wants a two-year pay-off on any expenditure. We've got a much more streamlined organization now but the middle management turnover is a bit worrying.'

The visitor passed on, wondering whom he would meet there on his next visit.

The Hard S's

Strategy – the plan of action which allows it to allocate its resources in order to get food from here to there.

Structure – the way the boxes or clusters fit together.

Systems – the way information moves around and is collected, by forms, computers, meetings or networks.

The Soft S's

Staff – the array of people and the kinds of people that work the organization.

Style – the way things are done, the 'cultures' of Chapter 7.

Shared values – the set of beliefs, principles and priorities which characterize the organization.

Skills – the distinctive competences of the organizations.

The hard S's are easier to change, but the change can be illusory if the soft S's remain unaffected because each of the seven variables are interconnected one with the other. A businessman in Hungary noted that after the fall of the communist regions the one state bank had been replaced by fifteen others but, he ruefully reflected, it made no difference because 'all the bankers were still the same bankers'. Structural change on its own avails little.

Similarly, it is not unknown for consultants to draw up an imaginative plan for entering new markets or new technologies but without attending to the core competences (skills) the plan will be mere verbiage, left to gather dust in the chairman's bookcase. This so-called 'systemic' effect of treatment is obvious but easily forgotten. The seven S checklist is a reminder that life is complicated.

This is one reason for the interest in the soft S's, or what used to be called organization development. These S's are much harder to change, particularly to change quickly. A ruthless organization can replace staff and thereby change its skill profile but doing such a thing in short order will say much about the style – power rather than role or task in this case. That change of style may undermine the new found competences and destroy any sense of shared values, resulting in a lack of trust and commitment.

The newstreams discussed in Chapter 10 are a way of developing a new set of soft S's alongside the old set in the hope of infecting the old with the values, skills and style of the new. It will take time, but it is more likely to get results than a flurry of good intentions or vision and value statements from the boardroom. One organization once circulated all its managers with a statement saying that with effect from

---

Box 11.4 Money or . . . ?

A young millionaire, noted for his take-over activities, once attributed his success to the simple fact that he was interested in making money. Most of the people that he competed against in take-over situations were interested in making or doing things *for* money. The difference had a crucial effect on valuations. To take the simplest example – the latter would see a factory as a building for manufacturing toys and would value it, both psychologically and financially, in terms of its suitability for that purpose. He, however, would instinctively see it merely as a site. To call him an asset-stripper, he maintained, was only another way of saying that his aims were different from theirs.

today's date we are resolved to be an entrepreneurial organization. To their surprise, nothing changed. Good intentions on their own are never enough.

3.4 The implementation

The manager, therefore, has a choice of seven strategic variables. In the short or medium term he or she will be confined to the hard S's but the longer-term factors must not be ignored, particularly by the more senior people in an organization. But in considering treatment the manager will also reflect upon its feasibility, *the implementation*.

She will realize that whereas she may see it as a cure for a malaise, most others will regard it as change. She will know from past experience that change is to managers what motherhood is to men, 'something to be approved of but for someone else'. She will understand instinctively that many of the strategies she has considered are not feasible, because the point of initiation is one that she cannot influence, that the parts of the organization that she can influence are perhaps politically ineffective, that change which is imposed will not be change that will be self-maintaining. If she has read Chapter 5 of this book she will understand that the implementation of change is largely a matter of sources of power and methods of influence, that organizations react psychologically rather than logically and that persuasion or rational argument is only a possible method of influence when she is regarded as the appropriate expert. Having realized all this she may well begin to feel that the ends are not worth the very troublesome means. But having recovered from her initial depression she will see that the appropriate psychological progression would be to:

1 Create an awareness of the need for change (preferably not by argument or rationale but by exposure to objective fact).
2 Select an appropriate initiating person or group ('appropriate' in this context refers to sources of power as perceived by the recipients of the strategy).
3 Be prepared to allow the recipients to adapt the final strategy. (That which one adapts one can more easily call one's own. Ownership equals internalization, i.e. is self-maintaining.)
4 Accept the fact that, like the good psychoanalyst, the successful doctor gets no credit but must let the patient boast of his sound condition. Good managers live vicariously.
5 Be prepared to accept a less than optimum strategy in the interests

of achieving something rather than nothing. Compromise has its own morality.

(Effectiveness=strategy × likelihood of success.)

Change is not to be advocated for its own sake. But the organization that can adapt to changing situations and requirements is the organization that survives. The assumption that a given organizational form which works today will still be right in five years' time is too often a misplaced assumption. The adaptive manager is the one who knows when change is needed, what change is needed and how to bring it about without disruption. The wise manager will not sit in the consulting room awaiting the onset of an epidemic, but will invest in a degree of preventive medicine.

4 The managerial dilemmas

4.1

There is usually some crude justice somewhere in the divisions of society. Managers are paid more than workers but in return they find themselves faced with a set of constant dilemmas. These dilemmas can be described in a book, but they can only be resolved by the person in the middle of them, the manager. The principal managerial dilemmas are:

The dilemma of the cultures;
The dilemma of time-horizons;
The trust-control dilemma;
The commando leader's dilemma.

Each of these needs a few words of explanation and description.

4.2 The dilemma of the cultures

In Chapter 7, the organization was described as being made up of a set of cultures. The role culture was suggested as appropriate for steady-state activities, the task culture for developmental work, the power culture for emergencies, crises and breakdowns. The manager, as he or she climbs the seniority ladder, will find that the job embraces all three of these cultures. There is a management style and a set of behaviours, or procedures and attitudes appropriate to each. A failure to behave in a culturally appropriate manner will result in a breach of the psychological contract, in lack of trust, in ineffective management.

The manager must, therefore, be flexible in both style and behaviour, and must cover all three cultures. Worse still, he must, if he wishes to preserve his own identity and to claim that 'he' makes a personal difference, retain some elements of the person culture. Without some elements of this Dionysian set of beliefs he will have little personal power and will add little 'character' to the organization. In short, the effective manager must be culturally diverse and culturally flexible. But he must at the same time avoid the sin of unpredictability. He must be flexible but consistent, culturally diverse but recognizably an individual with his own identity. Therein lies the dilemma. Those who fail to resolve it, who relapse into one culturally predominant style, will find themselves rightly restricted to that part of the organization where their culture prevails. Middle layers of organizations are often overcrowded with culturally rigid managers who have failed to deal with this cultural dilemma.

4.3 The dilemma of time-horizons

The manager is, above all, responsible for the future. For most of the time the present, for good or ill, is under way. There is often very little he, as manager, can do about it. He can, with greater ease, influence the future. Much of his time should be given to anticipating the future, making assessments of contingencies, and adjusting his plans and his resources accordingly, setting the culture and the climate, picking and developing his people. In general, the higher a person rises in an organization, the longer needs to be his time-horizon and the more of his time he should spend thinking about it.

But this management of the future has to go hand in hand with the responsibility for the present. Whilst it may be true that we can do little to change the present and can only comment on the past, we must nevertheless preside over both, must be interested in today as well as tomorrow, must inspire and control, know enough of what is happening to be able to judge whether an intervention might after all be profitable.

It is not easy to live in two or more time dimensions at once. It is hard to plan creatively for five years hence with a redundancy interview scheduled for one hour's time. Just as routine drives out non-routine, so the present can easily obliterate the future. By concentrating on the problems of the present the future becomes in its turn a series of present problems or crises, intervention by the manager in a power role becomes legitimate, even essential, there is still less time available for the future, the manager feels indispensable and legitimized by crisis. The cycle has become self-fulfilling. Unless the manager is able to live successfully in two time dimensions he or she will make the present more difficult than it need be and will unsuccessfully manage the future.

4.4 The trust–control dilemma

In Chapter 10 the issue of delegation was explored. The trust–control relationship was seen to be complementary. If control is increased, trust is decreased. An increase in trust is only believed and therefore only effective if accompanied by a decrease in control. Trust, it was pointed out, is a much cheaper way of running things as well as being more fitting to the dignity and rights of humankind.

The managerial dilemma is always how to balance trust and control. The dilemma is particularly acute for the manager in the middle, most crucially so for the supervisor or first-level manager. Trust implies giving someone the right to make mistakes. The mistakes that you might tolerate in your subordinate may not, however, be tolerated by your superior. In other words, the degree of control is often dictated not by the manager but by the manager's manager. Ultimately the chain stops at the top. As in so many other ways the example of top management is crucial to the trust–control issue. It is noticeable, for instance, that in successful organizations there tends to be more trust and less control, junior managers perceive they have more influence over their work. This is usually interpreted as meaning that more shared influence (more trust, in our terminology) leads to more success. The sequence, however, is perhaps more likely to work the other way round. When things go well it is easier to relinquish controls. Trust flourishes with success. Maybe the trust in turn contributes to further success but one suspects that in many cases the cycle starts with success not with trust. The practical message for any middle manager must often be – 'First get your success record, then you'll be given freedom which amounts to trust.'

One of the pre-conditions of trust, it was noted in Chapter 10, was a knowledge of, a confidence in, one's subordinates. This most easily happened when the manager could select her own people. Usually this luxury is denied to the middle manager. Given a group, she has to learn to know them and they her. She has to experiment with trust. Too much control is expensive, time-consuming and self-defeating in motivational terms. Trust, however, can often survive only one mistake. Therein lies this dilemma. A manager will often find herself being more controlling than she would like to be.

4.5   The commando leader's dilemma

The commando leader likes to be given a clear objective (e.g. capture that bridge) but allowed great freedom as to how he does it. A commando group is a collection of expert resources; there is a high degree of group loyalty. Commandos often develop cults, special group norms, badges, uniforms or languages. There is a great amount of camaraderie, of mutual trust and shared objectives. It is in fact the epitome of a project organization or task culture. Many a manager, and almost all young managers, have a personal preference for a task culture. To lead a project group in an organization can well be an exhilarating and inspiring task, reviving all one's faith in the purposeful challenge of work. And organizations *need* commando groups, particularly in the developmental area. But few organizations, if any, can be made up totally of such groups. Organizations, like armies, have to have a steady state; and commando leaders, though valuable, are often perceived as a nuisance. It is not unknown for the GOC to heave a silent sigh of relief when he hears that the commando leader was taken prisoner in the final assault.

Individuals have to learn to adjust to the new mix of managerial

---

Box 11.5   'Thank you, John, but . . .'

John was a highly competent, resourceful young manager. Early in his career with the multi-national corporation he was identified as a man who could be trusted with an independent command at an early age. Soon he was manager of his own subsidiary company in one of those isolated but interesting corners of the old empire. Admired and respected by his local staff he was highly successful. Soon he was moved to a larger but equally interesting outpost. Again success was quick and impressive. He was beginning to acquire a reputation for unorthodox but successful trading methods. A striking figure, he dressed a trifle bizarrely and drove strange cars. He inspired almost a devotion among his staff. He was known to be a hard man to succeed in any post.

The years passed, and so did a succession of outpost jobs. Always glowing reports. He was 38 now, married with growing children and anxious to return to London. Head office, however, had no vacancies for him. 'Sorry, John,' they said, 'but we don't think you would fit in here. Not enough of a bureaucrat, are you? Perhaps you ought to take six months' pay and find yourself a niche back in the Indian Ocean where you've done so splendidly for us.'

roles as they move up and through organizations. There may be no substitute for the first independent small command but such things do not last forever and would become stale if they did. Advancement nearly always means adjustment. Similarly, organizations must not be too prone to type-casting. Just because someone has been consistently successful in one type of job it does not necessarily follow that he could not do other jobs equally well. John's dilemma (Box 11.5) was the organization's fault.

4.6 Dealing with dilemmas

There is no universal panacea for these dilemmas. They are present with most managers most of the time. The following points are more in the nature of reminders than remedies.

(a) *Stress heightens the dilemmas*. Stress shortens time-horizons, polarizes issues, exaggerates the importance of the present, makes difficulties into crises and inhibits creativity. Stress in fact is the one thing a person, and especially a senior manager, should be without. And yet, for many a manager stress is almost a battle honour. To succumb to it is weakness, to be without it is dishonourable. In a way, a heartless way perhaps, it is not the physical and medical outcomes of managerial stress that are the worries. If a man has a heart attack, develops an ulcer, has a nervous breakdown, he is himself a victim but he is also incapacitated as a manager, prevented from causing hurt to others. It is the less respectable symptoms of stress, the general impairment of judgement and the tendencies listed at the beginning of this paragraph, which can really foul up organizations and the lives of others. Managers, as a social duty, must manage stress, not court it.

Stress, as Chapter 3 demonstrated, is largely inherent in the managerial role. The managerial dilemmas are not only heightened by stress, they can also add to the stress. The factors that cause managerial stress cannot all, should not all, be avoided or eliminated. But the stress that they cause can be managed, can be mitigated. Some of the ways for achieving this are noted below.

(b) *Create stability zones*. Alvin Toffler in his stimulating book *Future Shock* notes how those people who live the most mobile and stressful lives do have what he calls 'stability zones' in their lives (see Box 11.6).

Decisions use up energy. New situations imply new decision rules. If one is to manage stress it is important to conserve energy, to reserve energy for the important problems and the strategic decisions. A 'stability zone' can be a place or time for rebuilding energy reserves. Holidays, weekends, days off – these are important stability zones. Not enough managers pay enough attention to them. Holidays are seen as self-indulgence. Conferences, overseas visits, courses – these are more respectable forms of 'getting away'. But they are less effective than a straightforward holiday as buffers to stress and considerably more expensive. Managerial holidays need to be clothed in a new respect-ability.

The family is for many a stability zone. Perhaps a demeaning role for the wife – to be manager of a stability zone – but a very important one for her husband and his colleagues and subordinates.

An important way of creating stability zones is through the creation

---

Box 11.6   'Stability zones'

One man I know has run through a series of love affairs, a divorce and re-marriage – all within a very short span of time. He thrives on change, enjoys travel, new foods, new ideas, new movies, plays and books. He has a high intellect and a low 'boring point', is impatient with tradition and restlessly eager for novelty. Ostensibly, he is a walking exemplar of change.

When we look more closely, however, we find that he has stayed in the same job for ten years. He drives a battered, seven-year-old auto-mobile. His clothes are several years out of style. His closest friends are long-time professional associates and even a few old college buddies.

Another case involves a man who has changed jobs at a mind-staggering rate, has moved his family thirteen times in eighteen years, travels extensively, rents cars, uses throw-away products, prides himself on leading the neighbourhood in trying out new gadgets, and generally lives in a restless whirl of transience, newness and diversity. Once more, however, a second look reveals significant stability zones in his life: a good, tightly woven relationship with his wife of nineteen years; con-tinuing ties with his parents; old college friends interspersed with the new acquaintances.

A different form of stability zone is the habit pattern that goes with the person wherever he travels, no matter what other changes alter his life. A professor who has moved seven times in ten years, who travels constantly in the United States, South America, Europe and Africa, who has changed jobs repeatedly, pursues the same daily regimen wherever he is. He reads between eight and nine in the morning, takes forty-five minutes for exercise at lunchtime, and then catches a half-hour cat-nap before plunging into work that keeps him busy until 10 p.m.

From Alvin Toffler, *Future Shock*, 1971

of routines. Routines are a way of coping with stress. Carried to extremes or applied inappropriately they inhibit creativity and change. But just because they are a way of coping with stress, they are useful in moderation as buffers. Many decisions can be taken by habit. What time do you get up in the morning? What train do you catch? What do you do for the first hour at the office? When do you have those meetings? To make each of these decisions afresh every day is energy-consuming, and will tend, just a little, to make you more prone to stress. Take them by routine or habit and that energy is conserved for more useful things. Does this make you a creature of habit, a predictable unexciting individual? In little things, perhaps, and much to the benefit of your colleagues. 'A creature of habit', as long as it is not inflexible, is often a creature of wisdom.

(c) *Be your own person.* He who wants nothing from anyone is no one's servant. That is easier to say than to achieve but it is crucially important for anyone who wants to be a manager rather than an institutional cog. Personal values, personal goals and personal wealth are the necessary steps to personal freedom within organizations. Those who know what they believe to be right and proper and who have a good grasp on what they really want from life come over as strong and not easily dominated. Personal wealth, which provides economic independence, is perhaps harder to achieve, particularly if organizations actively connive to tie it up in organizational perks and benefits.

Organizations would, in the long run, have stronger and better managers if they encouraged them to be personally and financially independent. Unfortunately, both power and role cultures foster dependency and relish conformity, sometimes cloaking it in the guise of loyalty. Unconsciously, as they do this, they force the individual to surrender a piece of himself to his role with the result that he can begin to feel that he is acting some kind of part in a play not always of his own devising. The sense of being imprisoned in a role only makes the dilemmas seem bigger.

(d) *Use catalysts.* Our vantage point will colour what we see. The blind man and the elephant, the wood unnoticed because of its trees, the Eskimo who thought a tree was a god; the folklore of the world is full of stories of how our past experience and present involvement affects and distorts our image of reality. The present undoubtedly can impair our vision of the future.

Outsiders can be valuable in restoring perspective. They can ask pertinent questions even if they do not know the answers. The self-confident manager will find it a stimulus to expose his thinking on his management of the future to interested outsiders. To the insecure the stranger is a threat, to the confident he is a catalyst. Consultants are the ritual form of outsider. To ask them for answers as well as questions is often to require, and pay for, more than you really need. It is their role as catalyst and stimulus that is often the most useful. It is no accident that many consultants' solutions lie gathering dust on bookshelves, whilst the organization evolves its own solutions to the problems the outsiders raised.

Non-executive directors on boards of companies are another institutional form of the outsider as catalyst. They perform other custodial duties as well sometimes, but their role as catalyst and stimulus can be the most rewarding. 'Boards,' someone said, 'are usually long, narrow and wooden!' Often, but not necessarily so. The outside director is becoming more common in the UK although he is still regarded more as a bearer of status than of stimulus. A pity, for a proper perspective on the future must be one of the major tasks of the board of any company. If outsiders are valuable anywhere they are valuable at this level.

The 'outsider' role does not, however, have to be so formally institutionalized. The requirement that a manager reveal thinking on the management of the future to anyone not immediately involved in the operation is a most useful discipline. The need to explain something to others will force you to understand it yourself. The best way to learn is to teach. Teaching others about one's job has been found by many to be more illuminating to the speaker than to the listener. We need, in organizations, to do more to encourage and promote the role of official listener. We need to institutionalize the inside outsider, the person from one section of the organization sitting as non-executive director on the 'boards' of the other sections. This is done under the guise of training and development by some organizations. Union Carbide in the US experimented with the idea at a higher level by requiring executives from one division to act as members of planning groups in other divisions. More perhaps could be done with divisional boards in large companies, usually composed of the senior divisional managers and head office representatives.

(e) *Compartmentalize*. Just because it is difficult to work in two time-dimensions at once, so one should seek to arrange it so that one does not have to. One way is, of course, to deal only with one of the dimensions, usually the present. The more desirable method is to organize the work so that it is sorted by time-dimension rather than by topic. Most meetings in organizations are topic-centred, e.g. overseas marketing, competition, salary review. Few are time-centred. As a result, the agendas of most organization meetings cover a variety of time-horizons.

A study of a number of senior managers' diaries has revealed that problems are juxtaposed, randomly, in terms of the time-dimensions which apply to them. An incident from the past is followed by a problem in the present, when the five-year forecast is required by that evening.

Box 11.7   A senior manager's diary

One senior divisional manager sat down to separate out what he regarded as the major responsibilities of his job. He listed six key areas for himself:

A Relationships with head office;
B Long-term and strategic planning;
C Operational responsibilities for particular ongoing activities;
D Co-ordinating function;
E Standard setting, performance, morale, priorities;
F External relations.

He then analysed his diary for the previous three months and came up with the following approximate proportion of time spent on each of the key areas.

A 20%   D 25%
B 10%   E 5%
C 35%   F 5%

Should he have been worried?

Ask any individual manager for his major continuing problem and he will normally reply 'time'. Time to think, time to plan, time to talk with my people. Yet the same person finds time for food and for sleep, for Sundays and holidays. But these are institutionalized priorities – time for the future is not. The organization of work in organizations is usually haphazard. Diaries get filled up on a first-come first-served basis. Meeting agendas look like a cafeteria menu.

Some organizations make some attempt to compartmentalize. Long-term planning meetings are held away from the office. Certain days are regularly annotated for review or for planning. Some individuals attempt to compartmentalize their days into immediate and long-term divisions. Some have two offices – different territories for different kinds of problems. On the whole, however, there is too much adherence to the maxim that a manager has the door ever open, that a manager's place is at the desk or in a committee room, that a manager should be available at all times. This is a recipe for stress, for putting the present in place of the future, for letting problems drive out plans. Why not, instead, compartmentalize your work? Stay at home occasionally if that aids your thinking. Use what academics call office-hours for seeing subordinates. Remember that if a manager is thought only to be working when he or she is seen to be working, then he is unlikely to be doing as much long-term thinking as he should.

Organizations can help by institutionalizing thinking. A library as a place for reflection, recognition that days at home are not 'slacking', the occasional sabbatical in addition to a holiday. This kind of measure will help individuals to compartmentalize the future into the present.

5   The manager as a person

5.1

The last quarter-century has seen the emergence of 'the manager' as a recognized occupational role in society. Management has become at least a semi-profession. It is not a profession in the sense of medicine, for instance, with formal admission procedures, a recognized body of relevant knowledge, codified and enforced standards of practice. Nor is it a profession in the sense that a member of it is entitled to ask a set scale of fees for his services from the public. It is, however, a recognized occupational role, and one that now embraces something like 10 per cent of the total work-force of the UK.

The emergence of a new kind of middle class, dependent not on property, nor on the earnings from the practice of their own trade or profession, but on the salary paid to them by another, has begun to create real dilemmas for society, some of which are only beginning to emerge. It is not the purpose of this book to analyse the emerging society, but there are some questions that are beginning to be matters of urgent importance to organizations which arise from the existence of the managerial middle class. For instance:

(a) Does an organization owe an individual a career, or only skill-related earnings? Before management became a semi-profession, organizations seemed to view themselves as latter-day villages with many of the accompanying responsibilities of squirearchy towards their tenants. If they admitted someone to their patronage they were thenceforth responsible for that someone unless that someone renounced the patronage. The emergence of managers as would-be professionals has meant that individuals now believe in transferable skills, wish to be rewarded for these skills and resent patronage or paternalism. The obverse of this, of course, is that the organization has no obligation to hire the professional when his or her services are no longer required. Earnings will increasingly be related to marketable skills, redundant skills will be cut from pay-rolls, organizations will feel less obligation towards their managers and managers less commitment towards an organization. Since skills become redundant there will be a tendency to try to gather a lifetime's earnings during the extant life of the skill. In short, salaries will tend to increase but more people will retire early. Alternatively, deferred salaries, i.e. pensions, will increase, thus permitting early retirement.

Employability is the new form of security, argues Kanter. Companies should help individuals build up 'reputational capital' so that they can survive outside the corporation. People who have been helped with education or with assignments that earn them a reputation outside the corporation not only have an easier time moving on and out if they have to but also value the company more highly – because it is investing in them.

(b) Should more managers be female? For a variety of reasons the answer should be 'yes'. There is the straightforward feminist argument that women have the same rights as men and should have the same opportunities. There is the simple statistical truth that, by not recruiting women managers, organizations are missing out on half of the population. There is the likelihood that women could bring more of the yin into the yang of organizations, as Nancy Foy puts it. Indeed, those cultures (advertising, parts of journalism and television, fashion merchandising) where women are easily acceptable in managerial roles are often noticeably more creative and task-cultured in their work. But the managerial class is a new one; it will not quickly or willingly open its ranks. The predominant male pronoun in this book is not just a linguistic convenience, it still represents the true position in many organizations. Ironically, as management becomes more professional and organizations see themselves as buying skills rather than lives, it will become less important which sex is behind the skill. The professionalization of management should eventually mean the enfranchisement of women in organizations. Wise organizations will get there first.

(c) Should the organization concern itself with the individual's family situation? Most people would instinctively say that the family and the personal situation of the manager are of no concern to the organization which, after all, has hired the individual not his ancestry and dependants. It is not, however, as simple as that. The home situation inevitably affects the work situation. Multi-national companies know from experience that unless an executive's family is happy with an overseas posting and can adapt to the new situation, they will have a problem executive on their hands. Some research on executives and their marriages suggests that husbands with supportive wives who identify with their husbands' careers do better in the promotion stakes. On the other hand, other research shows that those successful husbands can later feel cheated out of family life. Managers who refuse to move because it would not be in the interests of their family hamper an organization's flexibility. On the other hand, a manager separated from the family or with a resentful family to go home to each night is not going to be a productive manager. The problems can be further complicated if the manager is responsible, as many women managers are (and some men), for the care and upbringing of children. There will be times when family concerns become more important than those of the organization. Should the organization be co-operative?

Organizations have to be aware that their people all belong to more than one role set. They have to tread the narrow path between invading privacy and not caring. The psychological contract (and sometimes the formal contract) between individual and organization will need renegotiation over time as the individual's circumstances change.

5.2 The implications

The changing role of the manager has its implications for managers. They must become pro-active in the management of their careers. In a world of skill-related earnings it is of little use relying on the village elders to nurture and guide your upbringing. Increasingly it will come to be seen as our responsibility to maintain, alter or boost our skills, to find the right market for those skills and to sell them to the appropriate buyer. Traditional management development looked upon its managers as resources in whom it made sense to invest. The initial responsibility lay with the organization. The individual could rest assured that if he did that which was asked of him development and subsequent advancement was guaranteed. He was encouraged to be reactive, to respond to organizational initiatives. This concept of management development is fast being eroded. The societal *responsibility* of the organization is to offer opportunity and perhaps facilities for the individual to improve his skills, to re-qualify or re-align himself professionally. It is in the *interest* of the organization to see that it has first call on the individuals and skills it wishes to retain. It will retain them by, to some extent, paying for the future in the present. The rewards, in terms of higher salaries, stock options, deferred bonuses, pension schemes, will be intended to provide for an individual's future as well as his present. There will then be no obligation to continue to employ the individual when the benefits of his skills begin to be less than their costs. Managerial talent will thus become much more expensive, organizations will become more discriminating, management complements will be fined down, the average age of top and middle management will decrease. Managers of all levels of ability may expect to find themselves and their skills unwanted at their current rates of pay by their early fifties. They will *all* be 'redundant', although society will doubtless find a kinder word. The only difference between the more and the less successful will be that the former will have their future financially protected by their past earnings.

The individual must, therefore, look to himself. Are his current skills likely to be in demand in ten years' time? If not can he acquire new ones; if so what, and how? Going back to school is one alternative. But so many of the managerial skills, whilst they may be taught in the classroom, can only be tried and tempered by experience. Mobility, within or without the same organization, will be the major method of skill acquirement. Since organizations are unlikely, under the new conditions, to want to move individuals much before the expiry date of their current skill, it will be left to individual initiative to prompt and negotiate the transfers.

Self-development is not as easy to practise as it sounds. It implies:

A clear idea of ultimate priorities and directions;
A knowledge of one's own strengths and weaknesses;
A willingness to regard the present as an investment for the future.

1 *Priorities* may well change over time. Travel and variety may be important to the young individual, finance to the married man or w men with growing children, self-realization to the older individual. The career line will no longer have to progress steadily upwards in terms simultaneously of income, status and interest. Individuals may consciously start to plan for a second career. The portfolio approach to life may become more common, when individuals gain their income from one set of activities, their main interest and purpose from another.

2 *Self-knowledge* is uncomfortable at first. As Chapter 3 indicated, we are at pains to protect our self-concept, not to explore it. Yet we

may have so many talents and abilities which the zig-zag of our experience has not yet uncovered. What is called a defect in one environment (e.g. meticulousness) may be an asset in another. To make the most of ourselves we must expose ourselves to a range of opportunities and experiences, yet to do so may mean facing up to realities which we had hoped to ignore.

3 *Investment*. Culturally we are conditioned to a personal investment period that finished by the early twenties at the latest. In the new managerial world our stock of learning and conditioning will need continual replenishment. The formal classroom will be the least important of the sources, although it will have its place. The proactive individuals need to see every experience as a learning opportunity, they need to be able to learn from success as well as failure, to enrich their stock of concepts and skills as they work. How is this achieved? To learn from experience one must:

(a) Conceptualize the particular incident so that it becomes part of a general rule rather than an isolated anecdote. A collection of anecdotes is no more than a basis for some stories unless they can be linked by concepts.

(b) Apply the scientific method to life. Hypothesize, test, hypothesize again. In every significant event one should train oneself to make some predictions about the interplay of variables and the expected outcome. This procedure is the obverse of the first since here one is applying general rules or concepts to particular events. If the prediction is correct the hypothesis is confirmed, the general concept has had another concrete application. If the prediction is incorrect, do not leave it there. Some variable or mix of variables has been left out of account. Some explanatory concept is missing.

Box 11.8   Selfishness or . . . ?

I was a young trainee in the giant corporation. After three years of assorted experience I was back in the head offices, sitting in the waiting room of the personnel department, waiting to hear how they proposed to dispose of the next three years of my life. As I was sitting, expectant yet unsure, an old Scotsman on the point of retirement came by, saw me and paused:

'What are you waiting for, laddie?'

'To hear what they've got in store for me,' I replied.

'Ah, invest in yourself, my boy, invest in yourself. If you don't no one else will.'

6   In conclusion

6.1

This chapter has looked at:

The manager's job:
The roles of a manager.
The manager as GP:
The recognition of symptoms;
The meaning of diagnosis;
The types of strategy;
The implementation or treatment.
The managerial dilemmas:
The dilemma of the cultures;
The dilemma of time-horizons;
The trust-control dilemma;
The commando leader's dilemma;
Some ways of handling the dilemmas.
The manager as a person:
Management as a semi-profession;
The need for self-development.

6.2

This chapter has been very much a personal anthology culled from many years of dealing with managers and of being a manager. Other people's anthologies are of interest but are seldom taken to heart. Wise readers will now write their own Chapter 11. You should now set down in some more permanent form your own conclusions about the work and management of organizations, your own sets of precepts and heuristics. It is pointless to re-invent the wheel but some chiselling and hammering may help to make it your particular wheel. What we own we value, and are that much more likely to use.

12 ⟶ On the Future of Organizations

1 Introduction

Fashions change, not people, and Part Two is really about organization fashion or the ways in which we currently see fit to deck out the truths about people in organizational dress. Some fashions are fleeting, others enduring, because some fit our underlying needs and the circumstances of the times better than others. Different times emphasize different priorities which in turn underline some of the truths and ignore others. Wars have always been great disturbers of priorities, and therefore of fashion, but a creeping change in a society's age profile or a major piece of social reform may be just as pervasive. The speed of universal suffrage and the progressive emancipation of women have probably had more to do with changing the ways we run organizations than any refinement of the basic truths or any research into effectiveness. Who would care to predict the impact on organizations when the babies of the post-war boom, which flowered in 1968, reach middle-age in 2010? Organizations have to be the mirrors of our societies however much we may regret that fact and yearn for other times and other places.

This chapter, therefore, is an attempt to be a guide to future fashion. It will look at some fashions on their way out and try to discern some on the way in and to show what this will do to the way we run our organizations. It will then examine some of the problems and possibilities that these changes will present to the manager and to society as a whole. The Chinese ideogram for crisis combines the signs for danger and for opportunity. We need to see both signs clearly when we look into the future lest we be carried away by enthusiasm into extravagant experiment or by dismay into dogged reaction. Two things at least we can be sure of: organizations of some shape and size will still be needed, and people will still be people however we present them.

2 The changing assumptions

2.1

The late Dr Fritz Schumacher was a great believer in curvilinear logic.
He argued that many graphs flatten out after a time; they may even
turn back on themselves. Every graph is based on a relationship between two factors. The more you have of one the more (or less) you
will have of the other. Curvilinear logic does not say that the relationship ceases, it only claims that you can no longer rely on more of one
factor producing more of the other; it may only produce the same or
even less. Fertilizer improves crops – up to a point. Too much fertilizer
will damage not improve. The basic proposition (that fertilizer improves crops) is not contradicted by the obvious fact that you can have
too much of a good thing. We automatically apply curvilinear logic to
domestic life – to sleep, food, even work. We believe Herzberg when
he uses it to create his hygiene factors in motivation. We are less good
at seeing the logic *before* it begins to work, in the unfamiliar. It is not
to be wondered at. When one of our basic assumptions runs out of
steam there is no longer any confident basis for predicting the future.
We then enter a condition which has been variously called Discontinuous Change, a Paradigm Shift or even the realm of Catastrophe
Theory. It is an uncomfortable situation until some new assumptions
have emerged.

I want now to argue that some key assumptions in organizational
thinking have reached the end of their useful life. They were only true
up to a point, or for a time. We can no longer rely on them for the
future. We need a new fashion, maybe a new paradigm.

There are four common assumptions which now need reconsider-
ation. Each of them has heavily influenced the way we have run organizations in the past. They are all now open to question. The first two,
however, are still valid, but only up to a point, and in many cases they
have reached that point. The second two may need to be abandoned
altogether. These assumptions are:

That concentration plus specialization = efficiency;
That hierarchy is natural;
That labour is a cost;
That an organization is a form of property.

We shall consider each in turn.

2.2   Concentration plus specialization = efficiency (the first assumption)

This formula has been at the heart of industrial organizations for at least two hundred years and from there it has spread into other forms of organization where, arguably, it has had less validity. Concentrate your activities, then specialize. That way came the economies of scale which pulled down costs, made yesterday's luxuries today's commonplaces and turned production into the servant of the consumer society.

Box 12.1   Paradigms

The word paradigm was given a new dynamism by T. B. Kuhn in his book *The Structure of Scientific Revolutions*. A paradigm is a conceptual framework, a way of looking at the world, a set of assumed categories into which we pile the facts. When Copernicus suggested that the earth was not at the centre of the universe he was, though he knew it not, a paradigm revolutionary. But it was the minds of men that changed, not the motions of the planets, and the way in which they now viewed that same universe had a profound effect on their beliefs, values and behaviour.

Economic surplus is another example. Today, and for many centuries, it has been assumed that surplus is good. Called 'profit' or 'wealth' it is every man's and every community's legitimate goal. It was not always thus, however. When distribution was difficult, in the early Middle Ages, and markets did not exist for the great majority of products, then surplus meant waste. There was no point in producing more than you and your family and friends needed because you could not dispose of it. Work in those days was necessary, not good. You did as little as you could because more than enough was of no benefit. But with better distribution methods and proper markets things began to change. Luther and Calvin made the notion of surplus respectable, the modern industrial age was born and the Protestant work ethic created.

Social paradigms seem to change when a new technology coincides with a shift in values or priorities. The new paradigm then needs its articulate exponent to spell out and legitimize the new assumptions on which we can begin to build a new era of continuous change. Capitalism, and the concept of money, not land, as the key form of prosperity, needed the two technologies of mass-production and limited liability to make it work. It needed Adam Smith to make it understood and respectable. The result was the rise of the merchant and managerial classes and all the values and social changes which that gave rise to, including exponential economic growth.

Could it be that a new technology of information will combine with a new value system to give us a new paradigm, a paradigm only awaiting its prophet?

Management became in effect the art or science of co-ordinating the right specializations with the appropriate concentrations. It should be noted that both components had to be present. Concentrations without proper specialization only increased the overheads (as many mergers have demonstrated), while specialization without the necessary size only produced high unit costs.

There are, however, three flaws in the formula, which impose their own limits on the equation. Specialization demands specialists and breeds them. Today's society is a society of specialists whether they have degrees to prove it or a union card. 'Respectable' specialists belong to professions and have associations. Less 'respectable' ones have closed shops and belong to unions. The difference is often only semantic. Now this desirable combination of concentration and specialization has produced those tightly designed organizations which are the joy of the organizational draughtsman in which every cog in the machine has a valid part to play. This is excellent until one of those cogs seizes up, in which case the whole machine grinds to a halt. We see the effect of the tightly designed organization often enough today, for various groups of specialists have come to see that if they can co-ordinate themselves they have the means to hijack the organization. The principle of concentration therefore yields ripe plums to any greedy group of specialists, for in the short term it nearly always pays to buy off the hijackers provided they are not too selfish or avaricious.

The preferred method for dealing with selfish specialists is to appeal to their commitment to the total enterprise, but here the principle of concentration works against us. Humans find it hard to identify with groups in which (a) they do not know everyone at least by sight, or (b) they have no power, formal or informal, to influence events. Concentration too often requires unit sizes and methods of co-ordination making both of these conditions impossible. Only in times of crisis will the individual identify his or her needs with those of the organization and even then the tale of crisis may not be believed. Imaginative leadership and skilful communications can do something to help out but they are fighting against heavy odds.

The second flaw lies in the changing nature of work. The assembly line has largely been automated; brains have replaced muscles as the key component of added value; we are all knowledge workers now, or will be soon. No longer, then, does concentration produce such obvious economies of scale. In fact, too many brains in one place can be counter-productive. Penetration not concentration, is the aim now; penetration of the market-place, penetration of the technology, penetration of the future. To be lean and flexible rather than big and cheap is what most organizations want. But it is hard to be lean if you are concentrated and hard to be flexible if you are too narrowly specialized. The old formula has had its day in the new automated and fast-changing world.

The third flaw in the argument has already been outlined in Chapter 9. Another name for specialization is 'the micro-division of labour', and the psychological costs of this have been well established. Specialization, after all, does mean limitation. This can be marvellous if you are a medical consultant, a professor or an R and D expert when there are unplumbed depths to explore within the small plot you have been given or have chosen. Every day can be new even if your focus remains unchanged. Try, however, digging a plot when there is concrete all around and one foot down. It does get boring – even alienating. Yet specialization has to be defined and confined if the benefits are going to be achieved.

The results are predictable. Work becomes instrumental and is done only for its extrinsic rewards. Therefore, the incentive to exploit any hijack opportunities is much greater. Alternatively, give work a miss. The levels of absenteeism and sick leave are now running at a fairly uniform rate in Northern Europe – fifteen days annually per worker. This exceptionally large figure must be an index of alienation. To the organizations it is another straight seven per cent on the labour bill.

Box 12.2   The knowledge worker

Peter Drucker comments

- In the nineteenth century only one of America's business builders had any advanced schooling – J. P. Morgan, and he dropped out of Goettingen University half-way through.
- Even after the Second World War the quickest and easiest route to a good job and good security was to start as a semi-skilled worker in a mass-production factory. Within a year that worker would earn more than a university graduate could expect to earn for fifteen years.
- This century the American population has tripled but the number of teachers has multiplied fifty times. So have all the other categories of knowledge workers – accountants, doctors, analysts, managers.
- Knowledge has now become the capital of a developed economy and the blue-collar workers are now a social problem. So much has our world changed in one generation.

Drucker, *The New Realities*, 1989

2.3 Hierarchy is natural (the second assumption)

Organizations have long assumed that one person had to be placed above another to make things happen. It is possible, however, that they were confusing the logic of organizational design with the messages of history. It is true that any organizational work has to be arranged in a logical sequence which roughly corresponds with the order of decisions. The nature of the task must be decided before it is actually embarked upon, the raw materials must be ordered before they are treated. But there is no *logic* which says that this horizontal decision sequence needs to be turned into a vertical ladder so that those who take the necessary earlier decisions are higher in the hierarchy than those who implement them. That is where history comes in, for those who got there first obviously set things up that way. Elliott Jacques, in work referred to in Chapter 9 (2.4), has demonstrated that those whose jobs involve a 'longer time-span of discretion' do in fact receive more pay. In other words, those positioned earlier in the decision process are in fact higher in the pay league and usually in the authority league. Jacques has gone further; he has turned this into a principle, arguing that those with the larger decisions *should have* proportionately more money.

So far he has had the instinctive support of nearly everyone but as organizations have got larger the worm has begun to turn. Individuals are less prepared to accept *impersonal* authority, less prepared to accept that people they have never met or known and over whom they have no control should have the right to take decisions which affect their own working lives. When the decision sequence is clear, when the decision-makers are known, when there is some way of influencing those decision-makers if need be, then there is acceptance that greater responsibility should have greater rewards and that the hierarchy of command is necessary and appropriate. No one, however, likes to be at the receiving end of a bureaucracy, particularly when those at the other end appear to be disproportionately better off. Time was when the disaffected could do little about it, but the advent of hijack power has meant that those at the receiving end have negative power at least equal to the positive power of those at the other end.

To call all this 'industrial democracy' is to risk losing the point in a label. The point is that authority increasingly has to be earned – it cannot be assumed. The idea that one's role gave one sufficient position power to do one's job is becoming less and less true. This means:

1 That the game of organizational chess which top managers like to play with positions and people is no longer so straightforward, when

it is only expert or personal power that is effective, for these forms of power (see Chapter 5) have to be earned.

2 That the number of levels in a given hierarchy is restricted to the number which can be self-justifying, so that the person at the 'top' can be known and, one hopes, respected by those at the bottom. This is vastly different from the current situation in operating groups.

3 That any decision must increasingly be taken with the consent of those who will have to implement it. This does *not* mean that they have to participate in it (for that would be to ask for more responsibility than is in their psychological contract) but it does mean that they must *know what* is happening and have the chance to comment.

When these principles are followed there is effective industrial democracy. When they are not, the diminishing returns of the old assumption that hierarchy is natural are soon apparent. The assumption is not false but it has its limits and these limits have been exceeded in too many instances.

2.4 Labour is a cost (the third assumption)

Managements have long been accustomed to representing their labour as a cost and recording it as such on their profit and loss account. This is another historical situation which is hard to justify logically, but which has had an unquantifiable impact on the way organizations are managed. Costs, after all, are something you minimize and would ideally like to dispense with. Substitute the word 'people' for costs and it is very easy to see how labour can be alienated once it becomes figures not individuals.

Traditionally labour was a variable cost and people could be laid off

---

Box 12.3 Bertrand Russell on work

Work is of two kinds: first, altering the position of matter at or near the earth's surface relative to other such matter; second, telling other people to do so. The first kind is unpleasant and ill-paid; the second is pleasant and highly paid. The second kind is capable of indefinite extension: there are not only those who give orders, but those who give advice as to what orders should be given.

From *In Praise of Idleness*, Unwin Paperbacks, 1976

without notice. Today it is a fixed cost and some organizations even find it profitable to pay an attendance bonus. Gradually, however, some people have begun to query the different ways in which property or capital is handled compared with labour. In 1978 Dunlop proposed to close their tyre factory at Speke in Liverpool. The workers found it natural to argue 'if tyres don't sell that well any more it is management's responsibility to find something which we can make which will sell'. The Dunlop management took the argument seriously enough to set up a joint task force to look for projects. They failed to find any but a point of principle had been established. Excess assets are not returned to the market until management has fully explored all possible alternative uses for them, and even then there are reasonably efficient markets both for money and for property. Labour, on the other hand, has traditionally been dumped on an inefficient market as soon as it is surplus to immediate requirements.

There are those who would argue that if only the labour market were truly efficient we could return to the concept of labour as a variable cost which would undoubtedly make things much easier for management. We must suspect, however, that this assumption (that labour is a cost) is not one of those assumptions which has reached its limit but one of those which has been reversed. It is hard to see how it will ever be turned back again. Labour may remain on the profit and loss account, not the balance sheet (as with the football clubs mentioned in the introduction to Chapter 8), but it must henceforth be treated as an asset to be disposed of only after proper thought has been given to its alternative uses.

Many would see this development as right and proper but it significantly affects the way organizations go about their business. For instance:

1 Recruitment and selection become key activities at all levels if you have to keep what you take. It would be logical to expect those jobs to become more important and more highly rewarded.
2 The variables which management can play with in their planning must become the products, not labour or even plant. It is equivalent to saying that you cannot easily change your family, only the things it does. To a management which regards the ending of a product line (with its associated labour) as a purely economic decision, this change in thinking will be hard.
3 Since the labour force is less easily replaceable (because you cannot get rid of it) it will in future make more economic sense to invest time and money in building up the skills and commitment of the

individuals even though the pay-off is long-term. In the past you could buy in skills, now you will have to develop them.

2.5   Organizations as property (the fourth assumption)

The Marxist complaint has always been that organizations have been viewed by society as the equivalent of land. Those who provide the money are the owners and can dispose of it as they please. They are, in company law, very privileged owners since they can ruin the property without ruining themselves. The limited liability of companies may have been a most imaginative device to encourage the entrepreneurial use of capital but it has always seemed to some to be an unearned privilege.

Ownership has traditionally entailed both rights and responsibilities. Historically the rights have been better protected by the law, leaving the responsibilities to be taken care of by conscience. In particular, the owners have always had the right to all the residual profits and the right to make decisions on new expenditure and the choice of staff – the critical decisions.

Progressively, the responsibilities of ownership have become enshrined in law. Conscience was in many cases demonstrably not enough. Employment and financial legislation, product liability and consumer protection laws, environmental requirements and disclosure provisions have all proliferated in the last two decades until owners feel more like puppets than free men.

Recently, however, the whole concept of ownership has come into question. Does it really make sense to regard the shareholders as owners when these shareholders are principally institutions representing thousands of anonymous individuals who have no way of knowing what part of what company they own, nor any way of representing their views? Is it not more sensible, it is argued, to regard shareholders only as the providers of finance, with financial privileges proportionate to the risk they run, rather than owners? Who then are the owners? Or does ownership no longer have any real meaning? Is stakeholding the new concept, implying that there are a number of interested parties each with rights and duties appropriate to their interest? In most countries company law is still behind leading practice but more and more an organization is coming to be thought of as a *community* rather than a *property*. The difference is more than semantic. A community belongs to no one, instead one belongs to a community. People have different interests in regard to the community and play different roles within it but no one is owned by anyone else. The fruits of success belong in a sense to all the interested groups. The consumer is entitled to some surplus profit invested in a better or cheaper product, the employees (who now include all the managers) to some bonus, the financiers to a return proportionate to the risk, the state to a higher amount of tax, etc.

Box 12.4   Profit-sharing

Martin Weitzman has suggested that pay should float to reflect company performance. If *everyone* was paid their share of the profits or revenues and if that was their only pay then when times were bad pay would automatically be cut before people were laid off and in good times new jobs would be created since the new workers would be paid only in proportion to what they brought in. (Weitzman, *The Share Economy*, 1984)

Some are going part of that way. Lincoln Electric in the US sets aside six per cent of profits as a dividend to stockholders – what it calls 'the wages of capital'. The balance goes to employees and can reach 120 per cent of wages or salary in a good year. (Lincoln, Incentive Management 1957)

Watts, Blake Bearne in Devon, England allocated 60 per cent of value added to employees, with their wages being, in effect, payment in advance. In good years the 60 per cent was well above the total cost of wages. In bad years they got their wages anyway. The point is that the commitment to 60 per cent of value added was made in advance, as an indicator of the employees' worth.

Gain-sharing attempts to measure the value added by particular groups. General Motors' Saturn plant in Tennessee is the best-publicized example. Hermann Miller, the furniture company, uses the Scanlon Plan, described in Chapter 10, which it describes as a 'way of life' for the company.

For further examples see Kanter, *When Giants Learn to Dance*, 1989

Organizations have readily recognized the legitimate constraints placed upon them by the stakeholder concept but they have been less ready to recognize that the old patriarchal ideas of property are dying, if not dead, and will be replaced by the notion of community.

2.6

Paradigm shifts are uncomfortable. It is not easy when the assumptions with which one grew up turn out to be less true or less certain in maturity. It is understandable that those in the centre of things resist any changes in their assumptions for as long as possible. It is only realistic to expect that any new assumptions will come from the young outsiders and the newer organizations and will be resisted as rash experiments, dreams or unrealistic philosophies for as long as possible.

Some, of course, will be just that but assumptions do change when new technologies and new values arise. Military history is full of the lessons of those who fought the next war with the strategies of the last. The stubborn insistence of the French in the Middle Ages that warfare was essentially a combat of knights blinded them to the potential of the longbow as a weapon of war and set them up as easy prey to the English for a hundred years. The reluctance of the generals in the First World War to acknowledge that the machine gun had altered for ever the tactics of war wiped out a generation of Europe's manhood. Let us hope that today's organizations will not persist too long in fighting the challenges of tomorrow with the methods of yesterday.

3 Clues to the future

3.1

So much for the bad news. Is there any good news? What assumptions will emerge to take the place of the outworn ones? What new paradigms are in the offing? No one sensibly sets himself up as a seer. The future is yet to be created and any sketch plans are bound to be modified by events. However, there do seem to be various clues to some new influences on organizations. Some of these clues may turn out to be false (others have obviously been overlooked) but taken together they do contribute a hazy outline of a new kind of organizational thinking. The clues are:

The communications revolution;
Fees not wages;
Tools not machines;
The economics of quality.

We shall examine each in turn before trying to sketch out what they imply for organizations.

3.2 The communications revolution (the first clue)

The principle of concentration maintained that you pulled everything into the centre and pushed it out again. Rationalization used to mean closing depots and any outlying facilities. This procedure looks like going into reverse. The costs of physical transport will almost certainly go on rising faster than others, mainly because there is at present no practical general alternative to fossil fuel and this is bound to get more expensive as supplies run down, even if each new price rise brings in additional resources, but also because the realistic limits of size and specialization have already been reached in most forms of physical transport.

On the other hand electronic communications systems are getting cheaper in real terms every year, as well as becoming more adaptable and more relevant to our actual needs. Just when it is getting more expensive to move people and things around it is getting cheaper to move information around. It used to be just the opposite; to control operations you needed to have them under your eye. There is some sort of revolution of assumptions going on.

There may soon be very strong *economic* arguments for separating physical manufacture from distribution but linking it electronically to central design and control facilities. Sub-assembly would then become much more common, with the prime manufacturer selling very sophisticated kits to regional agents or even to the actual point-of-sale. Mobile factories or community workshops could proliferate, bringing the manufacturing to the locality in its simplest form.

It will certainly be sensible for organizations to think again about siting new manufacturing facilities as close as possible to the region they will serve. The design and control functions can still be kept in the centre, where the economies of scale and co-ordination can still apply. Many technical operations can now be scaled down without greatly affecting the economics, certainly when the economics of manufacturing are set against the new economics of distribution. New manufacturers entering the UK are setting up networks of small plants in the different regions believing that any extra cost in the replication of some facilities will be more than compensated for by the lowered distribution costs and the greater ease of running small plants from a human point of view.

3.3 Fees not wages (the second clue)

This is a shorthand way of saying that the contract between man and organization may be due for a change. At present most people receive a wage or salary. Wages are money paid for time spent and most people effectively sell their *time* as employees. The employer decides, ultimately, how that time should be spent. Fees, on the other hand, are money paid for work done. Professionals and craftsmen charge fees. The calculation of the fee may be based on the time spent but as far as the customer or client is concerned he is paying money for a finished job. When the surgeon has taken out your appendix and presented a bill you are not interested in how much time he took but in whether the job was properly done.

As the costs and the bureaucracy of employment continue to escalate (as they will), more and more organizations are discerning that much of their work can be contracted out to individuals, specialist groups and other organizations. There are three advantages to this:

1 The organization avoids the overheads and the responsibilities of employment (see the argument in the preceding section that labour must now be treated as an asset).
2 The organization can concentrate its control function on quality and price and does not have to worry about all the hygiene factors of management.
3 The relationship between organization and individual becomes much more one of adult-to-adult than parent-to-child. If a piece of work is unsatisfactory the organization refuses to accept it. This is felt to be a more acceptable statement than the criticism of a superior or senior manager that one's work is not up to standard.

There are, of course, some costs. The organization must devote more attention to planning, scheduling and contract setting. Their skills at costing and inspection will be crucial. It is managerially simpler to have all the work under one's direct control; theoretically this permits greater flexibility. In fact it also lays one open to hijack power as well as all the overheads involved. Subcontracting takes many forms:

1 There is franchising. Marks and Spencer in England franchise their production although they do much of the designing and can provide much of the finance. Hamburger chains franchise their product. Other organizations franchise their sales. Some organizations franchise both production and sales, keeping only research and design as the critical functions. Publishing is a long-established example of total franchising although publishers might not call it that.
2 There is specialist subcontracting. The construction industry has long realized that it does not make sense for any one organization to attempt to provide all the skills needed in a major construction job. The boards outside any major building project provide a vivid example of the contractual organization. On a smaller scale, new businesses frequently contract out accounting and pay-rolls, their market analysis, their delivery. The advertising world is built on a monopoly of subcontracting and is itself beginning to realize that many of its own skills can be subcontracted in turn, leaving the agency very much in the position of a privileged broker.

3 There is group subcontracting. The organization contracts with a group of actual or potential 'employees' to do certain work for a certain price. The 'lump' in the building industry used to be an example of this form of subcontracting until it was outlawed by the trade unions. A shipbuilding firm in the north-east of England has an interesting variation. It negotiates a rate per hour wage for its labour force. It then contracts with a group to do a certain job (e.g. welding the stern of a ship) for a given number of hours to be paid for at the agreed rate. The currency in the contract has become hours not money but the principle is the same.

When contracting with its own employees the organization is in fact treating the wage as a retainer and paying a contract fee in addition. In this way it gets the motivational benefits but still retains all the costs and problems of employment. It is really an extension of the old piece-work system and can easily inherit all the same problems and difficulties.

In the era of the big organization, self-sufficient in all its aspects, we have forgotten that most businesses have always been based on the principle of contracting. Even today most manufacturing companies are in fact assembly operators with often over 1,000 suppliers of parts or pieces. The contractual organization has always been with us. We need now to recognize the principles and practices involved and extend these to individuals and small groups as well as to other organizations. Many of an organization's specialist skills and services could be placed on a contractual basis, using the same people to the mutual benefit of both parties.

3.4   Tools not machines (the third clue)

This distinction was emphasized by Schumacher in his book *Small is Beautiful*. A tool is something which extends the capacities of the individual. A machine is another thing again, greater than a man, needing men to service it but essentially independent of them. The industrial revolution substituted machines for tools, introducing mass-production and the micro-division of labour. The next stage in the industrial revolution, founded on the silicon chip, is likely to be a return from machines to tools. Today anyone can purchase an auto-mated sewing machine which effectively puts the textile factory of a hundred years ago into a suburban bedroom. Machines can now, in many cases, be reduced in scale until they are the equivalent of a very sophisticated tool, to be used as an extension of a man. The robots of the modern factory are, in effect, the tools of modern man.

The impact of this switch back from machines to tools has yet to be appreciated by organizations and society. Within organizations it allows the whole process of splitting up the work into its component parts to be reversed. A man or a small group can once again be responsible for a complete piece of work. True, the tool will do most of it, but tools are ultimately the servants of man, while machines have been his masters. The robot will weld the car body, but man will have trained the robot and can retrain it.

The advent of these sophisticated tools, however, permits yet more adventurous ideas. The work need no longer be done under the same roof. While men had to come to machines, tools go with men. There could be a return to a sophisticated network pattern, with organizations providing the tools and the raw materials and the individual using them at home, at a communal workshop or at the old factory if he so chooses. Such a concept of out-work fits well with the other pressure, to substitute fees (for work done) for wages (for time spent).

It could go farther still. J. Gershuny has argued that we are heading for a self-service society in which the manufacturing sector increasingly produces capital goods for use in the home. Just as the automatic washing-machine displaced the laundry, so other forms of domestic capital equipment will allow us to do for ourselves things that others at present do for us. The average household now contains more capital

---

Box 12.5   The household economy?

[A] third strategy is . . . to start to consider the redesign of the household. Consider: if more time were available there would be no need to make the use of household capital so unrewarding. Take cooking for example: it is potentially the ultimate in non-alienating production. A pleasurable task in itself, it uses one's own capital and one's own labour for one's own consumption. So why stop at cooking? The level of investment in a middle-class kitchen could easily provide an adequate basic carpenter's or metal-working shop, or a pottery lathe and kiln. A very wide range of needs could be provided for in this manner, and a small commune or co-operative could provide an ever wider range . . . As production in the money economy gets more efficient and simpler capital goods get cheaper, the facilities for me to do this get ever more readily available.

From Gershuny, *After Industrial Society: The Emerging Self-Service Economy?*, Macmillan, 1978 equipment per head than the average factory at the turn of the century.

This last phenomenon will have a big impact on the product strategy of business organizations. There may be an increasing market for sub-assemblies, leaving the customer to do the final work for himself. Many service occupations (e.g. automobile servicing) may return to the customer to do himself with new tools. A form of domestic import substitution may actually reduce the total number of transactions while increasing output. It is a technologically sophisticated route to self-sufficiency.

Box 12.6 The unions and the new society

The role of the unions becomes interesting as fees start to replace wages. At present they are essentially pay brokers in the wage economy. As this diminishes their role will shrink, unless they change it. At first, therefore, they may be expected to resist any trend towards the contractual organization but ultimately the economic and social pressures are likely to prove too strong for them. There is, however, another role waiting to be taken up, that of certificating the growing number of independent workers. How will one know that plumbers, fitters, maintenance-men or carpenters are competent unless there is some certificating body? It is a role that the professional associations perform for the professions. It is a role that the old guilds used to perform. It is already badly needed in the growing 'informal economy' where a variety of trades, unpoliced and unregulated, are practised. Will the unions become certificating bodies?

Combine this new self-sufficiency with a capacity for more out-work and more subcontracted service work and you end up with the notion of *flexilives*, with individuals able to make more independent choices as to how, where and when they work. This new-found choice may mean great freedom for those who take it. It may not be so great for those who find flexilife thrust upon them as conventional employment is reduced. It will not make the management task any simpler but it will certainly make it different and, with care, more efficient.

3.5 The economics of quality (the fourth clue)

Economics is the study of value added. Traditionally this added value has been measured by the transaction price of the finished goods or services – what people will pay for them. A society's economic wealth is measured by the sum of all those transactions. It follows that the more of these there are the richer society is judged to be. As far as economics is concerned it makes no difference whether these transactions are in good commodities or bad, whether they involve building schools, nuclear power plants or guns. It is all wealth. The same concept was generally thought to apply to individuals. Individual wealth is conventionally measured by one's expenditure or one's capacity for expenditure. More wealth is good, for individuals and for societies. It has only been the distribution of that wealth within society which has seriously concerned politicians, and it has been assumed that all individuals, or at any rate most individuals at work, would like more personal wealth even if it did then bring difficult choices as to how to spend it. As a result, ideas built on the rationality of the Economic assumption have been heavily embedded in our societies and organizations for generations, even though everyone would acknowledge that the Economic assumption is only part of our complex psychological calculus (see Chapter 2).

There are signs, however, that the premises which underlie the economics of quantity may no longer be as valid as they once seemed. Let us look at some of the reasons.

(a) *Hirsch's theory of positional goods.* Professor Hirsch, in a book published shortly before his death in 1978, argues that after a certain stage in material growth societies achieve a state of prosperity in which most people have all that they need on which to live relatively comfortably. Of course, *relative* poverty will always exist and pockets of *absolute* poverty may still be found due to mismanagement or inefficient policies, but the bulk of the population is well provided for. For what, then, do people work? When you have one good washing-machine you do not really need two. Hirsch suggests that at this stage people work for the things that set them apart from their neighbours. At first these might be material things (a bigger car or better stereo system) but ultimately they want things that have a built-in exclusivity, such as a house with an uninterrupted view, privileged educational facilities or membership of an elite club. Because the value of these things lies in their exclusivity it follows that you cannot, by definition, have too many of them because they would then lose their appeal. Too many unusual houses and the house no longer has its uninterrupted view. This, says Hirsch, is the real limit to material growth. There is a built-in social limit to man's ambitions. Only the few, and not the many, can be satisfied by positional goods. What then do the others do? They may envy. They may even seek to disrupt a society that reserves its top rewards for a few. Many, certainly, will increasingly re-adjust their motivation calculus realizing that if the real rewards are unattainable, they must be content with what is available.

Quantity, Hirsch implies, is not eventually enough. This suggestion strikes at the heart of conventional economics.

(b) *A shift in values.* Another interpretation of the satiation of material ambition would give a new priority to non-materialistic goals. If people have all the money they actually need, if not want, and if they also see that more money does not actually bring the desired happiness, they may prefer to trade money for other things; for discretionary time, for instance, for better conditions at work including more freedom or autonomy as well as better lighting or better food.

Under this interpretation we may increasingly expect union agreements to feature shorter working weeks and provision for more autonomy at work. At present most people in Northern Europe, America and Australia still work the 'three forty-eights' (forty-eight hours per week, for forty-eight weeks a year, for forty-eight years of their life). We may well see this dropping to three thirty-fives as individuals increasingly trade money for time.

If this interpretation is correct one would expect the non-materialistic values to show up more markedly in the new generations who have grown up in affluence, particularly those who have been best prepared, through education, to take advantage of the materialistic society. Box 12.7 suggests that this is in fact happening. If the future leaders of our society have begun to turn from the economics of quantity to the economics of quality then the premises of economics must indeed be rewritten.

(c) *The personal economy and Micawber wealth.* Economics have always been principally concerned with the formal transactions of people, where goods or services are traded for money in one way or another, but a large slice of life has always taken place in the more informal economies of the household, the voluntary agencies and free recreation. Because nothing is officially traded, those activities, which add value of one sort or another, have never been counted. Indeed a slice of apparent economic growth has always been due to some of these informal, personal activities getting formalized and therefore counted. When you buy potatoes instead of growing them the formal, visible economy grows but the number of potatoes grown and consumed remains the same. Similarly if activities pass back from the formal economy to the household the economy may appear to shrink even though the same activities are still performed. There are at present signs that the personal economy may be growing in all the industrialized countries now that more people have further discretionary time, better education and more tools and equipment to do things for themselves.

Box 12.7   Three in one

The International Research Institute for Social Change has been tracking the change in values in 19 different countries for two decades. Based on the original work of SRI in California and Taylor Nelson in the UK they divide people into three categories.

1 Sustenance driven – people whose prime motivation is the need for security. Their concern is with just getting by from day to day and with belonging to a supportive group of their peers. Although a subgroup, the 'survivors' are economically disadvantaged, most are comfortably off, clannish and conservative in their tastes.

2 Outer directed – the flower of the mature industrial society, whose motivation is the search for esteem and status. They want to marry the right person, live in the right part of town, have the right job. They want their children to be a credit to the family. They want to improve their position in financial and social terms and they measure their success through the eyes and the opinions of those like themselves.

3 Inner directed – people who find the criteria for their success within themselves. Often the children of outer-directed parents, they are largely unconcerned with what other people think of them. They are often less materialistic than the other groups, although they do not consciously choose poverty. Self-expression, sensibility and the quality of life are key concerns.

There is a general shift down the categories towards the inner-directed. Britain in 1989 was made up of 29 per cent sustenance driven, 35 per cent outer-directed and 36 per cent inner-directed. The Netherlands had 44 per cent of inner-directed people, but France, Germany, Japan and the USA were largely made up of outer-directed groups.

No country is, of course, uniform. In the USA for instance, the percentage of inner-directed people in New England and the West Coast is double that of the heartlands of middle America. Nor are the percentages the same for the different age cohorts. The younger are often more inner-directed and seem poised to stay that way.

It will make a difference.

See further: Kinsman, *Millennium*, 1991

This trend will not only conceal the true state of affairs from formal economics in government or elsewhere, it will introduce more people to a new concept of wealth. Those who live principally in the personal economy do not measure wealth by the capacity for expenditure. They instinctively look upon it much as Mr Micawber did in Dickens's picture of him. Mr Micawber was fond of saying that happiness was an income of twenty pounds when expenditure was nineteen pounds nineteen shillings and sixpence, which turned to misery if the expenditure was twenty pounds and sixpence. Wealth to Mr Micawber was not the capacity to spend but the difference between what you had and what you needed to spend. The difference is subtle but crucial. Under the Micawber definition you can increase your wealth either by increasing your income or by reducing your expenditure needs. In the personal economy the latter is often the most favoured as people, instead of buying something, learn how to make it or do it themselves.

If economic activity moves back to the household we may well see a big switch from the economics of quantity to the economics of quality.

For organizations the consequences are clear. They will no longer be able to rely on the wage packet to be the panacea in issues of motivation, relationships or authority and control. Pay will still matter, of course, but so will other things. When people only have to work a little to satisfy their material needs you will need to rely on the other parts of your calculus to get them to work more than a little.

4   Possibilities and problems

4.1

The changeover in fashions and assumptions opens up a mixed bag of possibilities and problems. We will look briefly at three of them:

The federal organization;
Spliced careers;
New patterns of planning.

4.2   The federal organization

Federalism is the way to combine the autonomy of individual parts with the economics of co-ordination. Many of the pressures described in the previous sections will push organizations towards a smaller size of spending unit. Opinions vary about what that optimum may be. It depends partly on the technology and the way the work has to be organized, but most people put the upper limit at around 500 people.

These individual units, however, can still be co-ordinated centrally provided that the right information is available at the right time. Information, however, is one of the few things that we seem to be certain to have in more abundance and in greater variety than ever before. It is just as well because one of the few consistent findings of the research on organization structures has been that more decentralization is always accompanied by more information.

Federalism, however, is subtly different from decentralization. The subtleties are not always well understood, particularly in those countries which do not have a tradition of federalism in their political life. The British, for instance, have always seen federalism as a way of weakening one's past enemies or, at least, as a form of compromise when a central government was unrealizable. In fact, the supposed compromise usually turned out to be a strength (in Australia, West Germany, even Canada for a long time).

Decentralization implies a delegation of power from an all-powerful centre. Federalism implies that the power really resides with the constituent parts (e.g. the states) who cede part of that power to the centre for the benefits of all. Thus, in federal states, the capital is seldom the most important city – it is there only for the co-ordination of government and is usually not a centre of economic or artistic activity.

Federal organizations, similarly, will rely on a small nerve centre co-ordinating a range of small, nearly autonomous operations which

---

Box 12.8 Federal organizations

It is interesting to speculate on some of the more successful federal organizations and states.

The International Postal Federation is an impressive organization. In spite of the increasing inefficiency of most national postal services it is still taken for granted that the letter you mail in Paris to Santiago in Chile will reach there in a reasonable time, safely and still comparatively cheaply. As a model of co-ordination and efficient operation it ranks high and yet who knows where its head office is or who might be its chief executive?

Switzerland, similarly, is a very efficient country. Whether one shares the values of the Swiss or not, no one denies that it is a country that works well, in spite of four different languages, some of the most difficult terrain in the world, and a record of independence in the cantons for many centuries. Yet who could tell you the name of the first minister in the Swiss government? How many are even sure of the name of the capital city?

can be widely dispersed geographically. The concept of a holding company which has been a financial and legal reality will begin to mean more in strict organizational terms and will be as common in the integrated manufacturing company as it is in the financial world.

Unlike the traditional holding company, however, the federal centre may not always *own* the autonomous parts. In order to give proper expression to the ideas of stakeholders and community the ownership of those autonomous parts may well be more widely distributed (amongst employees and stakeholders) than is currently fashionable. The power of ownership will not therefore reside in the centre but in the parts. It is this shift in power which will make federalism a reality, making the centre truly the servant of the whole, not the master of it.

Dovetailing into the federal organization is the concept of the contractual organization. The contractual organization is built on the notion of fees rather than wages and on the principle of subcontracting. One way to keep the staff of the mainstream operations under 500 is to hive off as much of the operation as you can to outside individuals, groups or organizations.

The organizations of the future are increasingly likely to have three different categories of workers. There will be the professional core of managers and specialists performing the critical functions of designing, controlling and co-ordinating. To them the organization will offer careers, security and special terms and conditions. In return it will expect flexibility, mobility and commitment. The second category will be the contractual fringe of individuals and groups doing work that can be done more cheaply by outsiders, either because they are only required intermittently or because they can specialize and concentrate on a particular operation – be it market research, cleaning or the manufacture of a sub-assembly. Third will be the basic work-force, increasingly working part-time or in shifts to provide the necessary flexibility. This will be a purely instrumental relationship, money in return for time; they will not expect careers or development but will bargain hard for better pay and conditions, will move readily if better conditions are offered elsewhere and will expect to find the other satisfactions of work in other parts of their lives.

Each category will have a different psychological contract with the organization as well as a different formal contract. Each category will therefore have to be managed differently. The professional core will want a task culture, flat structures and lots of consultation. The contractual fringe, often person or power cultures themselves, will need a role culture to control and co-ordinate their services to the organization. The work-force will be more fragmented and will also need the disciplines of a role culture combined with the personal touch of a Zeus at the supervisory level. Federal contractual organizations pose problems as well as possibilities.

4.3   Spliced careers

Today it is still true that 90 per cent of those who work do so in an organization. Most of those will assume that they will continue working in that organization, or one very like it, until they retire at some age around sixty. This will soon be an uncommon assumption. The 'three forty-eights', as we have already noticed, are probably on the way out.

In years to come people may look forward (with mixed delight and apprehension) to a more varied work career. For some it will still be true that they will work for an organization for forty years. For more, however, it will be a mix of employment and self-employment. This mix could happen in various ways:

(a) *End-to-end*. Employment will give way to self-employment as people in their forties or early fifties begin to see the advantages of more flexible contract work outside the firm. For many people such self-employment may happen involuntarily as firms begin to retire employees even earlier, perhaps substituting a capital sum for a pension. In case this seems odd or inhuman it is wise to remember that the Armed Services in Britain have been pursuing such a policy for many years. Of course, most of those leaving the forces have opted for more employment, but this option may not be so readily available in the future. We may see it becoming increasingly common for 'responsible' employers to prepare their people for exit by ensuring that they have the necessary skills to stand on their own before they leave employment. In-company courses geared to exit may become more frequent.

(b) *Alternating*. The more professionally skilled may choose to alternate periods of employment with periods of self-employment, rather as some married women do today, opting in and out of the full-time work-force to suit their domestic circumstances. For some the idea of a sabbatical, or re-training, will be an increasingly necessary and attractive possibility and the development of continuing education, paid for by either the state, the firm or the individual, must be one of the growth areas of the future, along with new certificating bodies.

(c) *Complementary*. There will almost certainly be a growth in part-time employment. When organizations need extra labour or skills they will be increasingly tempted to look for part-time employees who will not require the same kind of organizational guarantees that apply to full-time workers. Many people will make up the balance of the work they require with self-employment. Because it is marginal, both to society and to the individual, much of this work will take place in the so-called informal economy. Rather than disparage this economy, society may well find that it provides a useful alternative to unemployment and is indeed a preparation for eventual full-time legitimate self-employment. A shorter working week will give everyone the opportunity for some part-time self-employment. This will not necessarily be undesirable.

The 'spliced careers' of the future will bring fundamental changes to the personnel functions in organizations. The counselling side of their work is bound to increase as the options for the individual multiply. The variety of employment and contract arrangements, although they will increase flexibility, must also bring administrative headaches. The question of training (for the individual and for the organization) will be a major issue with smaller organizations undoubtedly seeking to ride on the backs of the bigger ones by poaching their people in mid life. The whole question of pensions and individual rights will become more complicated and some major rethinking will be necessary if we are to avoid the situation where a small number of present-day employees are supporting three or four times their number of past employees in an inflationary age, unthought of when the schemes were originally funded. As *self-employment* of various sorts becomes more common the notion of *unemployment* may be of decreasing relevance and importance – the world does not have to be divided between employed and unemployed when there are so many variations on the theme of work.

4.4 Patterns of planning

Discontinuous change makes planning difficult. When change is in a continuous pattern it is possible to project the trends and to make some reasonable assumptions as to the actions and reactions required. But when the trends run off the graph paper, or reverse themselves, the process no longer works. What does one do when the facts run out? Many people do nothing or, rather, they do the same only more so. If aggressive advertising has always helped in the past it seems reasonable to do even more aggressive advertising when the situation seems even more dismaying, but if the problem has changed there can be no guarantee that yesterday's solutions will work tomorrow.

Under conditions of discontinuity change comes in from outside and new ways can overtake you before you are aware of what is happening. You are by-passed unless you change your approach to the future.

Organizations have traditionally approached the future by attempting to reduce uncertainty. Whole theories of management have been based on reduction of uncertainty. Such an approach works out well when you can control, or at least predict, your environment. It is potentially self-destructive when change is discontinuous and the environment unpredictable. In such situations organizations have no alternative but to adopt the experimental approach. This approach is akin to systematic gambling. Different openings and possibilities are explored. Initial success is re-inforced and failures are discarded. Expensive bids are laid off through alliances and security is sought in variety rather than certainty. Oil companies bidding for exploration contracts in the English North Sea understood the concept.

The experimental approach puts planning back into the boardroom for it is a matter of sequential decisions rather than scenario paintings. Estimates, scenarios and careful monitoring are all necessary but on a

---

Box 12.9   The vanishing laboratories

I was meeting with the board of a firm which ran a number of photographic laboratories, processing camera films for various chemists and photographic dealers who collected and returned these films to the private customer.

The discussion that morning concerned the new technologies which were beginning to affect the industry. There was general agreement that the day was not far off (five to seven years) when a large box could effectively replace the laboratory. This box could be placed in a corner of a shop and would process any film dropped into it, making the laboratories and the collection/delivery system obsolete.

After a break for coffee the board started to discuss the next item on the agenda – the long-term plan. This was discussed without any apparent reference to the previous topic except that they agreed that increased emphasis on efficiency was desirable in the light of probable 'new competition'. In other words, no real action was taken to deal with the discontinuous change which they all foresaw. Within ten years, though, such a box will have been developed by some newcomer to the industry and all the traditional structure of that industry will be outmoded and by-passed. Yet that board was not in the box-inventing game. They ran laboratories and all they knew was how to run them better. Was it their fault if discontinuous change made their laboratories irrelevant? Can you plan for discontinuous change?

walk into a fog a light is not much use – you have to stop and feel your way. Loose-linked organizations help to contain the risk and to provide the flexibility for experiment. The federal contractual organization which may be thrust upon us for other reasons may be well suited for discontinuous change but the managers in them may not adapt so readily. They will have to adjust to the fact that the area of choice in most jobs is going to become larger and that more risks will need to be taken. They must learn to live with their mistakes and to profit from them. Successful organizations will encourage their managers and will not punish mistakes provided they are the outcome of a conscious strategy.

5 In conclusion

We have argued that fashion is as important to organization design as any underlying theory of behaviour. Changing values in the environment linked to a changing technology will affect current assumptions of what makes organizational sense. What has appeared to be true for ever may turn out to be only partially true. When that happens change is discontinuous and disconcerting. You can then no longer run to-morrow's organizations on yesterday's assumptions.

The assumptions which appear to be losing their value are:

That concentration plus specialization = efficiency;
That hierarchy is natural;
That labour is a cost;
That an organization is a property.

Four clues to the future are:

The communications revolution;
Fees in place of wages;
Tools in place of machines;
The economics of quality.

These will produce new challenges to organizations, including:

The idea of federalism;
Spliced careers;
New patterns of planning.

It will, one hopes, be an evolution not a revolution. Technologies, products, ideas – they all have life cycles. They flourish then wane. So it is with organizations and the assumptions on which they have been built. The trick is to manage the switch from the end of one life cycle to the start of another. Firms which can do this with their products remain in business. Organizations which can allow old ways to die and new ways to grow will survive and have the chance to prosper. The acceptance of death as the prelude to new life is an age-old recipe for the survival of nature, society and the human race. It also applies to organizations.

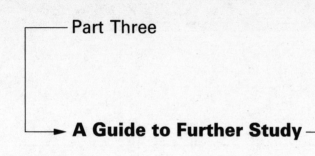

Part Three

A Guide to Further Study

→ Introduction to Part Three

The many writers on aspects of Organization Theory are particularly prolix. It is a full-time occupation to keep abreast of all the outpouring of research, theory and speculation in even one of the subdivisions of the field. Anyone who, like myself, is interested and involved over the whole range of topics must settle for selectivity in his reading and further study.

This part of the book is a signpost to one brand of selectivity. Others could list several totally different selections; they might all be equally good. I have tried to keep my lists of references short and yet to include in each list some overview of the field, some of the classic works, as well as references to any of the really crucial research studies. But I have above all sought to share with the reader my perceptions of the most interesting and thought-provoking works.

Those already knowledgeable in the literature of the field will no doubt be amazed at my omissions and puzzled by some of the inclusions. Whilst I feel that no apology need be made for a personal anthology, anyone following the trail I have laid should always remember that it is indeed very personal and makes no claim to be all-encompassing.

In addition to providing lists of references this part of the book also contains some short discussions of a few of the underlying assumptions in the area. I have not always found myself satisfied with the premises on which some of the research and theory is founded and have thought it proper to share with any reader my doubts and preconceptions since these undoubtedly colour the interpretation taken in the main text.

The comments, and the references, are listed by section and chapter. Many of the references date back to the 1960s or even earlier because this was when the original studies were undertaken or the concepts formulated. These by now classic pieces will often be found in more recent collections of articles or extracts of articles if they are no longer available under their original title.

→ **Chapter 1**

1 **The philosophical base**

I have taken the view in this book that the study of organizations is more akin, philosophically, to the study of history than to the study of the physical sciences, that there are no precise and verifiable and unvarying laws governing the behaviour of people, and that we must look for our understanding and our comfort in other ways.

That used to be a controversial view. John Stuart Mill, for one, disagreed; but then he lived in a simpler world. Nowadays the social sciences are generally reckoned to be different from the physical ones. Winch, in *The Idea of a Social Science*, explains why. I was pleased, too, to discover Bertrand Russell's views on the philosophy of history, given in a lecture towards the end of his life, entitled 'Portraits from Memory'. In it he makes the following points:

1 History is both a science and an art. When it is described as scientific two things are meant:

(a) The ascertaining of facts in a scientific manner;
(b) The search for the discovery of causal laws.

Although (b), as well as (a), is entirely laudable it is not what gives most value to historical studies. In history we are interested in the particular fact as well as the causal sequences.

Even when causal sequences are established as regards the past, there is not much reason to expect that they will hold in the future, because the relevant facts are so complex that unforeseeable changes may falsify our prediction . . . For these reasons I think that scientific laws in history are neither so important nor so discoverable as is sometimes maintained.

2 If history is to be of value to any besides historians it must be interesting. This means that it must be well presented and presented with feeling. The historian writing for non-historians is encouraged to have views. His examination of the facts should be impartial but his interpretation is allowed, indeed encouraged, to be personal.

Russell is not advocating intellectual idleness. He sees a division of labour in the study of history. There are those whose time is spent in the unearthing and definition of basic facts and observations. But just as Einstein did not himself make the observations on which his doctrines were based, just as Kepler's laws were based on the observations of Tycho Brahe, so there is a need for the interpreter, the man who can hold a multiplicity of facts within the unity of a single temperament.

Russell was talking of history. We are concerned with organization theory. I would hold that his remarks are just as pertinent to the latter. Scientific observations and the scientific unearthing of the facts of organizational behaviour are most important; so is the establishment of any causal sequences that can be traced. But we should not expect such causal sequences to be endlessly repeatable, to hold good for all time, nor should we look to them for a total understanding of organizations and what happens within them.

The distinction between those who work for other theorists and those who interpret the basic findings is also important. Those who seek to do both will tend towards a perceptual bias. They will inevitably seek to interpret the world in the light of their particular discoveries. Interestingly, as with historians, the organizational interpreters are assessed by society not so much on the scientific validity of their work but on whether leading practitioners find it interesting and meaningful.

This book is clearly an interpretative approach and must be judged as such. For those who wish to explore further into the scientific side of the field and its methodology I would recommend Kaplan, the first few chapters and the section on Methodologies in March, which has a wealth of further references.

2 Organization theory

This field of study has in the past been bedevilled by the fact that for many years the leading theorists grew up in one or other of the supporting disciplines of anthropology, sociology, psychology or social psychology. Inevitably their theoretical perspectives and their research training coloured their approach to this area of problems. Thus the sociologist tended to regard individual differences as deviations from a norm of zero, whilst the psychologist tended to relegate all the organizational determinants of behaviour to the category of 'the environment', something that should be held constant as long as possible in order to permit the study of individuals. The advent of 'systems theory' at least meant that a wide variety of disciplines appeared to be talking in approximately the same language about similar problems. However, an inter-disciplinary approach, respectable in its own right, is beginning to emerge. Pugh's paper 'Modern organization theory', to be found in numerous anthologies as well as under the original citation, is a very good overall view of this problem although it is, in my view, slightly coloured by the Weberian philosophy on the social sciences.

Pugh distinguishes between the following categories:

Management theorists;
Structural theorists;
Group theorists;
Individual theorists;
Technology theorists;
Economic theorists.

Other reviews of the field take either an historical perspective (Box 1.5 gives one such summary). Others focus more on the individual theorists. The Penguin book of readings on organization theory, edited by Pugh, is a useful way of tasting the original writings of the leading theorists, and contains references to further readings. Perrow takes a critical look at the various approaches to organization theories before coming up with a neo-Weberian approach. The book is a readable and knowledgeable review from a sociologist.

This book does not attempt such an overview, partly because it is available elsewhere, but also because this quasi-biographical approach to organization theory, though an interesting way of following the trends of thought, does not always seem to be particularly helpful. The viewpoints of these leading theorists will always be discussed where relevant, but anyone looking for a complete and systematic overview of the literature in this field could not do better than read the bibliographic appendix to Morgan's exciting book on the different ways of thinking about organizations.

There is still a shortage of good interdisciplinary works which cover the whole range of organizational variables. The latest editions of Leavitt's and Schein's standard textbooks, however, show an increasing interest in the systems and structures of organizations as well as in the individuals and groups who inhabit them. Hunt's excellent and readable book combines an overview of the research with lessons to be drawn from it by managers. Derek Torrington's *Effective Management* is a concise but comprehensive textbook, while for the more intellectually adventurous Ronnie Lessem's *Global Management Principles* is a voyage of discovery. America has, it is true, produced a shelf or more of compendious and expensive textbooks (often full of case studies and exercises) which aim to cover the whole field, but most of them are more like encyclopedias than guide-books. One of the best of these big books is Hall's. Nor should Peter Drucker's voluminous contributions to managerial wisdom be ignored. They are eclectic, based more on his experience than on theory and research, but are always interesting and useful.

Last, but by no means least, I would encourage people to read Aronson's stimulating and compulsively readable introduction to social psychology, dealing with topics such as conformity, prejudice, aggression and attraction, which underlie much of the material in the early part of the book.

References

ARONSON, E. (1976), *The Social Animal*, Freeman.

DRUCKER, P. (1980), *Management*, Pan.

EASTON. D. (1953), *The Political System*, Knopf.

HALL, R. (1972), *Organizations: Structure and Process*, Prentice-Hall.

HUNT, J. (1992), *Managing People at Work*, McGraw-Hill.

KAPLAN, A. (1964), *The Conduct of Inquiry*, Chandler.

LEAVITT, H. J. (1978), *Managerial Psychology*, 4th Edition, University of Chicago Press.

LESSEM, R. (1989), *Global Management Principles*, Prentice-Hall.

MARCH, J. G. (ed.), (1965), *Handbook of Organizations*, Rand McNally.

MILL, J. S. (1843), *System of Logic*, Longman. (This edition published 1971)

MORGAN, G. (1986), *Images of Organization*, Sage.

PERROW, C. (1972), *Complex Organizations*, Scott, Foreman & Co.

POPPER, K. (1959), *The Poverty of Historicism*, Routledge & Kegan Paul.

PUGH, D. S. (1966), 'Modern organization theory', *Psychological Bulletin*, vol. 66, pp. 235–51.

PUGH, D. S. (ed.), (1990), *Organization Theory, Selected Readings*, 3rd Edition, Penguin.

RUSSELL, B. (1958), *Portraits from Memory*, Allen & Unwin.

SCHEIN, E. H. (1980), *Organizational Psychology*, 3rd Edition, Prentice-Hall.

STEWART, R. (1970), *The Reality of Management*, Pan.

TORRINGTON, D., WEIGHTMAN, J., and JOHNS, K. (1989), *Effective Management*, Prentice-Hall.

WEBER, M. (1956), *Wirtschaft und Gesellschaft*, J. C. B. Mohr.

WINCH, R. (1958), *The Idea of a Social Science*, Routledge & Kegan Paul.

━► **Chapter 2**

I

The field of motivation theory is enormous, and the studies range widely. In Part One I have not attempted to list any of the studies or to give a systematic review of the literature but rather to pull some of the theories together into a reasonably coherent model. In doing so I found the book edited by Vroom and Deci to be an invaluable, concise collection of the principal source material.

2

Vroom, in his introduction, gives an overview of motivation theory which I have followed in part. Schein cites the principal research studies. Vroom's earlier book is a systematic and detailed review of the theories up to 1964. For studies prior to 1955 the Brayfield and Crockett review (in Vroom and Deci), on the relationship of attitudes to performance, is useful. All of these works, in their turn, list the primary sources.

Porter and Lawler's work gives a good overview of satisfaction theories, and suggests, amongst other things, that satisfaction is the result rather than the cause of productivity.

The essence of Maslow's approach is contained in an extract in Vroom and Deci's book of readings. McGregor and Likert are also represented in that collection, but since their principal works will tend to be referred to on several occasions in this book, I have listed them among the references.

Schein usefully discusses assumptions about man. Levinson's views are concisely presented in his 1972 article.

The motivation calculus model traces its ancestry back to three parents:

1 The Path–Goal approach originally suggested by Georgopoulous, Mahoney and Jones in 1957 and reproduced in Vroom and Deci.
2 Vroom's emphasis on valence, instrumentality and force in his 1964 book.
3 Porter and Lawler's expectancy model in 1968 which was built on the two preceding sources and tested by their own research.

All of these theorists were concerned to develop specific testable hypotheses arising out of their models. Desirable though this is, it did limit them to looking at fairly specific decision situations, usually where the individual was in effect choosing between two activities or two levels of activities. I have been concerned to extend the implications of their models and to link them with other concepts such as psychological maturity, the psychological contract, dissonance reduction, in order to give them wider, but less exact, predictability.

Porter and Lawler's work is most fully described in their 1968 book, but their 1968 article is a shorter description of their views and findings.

Herzberg's work is best described in his 1966 book. A lot of controversy has centred around Herzberg's work. Most of it has concentrated on his methodology and the fact that, given the way he asks his questions, you are likely to find the dissatisfying elements located in the conditions of work and the satisfying ones in the employees' contribution. Anyone interested in pursuing this controversy should read House and Wigdor. For my own part I find that his basic argument has a lot of face validity, given that motivation is essentially a subjective phenomenon, i.e. as the individual concerned sees it.

An interesting repeat of Herzberg's study in Texas Instruments is described by Scott Myers. Hunt's data on over 10,000 managers provides interesting comparisons between early environment and need profiles. He also shows how these profiles can change with age and experience.

McClelland's views are to be found in his 1961 book and are aptly summarized and commented upon in Kolb *et al*. Whyte has another approach called Sentiments and Symbols which it was not possible to summarize in Part 1 but is worth studying.

A motivation model based on McClelland's concepts is put forward by Atkinson and well described by Litwin and Stringer (1968). It is very similar to the motivation calculus.

Personality theory is a fascinating area which has not been linked closely enough to motivation theory. Argyris's discussion of the fusion of the formal organization and the individual is one such link. His book (1960) will direct the reader to the most relevant personality theorists such as Erikson, Kelly, Sullivan, Fromm and Horney. In this work Argyris also discusses the question of psychological growth. For more detail on personality theories it would be useful to start with Hall and Lindzey.

The importance of goal-setting will recur as a topic later in this book. A most interesting review of the research is contained in Dunbar.

4

It was probably Levinson who originally used the term 'psychological contract' but the principle of reciprocity has been around in sociology for some time. I have followed Schein's application of the concept.

The discussion on the type of contract has been much influenced by Etzioni's classification of organizations based on the predominant type of power and the type of investment of the members. He does not himself talk of a psychological contract and I have used the device of the contract to blur his distinction between the type of power used and the type of involvement, mainly because I have not found the distinction very helpful, nor all his words to describe them very illuminating. Nonetheless, his categorizations, though very broad, I have found a very helpful starting-point in the analysis of the underlying type of contract in any organization.

5

Many of the discussions of motivation assume that the style of leadership or the manner of the working of groups have a significant effect on motivation. They certainly have a significant effect on performances and this will be discussed in the relevant chapters. I prefer to regard the motivational assumptions as one of the factors to be considered when deciding on an optimum organization of work or style of leadership. To me it makes more sense to argue that a group-centred style of leadership is appropriate under a co-operative psychological contract than to maintain that a group-centred style is more 'motivating' in general terms. For this reason the studies and theories bearing on leadership style, group processes, productivity and morale, will be reviewed and analysed in Chapters 4 and 5 rather than under the heading of motivation.

Dissonance theory (mentioned in implication 4) is a most interesting set of concepts. Devised by Festinger in 1956 the theory states that when an individual finds himself in a situation when the cues he receives from reality do not accord with his prevailing image of what that reality should be, he will experience dissonance. He will either have to tolerate the dissonance, reduce it by altering either his image of reality or the reality, or find a way of explaining or rationalizing, the discrepancy.

For those who wish to explore the subject further, the best source is Brehm and Cohen's analysis and extension of Festinger's original work in this field.

A good, and reasonably concise, review of the literature on money and pay is provided by Opsahl and Dunnette. Their conclusion that nothing much is known about money is not, I think, justified by all the work that they review, although much of the work tends to be negative in the sense that it disproves some of the conventional myths.

There is a rich and varied literature on the concept of the 'self'. For those who wish to delve into it I have found that Mead's original work back in 1934 provided an excellent starting-point. Many of the studies in this area, however, have been concerned with the problems arising out of the self-concept and resulting in various forms of neurosis. Horney's 1951 book is a good example of this approach.

7

The concept of psychological success and a competent self-identity has been elaborated principally by Argyris, and by White. Hall used the concept to postulate certain hypotheses about career development. Attribution theory is well described by McElroy. What it all means for management comes across well in Peters and Waterman.

References

ARDREY, R. (1967), *The Territorial Imperative*, Collins.

ARGYRIS, C. (1960), *Understanding Organizational Behaviour*, Dorsey.

ARGYRIS, C. (1964), *Integrating the Individual and the Organization*, Wiley.

BREHM, J. W., and COHEN, A. R. (1962), *Explorations in Cognitive Dissonance*, Wiley.

DUNBAR, R. L. M. (1971), 'Budgeting for control', *Admin. Science Quarterly*, March.

ETZIONI, A. (1971), *A Comparative Analysis of Complex Organizations*, Free Press.

HALL, D. T. (1971), 'A theoretical model of career subidentity. Development in organizational settings', *Organizational Behav. Hum. Performance*, January.

HALL, G. S., and LINDZEY, G. (1973), *Theories of Personality*, Wiley.

HERZBERG, F. (1966), *Work and the Nature of Man*, World Publishing Co.

HORNEY, K. (1951), *Neurosis and Human Growth*, Routledge & Kegan Paul.

HOUSE, R. J., and WIGDOR, L. A. (1967), 'Herzberg's dual factor theory', *Personn. Psychol.*, Winter.

HUNT, J. (1992), *Managing People at Work*, McGraw-Hill.

KOLB, D. A., RUBIN, I. M., and McINTYRE, J. M. (1971), *Organizational Psychology*, Prentice-Hall.

LEAVITT, H. J., and MUELLER, R. A. H. (1951), 'Some effects of feedback on communication', *Hum. Rel.*

LEVINSON, H. (1972), 'An effort towards understanding man at work'. *European Bus.*, Spring.

LIKERT, R. (1961), *New Patterns of Management*, McGraw-Hill.

LITWIN, G. H., and STRINGER, R. A. (1968), *Motivation and Organizational Climate*, Harvard University Press.

McCLELLAND, D. C. (1961), *The Achieving Society*, Van Nostrand.

McELROY, J. C. (1982), 'A typology of attribution leadership research', *Academy of Management Review*.

McGREGOR, D. (1960), *The Human Side of Enterprise*, McGraw-Hill.

MASLOW, A. (1970), *Motivation and Personality*, Harper & Row.

MEAD, G. H. (1934), *Mind, Self and Society*, University of Chicago Press.

MYERS, M. SCOTT (1966), 'Condition for manager motivation', *Harvard Business Review*, January–February.

NILES, F. S. (unpublished), *The Influence of Parents and Friends on Adolescent Girls*, M. Ed. thesis, University of Manchester.

OPSAHL, R. S., and DUNNETTE, M. D. (1969), 'The role of financial compensation', in L. L. Cummings and W. E. Scott (eds.), *Readings in Organizational Performance and Human Behaviour*, Irwin.

PETERS, T. J., and WATERMAN, R. H. (1982), *In Search of Excellence*, Harper & Row.

PORTER, L. W., and LAWLER, E. E. (1968), *Managerial Attitudes and Performance*, Dorsey.

PORTER, L. W., and LAWLER, E. E. (1968), 'What job attitudes tell about motivation', *Harvard Business Review*, January–February.

SCHEIN, E. H. (1980), *Organizational Psychology*, Prentice-Hall.

VROOM, V. H. (1964), *Work and Motivation*, Wiley.

VROOM, V. H., and DECI, E. L. (eds.) (1970), *Management and Motivation*, Penguin.

WHITE, R. (1959), 'Motivation re-considered: the concept of competence', *Psychol. Rev.*, vol. 66.

WHYTE, W. F. (1969), *Organizational Behaviour*, Irwin.

→ **Chapter 3**

Role theory was introduced to the social sciences by Linton in 1936 but it was not until 1966 that Katz and Kahn were able to propose role concepts as 'the major means for linking the individual and organizational levels of research and theory'.

I

Role theory was a seductive but oft-discarded conceptual system in organization theory – discarded partly because there is very little agreement about the definition of the concept of role. Neiman and Hughes, after reviewing the treatment of the term by more than eighty writers, decided that the concept was 'vague, nebulous and non-definitive'. However there does seem to be some central core of meaning.

  Roles are associated with positions in organizations;
  Roles are involved in interactions.

I have avoided a precise definition of 'role' in the main text. A precise definition involves defining it in terms of behaviour, or expected behaviour, or relationships, when the dilemma truly is that role is all three. In 'role' the social scientist is using a language from the world of real organizations. Like many words in common use it has a variety of meanings, a variety that mirrors the complexity of the concept. To define away that variety is to avoid both the guts of the problem and the richness of the concept.

Another reason for its dismissal as a useful concept is what is called its lack of predictive power. By this, I think, is meant that statistical predictions of e.g. morale or tension cannot easily be made from situations of role problems. This is partly because the situations are hard to contrive experimentally, where many of the other variables could be controlled, and because in field studies too many other variables, particularly personality variances, intervene. Nevertheless it has generally been accepted as a very good explanatory concept and I have found it a good predictor of trends even if not of the magnitude of the trends. Thus one can predict that an individual will experience role ambiguity in a certain situation. The way in which he will respond to that piece of role stress will depend very largely on his personality and on his motivation calculus at the time. The outcome is not precisely predictable to an outsider – but knowledge of the existence of the role problem will certainly be helpful in any organization diagnosis.

The most useful of the sources in this area, and one to which I am greatly indebted, is Kahn *et al*. My language is not always the same as theirs but much of the thinking is. The authors, in this book, have gone a long way towards making role theory operational and advancing it as an analytical tool. In Katz and Kahn's book on organizational theory Role Set is made the core of their way of thinking about organizations and describing them. There is also a useful discussion of role theory in Krech, Crutchfield and Ballachey's basic text on social psychology. Similarly Hunt provides a useful and recent review of role theory. All these authors trace some of the ancestry of role theory back to the founding fathers – Linton, Newcombe and Menton. Pettigrew's writings on role and stress have also been of great help and stimulus to my thinking. Not all have been published but the short article in *Management Today* is well worth reading.

Cooper and Payne's collection of papers provides a good overview of research and thinking in the whole area of stress, while Marshall and Cooper's book focuses very helpfully on the practical problems for the manager, and Wright's looks at the medical side of the problem. Hopson's article provides a good set of strategies for the individual to use in managing stress and transitions.

5

The whole topic of people perception and interactions deserves much fuller treatment than I have been able to give it here. I found Hargreaves' analysis of the topic theory useful. As presented in his 1972 book it is applied to the educational world, but he does provide a good overall summary of the variety of approaches. Goffman's 1959 book is readable and exciting as is his later book which deals more specifically with role problems. Argyle provides a scholarly overview of the field, as does Hastorf, while Aronson's book provides a splendid introduction to all the issues. Rogers reviews the theory as it applies to education. There is another major approach to interactions not mentioned here, namely exchange theory, of which Homans is perhaps the leading exponent. This will be discussed briefly in Chapter 5 on power and influence. For other approaches, congruency theory and the so-called psycho-dynamic theories, see Zaleznik's chapter in March.

6

Eric Berne's original idea of the three ego states and roles of Parent, Adult, Child has since been built into the approach to inter-personal behaviour christened 'Transactional Analysis'. Transactional analysis is not discussed in this book in any detail, but Berne's original book is worth reading and Harris' later work.

Wallen uses the idea of individual roles in a group to form the basis for a whole theory of leadership.

References

ARGYLE, M. (1969), *Social Interaction*, Tavistock.

ARGYLE, M., *et al.* (1981), *Social Situations*, Cambridge University Press.

ARONSON, E. (1976), *The Social Animal*, Freeman.

BAGLEY, J. (1957), 'A cross-cultural study of perceptual predominance in binocular rivalry', as reported in H. Cantril, 'Perception and interpersonal relations', *Amer. J. Psychiat.*, vol. 2.

BERNE, E. (1964), *Games People Play*, André Deutsch.

COOPER, C. L., and PAYNE, R. (1980), *Stress at Work*, Wiley.

DEARBORN, D. C., and SIMON, H. A. (1958), *Selective Perception: a Note on the Departmental Identifications of Executive Sociometry.*

GOFFMAN, E. (1959), *The Presentation of Self in Everyday Life*, Doubleday.

GOFFMAN, E. (1962), *Encounters*, Penguin.

HARGREAVES. D. (1972), *Interpersonal Relations and Education*, Routledge & Kegan Paul.

HARRIS, T. A. (1969), *I'm OK – You're OK*, Harper & Row.

HASTORF, A. H., *et al.* (1970), *Person Perception*, Addison-Wesley.

HOPSON, B. (1981), 'Transition: Understanding and Managing Personal Change' in Cooper, C. L. (ed.), *Psychology & Management*, Macmillan.

HUNT. R. G. (1967), 'Role and role conflict', in E. P. Hollander and R. G. Hunt (eds.), *Current Perspectives in Social Psychology*, Oxford.

KAHN, R. L., *et al.* (1964), *Organizational Stress: Studies in Role Conflict and Ambiguity*, Wiley.

KATZ, D., and KAHN, R. L. (1966), *The Social Psychology of Organizations*, Wiley.

KRECH, D., CRUTCHFIELD, R. S., and BALLACHEY, E. L. (1962), *Individual in Society*, McGraw-Hill.

LEVINSON, H. (1970), *Executive Stress*, Harper & Row.

MARCH, J. G. (1965), *Handbook of Organizations*, Rand McNally.

MARSHALL, J., and COOPER, C. L. (1979), *Executives under Pressure*, Macmillan.

PETTIGREW, A. (1972), 'Managing under stress', *Manag. Today*, April.

ROGERS, C. (1982), *A Social Psychology of Schooling*, Routledge & Kegan Paul.

WALLEN, R. (1963), 'Three types of executive personality', *Dun's Rev.*, December.

WRIGHT, H. B. (1975), *Executive Ease and Disease*, Gower.

━► Chapter 4

I

Leadership has been a subject for speculation and research for centuries. As Warren Bennis once pointed out, it is remarkable that we should know so little about something on which so much has been written. We still do not really know in any detail how effective leaders should behave or how they are best developed. There are still many exceptions to any theory.

For a generation after the Second World War, 'leadership' went out of fashion as a word and as a topic. It seems to be staging a comeback. MacGregor Burns's big book on political leadership, largely based on American examples, may have started it. It has been followed by Maccoby, who brought a background of psychoanalysis and practical anthropology to bear on the tribal behaviour of organizations and their leaders. In Britain, Mant cast an iconoclastic Australian eye on Anglo-Saxon leadership habits and assumptions. Peters and Waterman have added to the folklore of American business leaders with some perceptive comment, while Hofstede's monumental study of cultural differences reminds us that not everybody is American. Hofstede's work is nicely summarized in his *Organizational Dynamics* article.

Adair's work on leadership development is widely used in Britain. His 1983 book is intended as a self-development course, is studded with exercises and examples and is very readable and sensible.

A collection of some of the research studies appears in the March 1971 edition of the *Administrative Science Quarterly* edited by Hollander. Hollander uses the terms 'style', 'structure' and 'setting' to describe the leadership variables, but the studies reported do not deal with the interaction between these variables. Stogdill provides a compendious analysis of the literature, for those who have the time to work through it. Hunt gives a good and practical overview.

2

The 'trait' approach has two kinds of advocates. The prescriptive theorists and the descriptive. Of the prescriptive, Barnard is perhaps the most noteworthy. Of the descriptive the studies by Ghiselli and by Wald and Doty are the ones that are most worth studying. Both are to be found in Huneryager and Heckmann's book of readings for managers.

3

Style theorists are best studied in their original works, e.g. Likert, McGregor, Blake and Mouton. A good review of a lot of the studies in this field is provided by Argyle *et al.*, in Vroom and Deci's book of readings. Kalman, in Cummings and Scott, has a good review of the Ohio State Work on considerations and initiating structures.

Although many of the style theorists pay lip service to the importance of the task and situational variables they tend to be advocates or prophets of the participative culture. There is too little critical evaluation of when it works and when it does not – most of the studies are primarily concerned to establish that it is correlated overall with satisfaction or with productivity and are insensitive to explanatory conditions.

The influence of some of these 'prophets' has been great but can, I think, be better explained on a cultural basis than on an efficiency criterion. They represented a more democratic humanistic approach to the use of man in organizations and came at a time of reaction against scientific management.

4

There is not space here for a detailed review of Fiedler's work. It is briefly described in his 1965 article, but that article does not describe the measures he uses to arrive at his conclusions. There is some doubt as to whether his measure of LPC really does measure what he says it does or whether it really is co-terminous with a structuring authoritarian style.

For a more detailed study of his work it is necessary to study his book and Mitchell's evaluation of his methodology. Fiedler has suggested that leaders who differentiate highly between co-workers have a differentiated approach to style; under stress they show consideration, under favourable conditions they show high initiation of structure. If this were so then Fiedler's measure of LPC is beginning to look like a trait of a 'good' or differentiating leader. Schein has a good discussion of the topic.

It is beginning to look as if differentiation could indeed be the beginning of a new approach to trait theory. Fiedler's other variables would then fit in well as determinants of the leader's freedom to differentiate in behaviour as well as cognitively. This is the sort of approach suggested in 5.4, although there is no research evidence to back it at this stage.

Vroom and Yetton have carried the contingency theories of leadership even further. They have looked at two aspects of a decision, its quality and the likelihood of its implementation, in terms of the nature of the task, the quality of the subordinates and their relationship to the leader. They have then produced a formal decision tree which minimizes the time taken for a decision after consideration of these other factors. By making the full contingency idea operational they have made it testable and teachable. So far they have found a lot of pragmatic evidence to validate it although it is perhaps too mechanistic and limited in that it deals only with formal decision-making acts of the leader. The whole procedure is well described in their book.

5

The Best Fit approach is an attempt to make operational the interactive nature of the three variables that have been postulated by many writers. In particular, Tannenbaum and Schmidt in a well-known article in 1958 list most of the factors and items. But they stop short at listing them and do not go on to suggest how the leader should attempt to rate them or what factors in the environment might help or hinder him. Rackham, Honey and Colbert describe how effective leadership behaviour was perceived quite differently in two different companies, BOAC and ICL and even within divisions of BOAC.

An article by George and Von der Embse takes into account some of the cultural and organizational factors and recounts a study which attempts to quantify their effect. Their approach seems reconcilable with that of the 'Best Fit'.

The implications and applications of the Best Fit approach are, as yet, a matter of conjecture. There is some good anecdotal evidence to suggest that this is in fact the way that leaders behave in organization settings and that the roles of ambassador and model are important. Guest's study of managerial succession, mentioned in the text, is one case which could be interpreted in the light of this general model, which is the reason for its inclusion in Part 3 in encapsulated form.

6

Bennis and Nanus's book on leaders and Bennis's follow-up study, *On Becoming a Leader*, are as valuable for their insights into the minds of particular leaders as for their general conceptual conclusions. Both books convey a good feel of what it means to be a leader. Kotter is another who has written perceptively about American business leaders.

Recent studies of leaders and leadership have concentrated more on setting a style for the organization than on leading a small group on a defined task. Maccoby's study of six leaders is interesting in this context, as is Nias' account of headship in schools. It is becoming more and more difficult to talk about leadership without also talking about power, about the style and culture of the organization and about its politics. This chapter should therefore be seen as just an introduction to the next four chapters.

References

ADAIR, J. (1983), *Effective Leadership*, Gower.

BARNARD, C. I. (1938), *The Functions of the Executive*, Harvard University.

BENNIS, W., and NANUS, B. (1985), *Leaders: the Strategies for Taking Charge*, Harper & Row.

BENNIS, W. (1992), *On Becoming a Leader*, Business Books.

BLAKE, R., and MOUTON, J. (1964), *The Managerial Grid*, Gulf.

CUMMINGS, L. L., and SCOTT, W. E. (1969), *Readings in Organizational Theory and Human Performance*, Irwin & Dorsey.

FIEDLER, F. E. (1965), 'Engineer the job to fit the manager', *Harvard Business Review*, vol. 43.

FIEDLER, F. E. (1967), *A Theory of Leadership Effectiveness*, McGraw-Hill.

GEORGE, N., and VON DER EMBSE, T. T. (1971), 'Six Propositions for Managerial Leadership', *Business Horizons*.

GHISELLI, E. E. (1963), 'Managerial Talent', *Amer. Psychol.*, October.

GUEST, R. A. (1962), *Organizational Change: The Effect of Successful Leadership*, Irwin & Dorsey.

HOFSTEDE, G. (1984), *Culture's Consequences* (Abridged Edition), Sage Publications.

HOFSTEDE, G. (1980), 'Motivation, Leadership and Organization: Do American Theories Apply Abroad?', *Organizational Dynamics*, Summer.

HOLLANDER, E. P. (1964), *Leaders, Groups and Influence*, Oxford.

HUNERYAGER, S. G., and HECKMANN, I. L. (eds.), (1967), *Human Relations in Management*, Arnold.

HUNT, J. (1992), *Managing People at Work*, Pan.

KOTTER, J. (1982), *The General Managers*, The Free Press.

LIKERT, R. (1961), *New Patterns of Management*, McGraw-Hill.

MACCOBY, M. (1981), *The Leader*, Simon & Schuster.

McGREGOR, D. V. (1960), *The Human Side of Enterprise*, McGraw-Hill.

MACGREGOR BURNS, J. (1978), *Leadership*, Harper & Row.

MANT, A. (1983), *Leaders We Deserve*, Martin Robertson.

MITCHELL, T. R., *et al.* (1970), 'The contingency model', *Academy of Management Journal*, 13.

NIAS, J. (1980), 'Leadership Styles and Job-Satisfaction in Primary Schools', in Bush, T., Glatter, R., *et al.* (eds.), *Approaches to School Management*, Harper & Row.

PETERS, T. J., and WATERMAN, R. H. (1982), *In Search of Excellence*, Harper & Row.

RACKHAM, N., HONEY, P., and COLBERT, M. (1971), *Developing Interactive Skills*, Wellens Publishing.

SCHEIN, E. (1980), *Organizational Psychology*, 3rd Edition, Prentice-Hall.

STOGDILL, R. M., and SHARTLE, C. L. (1956), *Patterns of Administrative Behaviour*, Ohio State University.

TANNENBAUM, R., and SCHMIDT, W. (1958), 'How to Choose a Leadership Pattern', *Harvard Business Review*, March–April.

VROOM, V. H., and DECI, E. L. (eds.), (1970), *Management and Motivation*, Penguin.

VROOM, V. H., and YETTON, P. (1973), *Leadership and Decision-Making*, University of Pittsburg.

WALD, R. M., and DOTY, R. A. (1954), 'The Top Executive – A First Hand Profile', *Harvard Business Review*, vol. 32, no. 4.

⟶ Chapter 5

I

The literature on power and influence is a growing one but not easy for the general reader to absorb. It has either had its roots in political theory and been concerned with the power bases of élites, or with revolutionary movements, with the changing nature of the power structures of whole societies, or the justifications for representative government. Alternatively, when it has delved into the *minutiae* of organizations it has done so in a piecemeal manner. No wonder that Dahl was able to describe it as 'a bottomless swamp'.

2

There is, however, a new interest in the power of the manager and its use in organizations, which has begun to generate a list of books with titles like *Power in Organizations*. Most of them are actually more concerned with the political processes in organizations and will therefore be listed under Chapter 8, but some of them provide a useful discussion of the relationship between power, influence and authority. The most comprehensive is by Mintzberg, who develops a comprehensive theory of power which he works through into different organizational forms and cultures. It is almost too near to be true but the systematic approach is helpful. Pfeffer or Swingle are more earthy. Hunt provides a practical check-list for the power-conscious manager.

Peabody's article is a good review of the earlier writers on power, including Weber's classic work. Weber and others preferred to use 'authority' as a substitute for 'power' but that, in my view, is to confuse the issue by suggesting that all power is somehow legitimate.

The best overall review of all the earlier literature relevant to power in organizations is that by Cartwright in March's *Handbook of Organizations*. He reviews a wide range of theories and studies and suggests some of the lines of approach that I have used. Likewise his earlier book, *Studies in Social Power*, is a useful compendium. Katz and Kahn in *The Social Psychology of Organizations* have much to say about the range and domain of various types of influence. Pettigrew has a growing body of work in this field, and the book of readings edited by Thomas and Bennis provides a useful overview.

3

Ecology as a method of influence has something in common with Skinner's ideas on human conditioning. He, however, sees it as much more powerful in its potential than I do.

Examples of ecology would be Herzberg's 'job enrichment' approach or Trist's work on the modification of work-flow patterns. Steele's writing on the importance of the physical environment is interesting and provocative.

Not everyone would distinguish power and influence in the way that I have done, but French and Raven's article in Cartwright's study has a discussion of power bases that is useful. Their terms are slightly different from mine and do not completely overlap, but there is a lot of convergent thinking. Homans too, the leading exchange theorist, merits study, particularly his 1961 book. His view of interactions as exchanges of rewards and costs I find almost too all-embracing to be useful but his description is certainly stimulating.

4

In dealing with responses to influence I am heavily indebted to Kelman's discussion of attitude change in his article. I have in several fields found this a most helpful categorization. The thoughts on the results of identification are, however, my own conclusions from personal experience.

The role of 'gatekeeper' in organizations, particularly in regard to information flows, is discussed by Pettigrew who describes an interesting case-history of the use of this role to influence a major investment decision. Allen has also described the role of technological gatekeepers in R and D establishments. Both of these writers are more interested in the positive aspects of their role than in the potential it gives them for negative power.

March and Simon's book *Organizations* is lucidly summarized from the perspective of 'vocabulary' by Perrow in *Complex Organizations*.

Cohen and Bradford's book *Influence Without Authority* has a timely title and contains much wisdom.

4

Hargreaves, in his social-psychological treatment of education, gives a good discussion of the various approaches to attitude change – a subject that has produced more literature and research than almost any other part of social psychology. I have used dissonance theory as a way of explaining most of the work in this field. I do not find that dissonance theory explains anything that cannot equally well be explained by concepts of power and influence, group process or the motivation calculus, but it is a good way of joining these together and seems to have some appeal to the newcomer to social psychology. Festinger's original 1957 book is the prime source, but Brehm and Cohen's later collection of all the research is perhaps more useful.

References

ALLEN, J., and COHEN, S. I. (1969), 'Information flow in research and development laboratories', *Admin. Science Quarterly*, 14(1).

BREHM, J. W., and COHEN, A. R. (1962), *Exploitations in Cognitive Dissonance*, Wiley.

CAPLOW, T. (1964), *Principles of Organization*, Harcourt, Brace & World.

CARTWRIGHT, D. (ed.) (1959), *Studies in Social Power*, University of Michigan, esp. French and Raven's article.

COHEN A. R., and BRADFORD, D. L. (1990), *Influence Without Authority*, Wiley.

FESTINGER, L. (1957), *A Theory of Cognitive Dissonance*, Stanford.

HARGREAVES, D. (1972), *Interpersonal Relations and Education*, Routledge & Kegan Paul.

HERZBERG, F. (1968), 'One more time: how do you motivate employers', *Harvard Business Review*, 46.

HOMANS, G. C. (1961), *Social Behaviour: Its Elementary Forms*, Routledge & Kegan Paul.

HUNT, J. (1992), *Managing People at Work*, McGraw-Hill.

KATZ, D. (1960), 'The functional approach to the study of attitude change', *Public Opinion Quarterly*.

KATZ, D., and KAHN, R. L. (1966), *The Social Psychology of Organizations*, Wiley.

KELMAN, H. C. (1958), 'Compliance, internalization and identification: three processes of attitude change', *Journal of Conflict Resolution*.

MARCH, J. G. (1965), *Handbook of Organizations*, Rand McNally.

MINTZBERG, H. (1983), *Power In and Around Organizations*, Prentice-Hall.

MUMFORD, E., and PETTIGREW, A. M. (1975), *Implementing Strategic Decisions*, Longman.

PEABODY, R. L. (1969), 'Perception of organizational authority' in Cummings and Scott (eds.), *Readings in Organizational Behaviour and Human Performance*, Unwin.

PERROW, C. (1972), *Complex Organizations*, Scott & Foreman, Glenview.

PETTIGREW, A. M. (1972), 'Information control as a power resource', *Sociology*, May.

PETTIGREW, A. M. (1973), 'The influence process between specialists and executives', *Personnel Review*, Winter.

PFEFFER, J. (1981), *Power in Organizations*, Pitman.

SIMON, H. A. (1947), *Administrative Behavior*.

SKINNER, B. F. (1973), *Beyond Freedom and Dignity*, Penguin.

STEELE, F. I. (1971), 'Organization development and sticks and stones' in H. A. Hornstein, *et al.*, *Social Interventions: a Behavioral Science Approach*, Free Press.

SWINGLE, P. G. (1976), *The Management of Power*, Wiley.

THOMAS, J. M., and BENNIS, W. G. (1972), *Management of Change and Conflict*, Penguin.

TRIST, E. L. (1960), *Socio-Technical Systems*, Tavistock.

WEBER, M. (1947), *The Theory of Social and Economic Organization*, Free Press.

━► Chapter 6

Much of the literature on groups is closely linked with that on leadership and motivation. For instance, a lot of the work on participation is really work on the effectiveness and motivation of groups under differing leadership styles. Most of the work on groups focuses on what, in the chapter, I have called the 'intervening factors'. Few studies look at the more comprehensive model studied here. One of the few that does is the little book by Zander, one of the giants in this area of study. Schein also takes a more comprehensive approach. The basic sources for the study of groups are:

1 The study of group processes – in particular Bales with his extensive way of recording group interactions, and the Leavitt-type studies of communication links.
2 The group-dynamics school, derived from the concepts of Kurt Lewin, and resulting in a whole range of training and group development methods. Schein and Bennis' book on group methods is a good overall description.
3 Field studies of group relations and the informal organization. In particular Mayo, Roethlisberger and Dickson, followed by Whyte and Homans particularly. Whyte has detailed some most revealing studies of groups in a wide variety of settings. They are described and interpreted in his book on organizational behaviour. Homans' *The Human Group* is a classic in the field, although I have not found his conceptualizations as interpretatively helpful as I expected.

Although I have tried to draw together the more useful of the research studies, I have found in my experience that the things that determine how groups operate are often more simple and more fundamental than many of the studies suppose. Much of the chapter therefore represents a conceptualization of my experience as well as an interpretation of the available research.

2

The early group studies, e.g. the Hawthorne studies and Trist's coal-miners, were the foundation for a whole approach to organizations in which a man's needs were assumed to be very largely satisfied and determined by the norms of his work group. Mayo, in particular, was so impressed by the Hawthorne studies and subsequent interviews that he concluded:

1 Man is basically motivated by social needs.
2 As a result of the rationalization of work, meaning has gone out of work and must be sought in the social relationships on the job.
3 The focus of the work group will do more to influence behaviour than the incentives and controls of managers.
4 A supervisor will only be effective to the extent that he can satisfy his subordinates' social needs.

This approach had a big impact on management theory and practice, especially because it was so contrary to the presumptions of scientific management. The impact was so big that the cult of the group began to dominate managerial thinking. The importance of the group definitely needed to be recognized but, like many of these approaches, it suffered from over-generalization and has now fallen back into its proper perspective.

For a long time it was thought that groups aided creative thinking through brain-storming. It was fifteen years before anyone thought to test it, and then it was only found to be true in certain respects. The results are reported by Taylor *et al*. Osborn's is the classical text.

The 'risky shift' phenomenon in group decision-making is interesting, partly because it was discovered in an experimental setting and has never been validated in the field. An enormous literature has grown up around this subject. The effect is so predictable that it has become a classroom exercise and most research now concentrates on trying to explain it. The most comprehensive review is Clark's article in *Psychological Bulletin*. Janis and Mann provide a general overview of the skills needed for solving group problems.

3

'Competence Motivation' is a term coined by Morse and Lorsch in an interesting article comparing motivation in high-performing and low-performing organizations.

The findings on group size are fairly predictable and very constant. For a good review of the studies see Lewenstein's article. The studies on homogeneity and heterogeneity are interesting, but seldom explore the dimensions of heterogeneity far enough until Schutz's studies in compatibility. Schutz's measures are complex and his research design intricate – sometimes so intricate that it is hard to draw any obvious conclusions from it. But he did try to assess the various elements of compatibility and he did draw attention to its relatively greater importance in tasks of complexity. His work is reported in his book. Heterogeneity of influence is discussed by Leavitt in his provocative article. Belbin's book describes his research which is summarized in Box 6.3.

The concepts of forming, norming, storming and performing are taken from an interesting article by B. W. Tuckman, which reviews a whole range of group process studies.

The T-group approach to developing group processes has already been referred to in these notes. For those who want to discover more about the current possibilities, The National Training Laboratories in Washington or The Group Relations Training Association in Great Britain are the best sources of information. Details of the Coverdale approach can be read in their 1961 booklet.

Very little research work has been done that is specifically related to the influence of the task on group design or performance. A pity because anecdotal experience suggests that it is a very important factor.

Fiedler's work on leader power and position has already been mentioned (Chapter 4). So has Festinger's work on cognitive dissonance (Chapter 5).

Festinger is also the co-author of a study of social pressures in a housing group which produced some conclusions about interactive patterns. The interaction thesis is supported by Homans. I have some worries about it, since any such research is likely to be self-fulfilling, i.e. increased interactions that did not lead to friendship would have ceased and would not therefore be known to the researchers.

Festinger's study is more longitudinal and therefore more reassuring on this count.

A good discussion of group processes and procedures and ways to improve them is included in Schein's excellent description of his personal consulting methods in organizations. This book also contains a short review of the history of group theory.

Deutsch looked at the productivity of co-operative well-maintained groups back in the early days of group studies. His conclusions are summarized in the text and reported in his 1949 article on human relations.

The interactions and communication patterns of groups have stimulated a vast amount of research. The comments in the text represent an amalgam and an attempted integration of the more important results. Unfortunately, not all the experiences used the same networks. Leavitt, in particular, who did much of the earlier work on this, did not look at the web pattern, being perhaps more interested in the communication distortion that results from links in a chain. The distortion effect was not mentioned in the text since it is not usually a feature of groups working together, but it is a well-established and well-known phenomenon. I have also used Guetzhow's work, following on Leavitt, on communication patterns.

Gaye Houston has produced a helpful book on groups and how to lead them, primarily aimed at those running an informal support group but useful to all.

References

BALES, R. F. (1950), *Interaction Process Analysis*, Addison-Wesley.

BELBIN, R. M. (1981), *Management Teams*, Heinemann.

CLARK, R. D. (1971), 'Group-induced shifts toward risk', *Psychological Bulletin*.

COVERDALE, R. (1967), *Training for Development*, Training Partnerships.

DEUTSCH, M. (1949), 'An experimental study of the effects of cooperation and competition upon group process', *Human Relations*.

FESTINGER, L., *et al.* (1950), *Social Pressures in Informal Groups: A Study of a Housing Project*, Harper & Row.

GUETZHOW, H., and SIMON, H. A. (1955), 'The impact of certain communication nets upon organization and performance', *Management Science*.

HOMANS, G. C. (1950), *The Human Group*, Harcourt Brace & World.

HOUSTON, G. (1990), *The Red Book of Groups*, The Rochester Foundation.

JANIS, I., and MANN, L. (1977), *Decision-Making*, Free Press.

LEAVITT, H. J. (1951), 'Some effects of certain communicative patterns on group performance', *J. Abnorm. Psych.*

LEAVITT, H. J. (1962), 'Unhuman organizations', *Harvard Business Review.*

LEWENSTEIN, E. R. (1971), 'Group size and decision-making committees', *Applied Soc-Studies.*

MAYO, E. (1945), *The Social Problems of an Industrial Civilization*, Harvard.

MORSE, J. J., and LORSCH, J. W. (1970), 'Beyond theory Y', *Harvard Business Review*, May.

OSBORN, A. F. (1957), *Applied Imagination*, Scribner's.

SCHEIN, E. H. (1969), *Process Consultation*, Addison-Wesley.

SCHEIN, E. H., and BENNIS, W. G. (1965), *Personal–Organizational Change Through Group Methods*, Wiley.

SCHUTZ, W. C. (1958), *FIRO: A Three Dimensional Theory of Interpersonal Behaviour*, Rinehart.

TAYLOR, D. W., BERRY, P. C., and BLOCK, C. H. (1958), 'Does group participation facilitate or inhibit creative thinking?', *Admin. Science Quarterly.*

TRIST, E. L., *et al.* (1963), *Organizational Choice*, Tavistock.

TUCKMAN, B. W. (1965), 'Developmental sequence in small groups', *Psychological Bulletin.*

WHYTE, W. F. (1969), *Organizational Behaviour*, Irwin.

ZANDER, A. (1983), *Making Groups Effective*, Jossey-Basy.

→ Chapter 7

I

Organizational cultures are the new vogue topic in a prescriptive as opposed to a descriptive sense. They paint vivid pictures but can seldom suggest what to do. The great advantage of the approach is that it starts with real organizations and behaviour as opposed to the simulated behaviour of many laboratory research experiments.

Peters and Waterman wrote a best-selling book on American companies which focuses on culture as its chief explanatory variable. It is a chatty, anecdotal book which makes up in true stories what it lacks in academic precision. Deal and Kennedy's book is in the same vein, with lots of examples. Schein's work is more conceptual, as is Pettigrew's article and Charles Hampden-Turner's studies. Hofstede has made a monumental study of national cultural differences, which he has summarized in a useful article as well as a big book. Maccoby, although looking at individuals, described corporate cultures in a very similar way to that used in this chapter. Finally, Harrison's set of four ideologies provided the starting-point for this chapter although he does not discuss the factors that influence the choice or mix of ideologies.

The 'contingency theorists' as they are termed are, principally, the following:

1 Lawrence and Lorsch in a famous book, *Organization and Environment*, first put forward the concept of a differentiated organization and tested it in the field. In a most perceptive and realistic book they emphasize four types of differences; orientations towards the market, orientations towards time, orientations towards people, and degree of formality in the structure. It focuses perhaps too much on the diversity of the market as the influencing factor, but has been the single most influential prod to my own thinking on organizations.

2 Burns and Stalker were in a way the forerunners of Lawrence and Lorsch in that they identified the need for a different structure when the technology of the market was changing. They did not, however, in distinguishing between mechanistic and organismic (later organic)

structures, discuss the problems of the mix, although they talked of it as a continuum.

3 Other forerunners of Lawrence and Lorsch are Fouraker, Chandler and Udy. These are discussed in Chapter VIII of Lawrence and Lorsch's work. Joan Woodward's was the forerunner of several 'technology' approaches. Her study of Essex firms set out to test whether traditional management principles in fact led to success. Her differentiated conclusions resulted. Attempts to replicate her findings have not always been successful, probably because technology is only one of the influencing factors and cannot be looked at in isolation. The replicating studies did not take into account the other possible factors.

4 Perrow has suggested that the essence of the technology question is whether the individual tasks are routine or non-routine. From this essential distinction flow the methods of control and co-ordination, the degrees of individual discretion and power, the type of social structure and motivation, the goals and the climate of risk. It is a complicated model which seems to suffer from the need to fill up, under each heading, all four cells of an assumed matrix. However, its general conclusions would fit well with the less closely defined cultural approach. In particular, his two most important cells fit closely with task and the role cultures.

Other approaches are:

5 Blau has published a systematic theory relating organizational size and structural differentiation. Katzell first demonstrated the cause of possible influencing factors and the need to find genotypic dimensions.

6 Homans wrote of the effect of the external system (physical, cultural and technological environments) on the internal system (activities, interactions and sentiments) and postulated that they are all interdependent.

7 Katz and Kahn in their discussion of open systems stress the linkages between the organization and its environment. They speak of the combination in an open system of a steady state and dynamic homeostasis and of a tendency towards differentiation. They are descriptive rather than prescriptive.

8 Miller and Rice of the Tavistock Institute have also advocated an open system model in which the activity system, the task group and the sentient group interact, and have presented a variety of organizational models evaluated on this basis. One of their suggestions is that task and sentient groups will coincide fully only when

the task is short-term, i.e. project groups make for high involvement.

9 Pugh and his colleagues have sought to measure more precisely some of the independent and dependent variables such as size, technology, dependence, formalization, centralization and their inter-relationships. They have shown that size is a major explanatory variable and, interestingly, that formalization does not have to accompany centralization.

For a good review of these and many other approaches to the description and categorization of organizations see Lichtman and Hunt's paper.

2

The cultures have not been rigorously defined in the text since a rigorous definition might destroy the 'flavour'. The questionnaire in Box 7.7 is an attempt to contribute a little more rigour and can be used as a set of definitions if need be. Self-completed questionnaires are, however, subject to cultural bias. Few people will accept a power orientation or a person orientation although to an outside observer that might be clearly their preferred culture. I have found the questionnaire more useful as a guide to my external rating of the organization after living with it for a time.

The task and role cultures appear frequently in the literature under other names. e.g. organic and mechanistic. The power and person cultures seem unrecognized by most theorists but to me seem significant realities. Similarly, the fit between a preferred personal culture and the dominant organization culture is one way of approaching the tricky question of establishing the psychological contract, but one which is not made explicit by many theorists. Etzioni's classification of organizations, mentioned in Chapter 2, is an approach along these lines, but his 'calculative' category can embrace all the cultures.

Mintzberg's ideas are in some ways similar but he has a more complete model and pushes it further in an attempt to embrace most of the characteristics of organizations.

3

The work by Pugh et al. on measuring some of the influencing factors and their effects has already been mentioned. Leading on from that,

Payne and Mansfield have investigated the effects of size and content on the perceived climate of the organization.

Trist and Bamforth's study of the changes from a task to a role technology (in my words) gave rise to the concept of the socio-technical system. the inter-relations of the technology and the social structure of the organization. A review of most of the studies of the impact of technology is contained in Mohn's paper.

Cyert and March in their *Behavioural Theory of the Firm* regard goals as the outcome of bargaining among potential members of a coalition about five classes of goal – production, inventory, sales, market and profit.

The impact of the environment on the organization, the link between the organization system and its content, has been the focus for most of the studies in this area. The important ones are those cited at the beginning of this set of notes.

4

Burns and Stalker have given a graphic description of some of the ways in which mechanistic organizations try to adapt to a changing technology. Galbraith's hypothetical account of how a matrix organization should evolve is interesting to set beside Burns and Stalker.

The concept of steady state is found in Katz and Kahn's text on social psychology. Leavitt and Whistler in an interesting article suggest that organizations of the future may look like a football on top of a bell – the football having characteristics similar to my power culture.

The discussion of integration is largely dependent on the study by Lawrence and Lorsch who talk of the integrator rather than the co-ordinator. The role stress associated with such a position is discussed in Chapter 3.

The studies by Lawrence and Lorsch and by Woodward have already been cited. The study by Morse and Lorsch is more concerned with motivation but is a good instance of the 'Best Fit' leadership approach.

Graham Turner's colourful descriptions of most of Britain's larger concerns, when read in the light of 'cultures', are very interesting and revealing.

References

BLAU, P. (1970), 'A formal theory of differentiation in organizations', *Amer. Soc. Review*.

BURNS, T., and STALKER, G. H. (1966), *The Management of Innovation*, Tavistock.

CYERT, R. M., and MARCH, J. G. (1963), *A Behavioural Theory of the Firm*, Prentice-Hall.

DEAL, T. E., and KENNEDY, A. A. (1982), *Corporate Cultures: The Rites and Rituals of Corporate Life*, Addison-Wesley.

GALBRAITH, J. R. (1971), 'Matrix organization designs', *Business Horizons*, Feb.

HAMPDEN-TURNER, C. (1990), *Corporate Culture*, Economist Books.

HARRISON, R. (1972), 'How to Describe Your Organization', *Harvard Business Review*, Sept.–Oct.

HOFSTEDE, G. (1980), *Culture's Consequences*, Saga.

HOFSTEDE, G. (1980), 'Managing Differences in the Multicultural Organization', *Organizational Dynamics*.

HOMANS, G. C. (1950), *The Human Group*, Harcourt, Brace & World.

KATZ, D., and KAHN, R. L. (1966), *The Social Psychology of Organizations*, Wiley.

KATZELL, R. A. (1962), 'Contrasting Systems of Work Organizations', *American Psychologist*, vol. 17.

LAWRENCE, P. R., and LORSCH, J. W. (1967), *Organization and Environment*, Harvard University Press.

LEAVITT, H. T., and WHISTLER, T. A. (1964), 'Management in the 1980s', in Leavitt and Pugh, *Readings in Managerial Psychology*, University of Chicago Press.

LICHTMAN, C. M., and HUNT, R. G. (1971), 'Personality and organization theory', *Psychological Bulletin*, vol. 76.

MACCOBY, M. (1979), *The Gamesman*, Simon & Schuster.

MILLER, E. J., and RICE, A. K. (1967), *Systems of Organization*, Tavistock.

MINTZBERG, H. (1989), *Mintzberg on Management*, The Free Press.

MOHN, L. B. (1962), 'Organizational technology and organizations', *American Psychologist*.

MORRIS, J. F. (1971), 'Developing managers structure and development management', *Admin. Science Quarterly* (2); *Personnel Review*, December.

MORSE, J. J., and LORSCH, J. W. (1970), 'Beyond theory Y', *Harvard Business Review*, May–June.

PAYNE, R. L., and MANSFIELD, R. (1972), 'Effects of organizational structure, organizational content and hierarchical position on perception of organizational climate'. Working Paper, London Business School.

PERROW, C. (1970), *Organizational Analysis*, Tavistock.

PETERS, T. J., and WATERMAN, R. H. (1982), *In Search of Excellence*, Harper & Row.

PETTIGREW, A. M. (1979), 'On Studying Organizational Cultures', *Admin. Science Quarterly*.

PUGH, D. S., HICKSON, D. J., HININGS, C. R., and TURNER, C. (1968), 'Dimensions of organization structure', *Admin. Science Quarterly*.

SCHEIN, E. H. (1986), *Organizational Culture and Leadership*, Jossey-Bass.

TRIST, E. L., *et al.* (1963), *Organizational Choice*, Tavistock.

TURNER, G. (1971), *Business in Britain*, Penguin.

WOODWARD, JOAN (1965), *Industrial Organization*, Oxford.

➤ Chapter 8

Personnel administration as a subject has generated a very mixed bag of literature, ranging from the 'How I did it', through cook-book-type prescriptive formulations, to detailed studies of particular phenomena or particular situations. There are good and bad examples of each variety; the problem often is to get past the allure of the title to the meat within.

In this chapter it is not possible, nor intended, to review all the systems of personnel management, but rather to look at some of their problems and implications in the light of the conceptual frameworks introduced earlier in the book. Much of the time, it is not the details of the system or the strategy that matters, but the intent behind it, the way it is introduced, the way it is handled, that is crucial. This is more the focus of this chapter.

Readings on Personnel Management, edited by McFarland, is one overview of the literature in the field, which focuses quite heavily on the prescriptive end of the scale. The book on managerial behaviour by Campbell *et al.* is a compendium and detailed review of all the research in this general area. Examples of 'How I did it' approaches are Robert Townsend's *Up the Organization*, and Carl Dueu's account of his career as a company doctor. A combination of these four very different books is perhaps an appropriate start on this vast and overlapping topic. Another overview is provided by Robbins, from an American standpoint. The Institute of Personnel Management in Britain provides a long list of publications on all aspects of the subject.

I

The implications of human asset-accounting have been stressed by Likert amongst others. Hekimian and Jones' article is the most concise treatment of the subject, although it does not really probe all the possible implications. Caplan also touches on the topic in his book.

2

Alfred's article 'Checkers or choice in manpower management' contrasts the 'Open' and 'Closed' systems of development and describes some examples. An overview of the various systems is provided by Markwell and Roberts' book. On the topic of manpower forecasting, Vether's book is a reliable introduction. Brown, in his book on organization, describes some of the formal mechanisms for management development that he recommends.

Schein's conceptualization of the career process and his concept of career anchors is most useful, but has not yet been given the practical push it needs. In Britain, the Stewarts have produced some of the best writing on the selection, appraisal and development of managers. Rogers, writing about schools, deserves to be read by a wider audience because he brings all the social psychological research to bear on a practical problem.

A good review of the research on pay is provided by Opsahl and Dunnette's article in the *Psychological Bulletin*. This is brought up to date in Campbell *et al.*'s larger work on managerial effectiveness. Jacques' system of differentials is described in his book *Equitable Payment* and discussed by Brown in his book *Organization*.

3

General approaches to individual development are provided by Schein in his article and by Markwell and Roberts.

This discussion of formal education is based very largely on my article in 'European Business'. Revans's views on formal education and its perils are well worth studying and are set out in his book *Developing Managers*. Other studies are reported and commented on in Campbell *et al.*'s review.

A good summary of the evaluation studies of group learning is provided by Morgan, in Rackham *et al.* Campbell *et al.* provide more details and further references. Morgan also provides a good description of the various types of group development methods to be found. Morris' article describes the use of team project learning within companies and business schools, along with other devices, as a way of developing managers for the development activities within organizations – a useful foretaste of possible future trends in management education.

There is, in general, a confusion in this area as to whether the object of development is the group or the individual. It can blur the issue to claim that both happen simultaneously, since there is no clear evidence that they do.

A good discussion of coaching as a mechanism for developing the individual is provided by Levinson. Berlew and Hall's article on the early careers of new recruits is a good study of the effects of high expectations on performance. Schein's studies of the early careers of new graduates is evidence of the possible detrimental effects of socialization if badly handled. Life-planning is one method for clarifying one's personal goals and objectives.

4

The whole topic of organization development should perhaps be given more space than a sub-section. The view I have taken is that organization development is really the whole topic of this book. The role of the manager in instituting change will be discussed in Chapter 13. Here we are concerned only with the techniques of OD as an alternative to individual development. Warren Burke's article is a good summary of the differences. For a fuller treatment of the methods of OD one should consult Beckhard's book. Paul Hill gives an interesting account of an OD programme in Shell, while Paul and Robertson describe the job enrichment programme in ICI. Both of these are good examples of changing the way of working in a large organization as a method of improving the effectiveness of the individual and his contribution to the organization.

Most of the writing and research of Chris Argyris has been taken up by the topic of the individual and the organization, with the need to integrate the objectives of the two and to allow for individual psychological development within the constraints of organizational goals. He is more concerned with the damaging consequences of most managerial practices and not especially interested in socialization. His 1964 book is the best statement of his views. Whyte's book remains the best polemic on the danger of socialization and is still relevant and stimulating reading. For more modern descriptions of socialization in American firms one need only turn to Peters and Waterman. For Japan, see Pascale and Athos, and Ouchi. Evans and Bartolomé's research on the relationship between organization and family is worrying but important.

References

ALFRED, T. M. (1967), 'Checkers or choice in manpower management', *Harvard Business Review*, January–February.

ARGYRIS, C. (1964), *Integrating the Individual and Organization*, Wiley.

BECKHARD, R. (1969), *Organization Development: Strategies and Models*, Addison-Wesley.

BERLEW, D., and HALL, D. (1966), 'The socialization of managers: the effects of expectations on performance', *Admin. Science Quarterly*, September.

BERRY, D. F. (1968), 'Applied research in motivation performance and assessment', Bath Conference.

BROWN, W. (1971), *Organization*, Heinemann.

BURKE, W. W. (1971), 'A comparison of management development and organization development', *Management Science*.

CAMPBELL, J. P., DUNNETTE, M. D., LAWLER, E. E., and WEIK, E. E. (1970), *Managerial Behaviour, Performance and Effectiveness*, McGraw-Hill.

CAPLAN, E. H. (1971), *Management Accounting and Behavioural Science*, Addison-Wesley.

DUEU, C. (1971), *Management Kinetics*, McGraw-Hill.

EVANS, P., and BARTOLOMÉ, F. (1980), *Must Success Cost So Much?*, Grant McIntyre.

FLAMHOLZ, E. (1971), 'Should your organization attempt to value its human resources?', *California Management Review*.

FORDYCE, J. K., and WEIL, R. (1971), *Managing with People*, Addison-Wesley.

HANDY, C. B. (1971), 'Exploding the myth of management education', *European Business*, Spring.

HEKIMIAN, J. S., and JONES, C. H. (1967), 'Put people on your balance sheet', *Harvard Business Review*, January–February.

HILL, P. (1971), *Towards a New Philosophy of Management*, Gower Press.

JACQUES, E. (1961), *Equitable Payment*, Wiley.

LEVINSON, H. (1970), 'A psychologist looks at executive development', in G. W. Dalton, P. R. Lawrence, and L. E. Greina, *Organizational Change and Development*, Irwin and Dorsey.

LIKERT, R. (1967), *The Human Organization: its Management and Value*, McGraw-Hill.

McFARLAND, D. E. (ed.), *Personnel Management Readings*, Penguin.

MARKWELL, D. S., and ROBERTS, T. J. (1970), *Organization of Management Development Programmes*, Gower Press.

MEYER, H. H., KAY, E., and FRENCH, J. R. P. jnr (1965), 'Split Roles in Performance Appraisal', *Harvard Business Review*, January–February.

MORRIS, J. (1971), 'Development management and management development', *Personnel Review*, December.

NICHOLS, R. G. (1967), 'Listening is good business', in Huneryager and Heckman, *Human Relations in Management*, Arnold.

OPSAHL, R. L., and DUNNETTE, M. D. (1966), 'The role of financial compensation in industrial motivation', *Psychological Bulletin*.

OUCHI, W. (1981), *Theory Z. How American Business can meet the Japanese Challenge*, Addison-Wesley.

PASCALE, R. T., and ATHOS, A. G. (1982), *The Art of Japanese Management*, Penguin.

PAUL, W. J., and ROBERTSON, K. B. (1970), *Job Enrichment and Employer Motivation*, Gower Press.

PETERS, T. J., and WATERMAN, R. H. (1982), *In Search of Excellence*, Harper & Row.

RACKHAM, N., HONEY, P., and COLBERT, M. (1971), *Developing Interactive Skills*, Wellens Publishing.

REVANS, R. G. (1971), *Developing Effective Managers*, Longman.

ROBBINS, S. P. (1978), *Personnel: The Management of Human Resource*, Prentice-Hall.

ROGERS, C. (1982), *A Social Psychology of Schooling*, Routledge & Kegan Paul.

SCHEIN, E. H. (1969), 'Management development as a process of influence', *Industrial Management Review*, May.

SCHEIN, E. H. (1980), *Organizational Psychology*, 3rd Edition, Prentice-Hall.

STEWART, A., and STEWART, V. (1981), *Tomorrow's Managers Today*, 2nd Edition, Institute of Personnel Management.

TOWNSEND, R. (1970), *Up the Organization*, Michael Joseph.

VETHER, E. (1968), *Manpower Forecasting*, Bureau of Industrial Relations, University of Michigan.

WHYTE, W. H. (1957), *The Organization Man*, Cape.

━► Chapter 9

The writing on organizational structure has been voluminous in the last ten years. There is no way in which it can be all encompassed in one chapter of this book. All I have sought to do is to point to the key principles and the main problem areas. Anyone wanting to go further will find much to choose from.

Mintzberg's big book, *The Structuring of Organizations*, is an impressive review of the literature built around a new analytical framework. Because it is so long and complex he produced a shorter version, *Structure in Fives*, which is still rather academic in tone. More accessible, perhaps, but equally authoritative is Child's book, rich with practical examples, or Galbraith's *Organization Design* (written explicitly for managers and employees). Karl Weick's short book is full of insight and well worth reading.

Lawrence and Lorsch's old classic, *Organization and Environment*, remains, for me, very influential – as will be evident from the text. They have been much criticized for using qualitative or perceptual measures rather than hard objective ones and there is some evidence, which Child discusses, that the environment is not always as causally important as Lawrence and Lorsch believe. Time has made a truism of their conclusions but the conclusions are crucial for there are still many managers who think that organizational structure is independent of what they are doing and where they are doing it.

Sadler's book provides a good approach to the practical problems of implementing a design and of the necessity for compromise in doing so.

2

Diversity in various forms has cropped up in several studies as a determinant of organization design. Weinshall's monograph is primarily concerned with the structural features of design, but he clearly depicts how structure is related to the scope of the design-making process. He cites the various other studies that support his contention, particularly Stopford's. I am not aware of writers who stress the other pole of my continuum 'uniformity'. 'Uniformity' is not a totally successful word. It has undesirable overtones. 'Consistency' and 'regularity' were two others that I have considered, but which equally fail to convey the full meaning required. Similarly diversity, as I use it, enhances more than Lawrence and Lorsch's differentiation. These semantic difficulties epitomize the dilemma of the social scientist when he seeks to use everyday terms to describe a precise feature of organization or of reality. The proliferation of newly invented terms, with definitions tailored to purpose, is understandable. Unfortunately, these terms, although they gain in precision, lose in ease of use by the non-initiate.

The matrix organization, its features and its problems, is well discussed in Galbraith's 1973 book on the topic. His way of looking at organizations as information-processing devices is interesting and full of implications, and is still relevant today.

Peters and Waterman's descriptions of American companies are full of examples of structuring for diversity. They are less eloquent on the control of diversity, partly because they seem reluctant to admit to any problems in their 'excellent' companies. Peters' new book is better.

Thompson's book, an old classic, is difficult but rewarding reading. It describes how successful organizations always seek to extend their control over their environment, not least by choosing the appropriate 'domain'.

Mills's advocacy of the cluster organization is compelling but will not be appropriate for all organizations.

3

Corning Glass undertook a detailed implementation of Lawrence and Lorsch right through from diagnosis, using the same questionnaires and interview schedules, to implementation. They have described this in a series of papers to the *American Psychological Association* in September 1971. Only the last of these papers, Hundert's on project teams, is referenced here.

Zuboff's book on the possible consequences of computers on the shape of work and power provides valuable insights and an important distinction between 'automating' and 'informating'.

4

Job enrichment, whether by data feedback, socio-technical intervention or re-design of the work, is a whole industry on its own. Pasmore's article is a good overview of what has been achieved which, in short, is not as much as you might expect. Child also has a good discussion of this topic.

4.3

The literature on participation is essentially that which was listed in Chapter 4 (on leadership). Tannenbaum and Massaryk's article is a good list of the practical problems, written for the manager rather than the theorist.

4.4

Delegation is one of those topics that has fascinated the practitioner and those who write for him, but has been largely ignored by the researchers, or at least incorporated into other topics such as job enlargement or participation. It is, however, in my experience, a different problem from these, and one that is a real and pressing dilemma for many managers. Drucker, inevitably, recognized it back in 1954, and with his original idea of management by objectives, suggested a mechanism for implementing it.

4.5

Trist et al.'s study of the Durham Coal Field is the classic work on the value of the autonomous work group. This, and other Tavistock Studies, is concisely reviewed in Hill's account of their attempt to create these groups in a process technology in Shell UK. In a sense, these authors were prophets of this philosophy of management. Although ideologically in agreement with them, I felt it necessary to spell out in the chapter the basic conditions for success which explain so many of the failures, of the lack of attempts to implement the concepts.

References

BAVELAS, A., and STRAUSS, G. (1961), 'Group dynamics and inter-group relations', in W. G. Bennis (ed.), *The Planning of Change*, H. Holt.

CHILD, J. (1984), *Organizations*, Paul Chapman.

FOY, N. (1980), *The Yin and Yang of Organizations*, Grant McIntyre.

GALBRAITH, J. R. (1973), *Designing Complex Organizations*, Addison-Wesley.

GALBRAITH, J. R. (1977), *Organization Design*, Addison-Wesley.

HARRISON, R., 'Effective organization for start-up', unpublished paper.

HILL, P. (1971), *Towards a New Philosophy of Management*, Gower Press.

HUNDERT, A. T. (1971), 'Problems and prospect for project teams in a large bureaucracy', paper presented to *Am. Psych. Assoc.*, 3 September.

LAWRENCE, P. R., and LORSCH, J. W. (1967), *Organization and Environment*, Harvard University Press.

MARCH, J. G. (1980), 'The Technology of Foolishness', in Leavitt, H., *et al.*, *Readings in Managerial Psychology*, 3rd Edition, University of Chicago Press.

MILLS, D. Q. (1991), *Rebirth of the Corporation*, Wiley.

MINTZBERG, H. (1979), *The Structuring of Organizations*, Prentice-Hall.

MINTZBERG, H. (1983), *Structure in Fives*, Prentice-Hall.

NYSTROM, P. C., and STARBUCK, W. H. (1981), *Handbook of Organization Design*, Oxford University Press.

PASMORE, W. A. (1984), 'Turning People on to Work', in Kolb, D. A., *et al.* (ed.), *Organizational Psychology*, Prentice-Hall.

PAUL, W. J., and ROBERTSON, K. B. (1970), *Job Enrichment and Employee Motivation*, Gower Press.

PETERS, T. J. (1992), *Beyond Hierarchy*, Alfred Knopf.

PETERS, T. J., and WATERMAN, R. H. (1982), *In Search of Excellence*, Harper & Row.

SADLER, P. (1971), 'Designing an organization structure', *International Management Review*.

SCHEIN, E. H. (1980), *Organizational Psychology*, 3rd Edition, Prentice-Hall.

STOPFORD, J. M., 'Growth and organizational change in the multinational firm', unpublished doctoral dissertation.

TANNENBAUM, R., and MASSARYK, F. (1950), 'Participation by subordinates in the managerial decision-making process', *Canadian Journal of Economics and Political Science*, August.

THOMPSON, J. D. (1967), *Organizations in Action*, McGraw-Hill.

TRIST, E. L., HIGGIN, G. W., MURRAY, H., and POLLOCK, A. B. (1963), *Organizational Choice*, Tavistock.

WEICK, K. (1979), *The Social Psychology of Organizing*, Addison-Wesley.

WEINSHALL, T. D. (1970), *Applications of Two Conceptual Schemes of Organization Behaviour, in Case Study and General Organizational Research*, Ashridge.

ZUBOFF, S. (1989), *In the Age of the Smart Machine*, Heinemann.

➤ Chapter 10

There is a growing list of writings on the politics of organizations. I welcome this, as it demonstrates that academics are getting more interested in how organizations actually work rather than how they might work if they were more logical and rational. The most comprehensive of these writings is Mintzberg's big book on *Power In and Around Organizations*, which seeks to pull everything into one all-embracing analytical framework. It is rich in insight and comprehensive in scope, but too detailed and complex for any but the specialist. A little easier is Pfeffer's work on *Power* which is also based on American research and therefore influenced by that cultural environment. More prescriptive, anecdotal and British is Kakabadse's work and Foy's iconoclastic look at organizations from the outside. We may expect to see a growing list of titles on this topic in the next decade.

'The management of differences' is the title of the last chapter in McGregor's *Professional Manager*, and provides a brief introduction to the whole topic. According to the editor, this subject was beginning to dominate McGregor's thinking when he died. A well-known paper by Schmidt and Tannenbaum explores the management of individual differences or disputes. Much of what they say is also applicable to groups. Lateral relations are fully discussed by Sayles in his book on managerial behaviour. He identifies several more sets of roles than I do in this chapter, but many of them seem to overlap. A good analysis of organizational conflict is provided by Dutton and Walton's article which also provides a review of the available literature. Dalton's *Men Who Manage* is a blow-by-blow account of the conflicts and differences in two organizations. His descriptive material is more abundant and more valuable than the conceptual analysis. Cyert and March's famous *A Behavioural Theory of the Firm* is relevant to this topic, although this treatment regards organizations and their constituent parts too rationally for my liking. Caplow, in his book on organizations, has a long chapter on conflict which has some useful concepts, although the examples are drawn more from international and national affairs than those of organizations. Thomas and Bennis's book of readings on change and conflict is a useful compendium. Ardrey's book *The*

Territorial Imperative, and Machiavelli's *The Prince* are of a different order. They both provide fascinating analogies and parallels from different worlds. One cannot look to them for precise and proven theorems in the field of organizations, but if we are concerned with insight as much as with scientific evidence, then these two authors should not be missed.

The exchange theory of power, which I personally find useful as far as it goes but ultimately inadequate, is well set out by Peter M. Blau. The work of Andrew Pettigrew, focusing on the political relationship between specialists and line executives, is stimulating and reality-based. Crozier's *Bureaucratic Phenomenon* is one of the best field studies of power relationships in organizations. Most of the other interesting studies have concerned themselves with such places as hospitals and prisons where the political problems are perhaps more obvious. Of these perhaps the most insightful is Anselm Strauss's study of relations between the various groups in the mental health world.

1

Rackham *et al.* in their book (1971) cite their investigation of key problem incidents as perceived by a range of British managers to explain the importance of interactive skills. The percentages on perception of conflict are taken from one of Argyris's studies, quoted and commented on by him most recently in his *Intervention Theory and Method*.

2

Much of the discussion in this section is based on Schmidt and Tannenbaum's *Management of Difference* which deals essentially with the resolution of particular disputes between individuals, is insightful and practical.

The topic of competition *within* an organization has not been extensively discussed. Zaleznik's article is one of the few to deal with it. He distinguishes between coalitions and collusions and cites several supportive instances, but otherwise the possible beneficial effects of competition are usually summed up in one paragraph as an introduction to the problem of conflict. I feel this does the topic less than justice, particularly since competition *between* organizations is one fundamental tenet of capitalism.

There is of course a wealth of literature on aggression, and whether it is innate or induced. Ardrey provides a readable but polemical introduction to this field. As I state in the chapter, I feel the need for the student of organizations is to recognize that man does have this tendency towards aggression, however acquired.

3

Dutton and Walton identify nine antecedents of conflict – mutual dependence, asymmetries, rewards, organizational differentiation, role dissatisfaction, ambiguities, common resources, communication obstacles. These are often the results rather than the cause of conflict. But they provide a good integration of the various studies on conflict.

Strauss's detailed analysis of the role of the purchasing agent is a useful example of many of the causes and symptoms of conflict, as are Seiler's study of relative status rankings and the oft-cited Lawrence and Lorsch's comparison of effective firms in these industries.

Some examples of Ardrey's thinking are given in the boxes. Anthony Jay and Robert Heller, amongst others, have recently picked up the idea of using the concepts of the popular anthropologists and zoologists in organizational contests (e.g. The Naked Manager). But a systematic application of Ardrey's concepts to organizations has not, to my knowledge, been attempted. I have found the metaphor of territory, and the assumptions underlying it, to provide many insights in organizational analysis.

4

Pettigrew's paper gives a detailed account of the use of information control to bring about a particular solution to an investment decision in an organization. The implication is not that this decision was right or wrong, but that information was used as a power resource to obtain it.

Kakabadse provides an illuminating insight into the ways that different cultural types handle conflict. His four cultural types have a lot in common with those discussed in Chapter 7. Cribbin, in a good, practical and prescriptive book on leadership, gives a useful list of strategies for conflict which goes into more detail than the lists I have given.

5

Dutton and Walton's study of conflict and collaboration in two contrasting divisions is most illuminating. It is nicely observed, and interesting conclusions are drawn from it, most of which are reflected in the chapter.

Schein, in his discussion of process consultation, gives a good description of what is involved in group confrontation. A whole set of intervention methods has grown out of his particular strategy. Argyris, in his book *Intervention Theory and Method*, goes into considerable depth on the conceptual underpinnings and practical applications of this method. Although sound in principle, the strategy is often applied too indiscriminately. If the cause of the conflict is rooted in the objectives or the allocation of territory, then better understanding and better communications between conflicting groups may help to remove stereotypes each of the other, but will really only paper over the deeper cracks.

Harrison's approach of role negotiation is a practical and viable way of getting rid of some of the unnecessary irritations of conflict and making it manageable. Particularly useful for individuals in small groups, it has been used in intergroup situations. He has described it in a paper for *European Business*.

Organization development, whose primary focus has traditionally been on improving the process of group and intergroup interactions, has sometimes proceeded as if unaware of the political reality of organizations, and in dealing with the symptoms of conflict rather than its causes, has earned itself, on occasion, the label of ineffective.

6

Change is one of the topics of the times. It gives birth to countless prescriptive and some descriptive tomes. Most are too anecdotal and too lacking in conceptual clarity to be of much value. Exceptions are Kanter's readable and thought-provoking book on what she calls 'post-entrepreneurial' management and Pascale's book based around the big automobile companies of the USA and Japan. It took the western world too long to discover Dr Deming's philosophy of a constant search for quality but once found his prescriptions will not be forgotten. Read him in the original or as seen by one of his disciples. Stewart's book is appropriately subtitled 'How to reclaim power and liberate your organization.' Largely based on British examples, it is both readable and practical.

References

AGUAYO, R. (1990), *Dr Deming*, Mercury.

ARDREY, R. (1967), *The Territorial Imperative*, Collins.

ARGYRIS, C. (1970), *Intervention Theory and Method*, Addison-Wesley.

BLAU, P. M. (1964), *Exchange and Power in Social Life*, Wiley.

CAPLOW, T. (1964), *Principles of Organization*, Harcourt, Brace.

CRIBBIN, J. J. (1981), *Leadership – Strategies for Organizational Effectiveness*, Amacom.

CROZIER, M. (1964), *The Bureaucratic Phenomenon*, Tavistock.

CYERT, R. M., and MARCH, J. G. (1963), *A Behavioural Theory of the Firm*, Prentice-Hall.

DALTON, M. (1959), *Men Who Manage*, Wiley.

DEMING, W. E. (1986), *Out of the Crisis*, Cambridge.

DEUTSCH, M. (1969), 'Conflicts: productive and destructive', *Journal of Social Issues*.

DUTTON, J. M., and WALTON, R. E. (1962), 'Interdepartmental conflict and co-operation: two contrasting studies', *Human Organizations* 20.

DUTTON, J. M., and WALTON, R. E. (1969), 'The management of interdepartmental conflict', *Admin. Science Quarterly*, March.

FOY, N. (1981), *The Yin and Yang of Organizations*, Grant McIntyre.

HARRISON, R. (1972), 'When power conflicts trigger team spirit', *European Business*, Spring.

KAKABADSE, A. (1983), *The Politics of Management*, Gower.

KANTER, R. M. (1989), *When Giants Learn to Dance*, Simon & Schuster.

LAWRENCE, P. R., and LORSCH, J. W. (1967), *Organization and Environment*, Harvard University Press.

McGREGOR, D. (1967), *The Professional Manager* (ed. W. E. Bennet and C. McGregor), McGraw-Hill.

MACHIAVELLI, N. (1967), *The Prince* (trans. G. Bull), Penguin.

MINTZBERG, H. (1983), *Power In and Around Organizations*, Prentice-Hall.

PASCALE, R. T. (1990), *Managing on the Edge*, Viking.

PETTIGREW, A. M. (1973), 'Information control as a power resource', *Sociology*, May.

PETTIGREW, A. M. (1973), *The Politics of Organizational Decision-Making*, Tavistock.

PFEFFER, J. (1981), *Power in Organizations*, Pitman.

RACKHAM, N., HONEY, P., and COLBERT, M. (1971), *Developing Interactive Skills*, Wellens Publishing.

SAYLES, L. (1964), *Managerial Behaviour*, McGraw-Hill.

SCHEIN, E. H. (1969), *Process Consultation*, Addison-Wesley.

SCHMIDT, W., and TANNENBAUM, R. (1960), 'The management of differences', *Harvard Business Review*, November–December.

SEILER, J. A. (1963), 'Diagnosing inter-departmental conflict', *Harvard Business Review*, September–October.

STEWART, V. (1990), *The David Solution*, Gower.

STRAUSS, A., *et al.* (1964), *Psychiatric Ideologies and Institutions, Glencoe, Ill.*, Free Press.

STRAUSS, C. (1962), 'Tactics of lateral relationship: the purchasing agent', *Admin. Science Quarterly*, vol. 7.

THOMAS, J. M., and BENNIS, W. G. (1972), *Management of Change and Conflict*, Penguin.

ZALEZNIK, A. (1970), 'Power and politics in organizational life', *Harvard Business Review*, May–June.

Chapter 11

1

This chapter is a little different. There is less analysis of other people's findings and more speculation on the problems and dilemmas of the managerial role. Too many books on organizations seem to be written mainly for other students of organizations. This book was written for those who work in and run them, in the hope that it might help them to understand them better. The chapter is therefore intended to be a way of putting the rest of the book into some sort of perspective.

2

There have been several studies of the manager's job. The most influential has probably been Mintzberg's but it must be remembered that his theorizing is based on his observations of five chief executives. Other people's jobs may not be so complicated or so interesting. Stewart's work, however, is based on a much wider sample of British managers, mainly at junior or middle levels. Another account of the way a manager works is to be found in Sloan's story of how he ran General Motors, which is fascinating partly because of the clarity of his organizational thinking more than fifty years ago. Maccoby's study of leaders in action also provides some good insights into the way different managers divide up their roles.

3

The seven S checklist appears in Peters and Waterman and in Pascale. It looks too simple to be true but I have found it to be a pertinent reminder of the complexity of organizations when it is time to change things.

4

Toffler's *Future Shock* and his later book, *The Third Wave*, provide a readable and anecdotal look into the future, some of which is very much with us already.

5

Evans and Bartolomé's research is of particular interest, based as it is on interviews with successful managers and their wives. The last part of Kanter's book is both relevant and very perceptive. There is also my own book. For self-development try Mike Woods' small and practical books.

References

EVANS, P., and BARTOLOMÉ, F. (1980), *Must Success Cost So Much?*, Grant McIntyre.

HANDY, C. (1989), *The Age of Unreason*, Business Books.

KANTER, R. M. (1989), *When Giants Learn to Dance*, Simon & Schuster.

LEAVITT, H. J. (1965), 'Applied Organizational Change in Industry', in March, J. G. (ed.), *Handbook of Organizations*, Rand McNally.

MACCOBY, M. (1981), *The Leader*, Simon & Schuster.

MINTZBERG, H. (1973), *The Nature of Managerial Work*, Harper & Row.

PASCALE, R. T. (1990), *Managing on the Edge*, Viking.

PETERS, T. J. and WATERMAN, R. H. (1982), *In Search of Excellence*, Harper & Row.

SLOAN, A. P. (1954), *My Years with General Motors*, Doubleday.

STEWART, R. (1983), *Choices for the Manager*, McGraw-Hill.

TOFFLER, A. (1970), *Future Shock*, Bodley Head.

WOODS, M. (1988), *The New Manager*, Element Books.

→ Chapter 12

I

Anyone looking into the future of organizations must first look at the literature on the possible future of society. There is a rich and constantly changing selection here; what is in vogue one year will be out of date the next. David Bell's classic book on the post-industrial society still remains very relevant. James Robertson's latest books argue for a rather optimistic steady-state world, with which all might not agree, but in *The Sane Alternative* he reviews the other possible scenarios and thereby provides a useful check-list. Hazel Henderson, in America, has a similar point of view. Higgins presents a more cataclysmic view, seeing the future as a set of possible disaster scenarios, which we shall only with difficulty avoid. Hirsch has a different viewpoint. His important book argues that materialism carries in-built limits which are more social than physical. His argument is not fully worked through but he raises interesting questions. Toffler and Naisbitt are two of the most readable futurists. They both postulate the West moving away from large hierarchical organizations and materialist values but they may have exaggerated the speed with which this is happening. Kinsman, writing in Britain, is also optimistic about a new set of values. Peter Drucker, as always, is thought-provoking and realistic.

2

Schumacher's book *Small is Beautiful* is well known. Much of his influence, however, was due to his talks and writings in small journals in his later years. These are inadequately captured in the two books published after his death. Kuhn's notion of paradigms is important; it is set out in his book on the history of science.

Elliott Jaques has summarized his work on organizations in a major work, *A General Theory of Bureaucracy*, which is serious reading but worthwhile for anyone interested in a full understanding of Jaques' position.

3

There is a great dearth of writing on the future shape of organizations. The general assumption seems to be that they will continue much the same as before, with minor genuflections to the expressed demands of a more sophisticated environment. Of those writing in this vein Mintzberg, in his set of proposed volumes under the general title of *The Theory of Management Policy* (the first, *The Structuring of Organizations*, came out in 1979), is perhaps the most useful. Lindblom's recent book on politics and markets is also full of implications for organizations although these are not spelt out; it is an investigation into the viability of enterprise in modern societies.

Another trend has been to investigate the more political nature of organizations, viewing them as mini-states. This, as was argued in Chapter 8, is a long-overdue emphasis, but it is not at present as future-orientated as it needs to be. An important but difficult book in this area is Williamson's *Markets and Hierarchies*.

Jonathan Gershuny's book on the post-industrial society is an interesting riposte to David Bell's hypothesis that we are moving into a service society. Gershuny's ideas could be of major importance to organizations.

Fred Hirsch's book on the social limits to growth is an interesting speculation which needs more thought.

The idea of the three forty-eights (section 3.5 (b)) comes from John Hughes, Principal of Ruskin College, Oxford.

4

These ideas are taken further in my books *Gods of Management* and *The Age of Unreason*, which postulate that a major change in the way organizations see their responsibilities is necessary if society is not to fall in on itself.

Federalism is a little-understood concept. In a small booklet, Derek Sheane has set out what is involved as well as anybody. If nothing else, the new Europe is teaching everyone something about federalism.

References

BELL, D. (1974), *The Coming of Post-Industrial Society*, Heinemann.

DRUCKER, P. (1989), *The New Realities*, Heinemann.

GERSHUNY, J. (1979), *After Industrial Society*, Macmillan.

GERSHUNY, J. (1984), *Social Innovation and the Division of Labour*, Oxford University Press.

HANDY, C. B. (1989), *The Age of Unreason*, Business Books.

HANDY, C. B. (1991), *Gods of Management*, Business Books.

HENDERSON, H. (1979), *Creating Alternative Futures*, Berkeley Publishing Corp.

HIGGINS, R. (1978), *The Seventh Enemy*, Hodder & Stoughton.

HIRSCH, F. (1977), *The Social Limits to Growth*, Routledge & Kegan Paul.

JAQUES, E. (1976), *A General Theory of Bureaucracy*, Heinemann.

KANTER, R. H. (1989), *When Giants Learn to Dance*, Simon & Schuster.

KINSMAN, F. (1991), *Millennium*, Penguin.

KUHN, T. S. (1962), *The Structure of Scientific Revolutions*, University of Chicago Press.

LINDBLOM, C. E. (1977), *Politics and Markets*, Basic Books Inc.

MINTZBERG, H. (1989), *Mintzberg on Management*, The Free Press.

NAISBITT, J. (1990), *Megatrends 2000*, Sidgwick & Jackson.

NAISBITT, J. (1983), *Megatrends*, Warner.

ROBERTSON, J. (1978), *The Sane Alternative*, Robertson.

SCHUMACHER, E. F. (1973), *Small is Beautiful*, Blond & Briggs.

SCHUMACHER, E. F. (1977), *A Guide for the Perplexed*, Cape.

SCHUMACHER, E. F., and GILLINGHAM, P. N. (1977), *Good Work*, Cape.

SHEANE, D. (1976), *Beyond Bureaucracy*, Management Research.

TOFFLER, A. (1981), *The Third Wave*, Pan.

WILLIAMSON, O. E. (1975), *Markets and Hierarchies: Analysis and Antitrust Implications*, The Free Press.

➤ Acknowledgements

For excerpts reproduced in this volume, acknowledgement is made to the following sources:

R. Ardrey, *The Territorial Imperative*, 1967: Collins, Publishers/Atheneum Press, New York

C. Argyris, *Personality and Organization*, 1948: Chapman and Hall Ltd

R. Blake and J. Mouton, 'The Management Grid', *Advanced Management Journal*: The Society for Advancement of Management, New York

E. H. Caplan, *Management Accounting and Behavioral Science*, 1971: Addison-Wesley, Massachusetts

N. Dornbusch, *The Military Academy as an Assimilating Institution*, 1953: University of North Carolina Press

P. F. Drucker, *The Practice of Management*, 1954: Harper & Row, New York

J. M. Dutton and R. E. Walton, *Interdepartmental Conflict and Co-operation: Two Contrasting Studies*, 1966: The Society for Applied Anthropology, Washington, D. C.

H. Garfinkel, *Studies in Ethnomethodology*, 1967: Prentice-Hall Inc., Englewood Cliffs, New Jersey, USA

D. Hargreaves, *Social Relations in a Secondary School*, 1967: Routledge & Kegan Paul/Humanities Press, New York

R. Harrison, *What Kind of Organization?*: Development Research Associates Kelly, 'The Organizational Concept of Leadership', 1970: *International Management*

F. Landis, *What Makes Technical Men Happy and Productive?*, 1971: American Society of Mechanical Engineers

P. R. Lawrence and J. W. Lorsch, 'Distribution of Influence in Two Organisations', 1967: *Organisation & Environment*, Harvard

R. Likert, *New Patterns of Management*, 1961: McGraw-Hill, New York

D. Miller, *Using Behavioral Science to Solve Organization Problems*, 1968: International Personnel Management Association

R. L. Peabody, 'Perceptions of Organizational Authority: A Comparative Analysis', *Administrative Science Quarterly*, 1962: Cornell University, USA

M. Sherif and C. W. Sherif, *An Outline of Social Psychology*, 1956: Harper & Row, New York

A. J. M. Sykes and J. Bates, 'A study of conflict between formal company policy and the interest of informed groups', *Sociological Review*, 1962: *Sociological Review*, University of Keele

R. Tannenbaum, I. R. Weschler and F. Massaryk, *Leadership and Organisation*, 1961: McGraw-Hill, New York

T. D. Weinshall, *Applications of Two Conceptual Schemes of Organizational Behaviour in Case Study and General Organizational Research*, 1971: Ashridge Management College, Herts.

➤ Index

Resource-investigator, 161
Results, knowledge of, 43
Revans, R. G., 242, 410
Rewards, 308. *See also* Incentives;
  Pay; Promotion
Robertson, J., 427
Roethlisberger and Dickson, 38,
  156–8, 398
Role(s)
  ambiguity, 63–5, 69, 72, 83
  classification, 84–5
  conflict, 65–7, 69, 227, 386
  culture, 185–7, 191, 195–6, 208,
    235, 296–7, 336, 405
  definition, 62–3, 84–5, 301–2
  expectations, 82, 85
  group, 91–2, 167
  incompatibility, 65, 69
  individual, 61–83, 161–2
    in groups, 162–7, 172
  interactions, 84–92
  negotiation, 312
  occupational, 76
  overload, 67, 70
  perception, 79–83
  pressure, 68
  set, 61–2
  signs, 63, 386
  simultaneous, 302
  stress, 65, 67, 68, 94
  territory and, 306
  theory, 61–8, 76, 94, 385–6
  transition, 94
  underload, 67–8, 70, 94
Rosenthal, R., and Jacobson, L., 82,
  83
Routine, 336
Row and Russell, 44
Rules and regulations
  conflict control by, 310–11
  influencing by, 134–5
  proliferation of, 299, 307–8
Russek and Zohman, 71
Russell, B., 351, 376–7

S checklist, 327–8, 425
Sadler, P., 414
Sales estimates, 221

Satisfaction
  group, 154–5, 175
  job, 234, 277
  mental health and, 31
  motivation and, 38–9, 175–6, 234
  productivity and, 31, 155, 156, 199,
    277
  success and, 43–4
  theories, 28–34, 37
  variables, 48
Sayles, L., 419
Scale economies, 186, 188
Scanlon Plan, 281
Schein, E. H., 34, 37, 158, 182, 231,
    378, 380, 398, 401, 403, 422
  and Bennis, W. G., 398
Schmidt, W., and Tannenbaum, R.,
    419, 420
Schools, 76, 114–15, 121, 136, 227,
    256, 296
Schumacher, F., 346, 358, 427
Schutz, W. C., 400
Seiler, 302
Self-activating man, 37
Self-actualization, 33, 35, 36, 100
Self-censorship, group-think, 164
Self-concept, 40, 53–7, 381–2
Self-development, 342–3
Self-employment, 367–8
Self-enlightenment, 240
Self-knowledge, 117, 342–3
Selznick, Philip, 22
Senge, P., 23
Seniority, pay and, 232
Sensitivity, emotional, 74
Sex and personality, 76
Shaper, group, 160
Sheane, D., 428
Shirom *et al.*, 71
Simon, H. A., 138
Simon and March, 22
Sin, G., 258
Size of organizations, 184, 192–3,
    404–5
Skinner, B. F., 228
Skynner, J., 317
Sloan, 425
Smoothing, 260

READ MORE IN PENGUIN

In every corner of the world, on every subject under the sun, Penguin represents quality and variety – the very best in publishing today.

For complete information about books available from Penguin – including Puffins, Penguin Classics and Arkana – and how to order them, write to us at the appropriate address below. Please note that for copyright reasons the selection of books varies from country to country.

In the United Kingdom: Please write to *Dept. EP, Penguin Books Ltd, Bath Road, Harmondsworth, West Drayton, Middlesex UB7 0DA*

In the United States: Please write to *Consumer Services, Penguin Putnam Inc., 405 Murray Hill Parkway, East Rutherford, New Jersey 07073-2136.* VISA and MasterCard holders call 1-800-631-8571 to order Penguin titles

In Canada: Please write to *Penguin Books Canada Ltd, 10 Alcorn Avenue, Suite 300, Toronto, Ontario M4V 3B2*

In Australia: Please write to *Penguin Books Australia Ltd, 487 Maroondah Highway, Ringwood, Victoria 3134*

In New Zealand: Please write to *Penguin Books (NZ) Ltd, Private Bag 102902, North Shore Mail Centre, Auckland 10*

In India: Please write to *Penguin Books India Pvt Ltd, 11 Community Centre, Panchsheel Park, New Delhi 110017*

In the Netherlands: Please write to *Penguin Books Netherlands bv, Postbus 3507, NL-1001 AH Amsterdam*

In Germany: Please write to *Penguin Books Deutschland GmbH, Metzlerstrasse 26, 60594 Frankfurt am Main*

In Spain: Please write to *Penguin Books S. A., Bravo Murillo 19, 1°B, 28015 Madrid*

In Italy: Please write to *Penguin Italia s.r.l., Via Vittorio Emanuele 45/a, 20094 Corsico, Milano*

In France: Please write to *Penguin France, 12, Rue Prosper Ferradou, 31700 Blagnac*

In Japan: Please write to *Penguin Books Japan Ltd, Iidabashi KM-Bldg, 2-23-9 Koraku, Bunkyo-Ku, Tokyo 112-0004*

In South Africa: Please write to *Penguin Books South Africa (Pty) Ltd, P. O. Box 751093, Gardenview, 2047 Johannesburg*

BY THE SAME AUTHOR

Understanding Voluntary Organizations

Applying many of the theories put forward in *Understanding Organizations*, *Understanding Voluntary Organizations* discusses the ways in which non-profit-making groups can function most effectively.

Voluntary organizations can vary greatly in their aims and structure; some, Dr Barnado's, for example, provide a service, others range from charities to self-help groups. Whatever the function of the organization, however, it must have have some form of 'management' if it is to operate successfully.

There are no easy answers to the challenge posed by these organizations. However, understanding the difficulties as well as the opportunities open to their leaders and officials will result in a more successful – as well as more enjoyable – operation and benefit everyone.